"This book casts an important light on t
world government as an evolutionary process.... The book is visionary
and appears at a time when the speed of change and the perceived
failings of current institutions call out for just such a vision."

—**Marc Pilisuk**, Ph.D., Professor Emeritus, Saybrook University;
     principal author, *The Hidden Structure of Violence*

"*One World Renaissance* is incredibly rich with insights, wisdom, and
scholarship. All of humanity should be reading this remarkable book,
which offers profound solutions to our global predicament."

—**Barbara Marx Hubbard**, futurist and author of
     Conscious Evolution

"Dr. Glen Martin is a global visionary who combines brilliance, heart
and integrity. He's a renowned activist for world democracy who
clearly outlines the practical infrastructures needed to create a just and
sustainable world. It is my hope that people everywhere will listen to
Glen's messages so that together we can go beyond the current global
crises to a new level of human evolution."

—**Philip M. Hellmich**, Director of Peace, The Shift Network;
     author of *God and Conflict*

"Dr. Glen Martin's realistic narrative concerning the present world
predicament must be seriously considered by all right-thinking people
on earth."

—**E. P. Menon**, author, global activist, and founder of
     the India Development Foundation

"This book by the well-known philosopher and humanist Dr. Glen
Martin is extremely important as it concerns the most critical issues of
our time including the question of the very survival of humankind. It
gives us hope that we won't finally lose control over events in our
troubled world."

—**Alexander N. Chumakov**, Professor of Philosophy and
     Department Chair, Financial University, Russian Federation

"A must read for all intellectuals, activists, and revolutionaries frustrated and shaken by perpetual war and chaos. Using the tools of philosophical analysis, Professor Martin helps us understand why the United Nations and the peace movement have been unsuccessful, and introduces the Earth Constitution as the powerful new social contract necessary to end global chaos and perpetual war."

—**Roger Kotila**, PhD., Senior Fellow, Institute on World Problems, USA Vice President, World Constitution and Parliament Association

"Drawing support from leading philosophers and scientists, Dr. Martin proves that a federated Earth is the wisest and only practical answer to our global problems."

—**Rev. Laura M. George**, J.D., Executive Director of the Oracle Institute

One World
Renaissance

One World Renaissance

Holistic Planetary Transformation Through a Global Social Contract

Glen T. Martin

The Institute for Economic Democracy

Institute for Economic Democracy
PO Box 309, Appomattox VA 24522, USA.

Library of Congress Control Number: 2015939597
Martin, Glen T., 1944- author.

One World Renaissance: Holistic Planetary Transformation Through a
Global Social Contract

ISBN 978-1-933567-50-1 (pbk. : alk. paper)
ISBN 978-1-933567-51-8 (ebook)

Contents

Dedication

God's joy manifests itself in nature and humanity. The human heart seeks to shape and express itself in literature. This process has no end and is remarkably diverse. Poets are mere instruments of this eternal struggle of humanity.

God's joyous poetry emanates from within itself; humanity's cultural products are a reflection of that force. The happy music of cosmic creation constantly vibrates the harp of the heart.

The song of the self, that creative impulse reverberating in tune with divine creation, is literature. Inspired by the breath of the universe, the heart, like a reed sings; literature attempts to capture that tune. Literature is not exclusively for the individual, nor is it for the author alone. Literature is divine utterance. Just as external reality ever seeks to express itself, with all its imperfection, so does literature struggle to manifest itself in different regions and languages.

—Rabindranath Tagore

This book is dedicated to all those who endeavor to express God's joy in their works, in their lives, and in their hearts: transforming our world by living the future now.

Prologue

NIETZSCHE claimed that all philosophy is really the hidden biography of the philosopher. I believe this idea carries some truth. But every philosopher is also a human being, something truly universal, and his or her biographically influenced meditation on existence therefore has implications for the rest of us. Our individuality and the wholeness of humanity are indivisibly one. And sometimes this meditation by an individual thinker may prove fundamental for the rest of us. I first began to learn this many years ago at age 19 when I read H.G. Bugbee's book *The Inward Morning*. I hope that this book may contribute to that role.

I began my systematic philosophical quest many years ago with the study of Nietzsche and the great modern problem of *nihilism:* the historical loss of meaning and value that has descended upon our modern world and threatens to end our human civilizational project in ecological or fiery death, or, what seems most likely, some combination of both. In the course of my studies in the thought of Wittgenstein, Buddhism, world religions, Western and Eastern philosophy, and through the practice of meditation, my own early nihilism evaporated in experiences and realizations that I called in *Millennium Dawn* "integrative mysticism."

I have never for a moment thought, however, that we can solve our own problems (as private persons, so to speak) and leave it at that, since we are ontologically, spiritually, and existentially bound to one another. The awakening of integrative mysticism (the unity of reason, intuition, and love) binds us as individuals to humanity, Earth, and the cosmos without which we could not be what we are and with which we are identical on the most fundamental levels. So my concern has remained the problem of nihilism in a very real way: how can the contemporary world move beyond its self-destructive attitudes and institutions toward a creative and transformed future, a human liberation that is itself ontological, spiritual, existential, and practical.

Thankfully, I am far from being alone, for there are many powerful thinkers and leaders (worldwide) who are speaking to the theme of human liberation and the possibilities for a transformation of human life on this planet. This book draws together the work of some of these thinkers and leaders under the theme of "transformative holism," a holism that has been pioneered by 20th century sciences of the cosmos, nature, and humanity. Together these thinkers and leaders are promoting a "new age," (a fundamental paradigm-shift) that can lead to a truly transformed human future.

I make concrete and detailed recommendations for how we must change our ways of living and thinking on this planet. I believe this vision of how to proceed into the future follows directly from the creative holism that this book elucidates. "It is the mission of civilization," Rabindranath Tagore writes, "to bring unity among people and establish peace and harmony" (2011: 214). My recommendations attempt to integrate a functionalist and systems approach with interrelated political, economic, ethical, psychological, and spiritual approaches to transformation. These approaches are mutually integral and ultimately inseparable. We are holistic expressions of *Being* and the quest for human liberation is not, on many levels, a matter of "either/or." All these paths to liberation belong together in the microcosm that is humanity.

In short, we need transformation in our institutions, our cultures, our spiritual lives, and ourselves. There is nothing "utopian" about this in the negative sense of this word. The possibilities for this transformation are very concrete, practical, and real. They are being expressed, implemented, and lived at this very moment in many sectors of human endeavor across the globe. We need to a "practical utopia," a pragmatic and concrete vision of how we can actualize our very real human potential. The fate of our Earth and the future of our children depends on our ability to make these changes in a significant way within the relatively near future.

I want to deeply thank those colleagues and friends who have willingly read the manuscript for this book and offered perceptive and important criticisms, corrections, and suggestions. They are Eugenia Almand, J.D., Rev. Laura George, J.D., Dr. Roger Kotila, Dr. Patricia Murphy, Dr. Richard Perkins, Dr. Mar Peter-Rieux, Prof. Courtney Ross, my excellent editor at IED Press: Dr. B. Sidney Smith, our brilliant publicist Byron Belitsos, and my wonderful wife, Phyllis Turk, CNM. They have all been wonderfully supportive and helpful. Any flaws that remain are entirely my responsibility.

Chapter 1

Emergent Cosmic Holism

There was a time when meadow, grove and stream,
The earth, and every common sight,
To me did seem
Appareled in celestial light,
The glory and the freshness of a dream.
It is not now as it hath been of yore—
Turn whereso'er I may,
By night or day,
Things which I have seen I now can see no more.

—William Wordsworth

1.1 The Universe Story and the Rediscovery of Harmony

THE principles of holism and harmony have deep roots in human civilization going back at least to the Axial Period in human history during the first millennium before the Common Era. For many thinkers and religious teachers throughout this history, holism was the dominant thought, and the harmony that it im-

1

plies has most often been understood to encompass cosmic, civilizational, and personal dimensions. Jesus, Mohammed, Buddha, Lord Krishna, Lao Tzu, and Confucius all give us visions of transformative harmony, a transformative harmony that derives from a deep relation to the holism of the cosmos. Human beings are microcosms of that holism and must seek ways to allow it to emerge within their lives and cultures.

Today, holism appears to us not only as a constant, abiding feature of our universe, but also as an emergent and evolutionary aspect of the cosmos and all life. In the face of the pervasive *disharmony* of much of human existence that we experience today worldwide, the principles of holism and harmony function, in the words of Ernst Bloch (1986a), as a gigantic "principle of hope." We recognize that disharmony threatens the very existence of life on Earth, that we face the possible end of the human project and higher forms of life on this planet.

However, even as the danger grows, as the poet Hölderin sang, the saving insight emerges within our hearts and minds and within human civilization. The creative and revolutionary holism of the emerging planetary paradigm becomes a vision of the very real possibilities for a harmonious and transformed human reality. Today, the holistic vision of the ancient spiritual teachers is reborn on a higher level—consistent with the deepest discoveries of modern science.

Holism is the most fundamental discovery of 20th century science. It is a discovery of every science from astrophysics to quantum physics to environmental science to psychology to anthropology. It is the discovery that the entire universe is an integral whole, and that the basic organizational principle of the universe is the field principle: the universe consists of fields within fields, levels of wholeness and integration that mirror in fundamental ways, and integrate with, the ultimate, cosmic whole.

This discovery has overthrown the early-modern Newtonian paradigm in the sciences, which was predicated on atomism, causal determinism, mechanism, and a materialism that was discerned, it was thought, by a narrow empiricism. The holism of the ancient and medieval thinkers was superseded by this early-modern Newtonian paradigm in the 16th and 17th centuries. This development generated a host of assumptions about the world and human beings that became determinate for the basic world view that most people and institutions continue to hold today.

Today the holism of the ancients has been rediscovered on a higher level. We understand, very much more clearly than these ancient thinkers, that human beings are deeply *historical* beings, moving from a past, through a dynamic present, toward a future that we are deeply involved in creating. We create our future through a vision and comprehension of its possibilities. Revolutionary holism is just that: a holism that can transform everything from disharmony to harmony, from war to peace, from hate to love. Ethics, law, education, and government are all historically grounded aspects of human life. This means they are subject to holistic transformation, to "a new heaven and a new Earth," that, indeed, has much in common with what the ancient teachers said about holism and harmony.

Holism is not simply an intellectual perception of harmony, for in holism we are included in the wholes, wholes we discern at the deepest levels with our entire being. We discern and embody the holism of humanity, of the Earth, of the cosmos, and of the divine. Holism means not only reason but love, indeed, it includes the synthesis of reason, intuition, and love, as we shall see. Theologian Matthew Fox affirms that "humanity as rational animal will no longer mean a dualistic rationalism but a harmonious animal, *ratio* originally meant harmony, one at its harmonious best *as* animal in search of harmony worldwide, self-wide and cosmos-wide" (1990: 266). In this sense, the paradigm-shift to holism can be akin to a religious conversion. Suddenly we see in a new way; we see everything in a new light; we discern reasons for hope, joy, and celebration everywhere. In their book *The Study of Religion in the Age of Global dialogue* (about the transformation of consciousness that is going on around us) Swidler and Mojzes write:

> The religious conversion means coming to know and love, and therefore truly to become one with, all Reality, not quantitatively, but qualitatively. This means becoming one somehow with its very structure, its Principle. (2000: 118)

The paradigm-shift to creative and revolutionary holism illuminates not only fundamental aspects of our world but something about ourselves as well: our participation, as D.H. Lawrence puts it, in this "magnificent here and now of life in the flesh that is ours, and ours only for a time," as part of the "living, incarnate cosmos" (1976: 125-26), that we manifest "its very structure, its Principle." It is the realization that we ourselves are manifestations of the "living, incarnate cosmos." Holism, we shall see, is not only the fundamental scientific discovery of the 20th century, but the realization of a new being and a new consciousness for persons worldwide.

Fox tells us that "the primary issue in spirituality is not redemption of the soul, but redemption of the world. We are both in the world and the world in us. To heal one is to heal the other. To redeem the one is to redeem the other" (1990: 268). Human beings are emerging into a new maturity, into new dimensions of love, meaning, and fulfillment. Spiritual thinker Barbara Marx Hubbard emphasizes a universal love that is emerging worldwide, connected with a love for "the whole of life" which is moving people to connect with others around the globe and create together a harmonious world equal to our highest human capacities. She writes:

> We are the crossover generation moving from one phase of evolution to the next! Although barely perceptible, as were the earliest humans in the pre-human world, a young Homo Universalis is emerging everywhere, in every culture, faith, and background. The signs of our emergence as universal humans include an unconditional love for the whole of life; a powerful, irresistible passion to unite with the spirit within; and a deep heartfelt impulse to connect with others and co-create a world equal to our love and our capacities. (In Henion, 2012: 18)

In this book I will first discuss fundamental aspects of the new, historically grounded, principles of transformative holism and harmony in order to elucidate these principles and show some of their significance in human affairs. We will examine the emerging holistic paradigm, especially in relation to the concepts of government, law, ethics, economics, and education. We will see that these principles do not deny the dynamism of conflictive interaction that takes place everywhere in nature and in human life, but that the *larger patterns* of this dynamic process reveal a deeply holistic process. We will also see that human beings may well be a key principle within this creative upsurge of the universe. We are microcosms of that creative upsurge, responsible for establishing a world and a future characterized by ever-greater holism and harmony.

By contrast, we also examine the early-modern scientific paradigm, and the institutions that emerged from that paradigm, to show some fundamental roots of the lack of harmony and civilization of conflict that dominates in today's economic, political, and legal institutions. A tremendous hope is emerging in those who live from the emerging paradigm of wholeness and harmony, a hope and a love that is worldwide and planetary. The dynamism of conflictive interaction that characterizes life on this planet, understood in terms of the emerging holistic principles that I describe in this book, need not lead to the destruction of the human project or of the nature that sustains us. A new future is opening up for human beings that had not previously been apparent.

We need to take up that future, let it inspire our lives, and transform the failed institutions by which we have organized our lives on this planet into living embodiments of holism and harmony. Like Wordsworth we have lost the "glory and freshness" of the "celestial light." However, unlike Wordsworth, "the years that bring the philosophic mind" can, indeed, recover the experience of the glory of existence and the special promise of the human project. What is emerging worldwide is truly a planetary *renaissance: one world reborn.*

The intent of this book is to help reveal both what is lacking in today's world and outline the process for establishing a harmonious planetary civilization: through drawing on the wisdom of the holistic thinkers of the past, through recognizing the immense paradigm-shift going on in the present, and through an analysis of the continuing causes of disharmony and fragmentation worldwide. Harmony and disharmony are correlative concepts. They apply not only to persons, but to the institutions and societies that structure persons' lives. Establishing harmony requires not only a positive vision of our higher human possibilities but also understanding the historical causes and conditions of disharmony.

In their 1992 book, *Universe Story – From the Primordial Flaring Forth to the Ecozoic Era, A Celebration of the Unfolding of the Cosmos*, Brian Swimme and Thomas Berry illuminate the emerging holistic understanding of human life and the universe through bringing the two together into a single, sweeping historical narrative: *"the universe story."* Beginning with the "primal flaring forth" of the big bang, through some 14 billion years of development, human beings emerge as an integral part of this process. Swimme and Berry trace the emergence of human consciousness from Neolithic and primitive beginnings through the mythological era and subsequent developmental eras down to the present in which the "ecozoic" era is emerging to replace the "technozoic" mode of human thinking.

Their story of the universe is one way of revealing the reintegration of human thought and feeling into the integrated holism of the cosmos. Human beings are not a cosmic accident within the universe, and our thoughts and feelings are not "merely" subjective epiphenomena somehow attached to an objective, mechanistic world of facts and deterministic natural laws. Rather, we are an emergent aspect of the cosmos intimately connected with the primal flaring forth and directly related to the deepest mysteries of existence and the evolutionary process. We need to examine what happened, the reasons why human beings continue to wallow in disharmony, violence, and chaos, and we need to understand evermore clearly the tremendous significance of emergent holism and our vital role within the new universe story.

1.2 Holism, Harmony, and Global Crises

THE principle of harmony that arises from transformative holism is associated in human thought with a number of complementary concepts that help articulate its meaning and implications. We associate harmony with peace, as opposed to conflict and war, with nonviolence, as opposed to violence and the mutual attempt of people to kill or harm one another, with cooperation, rather than forms of competition resulting in absolute winners and losers, with justice and fairness, as opposed to situations of injustice, exploitation, or domination, and with freedom—the freedom of people to live meaningful, flourishing lives in relationships with others and with society as a whole.

In past centuries, just as today, disharmony had terrible human consequences—as armies invaded the territory of others, legal systems persecuted innocent persons, class divisions in societies caused suffering to enslaved, oppressed, or marginalized peoples, and whole populations starved and perished in the midst of social settings abundant with food and other life-necessities. However, it was not until the mid-20th century that thoughtful people began to realize that disharmony was endangering the very existence of human civilization and the ecological ability of our planet to sustain higher forms of life.

Jonathan Glover's book *Humanity: A Moral History of the 20th Century*, details the terrible failure of human civilization to achieve any degree of peace or harmony. Instead, the 20th century provides a disgraceful record of evermore technologically sophisticated means of human beings mass exterminating other human beings. Glover writes:

> The twentieth-century history of large-scale cruelty and killing is only too familiar: the mutual slaughter of the First World War, the terror-famine of the Ukraine, the Gulag,

Auschwitz, Dresden, the Burma Railway, Hiroshima, Vietnam, the Chinese Cultural Revolution, Cambodia, Rwanda,
the collapse of Yugoslavia. These names will conjure up
others. Because of this history, it is (or should be) hard for
thinking about ethics to carry on as before. (2000: 2)

The same technological sophistication that has made mass
murder evermore efficient with push-button ease of execution has
also made the human impact on the environment of the planet
devastating for all the natural systems that make up its delicately
woven biosphere. Entire forests can be cut down in the time that
only 100 years ago appeared inconceivable to men working with
hand axes and two-person cross-cut saws. Today, entire moun-
taintops can be removed and chewed up by giant machines to ex-
tract the random veins of coal contained in them (as is happening
in West Virginia in the US).

Human beings begin to comprehend that we may be the cause
of our own extinction. In fundamental ways, it is clear that we
have been living in deep disharmony with one another and with
the natural world that sustains us."These tools," scientist Arthur
M. Young confirms, "provide not just the means for conquering
nature but...the means for man's own destruction, and, hence,
the challenge to achieve *self*-control, to attain the responsibility of
stewardship" (1976: 162).

A global consciousness has begun to emerge that was very
rare in human beings prior to the mid-20th century. It is a consciousness that we now face global crises and global issues that
threaten our existence on Earth. It began to dawn on thoughtful
people everywhere that we are faced with impending climate collapse—the transformation of our planetary climate into forms that
no longer sustain higher forms of life and that could, in the process of collapse, engender out of control patterns of devastation
such as mass extinctions or pandemics that wipe out the human
species and destroy civilization (Speth, 2005). "What we are experiencing today," philosopher Hans Jonas writes, "is the paradox

of excessive success that threatens to turn into a catastrophe by destroying its own foundation in the natural world" (1996: 53).

A second crisis of global proportions involves the problem of depletion of the most fundamental resources necessary to life such as agricultural lands, potable water, clean air, and planetary forests. As the human population vastly expands every year, the resources on Earth available to support its population continue to dramatically shrink. I documented these environmental crises in some detail in my 2013 book, *The Anatomy of a Sustainable World: Our Choice between Climate Change or System Change.* "System Change," we shall see, means that our survival and our future depend not only on a spiritual and cultural paradigm-shift, but on achieving a genuine global social contract, which is an integral part of the holistic solution.

A third crisis threatening human existence of which thoughtful people have been aware since 1945 is the development of weapons of mass destruction such as nuclear weapons, as well as the development of technologically advanced conventional weapons to the extent that entire countries can be devastated in a number of hours. Today, the entire human population could be devastated in the event of a major nuclear war and its environmental consequences. As German theologian and philosopher Jürgen Moltmann puts this: "When the atomic bomb was invented and dropped on Hiroshima and Nagasaki in August of 1945, it was not just the Second World War that was ended. The whole human race had entered its end-time as well" (2012: 46).

As global thinker Hans Küng expresses this: "Just as the human race came into being, so it can pass away again—and our generation is the first in the long history of the Earth which proves to be technically able to destroy itself, by nuclear weapons or by eroding the ecological basis of its survival" (in Schmidt-Leukel, 1989: 183). Theologian Gordon D. Kaufman declares that "With our enormous technological power we may be bringing human history to a close. Before it is too late, we must learn to develop a politics of peacemaking and of interdependence rather than one of self-protection and national sovereignty" (in Rouner, 1985: 134). In *Conscious Evolution,* Barbara Marx Hubbard writes:

> An irreversible shift toward conscious evolution began in 1945 when the United States dropped atomic bombs on Hiroshima and Nagasaki. With this dreadful release of power we penetrated one of the invisible technologies of nature— the atom—and gained the power that we once attributed to the gods. This capability, combined with other rapidly developing technologies such as biotechnology, nanotechnology (the ability to build atom by atom), and artificial intelligence, if used in our current state of self-centered consciousness could lead to the destruction of the human race. (1998: 9)

While poverty, misery, and disorder continue to grow everywhere on the Earth, the nations of the world spend well over one trillion US dollars each year on militarism and war preparation. While the resources of Earth continue to rapidly deplete, while climate change increasingly devastates entire portions of the Earth with droughts, hurricanes, floods, and rising sea levels, the militaristic competition of warring nation-states prevents any meaningful cooperation or collective action to prevent total disaster for Earth and its citizens.

These global crises demand analysis with regard to their causes and the background paradigm from which they emerged. We will see that this analysis reveals a consistent pattern—that I call the early-modern paradigm—in which modern man appears alienated, materialistic, secularized, and relativistic. But the convergence of scientific breakthroughs and philosophical insights today are reversing this entire picture that was fostered, for example, well into the 20th century by some Existentialist writers like the early Jean-Paul Sartre: the idea that human life appears as a useless passion vainly striving in a meaningless universe. "The pursuit of ends inspired by the Newtonian paradigm," philosopher Errol E. Harris writes, "has plunged humankind into a global crisis from which it can extricate itself only by thinking globally"

(2000b: 108). We are emerging from that nihilism into a new Renaissance, a new dawn of day, a new and exciting breakthrough of consciousness, insight, meaning, and a new love of life.

The question of harmony and its implications is clearly no longer merely a theoretical question for philosophers and cultural thinkers. Today, it is an absolutely vital question of survival, of restoring the possibility of a decent future for subsequent generations. We will see that dealing with the global crises that threaten human existence is directly related with the imperative to establish a world based upon human dignity and human flourishing, a world that will include both a spiritual renaissance and a practical, planetary social contract.

The emerging new paradigm understands that our situation at this point in history is unique. We must surely comprehend the ways in which the outdated early-modern paradigm remains an impediment to a viable and sustainable world order. Yet we must also realize the uniqueness of the present—there are few past precedents for how we are to move into the future because global awareness of our single fragile planet and the technology for destroying it did not previously exist in history. Today, we must envision a new, holistic future. We must start from this vision and allow it to guide our actions in the present, drawing us creatively forward toward a truly transformed future.

The revolutions in the sciences that have confirmed a universe that is holistic through and through, including the holism of our planetary ecology, have also confirmed the holism of our humanity in which our integrated capacities for reason, intuition, and love give rise to our ability to imagine a transformed future. In Paul Ricoeur's words:

> No doubt the understanding of the primordial first, then of the fallen in and through the primordial, requires a kind of imagination, the imagination of innocence or a "kingdom" wherein the quests for having, power and worth would not be what they in fact are. But this imagination is not a fanciful dream; it is an "imaginative variation," to use a Husserlian term, which manifests the essence by breaking the pres-

tige of the fact. In imagining another state of affairs or another kingdom, I perceive the possible, and in the possible, the essential. (1967: 170).

An immense world-transformative hope arises in those who have grasped the new holism, a new vision of a decent human future of peace and justice, and a human future in harmony and fulfillment in relation to our planetary biosphere. We will see that, like Ricoeur, many thinkers today are recognizing the power of imagination to identify something "essential" about human and cosmic holism, the actualization of which lies in the future as a very real human possibility. We will explore below the basic causes of our present planetary condition of fragmentation, disharmony, and ever increasing planetary disaster and outline some principles of harmony that are necessary for creating a decent human future, focusing especially on the questions of ethics, government, law, and the rule of law in human affairs.

1.3   The Age of Static Holism (Ancient and Medieval World Views)

IN their book, *The Universe Story*, Swimme and Berry attempt to bring together human knowledge from many scientific and cultural sources to provide a coherent picture of human life as an integral part of the emergent-evolutionary process from the originating explosion of the Big Bang to the present. This kind of endeavor may ultimately be what is necessary if we are to discover a path to harmony with one another and with nature. The sad history of the 20th century has made clear that we are in fundamental disharmony with both dimensions—with one another and with nature. The issue has to do with the historical emergence of human beings out of nature and into modes of self-consciousness that appear to make living in harmony impossible.

As Swimme and Berry express this: "the drama of self-consciousness takes place in five phases: the primordial emergence of the human; the Neolithic settlements; the classical civilizations; the rise of nations; and the Ecozoic Era" (143-44). Their book places the development of self-consciousness within the larger universe story and shows in what ways our present disharmony reflects the fact that we have not yet understood that story. The story is that of the contemporary scientific discovery of the holism of the universe and the articulation of that holism in the diverse development of human beings and human civilization.

Our disharmony with the planetary biosphere, and with other people, cultures, and nations, is the consequence of our limited view that fails to see the deeper *unity-in-diversity* of the entire process. Human self-awareness has emerged out of this evolutionary process, but this self-awareness remains trapped at the level of polar-opposites—my religion versus your religion, my nation versus your nation, my race versus your race—within a contemporary set of assumptions that Swimme and Berry call "Technozoic." Study of this historical development can bring us to an awakening to the *unity-in-diversity* of the whole. *The universe story*, in a very real sense, is also our story.

A number of thinkers who chronicle the rise of human self-awareness focus on the Axial Age as the historical era that was central to the emergence of our present level of self-awareness. Karl Jaspers (1953), for example, underlines the importance of the worldwide changes that took place approximately between 800 and 200 BCE, also emphasized by Swimme and Berry and by John Hick in his 2004 book, *An Interpretation of Religion*. During this period human beings became capable of clearly distinguishing their personal subjective beliefs, attitudes, and responses from the objective world around them that operated independently of this subjective dimension.

The objective world could be understood as governed by laws of its own, potentially discoverable by human reason, and the subjective world could be understood as providing a freedom of action in which humans could alter and manipulate their environment according to their subjectivity, according to their values, perceptions, and beliefs (Hick, 2004). The stage was set for the human drama that would be played out worldwide for the next twenty-five hundred years: the objective laws of nature in relation to human freedom of action. With the Axial Period, therefore, a new dimension develops within our universe—openness to the future. A creature has emerged much less determined by its past but open to new possibilities in the future.

My 2008 book *Ascent to Freedom: Philosophical and Practical Foundations of Democratic World Law* traces this drama as it moved from the Axial Age through three broad civilizational paradigms from the ancient world to the present. It names the first civilizational paradigm the "Age of Static Holism." Through the Ancient and Medieval eras the dominant paradigm looked at the world and human life in terms of a static, integral unity. In the West, prior to the rise of Christianity, Plato and Aristotle articulated versions of this unity in which the order and harmony of the cosmos were discoverable by, and reflected in, human reason.

There was, therefore, an integral continuity between the harmonious constitution of the cosmos and human life. For both Plato and Aristotle, each in their own way, leading a "philosophical" life meant using reason dialectically and dialogically to move up a ladder of ever-greater maturity and understanding toward true intellectual and spiritual harmony with the laws of the holistic cosmos. For Aristotle, all living things were ensouled, and understanding the human soul (as the form of the body), was part of understanding the holistic and organic order of the cosmos itself. The primary impediment to harmonious and just society for these thinkers was *ignorance*, and the key to promoting harmony on the Earth was both education and the construction of good human institutions that mirrored the harmony of the cosmos.

The ancient masters, prophets, and religious teachers predominantly understood the universe as a cosmic whole and both intuited and reasoned the many human connections with this whole. Human beings were most often understood by them as a microcosm of the macrocosm. They developed various forms of intellectual and meditational discipline to bring students into harmony with the higher order of things. Within ancient Greek cultures centering on the 6th century BCE, Parmenides declared that "thinking and the object of thought are the same," Democritus concluded that "man is a small 'ordered world' [*kosmos*]," Anaxagoras stated that "mind set in order all that was to be, all that ever was but no longer is, and all that is now or ever will be." (Wheelwright 1966: 98, 184, 163). For these thinkers, the human mind *participated* in the larger mind of the universe.

In this same ancient Greek culture, Heraclitus concluded that "man is not rational; there is intelligence only in what encompasses him" (ibid. 74). Human intelligence, for Heraclitus, is activated when we attend to the divine *Logos*, hidden within the flux of phenomena. For Pythagoras, the relation of the human mind and the cosmos was confirmed through study of the sacred, mathematical cosmic order, for Plato it was through the practice of dialectic leading from the flux of phenomena to the intelligible forms (*eidos*), for Aristotle illumination came through contemplation of the increasingly perfect harmony of the intelligible world ascending to the Unmoved Mover, for Plotinus, the holistic principle at the heart of all things was directly experienced through contemplative and philosophic meditations leading to union with the *One*.

The paradigm articulated by these thinkers became fundamental to ancient Western civilization moving into to the Christian era that followed. For the latter, the static harmony of the cosmos was the creative product of an all-wise and all-good God concerned with human redemption, harmony, and flourishing. It is true that this vision of harmony was somewhat undercut by the Augustinian doctrine of original sin according to which the original natural harmony created by God was disrupted by human sin, making it impossible for human beings to live in harmony naturally, and requiring an external divine interference and a cosmic redemption. As we shall see, however, the concepts of grace and redemption need not be understood in terms of a *deus ex machina* judging, condemning, and/or redeeming the world from outside.

Indeed, not only did Judaism and Christianity develop a messianic vision of a future holistic redemption, a concept of natural law also developed within that tradition that continued even during the era of original sin. Just as the cosmos was structured in a holistic and lawful fashion by God, so human beings could discern and live by ethical principles that likewise came from the supreme source. St. Paul writes in Romans 2:14 that "when Gentiles who do not have the law do by nature as the law requires, they show that the law is written on their hearts." Harmonious social and personal life was theoretically possible on Earth since its natural laws were available to every person as moral laws written on the human heart. Today, the work of Paul Ricoeur, for example, studies the natural dynamic of the "fallenness" quality of human experiences and illuminates the possibility of experience deriving from a primal openness to being that does not confuse "this spontaneous and tendential attachment to living with a real, actual and prior downfall" (1967: 143).

The ancient paradigm of static holism is also found at the heart of all the other great world religions: Judaism, Islam, Buddhism, Hinduism, Shintoism, Confucianism, and Taoism. In the most ancient of scriptures known as the Vedas, for example (which form the spiritual roots of the multiplicity of religions known as Hindu) the emphasis is on both spiritual and material harmony with nature. In Buddhism, the holistic concept of the "interdependent co-origination" of all things is fundamental, as is the famous concept of Tao (cosmic interdependence and harmony) in Taoism. The Shintoism that the present writer experienced in Japan is replete with a sense of harmony in nature and between humans and nature. For Confucius, the concept of *jen* or 'compassionate humanness' was essential for harmony and was embraced by the reality of *li* indicating a sacred order of social and cosmic harmony (cf. Fingerette, 1972).

The core ideas of holism are found in the ancient scriptures of all these religions. This holism is being reborn today as a creative, dynamic, evolutionary holism that sees universal holism as emerging ever more profoundly through the world process itself. We no longer look to unchanging structures of divine, cosmic, and human law. Instead, we look forward to an emergent future transformed by ever-deeper relationships of harmony, peace, and ecstatic bliss.

Today, the vision of one world, and a future fulfillment within that one world, implicit in the ancient texts, must become an actuality if we are to survive on this planet. We have reached tipping points, limit points, beyond which there is no viable future without holistic transformation: institutional, cultural, psychological, and spiritual. Our task, our "imperative of responsibility" in the words of Hans Jonas (1984), is to make the ancient holism actual and concrete for all of us on this tiny planet Earth. Our task is "practical utopia," with emphasis on the practical: the unity of the human project actualized in one world of institutionalized and actualized unity-in-diversity.

1.4 The Age of Fragmentation (Early-Modern World Views)

THE Age of Static Holism began to disintegrate in late medieval times, not in the least because of the Black Death that wiped out well over 30 percent of the population of Europe during the 14th century. During the subsequent two centuries, however, developments took place that had worldwide implications. Thinkers such as Tycho Brahe, Johannes Kepler, and Galileo Galilei discovered the systematic applicability of mathematics to nature. "The book of nature is written in the language of mathematics," proclaimed Galileo, and creative thinkers from Spinoza to Descartes to Hobbes, to Newton attempted to work out the epistemology and cosmology that made this truth possible.

A new paradigm was in the process of being born. In the 17th century, the holism of Spinoza's thought ultimately lost out to a struggle between the mind-body dualism of Descartes (whose

Meditations on First Philosophy was first published in 1641) and the materialist monism of Hobbes (whose *Leviathan* appeared in 1651). These two options seemed to be the primary alternatives. For Descartes, the physical world of extended substance (which included the body) was singularly subject to mathematical determinism, but the mind was of a different non-material substance altogether. For Hobbes, on the other hand, the mind was simply part of the deterministic world of matter.

These epistemological and cosmological developments culminated in the 18th century triumph of the Newtonian world view that seemed to provide an explanatory framework for all bodies in motion anywhere on Earth or in the universe. They also triumphed through the adoption of a dogmatic empiricism first systematically formulated by John Locke, George Berkeley, and David Hume. Even Immanuel Kant, who reacted against the apparent skepticism implied in Hume's radical empiricism by positing *a priori* structures of the human mind that restored the universality and credibility of knowledge, still retained the assumption that all knowledge of the physical world was a product of the empirical senses, resulting in a Newtonian world view.

The Newtonian or early-modern paradigm was in the process of emerging that (because it appeared so evidently successful in predicting, controlling, and understanding the world) rapidly spread worldwide. The world was conceived as a gigantic mechanism, built up from indivisible simple parts called atoms, and governed deterministically by the mathematically precise laws of universal gravitation within a framework of absolute space and time. In contrast to that objective "external" world was the human mind. And its values, desires, and thoughts were often considered "merely subjective." Matthew Fox writes:

> For Descartes, since body is machine, people are souls that are bodiless. The soul was *res cogitans* as distinct from *res extensa*. Like Plato, Descartes posited soul as a distinct substance weighed down by body, saying, "our soul is in its nature entirely independent of the body." From his time

on, "Western thought fell victim to a dualism of body and
soul hitherto unknown" and soul was now considered exclusively as subjectivity. (1990: 261)

In *Apocalypse and Paradigm*, Harris studies the early-modern
paradigm at length. He concludes that there were eight cosmological assumptions behind this paradigm: (1) an absolute frame
of space and time, (2) materialism and mechanism, (3) atomism,
(4) reductionism, (5) the assumption that all relations are external,
(6) the demand for unbiased observation and value free science,
(7) rejection of teleological explanation, and (8) complete matter-
mind dichotomy (2000b: 21-22). We will see in due course why
every one of these features has been superseded by contemporary
science, even though many of these features continue to cling to
us in the forms of our dominant institutions and mental habits.

As Harris points out, this early-modern cosmology included
an epistemology demanding detached, value free observation and
"objective," scientific investigation. It assumed the materialism of
the physical cosmos and the idea that physical bodies and atoms
existed independently of one another in purely external relationships. Reason was to observe this mechanism "objectively," ignoring its own values, feelings, intuitions, and desires. This approach appeared immensely successful in terms of this set of assumptions, as creative individuals discovered how to apply observation and mathematics in ways that transformed our physical
environment through inventions of all sorts.

It also engendered the rise of capitalist economic relations, beginning with the goldsmiths and entrepreneurs of the 15th and
16th centuries (a system that appeared to promote unlimited economic growth). And it gave rise to the birth of the modern system of sovereign nation-states, usually dated from the Treaty of
Westphalia in 1648. It led to the industrial revolution during the
late 18th and early 19th centuries (which appeared to promise ultimately making the cheap manufactured goods and scientifically
grown foods necessary for life available to everyone on Earth).

Even though the Newtonian cosmology did not appear able to explain mind, that is, human moral choices, human freedom, or rational capacity (except either as an unconvincing reductionism that equated all these things with deterministic brain processes, or a metaphysical dualism that saw mind and matter as entirely different things), its success in controlling the material world allowed it to spread very rapidly throughout the globe. As physicist Henry Stapp asserts:

> In a coherent understanding of nature, all parts must stand together in a way such that none can stand alone. Yet classical physics is so internally coherent as to preclude any rationally ordained coupling between the physical reality it describes and anything else. Classical physics not only fails to demand the mental, it fails even to provide a rational place for the mental. And if the mental is introduced *ad hoc*, then it must remain totally ineffectual, in absolute contradiction to our deepest experience. (In Kitchener, 1988: 38)

Classical physics of the early-modern period was "internally coherent" but incomplete. It had no place for mind or values within its conception of nature and the scientific method. Today, evolutionary thinkers and scientists overwhelmingly see "mind" and "consciousness" as aspects of the space-time-matter-energy processes of the universe itself. As complexity develops so do emergent levels of mind-consciousness, already implicit in the simpler processes that predate life. Jay McDaniel sums this up:

> Even ostensibly inorganic matter, at least at the quantum level, has mind-like properties, meaning that consciousness is an expression of, not an exception to, the kind of energy from which the universe as a whole emerges. There is an ontological continuity between physical energy and consciousness, a continuity of matter and mind. (2005: 51)

In classical physics, even God was relegated to the role of cosmic watch-maker by Deism and Enlightenment thought. Since the world was totally determined by the laws governing bodies in motion, there was no role for God except as a demiurge-creator who set the entire process in motion at the beginning and subsequently played no role in its functioning. As the French mathematician and astronomer Pierre-Simon Laplace famously remarked when asked about a role for God: "I have no need for that hypothesis," manifesting, in the words of Ken Wilber, "the empiricist (and behaviorist) psychology that would seize and freeze the Western soul for almost three centuries" (1998: 79).

God was relegated to an apparently contingent role in relation to the mechanistic universe, and mind remained an apparently insoluble mystery. Nevertheless, the scientific revolution of those centuries had placed great technological and instrumental power into human hands. Physicist Fritjof Capra, on the other hand, describes the reintegration of mind into our contemporary scientific concept of nature, extending beyond self-conscious reasoning to nature and the entire cosmos:

> The fact that the living world is organized in multileveled structures means that there are also levels of mind. In the organism, for example, there are various levels of "metabolic" mentation involving cells, tissues, and organs, and then there is the "neural" mentation of the brain, which itself consists of multiple levels corresponding to different stages of human evolution. The totality of these mentations constitutes what we would call the human mind. Such a notion of mind as a multileveled phenomenon, of which we are only partly aware in ordinary states of consciousness. . . .
>
> In the stratified order of nature, individual human minds are embedded in the larger minds of social and ecological systems, and these are integrated into the planetary mental system—the mind of Gaia— which in turn must participate in some kind of universal or cosmic mind. The conceptual framework of the new systems approach is in no way restricted by associating this cosmic mind with the traditional idea of God... In this view the deity is. . .nothing less than the self-organizing dynamics of the entire cosmos. (1982: 291-92)

The inability of the mechanistic Newtonian world conception to include mind into its picture of nature gave rise to a split between the "objective" world characterized by causal laws and mechanical interactions, and the human "subjective" world of "mind" dominated by desires, purposes, moral reactions, cultural ideas, etc. This inner world of the human mind was "merely" subjective, not part of the physical world studied by science, even when science turned toward the human being it was in terms of the brain and the physical make-up of the human being. Reason was *devalued* from the high place it had held with the ancients to a merely instrumental and strategic figuring out how to satisfy human desires and purposes, the desires and purposes themselves being a-rational. Similarly, human values often appeared merely subjective or merely cultural to the early-modern thinkers like David Hume or Thomas Hobbes.

Our contemporary scientific world view (as we will see in more detail in Chapter Nine) understands that mind is a pervasive *natural* phenomenon of the entire universe, a phenomenon that includes, but is not limited to, the human mind. Ancient thinkers like Plato, Aristotle, and Plotinus viewed the holism of the cosmos as including mind—the human mind was microcosm of the cosmic mind. Hence, thinking and reasoning could discern real value in the universe and could determine the ethical ends or goals intrinsic to human life and its holistic cosmic framework. The early-modern paradigm, however, saw no cosmically embodied ends or goals, no *telos* or lure toward values, only blind mechanism. Ends or goals were now reduced to a-rational human desires, and reason was now merely an *instrument*, a *technique* for pursuing non-rational goals.

Sociologist Max Weber (1954) studied the development of the early-modern world system under the explanatory concept of "rationalization," which he understood as a predominantly *instrumentalization* of human reason. Since overcoming the "enchanted" medieval era of faith, society was oriented to "rationalizing" human life, to its progressive "disenchantment." The process of rationalization, according to Weber, supplied the explanation of the success of capitalism in which quantification, predictability, and regularity were essential to the expansion of a systematic and reliable profit-making regime. This regime was aided by the elaboration and bureaucratization of nation-state administrative systems.

The same calculability and capacity for mastery that early-modern science made possible for nature was now applied to human beings through the rationalization process. The domination of this "formal-procedural" rationality did not necessarily cohere with the possibility of a "substantive-value" rationality that had been prominent during ancient and medieval times and had provided a deep meaning and value for both thinkers and religious believers. A substantive-value use of reason to perceive the intrinsic values and goals of human life would have to await the 20th century rediscovery of holism.

The rationalization of capitalism and the bureaucratization of the nation-state undercut the medieval belief that both faith and reason could discover substantive value in the cosmos. Reasoning became merely instrumental. Reason, it was thought, did not provide objective ends of human action (or anything valuable in itself). It provided only the means for satisfying human desires. The ends became "subjective"—human desires, instincts, wants and needs were thought to determine the ends of action. After several centuries of this development, according to Weber, the over-all effect of this process of rationalization on human beings was the "loss of freedom" and "loss of meaning" inside the "iron cage" of late capitalism. Technique and instrumentality had dominated over freedom and any possible discernment of intrinsic values in human life.

Capitalism, as a pervasive economic system and pattern of life, developed as a global institution as part of this same early-modern paradigm: a process of rationalization in which reason was understood instrumentally, in terms of regularity, predictability, the development of administrative and bureaucratic systems, and the evermore effective mastery of both nature and human beings. "Reason" was considered a methodological practice applicable to the calculations of profit and loss, production and consumption, and human beings were also viewed as "rational" in this way: as atoms or units (whether individual or corporate) who calculated costs and benefits to themselves from their economic (and other) interactions and made choices on the basis of such self-interested calculations. Nothing else was allowed to interfere with this dogma. As Ernst Bloch expressed this:

> The economy works like a detached and artificial being that runs and stops all by itself. This economy—which is the economy of abstract mechanization—does not work concretely and as a whole abstractly according to scientific laws. This is why the economic law of the circulation of goods is, as Engels said along with Hegel, a pure law of chance.... Capitalism was obviously equally interested in what could be well formulated and guaranteed as its juridical determination (significantly, it is the law of exchange that is the strictest); calculability demands that it not be interrupted by any rights of privilege whether they be of the feudal or other type. (1986b: 134-136)

The ends or goals to which human beings direct themselves were considered non-rational or irrational. Reason was instrumental and involved a calculation of means to such ends. The non-rational ends, typically understood, were wealth, worldly success, power, and pleasure—a perfect fit for capitalism and often considered to be fundamental drives of our "human nature." This required "calculability" and embracing the illusion that the laws of capitalism were scientific and impersonal. Morality had no place interfering with these "scientific" laws.

Karl Marx in *The Holy Family* refers to the ruling class under capitalism as equally alienated from their true human possibilities as the working class. However, the property-owning class, he declares, is "satisfied" with its illusion that the ends of life are success, power, and wealth. The process of rationalization had created a materialistic civilization governed by deterministic instrumental, technical, and strategic forms of rationality that was incapable of seeing its own dehumanization. Following Marx, Herbert Marcuse remarks that:

> The intoxication with power has caused people to overlook the fact that, in spite of the progressive technicization and rationalization of contemporary society, man's *human* power over nature and "things" has diminished rather than increased!.... This is only one aspect of the fact that in capitalist society all human values are lost or placed in the service of technical and rational "objectivity." (In Wolin, 2001: 146)

A second institution studied by Weber that emerged as part of the same development of the early-modern paradigm was that of the system of territorially-based sovereign nation-states. As he points out, the elaboration of administrative and bureaucratic systems in these states, the keeping of accurate records, and the passage of private property and contract laws, vastly enhanced the advance of capitalism. And, as Karl Marx had also forcefully pointed out, the governments of these nation-states served as agents promoting the advance of their respective capitalist ruling classes. Capitalism and the nation-state system became two sides of the same coin. As contemporary social scientists Terry Boswell and Christopher Chase-Dunn conclude: "A system of sovereign states (i.e. with an overarching definition of sovereignty) is fundamental to the origins and reproduction of the capitalist world economy" (2000: 23).

Scholars commonly recognize that this system of territorially bound sovereign states was first implicitly formalized in the 1648 Treaty of Westphalia at the heart of the development of the early-modern paradigm. This system involved the same set of assumptions that characterized the rest of the emerging global civilization based on this paradigm: the nation-states were conceived of as atoms, as inviolable territorial units that stood in external relations to one another. Each state was autonomous over its internal affairs, just as the early-modern paradigm looks at individual human beings as autonomous over their bodies and subjective thoughts and at corporations as autonomous over their employees (who obey the commands of management in the service of profits for investors).

Each state was independent in its foreign policy, and governed, it was assumed, by calculations of rational self-interest. Hence, like individuals and capitalist corporations, states were assumed to be governed by the same instrumental rationality that calculates self-interest in terms of non-rational values such as power, prestige, and economic advantage. The self-interest of smaller and weaker states is to ally themselves strategically with bigger, more powerful states, and the self-interest of bigger states is to prevail in the global competition for markets, resources, and cheap labor.

With the development of this early-modern paradigm, the Age of Static Holism had now been replaced by what I called in *Ascent to Freedom* the Age of Fragmentation. The system of capitalism is considered an amoral system governed by impartial economic laws (while it was thought that individual capitalists, on the other hand, may or may not be moral persons). Atomistic corporations and self-interested individuals struggle in competition with one another in external relationships, following these economic laws. As Wilber describes this Age of Fragmentation: "And so it came about, in this fractured fairy tale, that the interior dimensions of the Kosmos were simply gutted and laid out to dry in the blazing sun of the monological gaze." (1998: 79)

There is no cosmic, social, or moral unity embracing it all that generates a harmony of the whole, only absolute winners and losers. The same is true of the system of sovereign nation-states. They are in economic and political competition with one another, governed by strategic self-interest, and there is no effective system binding them all together that would prevent absolute winners and losers. War can destroy an entire country and turn its remaining citizens into slaves of a foreign power. That is just the way things are in the amoral world of nation-state power relationships.

The conflict, in both cases, can become truly absolute, resulting in the death of millions: economic warfare can result in mass starvation for entire populations, and militarized warfare in the violent wiping out of entire populations. After perhaps 60 million dead in the Second World War, the Korean War is estimated to have killed between 1 and 2 million people, the Vietnam War killed 3-4 million people, with no end in sight for the war system. According the one website, there are at least 70 wars going on in the world at the present time (www.warsintheworld.com). There is no sense of a redeeming *unity-in-diversity*, and no depths to human existence, that might mitigate the carnage.

Finally, as often pointed out in the critical academic literature, the economic competition and wars are far from independent of one another but are most often directly correlated (Petras and Veltmeyer, 2005). Wars have always been about markets, resources, slaves, cheap labor, or oil. The drive to domination or hegemony has always served such practical purposes. Capitalism and the system of sovereign nation-states form parts of a single world system based on early-modern premises that result in these kinds of patterns of fragmentation, mechanism, and conflict.

1.5   Some critiques of the Early-Modern System

I want to introduce these critiques of the Early Modern System in order to illustrate some commonalities revealed by the critical literature (of which we will see more in subsequent chapters) and to show the depth of influence of this paradigm through the present. These following critiques arise from somewhat different background perspectives, but nevertheless resonate with one another. In this volume, I am not attempting to offer a specific, detailed critical theory of all our modern difficulties, but rather a general overview of the civilizational characteristics in the present influenced by the Newtonian set of assumptions inherited from past centuries.

Russian Orthodox Christian philosopher Nicolas Berdyaev in his 1936 book *The Meaning of History* argues that the immense promise of the European Renaissance as an affirmation of life, beauty, and creativity was derailed by a process of progressive "mechanization" of human life. By the 19th century the spirit of the Renaissance had been overcome by the spirit of the machine. The domination of machines over nature also resulted in the domination and destruction of the creative human spirit:

> The conquest and subjection of external nature brings about a change in human nature itself; and, by its creation of a new environment, modifies not only nature but man himself. The invention of machinery and the resultant mechanization of life while in some ways enriching him yet impose a new form of dependence on him, a dependence, perhaps, even more tyrannical than that exercised by nature. A new and mysterious force, alien to both man and nature, now makes its appearance in human life; and this third, unnatural and nonhuman element acquires a terrible power over both man and nature. It disintegrates the natural human forms. (1936: 151 & 153)

For Berdyaev both modern capitalism and its response in an oppressive, uncreative socialism are the results of this mechanization of humanity in the modern era. Neither recognizes the spiritual depths and mystery of life and both disintegrate the human spirit within systems of domination (ibid. 218-220).

P.A. Sorokin, in his well-known 1941 book, *The Crisis of Our Age*, contrasts the "Ideational" system of truth that predominated in Medieval thought, and its subsequent development as an "Idealistic" system of truth, with the "Sensate" (empiricist) system that dominated the thought of the modern world. In the Sensate system, all knowledge, truth, and value are reducible only to what is confirmed by sensation, through empirical methods (1941:30-36). The crisis of the modern age is due to the fragmentation engendered by the Sensate system that attempts to reduce all truth and value to materialist and empiricist assumptions. He writes (in italics) that "from *the integralist standpoint, the present antago-nism between science, religion, philosophy, ethics, and art is unneces-sary, not to mention disastrous*" (318). We need to restore wholeness to human understanding and sensibility by restoring an idealistic or "integral" mode of perception: "Human reason likewise com-bines into one organic whole the truth of the senses, the truth of faith, and the truth of reason. These are essentials of the idealistic system of truth and knowledge" (82).

In 1941 Sorokin was writing with a clear awareness of the rise of the Nazis to power in Germany and of the horrific atrocities of the Stalinist Soviet Union. He was trying to penetrate to the core of the civilizational problem that can make such inhuman social systems possible. He sees these systems, as products of a funda-mental early-modern paradigm that denies reality and value to anything beyond the sensate. For Sorokin, the "integral" orien-tation functions as a fulfillment both for civilization and for indi-vidual life. The modern world, as he found it in the mid-20th cen-tury, was a world of fragmentation and loss of meaning, a world in which both the holism of harmony, the integration of percep-tion, reason, and faith, and awareness of the depths of existence were missing.

Similarly, in his 1931 book *Man in the Modern Age*, philosopher Karl Jaspers reflects on the facts of the degradation and diminish-ment of individual human beings by mass culture:

> In the rationalization and universalization of the life-order there has grown contemporaneously with its fantastic suc-cess an awareness of imminent ruin tantamount to a dread of the approaching end of all that makes life worth living. . ...
> Man seems to be undergoing absorption into that which is nothing more than a means to an end, into that which is de-void of purpose or significance. But therein he can find no satisfaction. It does not provide him with the things which give him value and dignity. (62 & 83).

Again, for Jaspers, the inherently valuable ends and depths of human life are buried by the modern process of rationalization.

Within a civilization which is effectively organized to deny the value and dignity of the individual, persons seeking the restoration of meaning and freedom in life will need to be in rebellion:

> If man is to be himself, he needs a positively fulfilled world. When his world has fallen into decay, when his ideas seem to be dying, man remains hidden from himself as long as he is not able to discover on his own initiative the ideas that come to meet him in the world.... The mental situation today compels man, compels every individual, to fight wittingly on behalf of his true essence.... The first sign of awakening circumspection in the individual is that he will show a new way of holding himself towards the world. Selfhood or self-existence arises out of his being against the world in the world. (194-195)

For Jaspers, the quest to discover one's "selfhood or self-existence" includes becoming open to the depths of being that define and empower that selfhood. There is a cosmic framework, Being itself, that defines and illuminates personal selfhood and provides a holistic framework of harmony with oneself and the cosmos. This same "Encompassing" (awareness of the depths of Being) could also provide a framework for harmony and peace within human civilization. However, modern mass culture, with its domination of technique and instrumental reasoning irrespective of any substantive meaning and value for human life, threatens the integrity of the human self. It must be opposed.

A fourth philosopher concerned with what I have called the "Age of Fragmentation" is French thinker Jacques Ellul in his 1965 book, *The Technological Society*. The discovery of the mathematical structure of bodies in motion, and its applications to industrial and military uses, placed evermore power in the hands of the big capitalist corporations and the governments of militarized nation-states. As the analysis by Max Weber had shown, the purpose of the process of rationalization of society was power and the mastery of nature.

As Martin Heidegger put this in his 1950 lecture, "The Question Concerning Technology" (English publication 1977), the subject-object split in the modern world had developed into a division conceived of as "the autonomous will and its desires," on the one side, and the world as "standing reserve" on the other. This split, reductionistic at both poles, is what passes for reality, according to Heidegger, in our age of "the oblivion of being." An arbitrary "will to power" now faces a world that is simply a reserve for its manipulation and exploitation. No morality, no depths to being, no intrinsic values of any sort, no harmony.

Ellul examines our technological civilization from a similar perspective. Weber had already shown the predominance of instrumental rationality within the early modern paradigm. Ellul shows that technique, the extreme consequence of Weber's process of rationalization, has become an end in itself. What was *the means* to the realization of human interests (following Bacon's maxim that "knowledge is power") has taken on its own imperative—the technological imperative—and now dominates civilization regardless of human wishes. It operates not only throughout the mega-corporations of capitalism but through those technological power-systems called sovereign nation-states. Ellul writes:

> The interplay of the technical censorship with the pretended "anarchic" spiritual initiatives of the individual automatically produces the situation desired by Dr. Goebbels in his formulation of the great law of the technical society: "You are at liberty to seek your salvation as you understand it, provided you do nothing to change the social order." All technicians without exception are agreed on this dictum. It is understood, of course, that the social order is everywhere essentially identical: the variation from democracy to Communism to Fascism represents a merely superficial phenomenon. . ..
>
> For a long time it was believed that technique would yield a harmonious society, a society in equilibrium, happy and without special problems. This society would resign itself

to an easy life of production and consumption based on an untroubled commercial ideology. This model of bourgeois tranquility seemed to correspond exactly to the preoccupations of technology. The *summum bonum* was comfort, and the ideal type was capitalist Switzerland or socialist Sweden. The sudden plunge of the technically most advanced societies into war and mutual destruction was a rude awakening for the bourgeois. An aberration? Scarcely. It had been forgotten that technique means not comfort but power. The bourgeois countries had developed their technical systems at a comfortable pace, until these systems had fully exploited their possibilities of orderly growth. Then technology, with its accelerated tempo, took over. The smaller nations were unable to keep up. And the great technical countries had willy-nilly to abandon their languid pace so they can accommodate themselves to the real tempo of the technical society. The result was that disproportion between the leisurely bourgeois mentality and the explosive tempo of technique to which we give the name war. A by-product of this ecstasy was a certain mystique. The American myth was born, presenting exactly the same religious traits as the Nazi or Communist myth. But it is different, as we have often noted, in that it is still in a spontaneous phase; it is not yet organized, utilized, and developed technically. (1965: 420-22)

Writing in 1965 of the myth of American exceptionalism, superiority, and manifest destiny, Ellul remarks that the American myth was not yet organized under the technological imperative (as happened to Germany under the Nazis and the Soviet Union under Stalinism), a totalitarian imperative that is the consequence of the supremacy of technique, for all technique is fundamentally about power. During the Cold War, the US claimed it felt "forced" to build evermore weapons of mass destruction (even though most thoughtful people were aware that substantial use of these weapons would wipe out civilization and possibly humanity itself) (cf. Harris, 1966).

Ellul points out that the imperative to manufacture these doomsday weapons goes substantially deeper than Cold War fears of an implacable enemy. The technological imperative is a power imperative, inherently totalitarian. Today, Ellul's insight is substantially more compelling as we witness the wiping out of the *bourgeois* culture of personal freedom in the US, the militarization of its police forces, massive government secrecy, the war on journalism and freedom of the press, the implementation of totalistic system of surveillance (Roberts, 2014), and the pursuit of foreign wars and military actions throughout the globe (Parenti, 2011).

If it was possible to use newly invented nuclear weapons to wipe out entire cities with a single bomb (even though Japan had been clearly defeated with the entire city of Tokyo having been destroyed by firebombing six months earlier), the likelihood was that they would be used. If it was technologically possible to wipe out the Iraqi army (or that of some other small country) in just days, to invade and destroy an entire country using the "shock and awe" of impressive weaponry, the chances are that this would be done, regardless of the human consequences. If it is technically possible to spy on all worldwide communications through massive NSA computer systems, it is likely that this would happen.

The technological imperative, originating within the dominance of instrumental reasoning described by Weber—an instrumental-power imperative itself rooted in the early-modern paradigm of mechanism and materialism—has come home to roost in a growing worldwide system of human enslavement: the loss of freedom and the loss of meaning. The dominators are clearly enslaved to the technological imperative of power, just as much as their victims are enslaved to the dominators. Systematic use of torture and humiliation follow naturally from such a paradigm. The early-modern paradigm provides no grounds for harmony. Its ultimate implication is disharmony—war, injustice, terrorism, destruction of the environment, and totalitarianism.

1.6 The Age of Evolutionary Holism and the New Universe Story (Today's Emerging World View)

THE natural and social sciences of the 20th century experienced a paradigm-shift—across the board—from atomism and mechanism toward evolutionary and emergent holism. Today scientists know that everything evolves: from the universe itself to galaxy clusters, galaxies, solar systems, planets, biospheres, species, individual living things, societies, institutions, and psyches. Yet at the same time, this evolving multiplex universe exhibits a seamless wholeness, manifested in all its evolving parts, the parts themselves participate in "fields" or overlapping levels of wholeness.

Today, science has deeply understood that the entire cosmos is an evolving whole, and that our planet and the living creatures on it are intimate parts of this whole, the heavy elements that make organic life possible having come from earlier generations of exploding supernova stars. The physical planet on which we live is itself an evolving whole, and its evolution is intrinsically linked to the networks of living things that form intricate patterns of interdependence and holistic overlapping ecological fields everywhere, from the bottoms of oceans to the upper atmosphere. Cosmologist and holistic thinker Ervin Laszlo declares:

> For the past three hundred and fifty years, Western science has been dominated by the materialistic Newtonian paradigm. Cosmologies based on this paradigm envisaged the universe as a vast mechanism, running on the energy— the negative entropy—with which it was endowed at its birth.... However, the staggering energy sea discovered at the quantum level of the universe challenged the Newtonian concept of a closed clockwork universe. Another concept has been emerging, grounded in the insight that a deep, quasi-infinite medium or matrix subtends the world. (2014: 32-33)

In the language of paleontologist Pierre Teilhard de Chardin (1959) (which has become commonplace in contemporary discussions of evolution), the *geosphere* as an evolving whole cannot be separated from the *biosphere* as an encompassing, evolving whole that emerges out of the former as an increasingly more complex phenomenon, yet which cannot be separated from the physical dimensions that it incorporates within this emergent process. Subsequently, from the awakening of an evolving consciousness within the biosphere, developing from primitive sensation to higher forms of sensibility and awareness, there slowly emerged the phenomenon of human beings: the sphere of mind, the *noösphere*, evolutionarily ascending from both the Earth and the cosmos.

From this process of evolving unification of the geosphere to the biosphere there emerged this other dimension of encompassing unity in diversity, inseparable from the process but also irreducible to its physical dimensions. Mind now becomes part of the same process of emergent evolutionary holism: a dimension inconceivable apart from the geosphere and biosphere from which it emerges. The human mind now begins to understand that the cosmos itself, and all emergent evolutionary developments within it, is guided by a single, intrinsic cosmic (or divine) principle of unity in complexity. Indeed, mind pervades the universe.

The paradigm-shift to holism in the sciences began as far back as 1905 with the publication of Einstein's Theory of Special Relativity in which he showed that none of the fundamental aspects of the cosmos, including space, time, matter, motion, and energy, can be understood separately, independently from the rest. From that time forward, one discovery after another has confirmed the holism in human society, in the human species, in all of nature, and in the cosmos itself. This work is summed up in such books as Fritjof Capra's *The Tao of Physics* in which he writes:

> Quantum theory has abolished the notion of fundamentally separated objects, has introduced the concept of the participator to replace that of the observer, and may even

find it necessary to include the human consciousness in its
description of the world. It has come to see the universe
as an interconnected web of physical and mental relations
whose parts are only defined through their connections to
the whole. (1975: 142)

Here we find the negation of all the fundamental elements of
the early-modern paradigm and the rationalized world described
by Max Weber and Errol Harris. Instead of objective, independent
observers, scientists are now "participators." Instead of atomism,
there is no notion of fundamentally separated objects. Instead of
materialism and the elimination of mind from the sensate world,
human consciousness is now an inseparable part of the unity. Instead of external relationships that characterize autonomous objects in relation to other such objects, we find "a web of physical
and mental relations whose parts are only defined through their
connections to the whole."

In other words, we find that the world and all its parts are
characterized by "internal" relations, not external ones. When
there is a change in one part, there are responsive changes in
other parts and in the whole, for reality is a seamless web of
relationships. Harris states that "the formulation of all physical
laws depends essentially on our own perception and conception"
(1988: 46). The technological imperative of instrumental power
for power's sake (as if the observer or participator were not part
of the equation) is fundamentally flawed and in complete contradiction to the deeper scientific reality that emerged during the
20th century.

Chapter Three of my book *Ascent to Freedom* quoted many contemporary sources concerning this holism, now conceived as an
"Age of Evolutionary Holism," and I will not repeat this material
here. However, *the universe story*, as told by contemporary cos-
mologists, is one in which the higher and more complex forms of
life, including human beings and human consciousness, emerged
as part of the process of "complexification"—from the evolutionary development of the whole as a moving and developing, but

nevertheless seamless, web. We have regained the holism of the
ancient world at a higher and much more sophisticated level. As
beings capable of openness to the future, we are capable of embracing this new paradigm and moving to a transformed, emergent relation to existence.

We have moved conceptually, in the words of Swimme and
Berry, "from an abiding cosmos to an ever-transforming cosmogenesis" (223), a cosmogenesis in which the emergence of human
beings was not an accident in a randomly developing evolutionary process. Rather, "this story incorporates the human into the ir-
reversible historical sequence of universe transformations" (238).
In other words, human beings as a single, emergent-evolutionary
species are constituted not only as body-mind wholes but are integral to the evolutionary structure of the cosmos itself. Fragmentation is overcome, and celebration of the marvelous wonder and
depths of existence can begin. In their book *The Conscious Universe: Whole and Part in Modern Physical Theory*, Menas Kafatos and
Robert Nadeau assert:

> To put it differently, it was presumed that reductionism was
> valid, and, therefore, that one could analyze the whole into
> parts and deduce the nature of the whole from the parts.
> With the discovery of non-locality that picture is reversed—
> it is the whole which discloses ultimately the identity of
> the parts. Non-locality...forces the assumption that the
> universe is at the most fundamental level an undissectable
> whole.... (1990: 121)

Human beings emerged as a necessary feature of this "undis-
sectable" wholeness. But perhaps celebration at this point would
be premature, since this new paradigm of wholeness has not pen-
etrated into the practices and institutions of civilization. The
power of capitalism, the system of sovereign nation-states, and
instrumental-technological rationality remain fundamentally en-
trenched. Even though we understand that we are committing
what is often referred to as "planetary suicide," the mass me-

dia and the mass mentality refuse to give up either capitalism or sovereign states. As Harris puts this in *Apocalypse and Paradigm:*

> If the implications of this scientific revolution and the new paradigm it produces are taken seriously, holism should be the dominating concept in all our thinking. In considering the diverse problems and crises that have arisen out of practices inspired by the Newtonian paradigm, it is now essential to think globally. Atomism, individualism, separatism and reductionism have become obsolete, are no longer tolerable, and must be given up. This does not mean that analysis is useless, or that the examination of detail is unnecessary, but it does mean that reduction to least parts and examination of these will not by itself afford explanation of the structure of the whole they constitute. (90)

In *The Universe Story*, Swimme and Berry tell the story of a universal creative holism "from the primordial flaring forth to the Ecozoic Era, a celebration of the unfolding of the cosmos." The whole story, as it has been discovered in the 20th century, is indeed the holistic story. The early-modern paradigm, a mere four centuries in duration, was an aberration, a discordant note, within the symphony of the whole story. They refer to it, we have seen, as the "Technozoic" era: "The greater part of contemporary industrial society, it seems, is oriented to the Technozoic rather than to the Ecozoic. Certainly the corporate establishment, with its enormous economic control over the whole of modern existence, is dedicated to the Technozoic" (249-250).

Like Weber, Sorokin, Jaspers, and Ellul, they recognize the Technozoic as "a deep cultural pathology" (251) and emphasize a transformed mode of consciousness: communion, relationship, sharing, participatory, and openness to the depths of the cosmos in a way "that seems to be a new comprehensive context for all religions" (255). The universe evolves in an emergent evolutionary fashion, and its miraculous unfolding can inspire our peaceful and celebratory transformation to people in harmony with one another and with the natural world. Disharmony (in the form of war, exploitation, violence, domination relationships, destruction of nature, and the objectification of others inuring us to their suffering) is overcome within the new, holistic paradigm embracing individuals, human civilization, the natural world, and the cosmos. Harmony prevails and internal relationships emerge into mindful awareness. Human beings can now come to recognize one another as brothers and sisters possessing a single human dignity and join together in a global social contract of unity in diversity. We are one with one another and with nature within an immense web of unity-in-diversity.

In his book *Global Responsibility: In Search of a New World Ethics,* Hans Küng agrees that the early-modern paradigm must be replaced by a "holistic way of thinking," by a "new covenant." He calls into question "the modern paradigm" which consists of "a science free of ethics; an omnipotent macrotechnology; an industry which destroys the environment; a democracy which is purely a legal form." "Modern scientific and technological thought," he says, "has from the beginning proved incapable of providing the foundation for universal values, human rights, and ethical criteria" (1991: 41-42). In the modern conception, he says, "reason, which is not involved in any cosmos and to which nothing is sacred, destroys itself." Harmony does not exist. On the other hand, in the new holism reason is again grounded cosmically and therefore can serve as a foundation for a new ethics of global responsibility:

> Even in the natural sciences, which for a long time regarded the world as a well-oiled machine, since Einstein's theory of general relativity, Heisenberg's quantum mechanics and the discovery of elementary particles, a holistic way of thinking has become established and with it a paradigm change from the classical mechanistic physics of the modern world. Instead of the domination of nature, what Ilya Prigogine calls a 'new covenant' between human beings and nature is becoming urgently necessary. (1991: 13)

The world, now understood as a holistic web of relationships, is a world in which all things exist in *interdependence*. Interdependence must not only be understood by a detached reason but must become the focus of values, passions, and loyalty. However, as Barbara Ward and Rene Dubos argue in *Only One Earth: The Care and Maintenance of a Small Planet*, the planet itself has yet to become the object of "rational loyalty" for most persons (1972: 220). Holism means "rational loyalty" to Earth, its citizens, and its living biosphere. As Swidler and Mojzes express this: "Never before did humanity possess the real possibility of destroying all human life—whether through nuclear or ecological catastrophe." Yet today, "there are solid empirical grounds for reasonable hope that the inherent, infinitely-directed life force of humankind will nevertheless prevail over the parallel death force" (2000: 83).

In her book *A Systems View of Education*, Bela H. Banathy defines "interdependence" as follows: "Interdependence of components within a system means mutual reliance and signifies that change in one component brings about change in others" (188). In his 1996 book, *The Web of Life: A New Scientific Understanding of Living Systems*, Fritjof Capra characterizes the ecological model in relation to the concept of interdependence:

> Interdependence—the mutual dependence of all life processes on one another—is the nature of all ecological relationships. The behavior of every living member of the ecosystem depends on the behavior of many others. The success of the whole community depends on the success of its individual members, while the success of each member depends on the success of the community as a whole (298).

In *The Liberation of Life* (1990), Charles Birch and John B. Cobb, Jr. write:

> The ecological model proposes that on closer examination the constituent elements of the structure at each level operate in patterns of interconnectedness which are not mechanical. Each element behaves as it does because of the

> relations it has to other elements in the whole, and these re-
> lations are not well understood in terms of the laws of me-
> chanics. The true character of these relations is discussed
> in the following section as 'internal' relations.... Internal
> relations characterize events. For example, field theory in
> physics shows that the events which make up the field have
> their existence only as parts of the field. These events can-
> not exist apart from the field. They are internally related to
> one another. (1990: 83 & 88)

The new universe story, now understood by scientists worldwide (the implications of which have not yet transformed our
dominant institutions or patterns of thought), is the story of creative evolutionary and emergent holism. The dynamic evolutionary movement from the primal flaring forth to the present exhibits
two interrelated dimensions of holism: First, the world exhibits an
abiding deep unity constant throughout its 14 billion year history,
what holistic thinker Ervin Laszlo (2007) calls the "Akashic Field"
(with reference to the abiding cosmic plenum described in classical Hinduism):

> We are all connected, intrinsically and permanently con-
> nected. That is the new paradigm, the Akasha paradigm,
> emerging at the cutting edge of the sciences. We only dis-
> regard this new insight at our own risk. If we can open up
> our mind and our heart to our oneness with the world we
> will come up with a solution. The precondition for this is
> to allow the wisdom that is in us to become operative. This
> wisdom has guided people through the age.... The only
> way we can do this is by acting together at a deep level.
> By sensing our oneness, by cooperating, by becoming co-
> herent. We are no longer coherent either with each other or
> with the world around us. (2014: 77-78)

Werner Heisenberg writes that "the world thus appears as a
complicated tissue of events, in which the connections of different
kinds alternate or overlap or combine and thereby determine the
texture of the whole" (in Harris, 2000b: 86). Second, the world

appears as an *emergent process* of complexification in which holism emerges on evermore advanced levels, the most complex of which known to us is the human level. Paleontologist Pierre Teilhard de Chardin writes:

> I doubt whether there is a more decisive moment for a thinking being then when the scales fall from his eyes and he discovers that he is not an isolated unit lost in cosmic solitudes, and realizes that a universal will to live converges and is hominised in him. In such a vision man is seen not as a static center of the world – as he long believed himself to be – but as the axis and leading shoot of evolution, which is something much finer. (1955: 36)

Philosophical cosmologist Milton K. Munitz writes: "The universe and human life are coupled. If we are to understand either, we need to move in both directions: from the universe to man and from man to the universe, since they are mutually involved in a very special way" (1986: 237). And theologian Jürgen Moltmann writes:

> The new emergence theories break down this frontier in the concept of evolution. They tell us that something new does come into being which cannot be explained from the already given components. ... The whole is a new organizational principle, which makes parts out of particles and links the parts to the whole and to one another. ... And in each qualitative leap we cannot explain the new whole from the given parts. (2012: 125)

Human life is clearly an evolutionary whole. But human institutions and consciousness have not evolved to manifest this wholeness. Rational loyalty and compassionate solidarity with the wholes of which we are a part is still missing. Rather, our institutions and ways of life are fragmented, broken, and endangering our future on the Earth. If human institutions reflected the wholeness of humanity, the transformation of consciousness would soon follow in a pattern that has been repeatedly shown throughout human history.

Holism is now the presupposition for the possibility and meaning of the parts on every level, from the cosmos to the planetary biosphere to human life. We must make a paradigm-shift from starting with the parts and trying to build wholes (peace, justice, sustainability, etc.) to an orientation that *starts from the whole* on every level. We must think of our individuality, our culture, our economics, and our nation as deriving from the holism of humanity, not the reverse. The transformation of the primary perspective, of our starting point, is one of the keys to human liberation.

Our consciousness and our institutions are reciprocally related to one another. And, according to the principle of holism on which the universe is constructed (articulated here by numerous thinkers) the uniting of humanity under democratic world law would engender a qualitative leap: the whole is more than merely the sum of its parts and new qualities would emerge with the wholeness of human institutions and consciousness that would be very powerful, liberating, and would give us our best prospect for a world based on peace, justice, and sustainability.

Chapter 2

Holism and Ethics

The task of reason is to fathom the deeper depths of the many-sidedness of things. We must not expect simple answers to far-reaching questions. However far our gaze penetrates, there are always heights beyond which block our vision.

The art of progress is to preserve order amid change, and to preserve change amid order. Life refuses to be embalmed alive. The more prolonged the halt in some unrelieved system of order, the greater the crash of a dead society.

—*Alfred North Whitehead*

2.1 Evolutionary Holism: The Emergence of Reason and Freedom

THE ethics of holism is scientific and cosmic, reflecting, as it does, the fundamental holistic principle of the universe as discovered by contemporary science. It recognizes human beings as integral to the cosmic process, not a mere accident of despair and hopelessness as modeled, for example, in much of Existentialism. A human being represents a new whole which is "a qualitative leap" that cannot be explained in terms of its parts. The ethics of holism encompasses traditional ethics but goes beyond the anthropocentric orientation of much traditional ethics (and beyond the transcendental command structure of much religious ethics) to affirmation of this cosmic framework, which means that a tremendous revolutionary hope is arising in humankind: the realization that "practical utopia" is indeed possible. Our gigantic hope is based on the vision of the very real possibilities for a new world, new institutions, and a new era of peace, justice, and sustainability for our planet.

Although some philosophers make a stipulative distinction between ethics and morality, for my purposes in this chapter this is not necessary. Ethics (or morality) is about relationships; it is about how human beings creatively behave in relation to others and to the world around them, not just toward other persons but toward all of reality. As Michael von Brück points out in his book *The Unity of Reality*, a person is not the same as an *individuum.* Individual unities are ontologically distinct from other such entities: "*Person*, on the other hand, is a center of relationships. The personal center unites within itself a theoretically infinite number of relational structures" (1991: 197). Each person lives as a developing, growing center of relationships whose very being (as self-aware) involves a synthesis and transcendence of those relationships.

Ethics today, therefore, is understood as deriving not only from human practical reason, and from the human rational will with its desire for basic human goods. Ethics is also derived from our place in the cosmos, from the emergent wholeness of our selves within the communities formed by humanity, nature, evolution, and the cosmos. Reason, intuition, and love emerge together within human life from the very heart of cosmic existence. Similarly, Moltmann concludes that "modern anthropocentrism is deadly for human beings themselves":

> The modern split into soul and body, subject and object, person and thing, does justice neither to the totality of human beings, nor to their natural living community with the

> Earth. If the modern fissure is rigorously pushed through,
> human bodiliness is destroyed and the natural community
> of life is ruined. (2012: 222)

Ethics needs to be cosmos-centered, reuniting fact and value, integrated into "the natural community of life." Unlike traditional virtue ethics (formulated by thinkers such as Aristotle, Thomas Aquinas, and our contemporary, John Finnis), the ethics of holism understands human flourishing not only as anthropocentric, linked only to claims about "human nature," or to human practical reason, but as truly universal and cosmic. This larger perspective by no means negates virtue ethics, but rather encompasses it within the holistic and cosmic framework that has emerged since the 20th century.

The principle that animates human reason is also the fundamental organizational principle of the cosmos itself, which is relational through and through. The universe is not only organized as a series of evermore complex and evolving systems of parts-within-wholes up to, and including, the ultimate, encompassing wholeness of the cosmos itself (and beyond that to the One beyond name and form), but human beings are themselves such wholes as individuals, while at the same time parts functioning within the holism of the human species, planetary nature, and the cosmos.

Human reason both discerns this holism everywhere in nature and is itself a manifestation of it. "The important point," Harris writes, "is that reflective intelligence and reason are seen as intrinsic and essential to the universe as a whole" (2000a: 280). The drive (or *telos*) within nature is toward ever-greater forms of holism and the *telos* within us is likewise toward ethical and intellectual holism. In Whitehead's language, this *telos* might be alternatively expressed as "the lure for feeling": "The primary element in the 'lure for feeling' is the subject's prehension of the primordial nature of God" (1978: 189).

In either case, the early-modern conception of a universal deterministic causality of the past over the future is broken and we are open to the "lure" or call of the whole. Jonas concludes: "Since the dissolution of classical determinism by quantum theory, this 'openness', i.e. the causal giving-way for such purposive spontaneous interventions, is no longer a prohibitive problem theoretically" (1996: 211). Here again, it is not "pure reason" alone that lures or functions as a *telos* for human ethical freedom. It is the wholeness of our being: including reason, intuition, feeling, desire, and love—these, in turn "lured" by the holistic structures of the cosmos. The wholeness of our responses to existence become integrated into the networks of relationships that make up our lives. As Kara Mitra expresses this:

> All of us, individually and as members of a group, culture, society, or in whatever way we want to identify ourselves, are what we are in relationship to all time, all space, all humans, all nonhumans, and we are not substantive in the sense of being independent and solely self-determined. We are all networks of relationships. Each individual or group is a specific yet dynamic network. Some of these networks may be more inclusive or less inclusive; yet each is a specific network, which is also in relationship to all the rest of the networks. (In Swidler, 1987: 252)

Holism means that mind, just as much as matter, is now understood as integral to the emerging complexity of the universe. Our "minds" are not simply autonomous subjective centers of thought and value. Rather, our minds are now inseparable from the dynamic relationships in which we participate: family, community, society, humanity, the natural world, and the cosmos. We participate in these relationships though the wholeness of our being, which includes reason, intuition, feeling, desire, and love. We need to articulate for ethics a new "*humanum*," as Hans Küng expresses this (in Swidler, 1987: 248), a *humanum* in which our common existential situation of relationship becomes expressed in values shared simply because we are all human.

The material that we have to work with is the rich historical material of the great religious and ethical traditions as well as the rich diversity of our capacity for creative participation in the relationships that make up our lives, especially reason, intuition, and love. What has uniquely emerged from the cosmic process in us that we call "reason"appears as a self-aware capacity to conceptualize, universalize, and represent our situation to ourselves (as I will discuss further in chapters Four, Eight, and Nine). From this self-aware reasoning process, it appears that freedom has emerged into the cosmos, freedom as a deeply mysterious openness to the future in which we now exist as centers of relationship not only to the many elements in the cosmos but in relationship to a future as well. We appear to be under a "lure" or, for many, a "command" to actualize a transformed future for human beings and the Earth.

This means that human desires, emotions, intuitions, and feelings must be included within the scope of our ethics, not separated off from the rational moral will as Kant insists in his 18th century dualistic ethics. Kant's "categorical imperative" (1964), however, correctly understood the intrinsic dignity of human beings. Recognizing this dignity, reason commanded that one should "always treat every person as an end in themselves, never merely as a means." This is indeed a fundamental principle of ethics. In formulating this principle, Kant understood that the only moral laws that can be obeyed without question are moral laws that we *legislate for ourselves* according to the principles of universality and logical consistency given by the categorical imperative. In this he represents a significant advance because he brings human creative freedom into the heart of living responsibly through responding to the multiplicity of our situations and relationships to others, society, nature, and the cosmos.

However, Kant conceived of the body and its desires as part of the determined, mechanistic, empirical world, a view he thought necessitated by early-modern science. Morality required that we do our duty "regardless of our inclinations." Holism overcomes this dualism between rationally willed ethical principles and irrational or arational emotions and desires. As John Finnis affirms in his 1983 book *Fundamentals of Ethics:* "When we fill out Kant's inadequate conception of humanity that must be respected in every act, and identify basic goods intrinsic to humanity...we are not adulterating or diverging from the principle of respect for persons. We are simply treating persons in their non-dualistic wholeness" (125).

Kant's tacit mind-body dualism took the form of a "reason versus inclinations" dualism: it was reason alone that understood the categorical imperative and required a "good will" to do what is right "regardless of inclinations." The body and its inclinations were part of the mechanistic, determined physical universe. However, such a dualism is not correct, and no longer rationally necessary to secure the categorical imperative. Freedom does not break into our determined world from the unknowable "noumenal" world, as Kant assumed. Bloch describes this situation:

> Kant himself, whose ethics developed completely as an autonomy of the *human will*, of a *human spontaneity*, posits freedom outside the realm of empirical appearances and its rigorously determined natural necessity. Freedom only comes from the "intelligible character," that is, man as a "citizen of intelligible worlds," and as the condition of moral behavior (as the faculty of conforming to the moral law in all circumstances), it is not an object of empirical knowledge, but a postulate of transcendent faith. (1986b: 161)

For Bloch, freedom is non-dualistically integral to our humanity. There is one aspect of Kant's thought, however, that recognizes holism and points forward to the holism of the self and the world. Kant explicitly recognizes that the "ideal of pure reason" (that is the ideal of knowledge and science) is the whole. The human being as knower *presupposes* the whole as the totality implicit in all investigations. The world appears to us as a coherent process of bodies and relationships within the totality we call the universe. Holism is implicit in the self-aware human mind from the beginning (1965b: 133-149).

Kant also recognizes that all the disparate thoughts and perceptions within the human mind could never represent a coherent world within which we could operate socially, culturally, technically, or scientifically without the "synthesis of the manifold of perceptions" in the unity of human consciousness. Thus a direct link is established in his thought between the holism of the universe (presupposed in the very concepts of knowledge and science) and the holism of the human self. Like the holism implicit in knowledge, the holism implicit in human consciousness is called an "ideal of pure reason" (1965b: 485-495). To be a "self" at all requires that the manifold of thoughts and perceptions be integrated into a coherent unity, and our perception of the unity of the world that we perceive is directly linked to that unity of the self. The holism of the self and that of the world imply one another.

Kant lived before Darwin, whose 1859 book *On the Origin of Species* propelled civilization forward toward the contemporary understanding that *everything* evolves, that everything is in *relationship* to everything else, and that everything is part of *the universe story*. Darwin's 19th century also began to understand the geological age of Earth, lending coherence to the general evolutionary thesis. By the 20th century, scientists realized that humans have biologically emerged from the very long process of the evolution of life on Earth. Like most other higher animals, we tend to be very social, ultimately developing the genetic predisposition to speak language, which ability cements us to the human community to the point where we understand that our personhood (our individuality) is inseparably united to all of civilization. Our very essence as human beings is to be both individual and inseparably bound to the human community. The holism of the human community and that of the human personality mutually imply one another.

What has evolved out of the cosmic process of evolution that resulted in the creation of Earth and our solar-system some five billion years ago, and in the "immense journey" of the evolution of life on the Earth over the past three and a half billion years, is

not only the human "mind," creatures self-aware who can become
an "object to themselves" as George Herbert Mead expresses this,
but the *social character* of language-speaking beings who are a necessary condition for the emergence of the human mind.

Our biological-psychological bodies and minds have evolved
over millions of years, and from this same process, human societies have emerged, exhibiting the coherence and order characteristic of mind. From this very long process (given that life itself
may be approximately one fourth the age of the entire universe) a
new level of mind has emerged: the self-aware capacity not only
to know, but to be self-aware that we know. As Jonas summarizes:
"It follows from this that final causes, but also values and value-
distinctions, must be included in the (not utterly neutral) concept
of the cause of the universe, and that they occur there as a potentiality for them and at the same time as a tolerant openness for
their intervention into the determining system of efficient causes"
(1996: 173)

Knowledge necessarily involves both a knowing relation to
the world and the self-awareness of that relation, a relation that includes final causes and values. We can now envision the world as
a whole as the ultimate object of human knowledge (although in
some respects the world cannot be "objectified" as we will see in
Chapter Nine). We can self-consciously know ourselves as know-
ers of this process through the unity of our consciousness, deriving final causes and values as part of this knowing.

Kant first clearly articulated what has been confirmed by the
20th century sciences. It is this capacity for self-knowledge that
makes each of us a human personality and gives us immeasur-
able dignity and human rights. The ultimate principle of interpretation, of truth, is *coherence,* the coherence of holism. The fact
(of holism) and human values (the values of harmony, peace, and
holistic integration) emerge together. "The ultimate principle of
interpretation," Harris states, "is, in consequence, the principle of
value." (1954: 206)

For Harris, this is because the holistic process of evolution in the universe can now be understood *teleologically*: progressively greater levels of coherence and order emerging out of the process. Processes are understood in terms of the wholes within which they operate and toward which they develop within the contexts of the holistic fields that make them what they are. In terms of evolution on planet Earth, a human being is the highest development of this process that we know. Teleological purposes in nature "constitute an order of ascending grades of value" (ibid. 205). A human being as the highest end of evolution that we know is also the bearer of intrinsic value. Indeed, through us the universe becomes aware of itself and blossoms into freedom and responsibility.

Reason, therefore, need not be a specific anthropocentric feature of humanity mysteriously linked to the unknowable intelligible world, as Kant concluded. Reason emerges as our self-aware ability to cognize relations in the world, to critically, empirically, evaluatively, and dialectically examine and participate in these relations, to build on the work of past investigators, and to produce books and other media that preserve our investigations for future generations. These in turn can be critically examined and integrated into the on-going process of articulating the multiplicity of relations and processes that make up the universe. Reason manifests the holism of the universe that has emerged to self-awareness in the human phenomenon. The hidden processes and relations of the universe emerge into greater actuality as they are articulated and embodied in human knowledge. Harris writes:

> The objective complements the subjective and supplies its shortcomings, confronting it as an opposite; yet each includes the other, and although the objective transcends the limits of the subjective, it also requires and depends upon it. The organization of social life is the work of reason, but rational self-consciousness can only arise within the social milieu. (1992: 40)

Cosmic evolution has produced the human body, society, mind, and reason as integral parts of this process. Individual reason and reason as embodied in civilization and in nature mutually imply one another. Descartes' opposition of mind and body as two different kinds of substance is mistaken. Mind and reason are as natural to the cosmic process as is bodily evolution. Mind and reason emerge as aspects of the cosmic "universe story" localized, as far as we know for sure, in the human phenomenon. This evolutionary holistic understanding applies to freedom as well. It is no longer necessary, as Kant thought, to posit freedom as breaking into the deterministic mechanistic world from the unknowable intelligible (noumenal) world. Freedom, responsibility, the ability to consider choices and alternative courses of action, all emerge with the concomitant emergence of society, mind, reason, and self-awareness.

Hegel recognized this holistic aspect of Kant's thought that I have been describing. However, he also recognized that the complementary and interrelated holisms of self and world were not static and timeless features of existence but that they were evolving dialectically—this holistic situation emerged, for Hegel, in the historical becoming of "being" and continued dialectically toward ever-greater knowledge and understanding of the whole. The differentiated parts within holistic fields relate to one another though dynamic conflicts that are transformed with the emergence of higher levels of wholeness in which the relations of the parts are simultaneously canceled yet preserved within the higher synthesis (a process he called *Aufheben*). He also recognized that freedom is integral to this dialectical process, not something that breaks into a determined world from an unknowable "noumenal" realm, as Kant had argued. In this regard, he argued, the history of humanity is the history of the emergence of freedom. Freedom naturally emerges from the world-process.

Today, we are beginning to understand that freedom indeed emerges out of the holism of the evolving universe. Laszlo writes: "There is more to human freedom in the world than a science based on the old paradigm would have us believe. We are an organic part of a nonlocally interconnected universe, and we interact not only with its manifest dimension, but also with its Akasha dimension" (2014: 61). Freedom can be considered an "openness" to the future, as Bloch puts it (1986b:162), in which the future is not merely a product of past deterministic causes but rather is teleologically (or eschatologically) summoned by the structures and meanings of the wholes in which all things participate. As Theologian Paul Tillich puts it (see Chapter Eight), we are summoned by the future, and our decisions can creatively respond, or not respond, to that summons.

Human responsibility, moral imperatives, and distinctions between right and wrong emerge from the evolutionary processes of the universe as part of the openness of the world itself toward the future. As von Brück describes this process: "Realization of the personal implies freedom and creativity. For while new relationships are integrated by being brought into meaningful connections with the present crystalized forms (without which no integration would be possible), integrating the new also alters the structure of the person: the person *is* the alteration, and its continuity is dialectical" (1991: 198). Each of us as persons, as a dialectical synthesis of relationships involving not only other persons but the whole of existence, moves into the future through a holistic process of integration. Ethics is in large measure our responsibility for this process, both its action in the present and its outcomes in the future.

Ethics, therefore, is transformed from a process of merely obeying principles formulated by some cultural or religious authority to a process of creatively responding to life. Each person, like the cosmos itself, becomes an emerging process of holistic freedom involved with innumerable relationships with persons, nature, society, and the world. Just has Kant had placed creative freedom at the core of ethics by affirming that the moral law is *self-legislated* by each free, rational being in relation to an ever-changing concrete situation comprised of inner inclinations and outer circumstances, so holism transcends Kant's dualism but not this immense responsibility for creatively, humanly, and compassionately responding to life in an on-going process of holistic development toward harmony, peace, justice, freedom, and sustainability.

Jonas even imagines the evolutionary process as the working out of the destiny of God: "entering into the adventure of space and time, the deity held nothing back of itself: no uncommitted or unimpaired part remained to direct, correct, and ultimately guarantee the devious working out of its destiny in creation" (1996: 134). For Jonas, this imagery suggests "the transcendent importance of our deeds." The human person becomes a "moral trustee of an immortal cause" (ibid. 128), for the future of the deity is, in part, delegated to us. However one imagines the deeper features of *the universe story*, the parameters of holism and the integral arising of mind and freedom as "natural" features of the cosmic process remain, today, widely accepted (cf. Chapter Nine).

It is important to observe that in all these formulations that freedom and responsibility exist as *my* freedom and responsibility. There is no impartial, objective "science of ethics," as Utilitarianism would have it, that can equate my responsibility with some objectively describable action that can be evaluated independently of me by some consequentialist calculus. In this some of the Existentialists such as Kierkegaard had it right: I am responsible for my actions; I am responsible to treat every person as an end in themselves; I am a free and responsible holistic center of relationships. Yet my freedom is also our (human) freedom. We are also collectively responsible for the kind of future that is now being created.

This world is a whole, and does not require appeal to another unknowable world to account for freedom—for this appeal carries the unfortunate consequence that human beings become a kind of wayfarer or sojourner in a world alien to their deepest needs and desires. *This world* is the place where the drama of an emergent and as yet unknown future is played out, requiring real consciousness-raising and effective participation by human beings themselves. We are not the playthings of another world, nor victims of an absolute determinism inherent in this world. Our burgeoning freedom makes us the emerging focus and "leading shoot" of evolution itself.

In saying this, I am not denying a transcendent-immanent dimension to the world, as I will make very clear in Chapters Eight and Nine. Traditional theology always recognized both the immanence and transcendence of the Infinite, as, for example, both Meister Eckhart and Nicholas of Cusa make clear in very different ways. Some thinkers have spoken of "immanent transcendence and transcendent immanence," suggesting recognition of the "depths" of things in ways that do not violate the holism of reality (Brück, 1991: 116). As Ken Wilber declares: "The Absolute is both the highest state of being and the ground of all being; it is both the goal of evolution and the ground of evolution; the highest stage of development and the reality or suchness of all stages of development.... If Spirit is completely transcendent, it is also completely immanent" (1996: 289).

But holism understands that the meaning of the present, and the meaning of the emergent future, are not mere appearances of some other world but are the genuine reality of whatever is happening in the universe. In *Process and Reality* Alfred North Whitehead called this movement the "consequential nature of God." Something (of which we now may only have a dim apprehension), having to do with the meaning of the whole, the Ground of Being, and human freedom is emerging through the process. In terms of planet Earth, some thinkers, such as Enrique Dussel, José Miranda, Mahatma Gandhi, and Martin Luther King, Jr., call this the eschatological demand for "the beloved community," the beloved community as local, human, planetary, and cosmic.

The reconciliation of mind and body does not mean that self-discipline and the sublimating of our desires and inclinations into the ends recognized by reason, intuition, and love are not necessary. Plato understood and outlined the necessary process for the development of virtue through Socrates' speech in the *Symposium*. Desire can be creatively sublimated at ever-higher levels consonant with our cognitive, spiritual and moral growth. And Kant also recognized that virtue requires the molding of desires and inclinations to conform with the principles of moral action.

However, the central *telos* within us is directed toward the same holism and harmony that reason also recognizes. The holism recognized by science and the *telos* for holism within us complement one another. We are the principle of holism manifest in human form, not simply some contingent cosmic accident. Irrational impulses and instincts need to be molded by reason and the *telos* for harmony into genuine virtues.

2.2   The Reintegration of Fact and Value

A fundamental concept in this new ethics is creative harmony. Unlike deontic and Kantian ethics, the ethics of holism does not create a dualism between the mind and body, nor between reason and human inclinations. It heals these problematic dualisms that have plagued much ethical thought for centuries. Similarly, unlike the alternative modern ethical tradition called Consequentialism or Utilitarianism (first formulated in the 19th century by Jeremy Bentham and John Stuart Mill and followed today by thinkers such as Garrett Hardin and Peter Singer), holistic ethics does not sacrifice the integrity of human beings: who can be used as a means for some imagined ideal end under the maxim: "what is right is what promotes the greatest good of the greatest number of people." There is no temptation to sacrifice this person or these people for the greater good of some abstract majority.

Holism sees every human being as having intrinsic and inviolable dignity, as does the UN Universal Declaration of Human Rights. This dignity does not separate us from the rest of the empirical world (as does Kantian ethics) but unites us to the dignity of existence inherent in all things, a dignity compacted like a laser beam in our human form. Each human being expresses both the dignity of his or her existence as a concrete, individual person (as Michael Rosen emphasizes in his 2012 book on dignity), and each shares the dignity of being part of humanity (as George Kateb emphasizes in his 2011 book on dignity).

For holism, such different dimensions are no longer mutually exclusive alternatives. Nor does holism necessarily deny the otherness of other persons, their infinite depths, so to speak, that is emphasized by Emmanuel Levinas (1969). Finally, holism has no need to deny Kierkegaard's existentialist sense of the infinite significance of making decisions and facing the absolute seriousness of this life in the here and now. There is, of course, for finite beings living time-bound between past and future, a level on which our decisions are either/or rather than both/and, as Kierkegaard insisted. As Jonas expresses this: "In *moments of* decision, when our whole being is involved, we feel as if acting under the eyes of eternity" (1996: 120). Nevertheless, holism remains the framework for all of this.

The human mind, like the human body, reflects the holism of nature and the universe and, in turn, discerns this holism. We are at once both all humanity and a unique perspective on that totality. Moreover, mind and body are not two different kinds of things but two aspects of one emerging reality. Fact is no longer separated from value, for what is valuable is now discerned by science and reason as holistic and harmonious: cosmic, ecological, economic, social, and personal harmony. The intrinsic dignity of parts cannot be separated from the intrinsic dignity of wholes. A totalitarian denial of individuality becomes as impossible as the egoistic denial of community. Errol E. Harris writes:

> The new metaphysic abolishes the opposition of fact to value, for the criterion of truth and value is the same: coherent order and unity. No fallacy is involved in deducing what ought to be, and to be done, from the general nature of the world and its organizing principle, which, when it becomes self-conscious, characterizes and defines human nature. For what ought to be done is what promotes health,

unity, and harmony, as well in the biosphere, as in human
history. (2000a: 261-62)

The pervasive positivism of much political and ethical
thought throughout the past century has derived in part from the
historic, apparently unbridgeable, distinction between fact and
value, between what is the case and what should be the case. This
distinction was made by such 18th century thinkers as Kant and
David Hume and is integral to the early-modern paradigm. This
paradigm, we have seen, found no place for the human mind
within its epistemology of objective observation and empirical
testing. A trained observer ignored his or her values, feelings, and
personal beliefs and just observed the facts. Subjective thoughts,
feelings, and desires had nothing to do with the objective facts.
Within the objective set of facts, no value was observed, attribu-
tions of value were considered merely subjective assessments imposed upon the impersonal reality of the situation.

The book that launched the career of Jürgen Habermas as a
major thinker, *Knowledge and Human Interests* (1972), by contrast,
effectively revealed the primordial connections between values
and facts in three major areas of concern: the technical interest
in the control of nature, the historical-hermeneutical interest of
the social sciences and humanities, and in the cognitive interest of
all humanity in human emancipation to freedom, autonomy, and
responsibility. Habermas summarizes this process as "the insight
that the truth of statements is linked in the last analysis to the intention of the good and true life" (1972: 317).

The contemporary holistic paradigm has discovered that the
human mind is an integral part of the reality investigated by science, that science, in relation to values, arises from a primordial
human "life-world" that includes an "intersubjective" dimension
from which the distinction between objectivity and subjectivity
subsequently arises. Jonas affirms that "to ground the 'good' or
'value' in being is to bridge the alleged chasm between 'is' and
'ought'" (1984: 79). A human being is an integral part of the
holism of the world, grounded in being, a "participator" as Fritjof

Capra puts it, not simply an objective observer. Mind has emerged from this process of evolutionary holism just as much as have life, sensation, perception, and feeling (all of which are aspects of mind that we share with other creatures on Earth). And this means that the values that arise from mind as part of its holistic response to life are a real part of the world, not "merely subjective." Capra writes:

> During the scientific revolution in the seventeenth century, values were separated from facts, and ever since that time we have tended to believe that scientific facts are independent of what we do and are therefore independent of our values. In reality, scientific facts emerge out of an entire constellation of human perceptions, values, and actions—in one word, out of a paradigm—from which they cannot be separated. (1996: 11)

The new holistic paradigm understands values as arising from human reasoning, intuition, and love just as much as scientific thought. Both modes of reasoning are part of the "entire constellation" of our response to the world and are intertwined with one another. Like mind itself, values arise naturally from human reasoning, social interaction, and our deeper relation to the ultimate principle of the Cosmos, and are not "merely subjective." Many traditional thinkers, such as Plato, Aristotle, Plotinus, and Thomas Aquinas, affirmed similar views.

The human mind makes value judgments and some of these, at least, derive from its being a creative expression of the fundamental organizing principle of the universe. In the words of Jonas, in them we hear "the voice of *being*," which is the voice of harmony, unity-in-diversity, and responsibility. The holism and rationality of the mind embody the same holism and rationality that are manifest in the order of nature and in the very fact of existence. Holism, we have seen, means that we participate in *internal relations* with other people, nature, and ultimately all things. Mind is no longer divorced from nature, and fact and value are now understood as integral aspects of the same holistic reality. Jonas writes:

> To ground the "good" or "value" in being is to bridge the alleged chasm between "is" and "ought." For the good or valuable, when it is this of itself and not just by the grace of someone's desiring, needing, or choosing, is by its very concept a thing whose being possible entails the demand for its being or becoming actual and thus turns into an "ought" when a will is present that can hear the demand and translate it into action. . . . In that case, axiology becomes a part of ontology. (1984: 79)

The consequence of this is that harmony and holism themselves have become the new "categorical imperative" of ethics. *Our responsibility is to discern our internal relationships with others and with the orders of living and natural things. From this careful assessment of these relationships, we can discern the principles of ethical action and apply these to specific situations.* What attitudes, actions, and institutions promote health and harmony in the family, the community, the nation, and the world? We confront a world of particular cultures, races, nations, and individuals that often appear antithetical to one another, but emergent and evolutionary holism discerns the larger patterns of wholeness and acts to unite the particulars into evermore encompassing harmonious wholes in ways that do not deny the integrity of the particulars but rather fulfills them. Stapp indicates the impact of the newfound wholeness on values:

> What we find, therefore, are not elementary space-time realities, but rather a web of relationships in which no part can stand alone; every part derives its meaning and existence only from its place within the whole. . . .

> More appropriate to this forum is a discussion of the impact on human values of the penetration into general human awareness of the quantum mechanical conception of nature. The importance of developments in this area can

> hardly be overstated. For human values control human de-
> cisions, and human decisions control the future of all life on
> this planet. (In Kitchener, 1988: 54-56)

The "static holism" of the ancients did not separate fact from value. For Plato, the ontologically real forms (*eidos*), such as justice, courage, beauty, etc., were also the source of value: we should discern their reality (*ousia*) and conform our lives to it. For the Stoics, the cosmos itself, the ultimate reality, was the source of the moral law. Rather than an anthropocentric ethics, Bloch points out, their ethics was a "cosmomorphic: participation in the reason of the universe" (1986b: 14). For the Stoics, the natural law involved "the *unity* of all people as members of the international community, that is, the rational empire of love. Stoicism is enormously democratic here: Its natural law is uniquely philanthropic, its state is brotherhood" (ibid. 13).

In his noteworthy book, *Fundamentals of Ethics*, John Finnis, who accepts the distinction between fact and value (but argues that *objective values* can be discerned by reason and need not be derived from facts to be objective), insists that Aristotle did not derive values from facts in spite of the fact that he is often interpreted that way by contemporary philosophers. Aristotle is often seen as identifying the characteristic activity of humans, our unique "function" (rationality) from which he derives the imperative to develop intellectual and moral forms of virtue. Finnis argues that this misinterprets Aristotle's argument in the light of a number of things he says elsewhere (1983: 10-23).

This may well be true. However, that Aristotle understood ethics in relation to a holistic universe that profoundly influenced his thinking should not be in doubt. Everything (in the static holism that characterized Aristotle's world view), from the Unmoved Mover (God), to the descending levels of being, to the entelechies inherent in all things, to the participation of human beings in the cosmic hierarchy of being, to the drive inherent in the human form to actualize its rational potential, provided material for how human beings should be living their lives. Fact and value appeared integrated and complementary to Aristotle.

Today, science has discovered a new holism, very different in its understanding of how the universe works, but the principles of holism in relation to ethics remain deeply similar. The new holism, however, is emergent and dynamic, not static. It understands that there are yet higher levels of holism that human beings can aspire to, that are not just a matter of conformity with "the way things are." Human freedom has a profound role in the development of a harmonious "Kingdom of Ends," as Kant put it. It has a profound role in bringing the Kingdom of God to Earth, as Jesus put it. Fact and value are again integrated, for they were never, in fact, actually separated, but we now have a critical social theory emerging that can help assess our deepest problems in terms of lack of holism and point to emergent levels of holism that can address these problems.

Our values, the values of our *humanum*, critically understand that the facts of war, violence, hatred, and terror that we experience in the world are wrong, immoral, in violation of the wholeness and harmony that should exist. Our reason, intuition, and love (and therefore our creative freedom) experience the demand for transformation, for moving into a future characterized by peace, justice, and harmony. Holism becomes an imperative for moving to higher levels, for individuals and for humanity.

Before the rise of the early-modern paradigm, facts and values were not systematically separated but considered part of both philosophical and everyday experience. Even today, our everyday experience is that the facts are value-laden for us: every aspect of our lives and our experience of the world elicits value judgments. Human beings are awakening to their relation to the wholes of which they are part: the family, the community, the nation, all humanity, the planet, and, ultimately, the truth of the whole cosmos (in which we participate and insofar as this can be known and/or experienced). Facts are not just isolated atoms of experience; they are elements of systems of relationships within which we are embedded: family, community, humanity, planet, and cosmos.

All of these elicit value responses in us, not as "merely subjective" reactions, but as integrated responses to the wholes within which we are embedded. Our values derive from these wholes at the same time that they are responses to these wholes. In any holistic relation values arise in this dialectical way. Fact and value were never separated in reality at all. The early-modern paradigm was mistaken in deriving this separation. As philosopher Joseph Kockelmans describes our situation:

> The importance of philosophy for any ethical view must be found first and foremost in the fact that it shows that man, existing in the truth of the Whole, must primarily concern himself with the Whole, and that only insofar as man is concerned with the Whole, can the assigning of all the directions which must become value, law, and norm for man come from the Totality of meaning itself. One could say, also, that this philosophy is inherently 'ethical' in that it urges man to be concerned with two things which are essentially connected with one another: his own authenticity and the unconcealment of the genuine meaning of the Whole in his world. . . ..
>
> Philosophy should certainly be concerned with the values things have for us, but existential philosophy suggests a completely different approach to the value problem. First of all it tries to convince us that the distinction between fact and value rests on an abstraction. On the level of our prephilosophical experience we never experience things without values, nor do we ever experience values which are not the values of things. . . ..
>
> But, more importantly, one must also realize that values are never experienced in isolation; we experience them in contexts, in a certain horizon of meaning, and, in the final analysis, within the totality of all possible meaning, as this now manifests and hides itself in our Western civilization. (In Wood, 1970: 246-47)

It is not entirely clear why Kockelmans identifies "Western civilization" as a horizon of meaning where the truth of the whole both "manifests and hides itself." For, by his own argument, meaning derives from wholes, and planetary civilization is a much more fundamental whole than Western civilization, as dozens of thinkers today are pointing out. Nevertheless, he clearly recognizes that the early-modern paradigm created a false "abstraction" in separating fact and value. The human mind is an integral aspect of reality, having evolved as a manifestation of the order and structure of the cosmos itself, and with that mind, value emerges into clarity, the values of practical and theoretical reasoning, integration, harmony, reciprocity, love, friendship, and compassionate justice. The wholes and systems of the universe both elicit and manifest value. As Kockelmans asserts, values are never experienced in isolation, but in contexts, as integral to the meaning of situations and the dynamic wholes of family, community, humanity, planet, and cosmos.

Of course, the emergence of value in and through human experience does not mean that the judgments of each individual or group are veridical. Just as the process of progressively accumulating scientific knowledge and philosophical understanding of the world is inherently communal and dialectical, so the process of articulating and clarifying values is communal and dialectical. (And, of course, each of us is continually growing and learning.) This is one of the fundamental insights arising through the work of Habermas: we are in a social process of articulating values; ethics, in some fundamental ways, is communicative.

No (describable) aspect of ourselves is entirely personal and separate from the social and biological construction of our selves. The criterion of objective truth (coherence) and the criterion of value (harmony and coherence through dialogue directed toward mutual understanding) are fundamentally the same. As Harris concludes: "Since objectivity has turned out to be systematically integrated wholeness, if that also proves to be the hallmark of value, its criteria will be just as objective and universal in their validity as are the standards of truth" (1987: 245).

There are exceptions to these statements that should be pointed out: in his *Tractatus Logico Philosophicus,* Wittgenstein identifies "what is true about solipsism" and in *Totality and Infinity* Levinas identifies an "infinity" reflected in the human face that *cannot be subsumed to the relations found in the totality of being.* Both of these exceptions bear on the question of value in fundamental ways, some of which we will explore further in Chapters Eight and Nine. Nevertheless, Habermas and Harris are correct in general that ethics is a communicative and dialogical enterprise. We are all involved with one another as parts of our common human project and need one another to clarify the value that we find arising all around us: in every culture, religion, community, ideology, and science. We need to discuss values through a perpetual asking of questions and dialoging with one another concerning the answers and through the attempt to actualize ever greater levels of harmony as we move into the future.

What kind of human actions promote the integrity and harmony of the biosphere? Again we find that the biosphere cannot be protected both while human actions are not in harmony with its delicate ecological patterns but also while human beings themselves remain fragmented and divided from one another. What is a sustainable relationship to the ecology of the Earth? How can we promote the emergence of human harmony in conformity with these scientific realities? What kind of political and economic institutions promote harmony with nature as well as integrity and harmony among human beings? How can love, friendship, and compassionate justice be promoted worldwide leading toward a peaceful, just, and fulfilled human community? We are in a holistic relationship with both nature and humanity, and these two aspects, human harmony and harmony with nature, necessarily go together.

The holistic emphasis is on the study of relationships and the fields within which these relationships operate with a view to maintaining, enhancing, and enlarging their harmony. The emphasis in ecology is on understanding the fields of interrelationships and interdependencies and conforming human activity to these patterns. The emphasis in human relationships is on seeing the issues from the point of view of the other person, culture, or nation with whom I realize I am internally related. In the process of understanding the other's point of view, we look for mutualities, larger unities, and commonalities that unite us, and then work to actualize these in ways that are mutually fulfilling. These principles today are fundamental to much of the work of peace studies programs worldwide and to theories of nonviolence, such as Marshall Rosenberg's theory of nonviolent communication (2005).

Perhaps the first principle of an ethics of holism is to realize that *the other is you and you are the other* on a very fundamental level. Or as Harris expresses this in a related sense: "Each is at once itself and all the rest" (1992: 19). As Whitehead affirms: "Every actual entity is present in every other actual entity. The philosophy of organism is mainly devoted to the task of making clear the notion of 'being present in another entity'" (1978: 50). We are already established in fundamental commonalities and need to evolve these commonalities into actualized, living wholes.

Fox writes that "the entire insight upon which compassion is based is that the other is *not* other; and that I am *not* I. In other words, in loving others I am loving myself and indeed involved in my own best and biggest and fullest self-interest" (1990: 33). Laszlo declares: "The other is also me and I'm the other. The world is not beyond or outside of me; it's inside me just the same way as I'm inside the world. There are no absolute boundaries between me and what I see as the world" (2014: 79). These are no mere values apart from facts, for fact and value arise together in authentic human experience. The truth of this process is revealed in a variety of ways in today's thought, and it needs to be elaborated and articulated systematically in ways that go beyond the present volume.

Already, philosophers of language such as Steven Pinker (1995), Noam Chomsky (1998), and Jürgen Habermas (1998) have shown the universality of language and its necessary connections with the selfhood of each of us. My self cannot be divorced from the human capacity for language that is part of our universal humanity. Similarly, biologists have shown that all human beings are more than 99.9 percent genetically identical, psychologists have shown that an amazing communion of human consciousness is possible between people (Laszlo, 2007), and anthropologists have shown the astonishing similarities of people everywhere (Brown, 1991).

On these holistic principles, my relationship with other persons will be *internal* relationships, not external as currently widely assumed. This means that my actions, beliefs, and goals affect the other and those of the other affect me, not simply externally but in our very being. My consciousness of myself is no longer that of an egoistic atom promoting my selfish interests, but that of a creative and cooperative participator, working with others to enhance the emergent well-being of all. We are internally related to one another and with the whole of humanity. To be a *person,* we have seen, is to be precisely a synthesis of such relationships. The principle guiding action should be that of harmony, operating at all levels, from the personal to the family to the nation to the world.

The traditional expressions of the Golden Rule, found in all the great world religions (Hick, 2008), form an early expression of this principle. But the ethics of holism would need to go deeper: it is not only a matter of doing to others what you would want done to you, but also the realization that what you do unto others you are doing to yourself. In *Oneself as Another*, Ricoeur writes: "*Oneself as Another* suggests from the outset that the selfhood of oneself implies otherness to such an intimate degree that one cannot be thought of without the other, that instead one passes into the other.... I should like to attach a strong meaning, not only that of a comparison (oneself similar to another) but indeed that of an implication (oneself inasmuch as being other)" (1992:3).

Mahatma Gandhi, in seeing every person as an expression of the Atman, lived from one understanding of this principle. Nonviolence is mandatory because the other person in a very real sense is me and I am him or her. Gandhi's ultimate goal was to actualize this awareness in the world. *Satyagraha* (clinging to truth) was his principle of action for creating ever-greater wholes and ever-deeper harmony on Earth. Something similar is expressed by Socrates' famous principle that "it is better to be a victim of evil than to do evil." For Socrates, if I harm you I am simultaneously harming myself, since both of us exist in internal relationships with one another, mutually participating in the "Good" (*Agathos*) that transcends us both. If I do evil to you, I am violating my own selfhood as well as yours, for we are united in deeper ways that transcend any apparent sayable differences.

While each of us includes a dimension that is deeply and ontologically individual (I am this *individuum* that is unique within the entire universe in a way that transcends all describable differences), each of us is simultaneously one with all the others. Ricoeur states that: "My field of motivation is open to the whole range of the human. My humanity is my essential community with all that is human outside myself: that community makes every man my like. My character is not the opposite of that humanity: my character is that humanity seen from somewhere, the whole city seen from a certain angle, the partial totality" (1967: 93)

Holistic ethics is the relation between myself as "partial totality" and that "essential community." There are some excellent contemporary formulations of a "global ethics" that articulate implications of these first principles, for example, the universal ethics suggested by Leonard Swidler and Paul Mojzes in their book *The Study of Religion in the Age of Global dialogue* (2000: 288-294). They correctly speak of both the Golden Rule as well as the "inherent equal dignity" of all persons and derive from this the Kantian principle that each person always be treated as an end, never merely as a means. And they add that global ethics must encompass this Kantian principle with a larger principle of "love." These are various expressions of an ethics of holism.

We have seen that Harris points out that the ethics of holism encompasses several of the traditional ethical theories as well as their identification of a positive role for emotions and desires within ethics. However, as above, there is a larger response that properly characterizes the ethics of holism that can be named "compassion"or "love." Matthew Fox says of compassion: "While it includes ethics, as all true spirituality must, it blossoms and balloons to something greater than ethics—to celebration of life and relief, where possible, of others' pain" (1990: 30). He quotes Thomas Merton's last lecture, two hours before his death, in which Merton says: "The whole idea of compassion is based on a keen awareness of the interdependence of all these living beings, which are all part of one another and all involved in one another" (23-24).

The more we embrace holism, the more we become directly aware of the interconnections, not only with living beings but with the whole of the cosmos, and the proper term for the response that this direct awareness elicits in us is compassion. A holistic ethics blossoms in love and compassion, in a solidarity with all of life and the fundamental principle of the cosmos itself. A global ethics recognizes the Golden Rule not from an egoism in which my self-interest dictates that I would not do what I don't want done to me, but from a compassion in which I realize that myself and the other are deeply one on multiple levels. The Kantian recognition of dignity undergoes a similar expansion in which I recognize the dignity of others, of living beings, and of the cosmos not only because human beings are free moral agents (as Kant says) but also because they participate in the dignity of all things as manifestations of the fundamental cosmic principle.

2.3   An Ethics of Liberation

MOLTMANN also points out that a global golden rule in itself is not sufficient for a global ethics, for it implies a world of equality in which people can really conceive of others not doing to them what they would not want done. In a world of vast inequality and injustice, the few live with structural impunity with respect to what they do to others. He argues that such a world requires that global ethics include an ethics of liberation:

> Without the liberation of the oppressed, the raising up of the weary and heavy-laden, and the rights of the humiliated and insulted, the golden rule cannot be realized. A 'global ethics' based only on this is an ideal, even if a fine one. A realistic global ethics in the face of the world's present conditions can only be an ethics of liberation on the side of the poor and the Earth. (2012: 176)

A holistic ethics of compassion is also an ethics of liberation that goes beyond the imagining of doing to others what I would want done to me to an envisioning of system-change. Ethics cannot be private morality alone (doing as you would be done by) since the systems of Earth make us all guilty, all beneficiaries or victims (or both in different ways) of unjust planetary systems. As Albert Camus (1986) expressed this, we do not want to be either "victims or executioners."

My compassionate identification with the victims of the current world systems (systems most notably identified as global capitalism and the system of warring nation-states) leads me to demand the transformation of these systems of injustice and exploitation to compassionate, inclusive systems of cooperation, sharing, and mutual participation. The ethics of holism under present conditions is creative and revolutionary holism: We are morally required to transform the systems of Earth to ones of justice, reasonable equality, respect for human dignity, and ecological sustainability.

Since nothing is excluded from the ethics of holism, it is clear that political life within democratic societies, international relations between nations, as well as economic and business relations, must be guided by ethical principles of holism and harmony. Harris compares the ethics of holism to the universal principle of love (*agape*) taught by Jesus: "Genuine rational love, therefore, must extend to the entire human race. .... Love of neighbor, in the full sense, transpires as love of the entire community and devotion to the ideal Kingdom of Ends" (1988: 163-64). Jesus taught the bringing of the Kingdom of God to Earth. Preparing the way for the kingdom of God means global system change. Dussel calls the present world system a "system of sin":

> In the totality of the systems of practices of the world, as objective and social reality, the "carnal" subject or agent desires the permanency of order, which, however, attempts to legitimate itself by appealing to the "gods" as its foundation. The "flesh" is idolatrized in the "kingdom of this world," and promulgates its own law, its own morality, its own goodness. .... This system is closed in upon itself. It has replaced the universal human project with its own particular historical project. Its laws become natural, its virtues perfect, and the blood of those who offer any resistance— the blood of the prophets and heroes—is spilled by the system as if it were the blood of the wicked, the totally subversive. .... Essential to an ethics of liberation is a clear understanding of the starting point of the praxis of liberation. The starting point is sin, the world as a system of sin, the flesh as idolatrous desire, and a system that nevertheless is "moral," having its own morality and a justified tranquil conscience. .... (1988: 30-31)

The system generates its own self-justifying ethics, its own conception of "natural" laws and virtues. These virtues normally include the golden rule as an ideal: "Do unto others as you would have them do unto you while ignoring the fact that you participate in global systems of injustice and domination that make this impossible." The ethics of holism requires critical analysis of systems of exploitation, hidden behind the "tranquil conscience" and self-justifying conventional morality of the dominant world order. The dominant world order generates "its own law" (so-called international law), "its own morality" (the naïve liberal idea that we can work within the system to evolve it toward greater justice), and "its own goodness" (e.g., the idea our military promotes and protects democracy worldwide).

Holism requires the critical social thought that was most clearly developed within the Marxist tradition. We do not want the illusion of holism (the false morality of the dominant system) but to establish real holistic systems of justice, dignity, and freedom for the Earth. Ethical holism is an ethics of liberation. The *fact* of global systems of violence, domination, and exploitation, exposed by those of critical integrity devoted to human liberation, generates a corresponding insight into *value*: the system must be transformed into one premised on universal justice, dignity, and freedom. Fact and value reunite in the authentic quest for human liberation. Authentic holism is *revolutionary holism*. Küng writes:

> In the past decades it has emerged more clearly than before that a religion can contribute not only to human oppression but also to human liberation: not only in psychological and psychotherapeutic terms, but also politically and socially. Here there is no longer propagation of a class morality (of a bourgeois stamp) of the kind that Marx and Engels rightly criticized in the last century; here—from Latin America to Korea, from South Africa to the Philippines, from East Germany to Rumania—there is a struggle for a humane society. (1991: 46)

Not only can religion embrace this new paradigm and the reintegration of fact and value, Kant taught that the social implication of the categorical imperative (that every person be treated as an end in themselves) is the ideal of the "Kingdom of Ends," the ideal of a union of all human beings in a community of moral relationships. The ethical principle of the categorical imperative alone necessarily also gives us the social-political principle of a universal, just human community. Harris (2005) also states that the ethics of holism, of rational love, implies the ideal of a moral world order of freedom, peace, justice, and harmony. To achieve this we must expose the lies of the self-justifying ideology of the current world system of sin. Küng states: "It has become abundantly clear why we need a new global ethic. For there can be no survival without a world ethic" (1991: 69).

A "world ethic" will by no means come from Christianity or Western thinkers alone. The work of such Eastern creative thinkers as Rabindranath Tagore (Martin, 2013b), Swami Vivekananda, and Sri Aurobindo is also fundamental. Insight into the interdependence of all being has long been a foundational theme of the great thinkers of Confucianism, Taoism, Buddhism, and Hinduism. As von Brück expresses this:

> Thus ethics has its basis not in a forever grounded ought, but in a real transformation, which includes being aware of the interdependence of all being, and this, in turn, has consequences for their behavior towards the whole of nature. . . Two aspects which such a new experience has to include are the "autonomous worth of creatures" and the "interdependence of all beings." If the West represents especially the "autonomous worth of creatures," Eastern thinking takes place in the context of the experience of interdependence. The dialogical community of the two could thus be important in working out our destiny. (1991: 273, 275-76)

Implicit in the new holistic paradigm is the vision of a cooperative and participatory world order in which war and exploitation have been abolished and replaced by peace, cooperation, rational love, and mutual economic and political efforts for the common good. And, indeed, it must be a *world* order, rather than one fragmented into autonomous warring economic and political units. The world of the early-modern paradigm, fragmented into conflicting national power interests and a multiplicity of conflicting economic interests, is gone forever from the most advanced conceptual and scientifically confirmable levels of holism. A true world *order* emerges that has truly emergent properties due to its higher levels of wholeness and integration. It will become clear that such a "true world *order*" necessarily involves planetary unity-in-diversity through democratic world law.

2.4 The Present World Disorder as the Denial of Internal Relationships

Y ET the nightmare of conflict and disharmony remain very much with us today in the form of the system of militarized sovereign nation-states and the exploitation and domination of global capitalism. Right from the very beginning of this system, Western thinkers have pointed out that the nation-state system is *inherently* a war system. It is not that nations sometimes go to war to promote their interests. Rather, the system is structured to make strategic manipulation, deception, economic rivalry, power struggles, and ultimately war inevitable in the relations between nations.

Thomas Hobbes maintained that all nations confront one another in the "posture of Gladiators." Baruch Spinoza pointed out that "Two [sovereign] states are enemies by nature." G.W.F. Hegel saw the relation of states as a conflict of wills that, ultimately, "can only be settled by war." Immanuel Kant concluded that sovereign nation-states were in a perpetual condition of "war" even when they were not fighting one another (see Martin, 2010a: 73-74). As Emery Reves expressed this: *"War takes place whenever and wherever non-integrated social units of equal sovereignty come into contact"* (1945: 121, italics in original).

The international structure is premised on an atomism of sovereign nation-states engaged in an amoral and immoral struggle of conflicting interests and power politics. So also, the global structure is dominated by transnational corporations with conflicting interests and competing with one another for control of cheap resources, markets, cheap labor, and political influence over governments. The dynamics of this system are best described by World Systems Theory as found in the works of such thinkers as Immanuel Wallerstein (1983), Christopher Chase-Dunn (1998), James Petras (2005), and others. Sociologist Thomas Richard Shannon sums up some of the systemic relations between global capitalism and sovereign nation-states:

> A central goal of international competition is for each state to obtain the best possible conditions and opportunities for its national capitalists. A successful national capitalist class contributes to state power by providing the necessary economic resources for state activities. World-system theorists point out that states in which the struggle for power resulted in a politically powerful capitalist class were the states that succeeded best in the quest for national power. The political power of the capitalist class reinforces the tendency for the state to support the national capitalist class. As a consequence of this interstate competition, the world-system has been characterized by repeated wars and shifting military alliances. (1989: 35)

World-systems theorists show that the capitalist system developing over the past five centuries is a *global* system that is simultaneously organized around sovereign nation-states competing with one another in the promotion of the interests of their respective capitalist ruling classes. The result has been unending wars and the division of the world into economic zones made up of collections of states: core states (wealthy, powerful, militarized, high tech), semi-periphery states (often in struggle to become part of the core), and periphery states (subject to super-exploitation of labor and natural resources) (ibid. 24-25). The relations between the states in this system is defined by economic and military "power," not by moral principles or respect for human dignity.

What paradigm or set of fundamental assumptions operates behind this system that makes possible such an unjust and violent world disorder? The system arose as part of the institutional development of the early-modern paradigm and the "rationalization" process that we have been exploring. Both sovereign nation-states and capitalist corporate entities claim to stand primarily in *external relationships* to their competitors and to their victims.

The world system is predicated on the idea of an economic and political atomism, as if the primary entities in the world (capitalists, corporations, and nations) existed as units relatively independent of one another in a competition that can result in abso-

lute winners and losers. And this set of assumptions is still defended around the world by outdated positivists, politicians, career militarists, academics, journalists, and economist mandarins
who place their professional lives in the service of arbitrary power
and wealth. We will see further in Chapter Eight that the system
"totalizes" itself to the point of rejecting any non-idolatrous forms
of transcendence from disrupting its puerile and outdated presuppositions.

Indeed, in recent decades, there have been many attacks on the
tradition of social democracy from the ideological proponents of
this system. The tradition of social democratic liberalism (which
has many links to holism) tends to assume, first, that politics is
and should be an extension of morality and, second, that government should regulate the economy in order to promote the common good and benefit as many citizens as possible. These attacks
on social democracy have come from both directions, political and
economic. On the one hand, theorists of unfettered capitalism,
like Joseph Schumpeter and Friedrich von Hayek, have argued
for a free market ideology, removing government interference as
much as possible from what they claim as truly free markets. They
affirm a competitive world animated by external relationships.

In contrast, Christian thinker Enrique Dussel points out in
Ethics and Community that the rich, under capitalism, try to deny
their internal relationships with the poor, internal relationships
that should be and are expressed within genuine "communities."
In their insistence on external relationships, on their "right" to enjoy the wealth they have accumulated at the expense of the poor,
they deny the human community, even though ultimately they
cannot deny their responsibility for this horrific situation:

> The life of the poor is accumulated by the rich. The latter
> live the life of the rich in virtue of the death of the poor.
> The life of the sinner feeds on the blood of the poor, just
> as the idol lives by the death of its victims. . .. The strength,
> wealth, beauty, culture, and so on, of the dominant group to
> which one belongs is consciously known, enjoyed, and af-
> firmed. Humiliation, weakness, cultural deprivation, serf-

dom, and so on, are consciously known and consented to by the despised poor. Thus it is that, day by day, dominators take on personal, individual *responsibility* for their sin of domination. After all, they daily assert the privileges and the potential (the opportunities) accruing to them in virtue of this inherited sin. And never again will dominators be able to claim innocence of that of which they have the use and enjoyment. (22-24)

Capitalism has been institutionalized as a *system* that supposedly operates according to objective, impersonal, amoral economic laws. Those who benefit from this system hide behind the ideology of impersonal economic laws to deny their personal responsibility for living off the blood, misery, and death of those whom the system uses to produce their wealth. The system emphasizes external relationships, embodied in the blind, mechanical operation of economic laws, behind which the rich take shelter. It denies the real internal relationships at the heart of capitalism.

Dussel makes this relationship explicit: "The life of the poor is accumulated by the rich." Your wealth is the condition of their poverty. Social democracy (brought now to a global vision through the new holistic paradigm) takes issue with this deception. It insists that both economics and politics fall within the scope of universal morality, the morality of social justice, peace, and universal harmony. Government and politics fall within the scope of morality and they are responsible to see that economics is also informed by moral principles.

Christian theologian David Ray Griffin calls this global economic empire, dominated by the United States, "demonic," a global evil that is covered over by free market ideology:

What other term can be used for a state that seeks to impose its will on the entire world, that oversees a system of global economic control that kills more people every decade than were killed by Hitler and Stalin combined, that refuses to eliminate the threat of nuclear holocaust, and that refuses to take action to reduce the likelihood that human civilization will be brought to an end by global warming within

the present century? If such a state should not be called demonic, than nothing should. (2006: 154)

As Griffin shows, this global empire operates according to the
principles of "realism" or "neorealism," which are also demonic
(ibid. 105-113). Attacks against social democracy not only come
from the advocates of an unfettered "free market" but also from
political theorists like Carl Schmitt and Hans Morgenthau, who
argue that there are major differences between morality and politics. The "demonic" quality of the empire includes both aspects.
Schmitt (who was the chief legal theorist for the Nazi regime)
makes the argument that the democratic ideal of rational discussion among informed parliamentarians concerning the content of
laws, the common good, and the best way to proceed into the future involves a false ideology obscuring what is really going on:
the struggle among the parties for power and influence.

Morality therefore plays no part in politics. Since law is inevitably *general*, Schmitt declares, its *specific* applications require
an arbitrary decision by some authority, whether judicial, legislative, or executive. Thus dictatorship, the development of "the total state," he asserts, is more realistic and preferable to democracy.
It effectively corrects the inherently indecisive character of the law
through issuing commands, enforceable by the authorities (1988).

Morgenthau (whose thought appears to serve as a chief ideological cover for US imperialism) also asserts the primacy of
power in his "six principles of political realism" developed in his
1948 book *Politics Among Nations: The Struggle for Power and Peace.*
Morgenthau's theory involves a form of positivism claiming that
political realism derives from *objective* laws of human nature, not
from moral ideals. The objective laws of human nature, when applied to international politics, reveal that the interests of nations
are defined in terms of power.

Moral ideals do not apply in international relations, only
power politics: the strong dominate the weak, might makes right.
The system of sovereign nation-states constitutes the objective
structure of world order through which the struggle for power in

the service of national self-interest takes place. This is the human situation, according to Morgenthau, and the attempt to moralize this situation only leads away from objectivity toward confusing the "autonomous" realm of politics with other areas of human life, or, if leaders of nations take moral principles seriously, toward failure of the nation within the international struggle for power, wealth, and national interests.

The many followers of such political realism today (as manifested in the worldwide relationships among nations) show that the fragmented early-modern paradigm is far from dead. On the other hand, holistic thinker Errol E. Harris writes:

> The notion of the field is holistic, for every variation in the field is determined by the pattern of the whole and is necessarily and inseparably connected with every other, and the field in principle extends over the whole of space-time. In wholes such as this, whose parts determine one another mutually and are interrelated in an ordered system, all relations are internal to their terms, a condition firmly established by the theory of relativity. (2000b: 77-78)

> Ethics and politics have never justifiably been separable, for the common good of the whole is as much a political as a moral end. Hence political obligation has a moral source which is not just the obligation to fulfill a contract but is the universal duty to serve one another and the good of the social whole. . ... It follows that the determinant of personality and its rights is the sociopolitical whole, and the result of thinking holistically in politics is far different from that of the individualism of the seventeenth century. (104 & 106)

> The economic health and success of every country is dependent on that of all the others, so the world economy has to be seen as a single system and must be treated as a whole. Further, the conception of profit must be transformed: It must be socialized rather than individualized. Production and supply have to be viewed as a cooperative enterprise rendering service to the community, rather than a venture undertaken for personal gain. (107)

Morality is no longer considered a mere subjective feature of human emotions operating within an objective, value free material world. It is an aspect of the internal relations that all things have with one another, and certainly that all human beings have with one another. The gigantic systems of which we are part (both capitalism and sovereign nation-states) tend to institutionally deny these internal relationships.

Under the emerging holistic paradigm, institutions that deny our ethical relationship with one another and with all of humanity are increasingly understood as *illegitimate*. Under the new holism, the absolute mind-body dualism has disappeared, as well as the reductionism of mind to matter, and with these the value-fact dualism. Out of the holistic scientific paradigm there arises a new ethics, a new politics, a new economics, and a new conception of human life and civilization.

Jonathan Glover, from whose book *Humanity: A Moral History of the 20th Century* I quoted in Chapter One, expresses a genuine perplexity over the ease with which ordinary moral persons slide into participation in genocides or massacres, from Cambodia to Rwanda to Sarajevo and beyond, throughout the century. We need to grow to a higher level of existence, to recover morality at a deeper level than that which we inherited from the early-modern paradigm, to overcome our assumption that our relation with others is merely external. Holism makes possible the transcendence of the outdated world-system of the past five centuries predicated on the struggle for naked wealth and power. It makes possible rapid growth toward a new planetary maturity.

A fundamental feature of our global crises today is that both capitalism and the system of sovereign nations institutionally deny this contemporary scientific understanding of holism, and, as we have seen, they have many articulate followers and spokespersons. These pundits actively advocate the war system worldwide. Gabriel Marcel declares that "the modern worship of the state, again, is simply one aspect of the extension of the notion of function; an extension which is really pathological in its extravagance" (1951: 38). The state is part of the early-modern obsession with functionalist, instrumental, and technological rationalization. Our future depends on rapidly converting to the new paradigm of holism and harmony: personally, culturally, ecologically, economically, and institutionally.

Emery Reves asserts that our situation (as of the mid-20th century) is a "Copernican" one: We need a "Copernican Revolution" that changes the disastrous outmoded paradigm. At the moment, he writes, the world is a multiplicity of incommensurable points of view between different nation-states: "A picture of the world pieced together like a mosaic from its various national components is a picture that never and under no circumstances can have any relation to reality" (1945: 22). Reality is the holistic integration of a world economically, humanly, and culturally interdependent.

The atomized world of sovereign nation-states and its so-called "realism" is sheer fantasy, Reves asserts. From a global and truly human point of view we need a truly planetary point of view and set of institutions that transcend the multiplicity of illusions that make up our pre-Copernican, atomized view of reality. This system institutionally denies our internal relationships with the rest of humanity. Each nation believes that the world around which "all the problems and events outside our nation, the rest of the world, supposedly rotate, is—our nation." To move beyond this "geocentric world of nation-states" (ibid. 26) and their demonic empires, we must create the Copernican revolution that understands that our problems are primarily planetary and human and that *realism* requires planetary democracy and the planetary rule of law, in other words, democratic world government (ibid. 139).

2.5 Realism versus Utopia

THE mistaken historical separation of fact from value has led some theorists, such as Morgenthau, to argue that being "realistic" is to objectively face the facts of human nature, human self-interest, and the inevitable conflicts among organized groupings such as nation-states. However, "realism" in their usage clearly becomes a normative term, a term of preference: it is supposed to be normatively better to be "realistic" than to be "hopelessly idealistic." The fact that "realism" is itself a normative term may illustrate the impossibility of separating fact from value. It may also illustrate that the distinction itself can be used as a cover for imperialism.

Human beings act from purposes. They evaluate and interpret their surroundings and their situation (the facts) in the light of their purposes, whether these be raising their children, survival by growing crops, altering their living conditions for the better, completing their jobs with satisfaction, gaining access to resources in another part of the world, or finding cheap labor to lessen the input costs of production. What we call "the facts," therefore, are always assessed in the light of human purposes, and this is true even within the sciences, as has often been pointed out.

We call people "unrealistic" who refuse to take their situation carefully or fully into account in their actions. They deny or do not face up to "the facts." Here "the facts" are themselves considered in an evaluative way: it is considered good to take certain conditions into account in determining one's course of action. What is valued by realists, therefore, is a careful and properly focused evaluation of the surroundings and situation and the planning of action in relation to these considerations. But this in no way shows that facts exist independently of values.

A scientist will carefully observe, classify, and record the data, but the scientist already does this within a theoretical framework that frames what is to be selected out as relevant data, and the scientist may creatively engage the data in the search for a new and more adequate theoretical framework. The facts and the purposive construction of theoretical frameworks are internally related. All human endeavor is value-laden. Our purposive frameworks not only condition what we select from the welter of experience that will count as facts, but the facts are also themselves theoretically conditioned by our purposes and frameworks. I am by no means arguing that the world does not exist independently of our purposes, nor that truth is somehow "relativisitic," but simply that human engagement with the world is always purposive and, therefore, always involves the pursuit of something that is valued. Fact and value are also inseparable in this way.

Morgenthau claims that there are "objective laws" of power politics and that nations pursue their self-interest within these laws or else fail because they have ignored the laws. But these conclusions already involve a theoretical construct of the world system that picks out "facts" from within that construct and privileges these as what must be taken into consideration. We saw that Morgenthau is using early-modern atomistic assumptions as part of theoretically envisioning a world-system of autonomous entities each struggling on behalf of its own self-interest, and that in this struggle, he argues, to be successful means to place ethical considerations in the background. His "realism" is therefore heavily value-laden.

By contrast we saw holistic thinker Errol E. Harris interpret this same world situation differently, claiming that the nation-state is constituted within a moral framework and that both politics and economics must be conditioned by that framework. The stance of "political realism" suppresses the evaluative basis of its determinations, the arbitrary nature of what it selects as "reality," and the way it frames the world-system in the light of this. Holism requires us to focus on the interrelatedness of facts and values with an eye to becoming ever more aware of their complex interpenetration. For our view of what ought to be always involves an evaluation and interpretation of what is.

The ideology of realism tends to criticize as "utopian" those who insist that our world system should be one of peace, justice, equality, freedom, and sustainability. As Enrique Dussel points out, this ideology is much more likely to be promoted by academic mandarins from wealthy and powerful countries than by those within the world's victim countries (1985: 4). However, we

have now seen that the values of peace, justice, equality, freedom
and sustainability derive from the deeper holism of our human
situation, and that "political realism" is based on a discredited
early-modern paradigm. While all assessments of our human situation are theory-laden, some are more adequate, coherent, and
comprehensive accounts of the world than others.

We may coherently define the word "utopian" as a theoretical account of the human situation that takes into consideration
our immense possibilities for holistic development and how to
creatively actualize these, while at the same time assessing our
disastrous current planetary situation as carefully and accurately
as possible. If this theoretical account is able to articulate credible options for a transformation from this disastrous situation to
a substantially more optimal one, than surely to be utopian in this
sense is the new realism, for "realism," even in the usage of its
ideologues, has positive evaluative connotations. In our current
human situation, facing as we are the end-time of human history
in the very real possibilities of nuclear holocaust or planetary climate collapse, to be utopian in the sense defined may be our primary moral obligation.

If the "categorical imperative" of holism is to create authentic democracy, harmony, justice, and peaceful living for the Earth
and its creatures, then we must envision what this would look like
and how to actualize it in concrete terms. Fact and value cannot be
separated as if the first were "realistic" (a good thing) and the second were hopelessly idealistic (a mere fantasy). When we assess
our current planetary situation as "disastrous" and deadly, we are
simultaneously generating a more or less coherent theoretical construct about how it could be different. Our very ability to see the
horror of the conditions of people living in the third world shows
that we know it does not have to be this way. There is nothing
"realistic" about passively accepting this. Pope John XXIII writes:

> Public authority, as the means of promoting the common
> good in civil society, is a postulate of the moral order. But
> the moral order likewise requires that this authority be ef-

fective in attaining its end. Hence the civil institutions in which such authority resides, becomes operative and promotes its ends, are endowed with a certain kind of structure and efficacy: a structure and efficacy which make such institutions capable of realizing the common good by ways and means adequate to the changing historical conditions.

Today the universal common good presents us with problems which are world-wide in their dimensions; problems, therefore, which cannot be solved except by a public authority with power, organization and means co-extensive with these problems, and with a world-wide sphere of activity. Consequently the moral order itself demands the establishment of some such general form of public authority. (*Pacem in terris*, 1963, Sects. 136-137)

Here Pope John XXIII speaks from a "Copernican" point of view similar to that of Emery Reves. He recognizes that our problems are "world-wide" and cannot be solved unless we envision a "universal common good" that is institutionalized in a "public authority" that has the "structure and efficacy" necessary to address these problems and secure that common good. Only five years after this encyclical appeared, 200 citizens from 27 countries and 5 continents were meeting in Interlaken, Switzerland and Wolfach, Germany to begin the process of developing a constitution for the Earth.

They elected a drafting committee of 25 persons and specified what should be included. During the next 23 years, between 1968 and 1991, three more Constituent Assemblies met, and drafts were repeatedly sent out worldwide for critical evaluation. At the 1991 Assembly in Troia, Portugal, the delegates voted the final changes to the draft of the *Earth Constitution* and determined that the world now had a finished template for a public authority, that could view the world from the point of view of a planetary realism, with the "structure and efficacy" necessary to actualize our universal common good (Martin, 2010b: 14-18).

This is why the *Constitution for the Federation of Earth* is perhaps the most important document produced in the 20th century. It sees clearly, to quote its Preamble, that humanity is on "the brink of ecological and social catastrophe," and that we have an obligation "to posterity to save Humanity from imminent and total annihilation." It carefully assesses the facts of our situation without illusions, and posits what is clearly within the range of our immense human potentialities: "a new age when war shall be outlawed and peace prevail" and "the Earth's total resources shall be equitably used for human welfare."

And it presents a carefully worked out design and plan for that new age with the means of actualizing it through a ratification and implementation process. It converts our present global institutions, based on the fragmented early-modern paradigm, into practical political and economic institutions premised on holism, inclusive of the Earth and all humanity. The moral authority demands the public authority, and the legitimate public authority itself embodies the moral authority. So-called "political realism" is immoral.

Boswell and Chase-Dunn recognize the crucial role of a utopian vision for establishing a global polity and democratic world system: "The lack of a 'utopian' goal against which to organize criticism and more importantly, to direct progress, has led erstwhile progressives and leftist intellectuals into the nihilism and endless relativism of postmodernism.... Getting past this impasse requires a theory of a realistic alternative at the global level, which we find in the idea of global democracy" (2000: 9).

The institutional conversion is crucial. It will not avail us if people personally and culturally embrace ethical holism while remaining globally organized according to capitalism and the system of sovereign nation-states. We need to make holism the presupposition of all our thinking and acting. We need new global institutions with a new, global government and universal rule of law. We need a global social contract democratically embodying the holism of humanity and the Earth.

Albert Einstein wrote that "there can be no compromise possible between preparation for war, on the one hand, and preparation of a world society based on law and order on the other" (in Fox, 1990: 187). There is nothing "utopian" in the negative sense about what Reves, Pope John XXIII, or Einstein are saying. It is strictly realism to make the Copernican paradigm-shift to a planetary perspective, with a planetary common good, and the planetary set of institutions necessary to address that common good. In Chapter Three, I try to elucidate these new holistic concepts of government and law.

Chapter 3

Legal Holism: The Rule of Law and Universal Harmony

> *There is only one justice, which constitutes the bond among humans, and which was established by one law, which is right reason in commands and prohibitions.*
> —*Cicero*

T HE fundamental issues with respect to the nature of government in relation to citizens have been elucidated at length within the tradition of political philosophy going back to Plato and Aristotle, but especially from the time of Spinoza, Hobbes, and Locke in the 17th century to the present. What is the source and justification for the authority of governments to make mandatory, binding laws for their populations and to claim a monopoly on the legitimate use of force in the administering of those laws? What rights do people retain with respect to the monopoly of authority and force claimed by the government, and where do these rights come from? What is the relation between the will of the people, or the common good of the people, and the authority claimed by governments? Where does sovereignty lie and how is it manifested? What is the relationship between ethics and politics?

The new ethics, politics, and economics, with its rationalistic and intuitive embrace of a cosmic perspective, goes beyond traditional social democracy in some ways (see Chapters Six and Seven). However, this tradition remains a good place to begin both because of its understanding that ethics universally applies to both politics and economics, and because of its emphasis on the role of government and law in relationship to social harmony. One key to understanding the relevance of this tradition involves its concept of "positive freedom."

The concept of positive freedom derives from the understanding that society is not simply a collection of atomistic individuals as 17th and 18th century political thinkers of the early-modern paradigm (like John Locke) would have it. The negative freedom of those who place the individual before society gives us so-called "liberal democracy," with the individual always in a struggle to defend personal autonomy against the community and against government. John Stuart Mill's famous essay *On Liberty* (1956, first published in 1859) illustrates this radical individualism.

However, we have seen that personality, individuality, is a product of society. You cannot separate particular individuals from the whole (claiming they have *a priori*, natural rights prior to society), for parts are only made possible by their relation to the whole. Moltmann states that "person and community are equally primal and condition each other mutually, just as, in the context of development history, a human being's individualization and socialization come into being at the same time" (2012: 220). As he points out, individual rights do not take precedence over social rights. The more adequate concept of democracy is not liberal democracy but "social democracy" in which our economic, social, environmental, and collective rights are protected along with personal integrity and autonomy. Legal holism recognizes its roots in the emergence of social democratic theory.

Reflection on the role of government and law have, there-fore, taken on another dimension that was minimized in tradi-tional philosophy of law. This dimension involves the fact that, as Robert Ornstein says, "The survival problems now facing us are collective rather than individual: problems of how to prevent a large nuclear war, pollution of the Earth, overpopulation. And notice that in these examples, a focus on individual conscious-ness, individual survival, works against, not for, a solution"(in Fox, 1990: 86).

Law, of course, still needs to include the classical focus on indi-vidual rights vis-à-vis the collective. Yet law must also recognize the holism of our situation and its necessary role in dealing with our "survival problems." Philosophy of law necessarily requires reflection on a *world law* that reflects the collective nature of our problems and the holism of our human situation. Such recogni-tion has been developing through a wide variety of thinkers, some of whom I want to identify as forerunners of legal holism.

3.1 Forerunners of Legal Holism

HOLISM focuses on the communities created and maintained by law and government. As Harris says, "Every organized society involves the regulation of the conduct of its members so as to make ordered cooperation possible" (2005: 83). Holism rec-ognizes that the communities thus created transcend a mere col-lection of independent individuals and groups. A common good shows up, a dimension of order, purpose, and meaning, that is not simply the sum of individually pursued goods. A "positive freedom" shows up, in which the freedom of each is empow-ered through the cooperation and community-consciousness of all the others. A number of philosophers have understood the significance of community in this sense, and have realized that the meaning of community points forward to the community of human beings living on Earth.

British philosopher Thomas Hill Green, for example, repudiates class society arguing that "no body of men should in the
long run be able to strengthen itself at the cost of other's weakness." The end or goal of society "is what I call freedom in the
positive sense; in other words, the liberation of all the powers of
men equally for contributions to a common good" (1964: 53). This
means that society should be organized to maximize my freedom
to develop my personal potential within a flourishing life, but this
level of freedom can only exist when persons develop "the conception of a well-being as common to self and others" for "the
right is one that belongs to every man in virtue of his human nature" (1964: 139).

For Green, as for Hegel, Ernest Barker, John Dewey, Jürgen
Habermas, and others in this tradition, the inseparability of human society from individual persons, that is the holism of humanity, means that government is only legitimately founded and
maintained as a vehicle for maximizing positive freedom. We are
in a holistic situation in which the maximization of my liberty depends on the common good of all humanity and a social order
organized so as to promote the maximum of everyone's liberty.
The liberty of all and my liberty mutually empower one another.
My internal relations with all other human beings make this conclusion clear and decisive. Barker writes:

> So far as the society of selves exists by formal rule, it ex-
> ists as a scheme for the adjustment of relations...; and
> while each is thereby limited for the sake of the freedom
> of all, each is also secured in a guaranteed freedom of ac-
> tion which he would not otherwise possess. This involves a
> system of law, intended to secure free agency and the con-
> ditions of such agency.... (1967: 18)

> But no organization is absolutely justified even if it pro-
> motes the freedom of all its members—but promotes *their*
> freedom only. It may do that, and yet be inimical to a
> broader liberty. That is why each partial organization needs
> the criticism of some higher organization, and why, ulti-
> mately, all other organizations of men come to the bar of the

organization of all men, if that can ever come to pass. We can imagine a high measure of general liberty under a system of national societies and national States. We can imagine a perfect liberty only in a world society and a world State. (1967: 28)

Barker here recognizes two essential features of the legitimate rule of law. First, law must serve human freedom in the recognition that the social whole (the organization of society as a whole under democratic government) is the true source of the liberty of all the individuals within society. Second, any territorially bounded society will be necessarily limited in the freedom that it can provide to its members by external relations of competition, scarcity, war, mistrust, economic pressures, etc. We can only conceive of a truly maximized and perfect liberty if government is organized to ensure the freedom of all human beings everywhere. The function of legitimate law (for all human beings) is to maximize liberty, and this function cannot be fully actualized within limited, territorially bound states that structurally and institutionally deny the wholeness of humanity.

For American philosopher John Dewey, the concept of democracy is equivalent with the actualization of our potential as human beings. Just as each person is a "personality" with a potential for actualizing his or her capacities for free flourishing, so the human species has the capacity for creating a world in which freedom, peace, justice, basic equality, and individual flourishing have been institutionalized for all of civilization. Dewey writes:

For Democracy signifies, on one side, that every individual is to share in the duties and rights belonging to control of social affairs, and, on the other side, that social arrangements are to eliminate those external arrangements of status, birth, wealth, sex, etc., which restrict the opportunity of each individual for full development of himself.... As an ideal of social life in its political phase it is much wider than any form of government, although it includes government in its scope. As an ideal, it expresses the need for progress beyond anything yet attained; for nowhere in the world are there institutions which in fact operate equally to secure the development of each individual, and assure to all individuals a share in both the values they contribute and those they receive. Yet it is not "ideal" in the sense of being visionary and utopian; for it simply projects to their logical and practical limit forces inherent in human nature and already embodied to some extent in human nature. It serves accordingly as the basis for criticism of institutions as they exist and of plans of betterment. As we shall see, most criticisms of it are in fact criticisms of the imperfect realization it has so far achieved. (1963: 497-498)

Democracy, in a word, is a social, that is to say, an ethical conception, and upon its ethical significance is based its significance as governmental. Democracy is a form of government only because it is a form of moral and spiritual association. (1993: 59)

From this central position of personality result the other notes of democracy, liberty, equality, fraternity—words which are not mere words to catch the mob, but symbols of the highest ethical idea which humanity has yet reached— the idea that personality is the one thing of permanent and abiding worth, and that in every human individual there lies personality. . ... Equality, in short, is the ideal of humanity; an ideal in the consciousness of which democracy lives and moves. (1993: 62-63)

The notion that organized social control of economic forces lies outside the historic path of liberalism shows that liberalism is still impeded by remnants of its earlier *laissez faire* phase, with its opposition of society and the individual. . ... Earlier liberalism regarded the separate and competing economic action of individuals as the means to social well-being in the end. We must reverse the perspective and see that socialized economy is the means of free individual developments as the end. (1993: 151)

Because Dewey's starting point is the holism of humanity, the ideal of democracy is a planetary ideal, implicit in human intelligence and personality. Democracy, he says, is "equivalent to the breaking down of the barriers of class, race, and national territory which kept men from perceiving the full import of their activity" (1993: 110-111). It involves seeing "the secondary and provisional character of national sovereignty" and emphasizing the superior value of the democratic ideal in which "the fuller, freer, and more fruitful association and intercourse of all human beings with one another must be instilled as a working disposition of mind" (ibid. 120).

Government and the rule of law arise from this planetary ideal. The idea of government starts from the social whole, the wholeness of humanity in which each human personality participates. It is a "planetary ideal" implicit in our common human potential. It derives from the rational, social, moral, and organizational nature of human beings. From this holism of humanity its moral character follows (it must maximize positive freedom for all persons) and its treatment of economics as an extension of this moral character (it must socialize economics for the benefit of all and end privatization for the benefit of the few).

As with T.H. Green and Ernest Barker, Dewey's holism elaborates into a holistic ethics, politics, and economics. Governmental and social harmony do not eliminate personal freedom or development of the human personality. Rather, the harmony arising from the recognition of internal relations makes this development possible and morally necessary. Emery Reves sums up something of this tradition when he writes:

> The founders of modern political democracy understood that freedom ... for which man had been struggling for five thousand years, means in practice only the proper regulation of the interdependence of individuals within a society.... Human freedom is *created* by law and can only exist within a legal order, never without or beyond.... At the present stage of industrial development, there can be no freedom under the system of sovereign nation-states. This system is in conflict with fundamental democratic principles and jeopardizes all our cherished individual freedoms. (1945: 34-5, 66, 163)

The wholeness of humanity demands that it be actualized in a planetary democratic government. At the same time that government expresses the holism of civilization, government is itself also an emergent principle of wholeness that must be actualized. Government binds people together within a common legal framework that is more of a cohesive whole than a society, culture, or civilization without government.

The purpose of government is to make possible the flourishing of the citizens of Earth: their freedom. Each individual is an emerging whole within the larger whole of the human project. We dialectically contribute to the emergent perfection of that project at the same time that we strive to perfect our lives, for the purpose of living, as Harris says, is "harmonious realization of the self in a complete life...what Aristotle defined as happiness or the good for man" (1987: 245).

Jürgen Habermas presents a contemporary version of social holism that sees human autonomy, personality, and moral capacity as arising from language: our distinctively social matrix that all human beings share (1971: 314). His theory of communicative action and his prolific writings spelling out the implications of this theory result from this insight. Language itself carries the rudimentary requirements for a universal ethics independent of human subjectivity. Here is another way in which the is-ought dichotomy is overcome. Human equality is presupposed in the communicative structures of language itself and results in universal ethical principles that include both politics and economics. He writes:

> A universalistic understanding of law and morality rests on the assumption that there is no definite obstacle to egalitarian interpersonal relations. Of course, our societies are marked by manifest as well as structural violence. They are impregnated by the micropower of silent repression disfigured by despotic suppression, deprivation of political rights, social disempowerment, and economic exploitation. However, we could not be scandalized by this if we did not know that these shameful conditions might *also* be *different*.

> The conviction that all actors, as persons, obtain the same
> normative status and are held to deal with one another in
> mutual and symmetrical recognition rests on the assump-
> tion that there is, in principle, a reversibility to interpersonal
> relationships. No dependence on another person must be
> irreversible. (2003: 63)

The fact that "all actors, as persons" have the same normative status (namely moral and communicative equality), reflects the holism of Habermas' "theory of communicative action" premised on the "mutual and symmetrical recognition" implicit in the "reversibility to internal relationships." Habermas here echoes similar conclusions made by Green, Barker, and Dewey. Understanding the deep structures of language forms the basis for universalistic conceptions of law and ethics. The logic of holism moves beyond the system of territorial states and the economic system of competition for private profit. Both law and morality are universal, and it is this universality that lays the groundwork for global harmony.

The concept of structural violence introduced here by Habermas goes back to the social scientific work of World Systems Theory of the past half century and to works such as Johan Galtung's 1971 essay "A Structural Theory of Imperialism" (in Barash, 2000: 42-45), further elaborated in his 2009 book, *The Fall of the US Empire—And then What?.* The *overt* military and terroristic violence of the world is just the tip of the iceberg. The world is structured according to a hierarchy of "center and periphery" in which the center dominates and exploits the periphery through economic and political institutions (deriving from the nexus of capitalism and the system of sovereign nation-states) that impose violence in the form of deprivation, misery, and early death on the majority of persons living on our planet. Being born within one of the peripheral territorial nation-states is like being born under a prison sentence and a death sentence. There is no easy way to leave, for the rich nations will not give you a visa even if you could afford transportation, and your life-opportunities are so vastly restricted that you will likely live in deprivation, with malnourishment, and face an early death (Leech, 2012).

But this harsh reality, Habermas argues, does not indicate a failure of the universalistic understanding of law and morality but, rather, our very capacity to be outraged by this institutionalized system of injustice is indicative of the universality of law and morality that exists in our awareness, deriving from the universal structures of language (1998). In attempting to deal with the problem of implementing decent regimes of democratic law and morality into the world since the democratic revolutions of the 18th century, countries developed as "welfare states," Habermas observes, in which mechanisms for redistribution of wealth, such as progressive taxes, were implemented through the 20th century. But we are at the end of the line now, for the territorially bound welfare state is no longer a viable option in the globalized world system:

> The welfare-state mass democracies on the Western model now face the end of a 200-year developmental process that began with the revolutionary birth of modern nation-states. We should recall this beginning if we want to understand why the welfare state has fallen on such hard times.... The phenomena of the territorial state, the nation, and a popular economy constituted within national borders formed a historical constellation in which the democratic process assumed a more or less convincing institutional form. And the idea that one part of a democratic society is capable of a reflexive intervention into society as a whole, has, until now, been realized only in the context of nation-states. Today, developments summarized under the term "globalization" have put this entire constellation into question. (2001: 60)

As with Green, Barker, Dewey, and Reves, Habermas envisions a world transcending the system of autonomous sovereign nation-states with its complementary system of class-based capitalism. This cannot but be the case for those who understand the implications of holism. These implications include not only universality but particularity: the value of the human personality and each individual. The holistic world order that constitutes "a seamless web" is simultaneously a world of diverse parts that make up the strands of that web. There is never a whole without parts, and the wholeness of humanity is made up of diverse nations, races, genders, cultures, ethnicities, and individual persons—all of which are evolving, and out of which are emerging higher levels of consciousness and freedom—the parts becoming more fully actualized, significant, and meaningful because of their relationships to the whole.

The principle here is often expressed as the principle of *unity-in-diversity*. *Unity-in-diversity* derives from the set of *internal* relations: you cannot separate individual persons from their "humanity" and you cannot have "humanity" apart from individual persons and groupings. As early as 1941 in a document called the *City of Man*, this principle was expressed by many leading intellectuals and thinkers who understood that democracy had to be a worldwide federal democracy or it could not be authentic democracy at all:

> Diversity in unity and unity in diversity will be the symbols of federal peace in universal democracy. Universal and total democracy is the principle of liberty and life which the dignity of man opposes to the principle of slavery and spiritual death represented by totalitarian autocracy. No other system can be proposed to the dignity of man, since democracy alone combines the fundamental characteristics of law, equality, and justice. (Agar, et.al. 1941: 27-28)

By contrast, the system of sovereign nation-states and the system of capitalism, assuming, as they do, the primacy of external relations, deny in principle the unity and dignity of humanity. They represent the fragmented early-modern paradigm because they claim to discover incommensurable differences: your nationality and your nation are *incommensurable* with ours because both are "sovereign," that is, both are autonomous and recognize no enforceable laws above themselves. If there is a fundamental clash of their apparently incommensurable interests, we may go to war and destroy your country. There is no one and nothing to stop us, for there is no law above the sovereign nation-state. The world system at present is a system of external relationships and of institutionalized structural violence.

Similarly, if I own capital and you live in a forest that your ancestors have occupied for generations, our interests may appear incommensurable. If I wish to purchase the forest as an investment in order to cut it down or mine its minerals, and you wish to continue living in your home as your ancestors have for hundreds of years, your interests and my interests appear to directly clash. However, my "right of private property" trumps your interests. I can buy the forest and force you to leave your home forever.

My relationship to you is an external one. I have the capital and it gives me the external prerogative to do what I wish with that capital regardless of most human or environmental consequences. Here again we encounter the structural violence engendered by the assumption of external relationships. Mexican thinker José Miranda speaks of "that mechanism of violence which we call the market, whether the consumer market, the wage market or both," which is predicated on the fact that, in today's world, "99% of all exploitation is legal" (1974: 12). If the law were predicated on holism and its internal relationships, the world system would clearly look very different from the way it looks today.

3.2 Legal Holism

THE paradigm-shift from fragmentation to holism has clearly not yet reached the dominant institutions of global society, and the institution of the territorially bound nation-state remains a fundamental assumption in much of today's philosophy of law. We have not yet achieved that global social contract that can institutionalize political and economic holism in spite of the fact that our "survival problems" cry out for such an expansion. The vision of transformative hope emerging from the new paradigm is not yet fully actualized. Nevertheless, contemporary philosophy of law has made great strides in moving in the direction of holism, and some of its formulations, even though developed within today's framework of territorial states, explicitly or implicitly claim a universality applicable to all humankind.

Before discussing my understanding of holism in contemporary philosophy of law, I wish to recognize the good work that was done between and immediately after the World Wars by thinkers such as P.C. Jessup, G. W. Keeton, Hans Kelsen, Hugo Krabbe, and H. Lauterpacht, who developed aspects of what may be termed "legal monism" (the concept that all law, including the laws of national states, derives from a single source). These thinkers questioned the concept of the sovereignty of nation-states, argued for a transformation of the fragmented world system toward one under enforceable world law, and developed the concept of a universal law in relation to the human community. Jessup, for example writes:

> Sovereignty, in its meaning of an absolute, uncontrolled state will, ultimately free to resort to the final arbitrament of war, is the quicksand on which the foundations of traditional international law are built. Until the world achieves some form of international government in which a collective will takes precedence over the individual will of the sovereign state, the ultimate function of law, which is the elimination of force for the solution of human conflicts, will not be fulfilled. (1948: 40)

These are important ideas that might be further elaborated. Chapter Nine of my *Triumph of Civilization* (2010), for example, articulates a conception of the proper function of the democratic state as "the elimination of force for the solution of human conflicts" in ways similar to what Jessup appears to be proposing. Nevertheless, despite the tempting antecedents found in the works of these thinkers, in this chapter I want to focus in the implications of more contemporary philosophy of law for a holistic understanding of law in relation to our common humanity and universal ethical principles.

Much of today's philosophy of law is similar in its situation to the philosophy of human rights developed at great length and in a wide-ranging literature since the ground-breaking formulation of the 1948 UN Universal Declaration of Human Rights. Human rights are said to be universal, to be "equal and inalienable" to all persons, to derive from the inherent dignity of every person, and to be "the foundation for freedom, justice and peace in the world." Yet the system of territorial nation-states has rendered their universal recognition and application nearly impossible. We will see that the philosophy of human rights and the philosophy of law imply one another in a multiplicity of ways.

The philosophy of law has become more nuanced and sophisticated since its early systematic versions as found, for example, in the 19th century works of Jeremy Bentham or John Austin. Bentham and Austin focused on the apparent unique feature of law as an imperative issued by a recognized authority designated as the "sovereign." They concluded that the essential nature of law involves the "commands of a sovereign." One person (such as the king) or a group of persons (such as a legislature) issue commands that are binding on the subject population. These commands are backed up by the sovereign (which assumes for itself a monopoly on the legitimate use of force), by the power to judge, and by the police to apprehend and punish those who violate the law.

But contemporary philosophy of law is much more sophisticated. H.L.A. Hart in his highly regarded 1961 book, *The Concept of Law*, shows that Bentham and Austin focused only on one feature of law, that law in actuality has multiple functions and dimensions that cannot be reduced simply to the relationship of a commander to one who is commanded. For one thing, it looks as though Bentham and Austin were privileging criminal law, with its arrest and punishment features, as the essential nature of law. However, Hart points out, the law has a multiplicity of functions that are just as much part of the law as is criminal law.

Property law, for example, defines what is to count as private property or public property, how this is legally obtained (through a paycheck or return on an investment, a legislative act, etc.), how property is transferred, how it is inherited, maintained, etc. The law here provides rules by which people can operate. It empowers and protects people by conferring on them rights with regard to property, its acquisition, transfer, etc. Secondly, there is the domain of tort law. The law not only regulates relations between government and the people, but in tort law it also regulates those that take place directly between people. Tort law governs my rights to be secure and to function without interference from others and defines the occasions when I can claim I have been interfered with or injured by others and the procedures I can take for redress of such grievances. Thirdly, there is also the domain of contract law, which again can be seen to empower and enable people to function within society. What is an agreement? When is it binding? How is an agreement altered, broken, or annulled? What are the implicit but nevertheless legal agreements, for example, between buyer and seller?

The essential insight provided by Hart and other contemporary philosophers of law is that law does not merely command, prohibit, threaten, and punish. The law is not simply "power over" a subject population. The law also *empowers* and enables human living across multiple dimensions. It enables me to marry and have children, to get an education and have this legally recognized by society, to vote or to claim social security benefits, to become legally certified to practice some specialty (such as doctor, lawyer, architect, engineer, or accountant), and to practice in that specialty governed by legal rules that enable and guide its operation. The law is not a contingent feature of human societies (that somehow might operate without it) but is a necessary feature of human civilization for all societies beyond the most primitive and elementary.

Hart analyzes the law into primary and secondary rules. The primary rules are the rules and regulations that enable and guide human living within society. The secondary rules are the rules by which society confers power on those who make up its government who are then enabled to make and enforce the primary rules. Hart divides secondary rules into those of recognition, change, and adjudication. What are the rules by which we can recognize who has the authority to make laws (e.g. election laws)? What are the rules by which those with executive power must step down so that others are chosen to take their place (e.g., term limits, office qualifications)? What are the rules by which judges decide cases in the courts? Hart also makes clear that authority may have multiple dimensions to it (checks and balances, etc.) and need not be located in a "unitary sovereign" such as Bentham and Austin appear to have had in mind.

Hart's pointing out the complexity and multiplicity of functions of the law helped the philosophy of law make great strides in the late 20th century. However, like Bentham and Austin, he remained a positivist who viewed the law as a set of social facts that did not include the moral dimension as a necessary feature of the law. In contrast to this, a number of prominent philosophers of law have insisted that moral principles are fundamental to the very nature of law. I will consider several of these thinkers briefly in order to show that much contemporary thought is tending toward a rejoining of the dimensions of fact and value that were so radically divided by the early-modern paradigm and its attendant positivism. I will mention David Luban, in his 2007 book, *Legal Ethics and Human Dignity*, Lon Fuller, in his 1964 book, *The Morality of Law*, John Finnis, in his 1980 book, *Natural Law and Natural Rights*, and Ronald Dworkin in his 1986 book, *Law's Empire*.

David Luban argues that the very existence of law in human civilization is inextricably interwoven with the value of human dignity. He writes: "Law enhances human dignity by knitting together thousands of details that make it possible for ordinary people to accomplish ordinary business smoothly" (2007: 4). He conceives of human dignity, not "as a metaphysical property of individuals" but in a "naturalized" way "as a relationship among people in which they are not humiliated. Non-humiliation plays a key role in my understanding of human dignity" (2007: 6).

I want to suggest that Luban's idea of human dignity coheres well with a holistic conception of human life and law. Like T.H. Green and the philosophers of "positive freedom" outlined above, individual persons are not seen by Luban as the bearers of *a priori* rights prior to being members of society, but rather their individual rights and dignity are integral to society itself. Dignity and non-humiliation arise from the social matrix with which our individualities are inextricably intertwined. The law is part of this holism intrinsic to human dignity and cannot be reduced, as positivism argues, to a set of social facts independent of that dignity.

Luban asserts that his own views are very much in accord with those of Lon Fuller (2007: 6). For Fuller, the law is about "the morality of duty," which he distinguishes from "the morality of aspiration." Human beings owe basic duties to one another and those who govern have basic duties toward those governed. These duties are the proper sphere of law and lawmaking. They provide the baseline for people living and working together in complex societies. The law makes possible human flourishing in the sense of enabling free pursuit of goals, goods, and plans to make our lives fulfilling. The area of freedom that the law leaves up to us, however, is the sphere of the morality of aspiration, where citizens are free to pursue what they take to be good in life, including human excellence.

Fuller emphasizes that law-making and law-enforcing are *activities* engaged in by people who are placed in these roles. As such, their activities, like those of all human beings, are governed by moral principles. As people engaged in these activities, they have a duty to do them well, and they have a duty to the people affected by their actions to do them morally. Fuller's list of features that the law will have if its makers have done their duty properly is well-known: the law will be general, it will not be retroactive, it will be promulgated so that it is known among the citizens, it will be clear and non-contradictory, it will be constant and not frequently changing, there will be the possibility of compliance, and there must be a coherence between the declared law and official action.

The key concept here is that, again, the morality of law is not separable from the moral responsibilities of those who make the law. There is a holistic relationship between the law, the lawmakers, and the citizens of any society. This holistic relationship includes the moral dimension of duty. The law is not a set of social facts independent of morality. It involves a moral relationship between the governed and the governors as well as a morality of duty for everyone to relate to one another in good faith within the framework set by the law. In addition, the function of the law is to free citizens to pursue the morality of aspiration in their personal lives. Fact and value appear intimately related to one another.

Ronald Dworkin elaborates the philosophy of law through focusing especially on the work of judges. Positivists hold that the law is a set of objective social facts, independent of morality or values. When judges are confronted with a unique and difficult case that does not appear to have any clear historical precedent to appeal to in their decision, therefore, a positivist appears forced to conclude that the judge's decision must be merely subjective and arbitrary. Dworkin argues that this is not the case: the responsible judge appeals to moral principles that are behind the law and that embody the intention and spirit of the law.

Dworkin examines specific cases, as well as the various arguments regarding the nature of law, with a view to showing what he calls "law as integrity":

> The adjudicative principle that governs our law enforces *inclusive* integrity: this requires a judge to take account of all the component virtues. He constructs his overall theory of the present law so that it reflects, so far as possible, coherent principles of political fairness, substantive justice, and procedural due process, and reflects these combined in the right relation.... He will therefore be aware of a different, more abstract calculation: *pure* integrity abstracts from these various constraints of fairness and process. It in-

> vites him to consider what the law would be if judges were
> free simply to pursue coherence in the principles of justice
> that flow through and unite different departments of law. . ..
> This purified interpretation speaks, not to the distinct duties
> of judges or legislators or any other political body or institu-
> tion, but directly to the community personified. It declares
> how the community's practices must be reformed to serve
> more coherently and comprehensively a vision of social jus-
> tice it has partly adopted. . .. (1986: 405-407).

As with Luban and Fuller, Dworkin invites a holistic interpretation of the human situation, transcending positivism with
its absolute division between fact and value. The law is part of
this holistic situation and cannot be separated from philosophical
considerations and reflection on values as this reflection should
be and is practiced by judges, legislators, and administrators. The
law gives rise to the vision of "the community personified." What
is the nature of our human community and what should it be?
Philosophical reflections, moral values, conceptions of our fundamental humanity, the principles of interpretation, and our existing
institutions all become relevant to the law and intrinsic to the law
as part of our integral human wholeness.

The "is" here cannot be coherently separated from the
"should." Under the emerging scientific paradigm of universal
holism, we have seen, the human mind, with its reason, values,
and desires, is not considered some accident of the blind forces of
evolution that contingently engendered in *Homo Sapiens* a spurious subjectivity. Rather, the reflection on values, on the principles
by which we should be acting, is as fundamental to the evolving
universe as is the universal law of gravitation or the principle of
entropy. Dworkin rarely ventures beyond British and American
legal traditions in his reflections and examples, but, like Luban
and Fuller, the presupposition of his philosophy of law is that
it applies to the entire human situation. For Luban, law is universally a fundamental aspect of human dignity; for Fuller, lawmakers universally have moral duties toward the governed; for

Dworkin, the "integrity" of value considerations is universally behind the worldwide phenomenon of law.

John Finnis is another prominent contemporary philosopher of law whose thought has made a huge impact. Finnis accepts the value-fact distinction, we have seen, but argues that the fundamental principles of practical reason (ethics) are immediately evident to our reason and do not need to be claimed as either facts (deriving, for example, from human nature) or values (subject to endless debate about what they are). Our practical reasoning power is based on immediately recognizing the basic elements that constitute human flourishing (the human good). Finnis formulates seven principles that fit into this category, all of which are primary goods and some (variable) combination of which constitutes human flourishing: life, knowledge, practical reason itself, sociability (friendship), play, aesthetic experience, and religion (that is, some coherent relation to the ground and meaning of existence) (1980: 81-90).

He argues, with great sophistication and knowledge of the relevant literature, that these primary goods are all intrinsically valuable in human life and participation in them (in various combinations) is what constitutes human flourishing. These intrinsic values are, therefore, the basis of both ethics and law. The function of law is to organize society to make human participation in these goods possible. It provides a framework both of freedom and *opportunities* so that citizens can pursue these goods in various combinations as part of a flourishing life. Unlike Austin, who conceived of law as the imperious commands of a sovereign, law for Finnis provides a framework for cooperative and common action for empowering the lives of citizens.

Finnis argues that it is especially important to recognize that these seven primary goods are *incommensurable* with one another. They cannot be amalgamated into some generalized conception of "the good" that can be pursued by individuals or society as a whole. This is why any form of utilitarianism or consequentialism is false, because such an ethical stance requires that we envision the ways in which our actions "promote the greatest good of the greatest number." But there is no such general good apart from the multiplicity of intrinsic goods that make up human flourishing. These intrinsic goods also form the basis for human rights, which are articulated as primary or secondary principles derived from these goods and are formulated to identify and protect our basic right to flourish as human beings.

Here we also find the basis for law and government. The nature and justification of law cannot be separated from the intrinsic goods known to our practical reason. The purpose of the law is to create the nexus of conditions that maximize our ability to pursue the variety of intrinsic goods that constitute human flourishing. The goal of the law is the "common good" in this sense. Just as with the principle of utility, the common good cannot be amalgamated into a unitary good that government uses as an excuse to interfere with the rights and freedoms of its citizens. Rather, the common good of society is "the various aspects of individual well-being in community" (1980: 214). That is, law and government must develop and maintain the conditions for humans to pursue the variety of goods within a framework that recognizes everyone's equal rights to these goods, and for which the law provides the rules and duties for the common action and cooperation that maximizes opportunities to pursue these goods for everyone.

The thought of these thinkers is related to what traditionally was known as "natural law," a perspective that has been revived in a sophisticated form in recent decades. It is no accident that Finnis' major book is named *Natural Law and Natural Rights*. Errol E. Harris agrees. Harris defines natural law as "the law of reason: namely, what prescribes the rational requirements of social living; for it is only the rational capacity of human beings that makes civilized society possible (whatever other propensities and characteristics human nature may include)." Today, Harris writes, "this is the conception of all law as belonging to one universal system, applying to the international (or better, world) community as well as to all subordinate communities included within it" (2005: 85).

Finnis' philosophy makes the important point, discussed above, that must be understood as part of the holistic view of law. Holism, unity, and universalism do not entail the abolition of diversity and differences. And when it comes to human beings and human rights, the diversity may be considered incommensurable in the sense that you cannot legitimately violate one innocent person's life in order to protect another person or for some overriding "common good" determined by government that amalgamates everything together under the principle of utility. There is no overriding general good that trumps the individual's rights to life, liberty, security of person, freedom from torture, etc. (cf. Finnis 1983: Chap.V). Nevertheless, the emerging world community embodies a common good that not only embraces and protects individuals, but supersedes all these parts in a higher unity–the right to flourish within the diversity of goods recognized by human practical reason.

The thirty different articles listed in the UN Universal Declaration of Human Rights by and large illustrate this diversity (1980: 214). Holism, on the other hand, enters when we consider that the individual does not hold these intrinsic goods, nor any *a priori* human rights, apart from being a human being and part of the human community (a truth correctly recognized by this declaration). Our relations with other persons and with government are internal relations. We are part of one another and must communicatively and nonviolently work together to create the universal dignity of equal opportunities for flourishing rather than war, conflict, and violence.

Legal holism points directly to the need for a planetary community governed by universal, democratic laws. As Harris points out, "a collection of sovereign states in mutual relation thus constitutes an association, but it can never form a community, because sovereign independence entails giving precedence to national interests over all others, while the defining characteristic of a community is that its members subordinate their own individual advantage to the demands of the common good" (2005: 83). Legal holism requires democratic world government defining and ordering the human community for the common good–the good of our universal right to lead flourishing lives. This community, now implicit in our common humanity, can only become actual through democratically legislated world law.

3.3 Consequences of this Paradigm-Shift in the Concepts of Government and Law

WE can learn the principles of the new paradigm not only from the scientific revolution that has taken place throughout the 20th century, but also from the critics of the old paradigm, as well as the most advanced contemporary thinkers concerning government and law. I have brought some of this literature together in this volume so that the following brief summary will make sense in terms of its background and larger context. Holism in government and law, therefore, exhibits the following general characteristics:

1. Government and law are the expression of *internal relations* among human beings. Governments need to be designed and laws enacted with this in mind. Democratic law is itself a fundamental component in the formation and maintenance of community within complex societies.

2. Law arises from these internal relationships. It harmonizes, empowers, enables, and regulates human activities in complex societies. Law is not reducible to the commands of a person or group having governmental powers. It is not incidental to human harmony but essential for harmony. Law is fundamental to transforming the collection of self-interested associations or individuals into a *political community* in which a common good supersedes individual goods.

3. Government and laws are, therefore, universal to human beings. However, they are incapable of fulfilling the goals in-

herent in law if divided among absolute, incommensurable
territorial states. The principle of emergent holism demands
that the nations of the world become administrative regions
within a holistic Earth Federation government, establishing harmony in diversity through binding themselves into
a larger whole, a planetary Earth community in which laws
are enforceable over all *individual persons*, and not solely
nation-states.

4. Holism in government and law, therefore, requires world
   government in the form of planetary social democracy, a
   global social contract. Once realized, as Dewey points out,
   human life will be brought to an entirely new level, since
   many of the impediments to the functioning of democracy
   imposed by today's global institutions will have been removed.

5. The ultimate end or goal of law is to empower human flourishing, that is, a free world society in which every person
   has genuine opportunities to pursue a life of fulfillment and
   well-being. It is also harmony: human beings flourishing
   within a creative and cooperative framework of peace, justice, and sustainability. Together these two constitute planetary "positive freedom."

6. Human flourishing entails a variety of incommensurable,
   but humanly universal goods. These goods include economic rights, political civil liberties, and the rights to peace
   and a protected environment. These goods are not reducible
   to one another and cannot serve as a justification for government to violate the fundamental human rights or dignity of
   innocent persons in the name of an amalgamated "general
   good." Within the holistic paradigm, the common interest
   will most often coincide with the individual interest, and the
   perceived need of government to claim priority for the general interest against individuals will be minimized. People

will realize that living in a cooperative, mutually supportive, sustainable community is in their interest.

7. Effective empowerment of human flourishing requires this
   "positive freedom," the enacting of laws that facilitate human cooperation, mutual understanding, and social harmony on a planetary scale. Unity-in-diversity mutually enhances both unity *and* diversity. This necessarily means a
   demilitarized Earth Federation.

8. Holism requires both a global cooperative civics and a global
   cooperative economics, for politics and economics are both
   based on the moral principles and internal relationships that
   exist among all persons. Human freedom and flourishing
   follow directly from actualizing these conditions.

Let me briefly elaborate some of these principles. The first
consequence of the paradigm-shift to holism with respect to government and law is recognition of the *illegitimacy* of the global
political-economic system that is today rapidly shredding the possibility for any viable future for human beings on Earth. The dominant political and economic system of the world today violates
wholeness, and, focusing as both nations and corporations do on
external relations, violates the possibility of harmony. For every
nation today, national and sectarian interests take priority over
planetary interests, but planetary interests are those of the whole
of humanity and future generations. They arise from our holistic
situation and require a holistic perspective and set of institutions
to address them.

People today are recognizing their rights to peace and a protected environment, and the system of sovereign nations is intrinsically incapable of providing these rights. As Harris expresses
this:

> National sovereign independence therefore has proved fa-
> tally inimical to the solution of world problems. Yet it is
> on the resolution of these global difficulties that the welfare

of peoples and the very survival of humankind depends. The national sovereign state can no longer effectively protect its citizens from devastation in war, nor can it protect their living standards and maintain the amenities of life in the face of environmental deterioration.... In short, the national state now lacks the one and only justification for the exercise of sovereign power, the fostering of national prosperity and security. Its ethical character has been undermined, and its title to be juristically supreme is no longer valid. (2000b: 70-71)

Nation-states can no longer function as the ultimate vehicles of government and law because they are incapable of actualizing the good for human life. Luban characterizes that good as protection of human dignity. Fuller sees it as the actualizing of a morality of duty on behalf of human flourishing. Dworkin sees it as actualizing human integrity throughout society, especially in the work of judges and government officials, and Finnis sees it as the promotion of the seven fundamental aspects of human flourishing. In every case, the nature of law and the role of government is universal: human dignity, the morality of duty, integrity, and the goods of practical reason apply to all governments everywhere and to all human beings.

A fundamental implication behind the thought of all these thinkers is that human beings (everywhere, as a world community) have the rights to peace and a protected planetary environment (cf. Wacks, 2006: 58). Without democratic world government, which alone can provide peace and truly protect the planetary environment, no government anywhere can fulfill its functions as identified by these philosophers. All national governments are therefore *illegitimate* as long as they claim to be sovereign. So-called "national self-determination" as an absolute "right" of nations explicitly denies a political community for humankind that recognizes these universal common interests.

The holistic paradigm of law and government identifies a new common good which is a planetary common good. It recognizes that the fate of all people is linked together, both because we are all human beings and because a globalized world has forced awareness of these rights to peace and a protected environment upon us all. Engendering a new global democratic order will establish government and law directed toward making the world a decent place for all its citizens, not just the one percent, not just those in the global north, not just those in North America, Europe, or Japan, and not just those within any particular nation. The very nature of holistic law demands this: the purpose of government and law is intrinsically moral and intrinsically demands universal application.

As we have seen, the units of the world (its diversity) are not abolished by holism but rather relegated to their proper places as unique elements within the whole. It is this proper functioning within the whole that constitutes harmony. You cannot have harmony among autonomous units that recognize no enforceable law above themselves, only the ability to do as they wish, and, ultimately, the right to go to war. The new world system, therefore, will convert the world from being an intrinsic war system to an intrinsic peace system. Peace is the proper functioning of whole and parts together within their common worldwide civilization. So-called "negative peace" (temporary absence of war within the current fragmented world system) is in reality no peace, since peace requires a holistic system for its actualization.

In no holistic field does the principle of peace mean the absence of conflict. The internal differentiation of many parts necessarily means a dynamic process of conflict and mutual adjustment. But the process of conflict is vital to the functioning of the whole and does not destroy that wholeness, as do war and the economics of absolute winners and losers. There are many ways the process of conflict can be mediated without mutual destruction.

On the level of individual human beings as parts of the human whole, proper functioning is the realization that my flourishing (in dignity, freedom, and peace) is linked to the flourishing of all others. Again, conflict is inevitable, but a holistic system of law mediates this through dialogue, mutual understanding, conflict resolution, arbitration, adjudication, voting, compromises, mutual loyalty to a larger good, etc. The health of the whole fosters the cooperation and health of each of the parts.

Given the emergent principle discussed above in which, in the course of evolution, wholes emerge that are not reducible to simply the sum of their parts, it is likely that the establishment of a global social contract uniting humanity will exhibit emergent properties (as we have seen a number of thinkers argue): a peace-system will not simply involve a toleration of the semi-autonomous parts for one another. Rather, it will be a genuinely new emergent level of human flourishing: the uniting of humanity in mutual respect, cooperation, and love. The synthesis of the parts results in a new, emergent level of wholeness (cf. Chapter Seven).

It is important to be clear that the process of emergence of this world peace system, and the planetary social democracy it entails, is not simply one arbitrary option among the various possibilities that we encounter as we reflect on our common future. We have seen that a dynamic principle of holism is fundamental to all the processes of the universe including human evolutionary development. Democratic world law is implicit within our emerging human holism. We can, of course, derail this process through environmental collapse or nuclear war, but the potential for harmony and *unity-in-diversity* of a nonviolent planetary legal order is at the heart of the emergent ethics of holism and the unity of our human condition.

This new world-peace system will not abolish national administrative and governmental units but will substantially remove the conflict of national partisan interests. National governments will then function more like states within the US or Pradesh within India. Holistic law recognizes that the cooperative regulation of everyone together engenders "positive freedom," a freedom for each that is so much greater than the so-called "freedom" of isolated units trying to serve egoistic interests while in conflict with others and while resisting governmental authority. The nations and peoples of Earth will begin working together in ways deemed unimaginable during most of modern history since the Renaissance.

War and conflict may or may not have something to do with the so-called weaknesses of "human nature," as popular thought believes, but they clearly have much more to do with the kind of institutions that encompass our lives and the kind of paradigm that we presuppose in our thoughts and actions. Capitalism and sovereign nation-states as institutions bring out our potential for fear, greed, conflict, and lust for power. They lead people to thoughts and actions presupposing external relationships. A social democratic world government will bring out our potential for cooperation and mutual participation. (We will see in Chapters Six and Seven that the idea of "social democracy" is articulated in a very specific way, not to be confused with many current ideas about this.)

For these reasons, the social democratic world government will provide a key element in engendering a new, holistic human civilization in which every person is recognized as a world citizen with all the rights and duties that this entails. People will begin literally to think globally as universal citizens, not as violent defenders of this or that sovereign territory. This will mean that the universal rights identified in the UN Universal Declaration will finally be actualized and universally protected—because the one key right (Article 28) that has never been fulfilled anywhere on Earth has finally come to pass: "Everyone is entitled to a social and international order in which the rights and freedoms set forth in this Declaration can be fully realized." The present world order of global capitalism and sovereign nation-states institutionally defeats the entire set of human rights precisely because it does not actualize the holistic world peace system that makes their actualization possible. The very existence of these global institutions violates Article 28.

The heart of Article 28 is precisely global democracy. Boswell and Chase-Dunn make very clear what is needed for a decent world system:

> Our fundamental starting point is one of global democ-racy. Global democracy has a dual meaning—democracy at the global level, with democratic institutions governing the ever more integrated world economy, and local democ-racy, with economic management and social administration as well as politics and the state open to democratic partic-ipation. Democracy includes civil and individual human rights, without which democratic institutions are meaning-less. (2000: 5)

The holistic system of government and law will naturally and peacefully disarm the world and make all war preparation, incite-ment, production, transportation, and investment illegal. People investing in, transporting, or building bombs or missiles need to be arrested and prosecuted, not rewarded through a lucrative re-turn on their investments. The conversion of the world to a holis-tic paradigm, which necessarily includes holistic government and law, converts human civilization to harmony across the board. Hence, human rights are substantially protected for the first time, war and war-preparation are abolished and a peace-system es-tablished, and universal moral principles such as integrity, trust, respect, justice, compassion, truth, and brotherly love are recog-nized among all peoples and taught to younger generations.

Transformative holism will protect and restore the environ-ment (to the extent still possible), something impossible within the current fragmented world system. Government, research uni-versities, and citizens will monitor the environment in all its com-plex, interrelated aspects and scientifically address the process of restoration. The many people worldwide formerly employed in military activities can now be employed in vast projects of replant-ing trees, reclaiming deserts, restoring potable water supplies, and converting to clean energy sources. As Herman E. Daly (a fore-most economist for economic sustainability) expresses this:

> One rather subtle yet very powerful moral force can be
> enlisted in support of the steady-state paradigm. That is
> wholeness. If the truth is the whole, as Hegel claimed, then
> our current splintered knowledge is so far from the truth
> that it is hardly worth learning.... Ecology is whole. It
> brings together the broken, analyzed, alienated, fragmented
> pieces of man's image of the world.... Unless the physi-
> cal, the social and the moral dimensions of our knowledge
> are integrated into a uniform paradigm offering a vision of
> wholeness, no solutions to our problems are likely. (1993:
> 357)

Holism integrates, as Daly asserts, the physical, social, and
moral dimensions. Physically the planet and its ecosystem form
a whole; physically the social democratic world government will
be a whole. Socially, the planet is and should be a whole, and
morally, we have seen, the planet is most certainly a whole. By
embodying social and moral wholeness, the world government
will transform people's attitudes, and the law will be liberated to
fulfill its primary function of providing the matrix for all people
everywhere to live flourishing lives. The law will, of course, address the structural violence of poverty and social injustice and
will establish a reasonable prosperity for all the citizens of Earth
(cf. Chapter Six).

One important function of the law in any society is its power
of conflict resolution, binding mediation, and impartial adjudication of issues before the courts. Democratic theorists have always
claimed that democracy is the one form of government that mini-
mizes violence, making it possible for people to nonviolently address their problems, conflicts, and desire for change through pro-
cedural, due process methods. A holistic world government will
necessarily set up worldwide mechanisms for conflict resolution,
mediation, and dialogue directed toward mutual understanding
among people to promote peaceful living among the world's diverse groups.

Much of the current hatred, fear, and misunderstanding now
rampant throughout the world will be rapidly mitigated. The dis-

information and false propaganda of imperial nation-states, along with their patriotic minions in the corporate mass media, will no longer breed misunderstanding, suspicion, and fear. For the first time in human history, the real import of democracy will be actualized. For, to date, under the economic and political system of sovereign nation-states, the real transformative potential of democracy has been systematically undercut.

Finally, the social democratic world government embodying the new holistic paradigm will itself be a place of dialogue directed toward mutual understanding for the people of Earth. Historically there has been no such thing. At the beginning of his 2005 book, *Earth Federation Now! Tomorrow is Too Late,* Harris states that "as we enter the twenty-first century C.E., humankind is threatened with extinction from numerous angles. . ... But, as human beings are intelligent animals, once they have been appraised of the menacing facts, they should be able to seek ways of countering the impending dangers, and, it is hoped, to find effective remedies" (9).

Harris' book continues investigating in detail the many "threats to human survival," showing that human intelligence has, indeed, failed to counter the dangers. But perhaps the chief reason for this failure is that we have never had institutions that allow human intelligence to effectively dialogue about these lethal issues and take effective steps to address them. Sovereign nation-states and global capitalism impede, rather than promote, our planetary intelligence.

The League of Nations was supposed to be a place for nations to talk out their differences and the world's problems rather than go to war, but such a nonbinding framework for militarized sovereign nation-states in aggressive economic competition with one another will necessarily fail to fulfill that purpose. The same thing is true of the United Nations with its undemocratic and powerless General Assembly and Security Council veto. Under the system of sovereign nations, the General Assembly becomes little more than a forum for ideology, posturing, and recrimination, not a forum for genuine dialogue, and clearly not a public space for effective use of human intelligence to address global problems.

But the functioning of a holistic democracy for Earth will give the people of Earth the necessary conditions for promoting genuine dialogue, communication, not only among one another, but among those from every corner of Earth who are participating in the world government. For the first time ever Earth will have a "brain." We need not only revolutionary, transformative hope, but a brain to guide us into that transformed future. Our planet will have a group of people from every corner of Earth dialoging with one another about the human situation, about our future, the common good, and how to deal with our lethal planetary crises—people who have the authority to take effective action as representatives of the human project itself.

Human intelligence will be focused and activated through real government, making real enforceable world laws. Through this process, it will be able to effectively deal with the lethal global problems that go unaddressed under the current fragmented world disorder. Moltmann writes:

> The era of the mechanistic world picture was also the era of subjectivity and of the sovereignty of human beings over against nature. The subjectivity of human existence and the reification of natural being conditioned each other mutually. If this bifurcation of the world we share is not to lead to the destruction of both nature and human beings, we must replace it by a new paradigm of a communicative community of culture and nature resting on reciprocity.(2012:68)

With the shift to the holistic paradigm in government and law we will finally be able to say: "the global brain awakens" (as Peter Russell put it in his 1986 book). A "communicative community resting on reciprocity" represents a level of wholeness fundamentally different from a system of private subjectivities dominating one another and the natural world. We will then be able, as a planetary civilization of dialogue directed toward mutual recognition and understanding, to engage in "conscious evolution" (the title of Barbara Marx Hubbard's 1998 book).

As long as we live under fragmented, disharmonious global institutions, there is little hope for the future. A global brain needs to awaken that will provide a higher level of integration and holism for humanity than has been hitherto known. The awakening understanding underlying the emerging global brain presupposes holism in all its thinking and acting. Under democratic world government, human intelligence will be directed to securing planetary peace and harmony. Under a holistic conception of government and law, which necessarily will be *world* government and *world* law, political, economic, and educational institutions will inevitably give birth to a new civilization.

3.4 The Presuppositional Status of Democratic World Law

LET us bring into focus the fundamental import of the work of the philosophers of law that we have examined in this Chapter. Common to their distinctive visions of the meaning of law is the *presuppositional* status of law as intrinsic to being human. Hence, despite the primarily particularized focus of these thinkers, the implication of their thought is universality. Law is presupposed by the human situation and the ultimate implication of this is democratic world law.

The rationality and sociality of human beings presuppose universal positive law. No complex society of any size beyond small groupings can function without law. Like grammar, and the translatability of all languages into one another, law manifests universal deep structures translatable into one another universally: the law in any human culture or language is recognizable and translatable by those outside that culture. Universal positive law is an *a priori* structure for human life, presupposed by human reason. This insight remains fundamental to the holism of our humanity.

The social-contract theorists of law and government from the 18th century Enlightenment (Thomas Hobbes, John Locke, Jean-Jacques Rousseau, and Immanuel Kant) all recognized the absolutely primary role of law and the governmental framework that makes positive law possible. However, theoretically Hobbes and Locke argued that law and government were created on utilitarian grounds: for Hobbes the positive law was needed to replace the "war of all against all" and for Locke positive law was needed to overcome the chaos of unreliable and subjective interpretations of the natural moral law made by people in the state of nature.

Such utilitarian interpretations of the law have it backwards—for the deep, universal characteristics of positive law cannot be derived from pragmatic, localized, or particularized justifications. For Rousseau and Kant, on the other hand, the positive law arises precisely from our universal humanity informed *a priori* by human reason and sociality. The law therefore is universal and prior to all particular cultures, nations, or social-systems. For Rousseau, the universal law, equivalent to the general will, derives from man's affirmation of himself as a universal, moral being prior to his unique, subjective particularities and differences. For Kant, the social contract (of positive law under a universal, "republican" constitution) is an absolute moral imperative deriving from man's rational nature and therefore an *a priori* requirement for all human societies, apart from any utilitarian or pragmatic considerations.

Some writers identify our planetary governmental situation under the descriptive phrase: "Hobbes' paradox." For Hobbes, we end "the war of all against all" by entering into a social contract in which enforceable positive law keeps the peace and allows for civilized living. But this social contract as Hobbes conceived it was and is confined to particular sovereign nation-states and therefore gives rise to the same condition of war that the implementation of enforceable law was intended to prevent: the state of war now exists among the multiplicity of sovereign nation-states.

To escape the condition of war requires the advent of the universal rule of law. All the social contract theorists are agreed on this. However, you cannot establish the universal rule of law by reinforcing the particularistic and subjective characteristics of the very entities whose warring existence needs to be overcome. Rousseau and Kant understood this—only by drawing on what is truly reasonable and universal can we really actualize the rule of law in human affairs. By trying to make the development of world law contingent on the voluntary agreements or treaties of sovereign nation-states, we are reinforcing the very resistance to law that needs to be overcome. We are exacerbating, not removing, Hobbes' paradox.

The paradigm-shift effected by the 20th century sciences, across the board, was a shift from the early-modern mechanism, atomism, and determinism to *holism*: 20th century science discovered that the universe and everything in it is characterized by a holism in which everything is internally related to everything else and there are no autonomous, independent atoms at the basis of any cosmic, social or natural structures. The cosmos is an integrated whole of unity-in-diversity, the planetary biosphere is likewise an ecological whole, and human beings are universally the same: our unique individuality and diverse cultures are inconceivable apart from our human rational, moral, and social universality.

The system of sovereign nation-states (usually dated from the Peace of Westphalia in 1648) derives from the early-modern assumptions about the atomism and mechanism of nature and society. These are false premises and the idea of a world divided into some 193 national sovereignties is based on these false premises. The truth of this is seen in the on-going destructive presence of Hobbes' paradox: there is war, environmental destruction, and social chaos everywhere on Earth. The United Nations is based on this outdated premise of "the sovereign integrity of its member states." The UN Charter must be replaced with a constitution based on correct presuppositions.

If we want to overcome the chaos of warring nations and planetary environmental and social chaos, our best option is to begin operating from the *a priori* status of universal law that is intrinsic to the human condition itself, not by reinforcing those incorrect premises behind the nation-state system as if they were the source of legitimate positive law and must be drawn upon to make universal law a reality. You cannot draw upon the false atomism that *prevents* universal law from becoming a reality by relying on those same illegitimate atoms as the basis for your endeavor. Yet people everywhere are still attempting to do this, for example, in the development of the International Criminal Court (ICC) or the newly emerging Court for Human Rights, people are relying on the "Assembly of States Parties" to legitimate these developments. But from incommensurable fragments you cannot generate holism. That is why the ascent to universal human and planetary law requires the paradigm-shift, made by all the 20th century sciences, from atomism to holism, in this case, the prior recognition and/or ratification of the *Earth Constitution*.

To actualize the universal *a priori* rule of law implicit in human sociality, rationality, and morality, we must *begin* with these presuppositions. You cannot succeed by presupposing precisely what *prevents* universal law from actualizing itself, namely, sovereign nation-states. That is why the *Constitution for the Federation of Earth* must be the presupposition of our endeavors to create a world court system and initiate the rule of universal positive law for humanity. By presupposing the holism and universality of law in all our endeavors (symbolized and concretized by the *Earth Constitution*), we bring our concrete, particular activities in the current state of fragmentation into actuality under premises that both give them legitimacy and progressively legitimize in the eyes of humanity the dimensions of universal positive law that constitutes our final goal.

To constitute a bench of the World Supreme Court in Costa Rica to try public cases such as the Ecuador-Chevron case (to actualize this particular element of emerging world law—to draw an example from work currently going on) will only prove really fruitful in the long run only if that particular court is framed within the foundational premises of universal positive world law, and not if one attempts to justify that court as a treaty among sovereign nation-states. We must begin with the correct presuppositions that are confirmed by the holistic revolution at the heart of all the 20th century sciences. We must begin by assuming what is presupposed in human rationality and sociality from the very inception. Appropriate assumptions will lead to the actualization of truly humane systems of world peace, sustainability, and justice. Inappropriate assumptions will continue to exacerbate the atomism and anarchy of the current world disorder.

The *Constitution for the Federation of Earth* is indeed a particular document that draws on these holistic universal premises concerning the framework of positive world law presupposed by human reason and sociality. As a particular document, there obviously could be other constitutions that embody these same universal presuppositions. However, in the face of our current planetary crises, potentially lethal and endangering the immediate future of the human project itself, we very much need to *concretize* the fundamental presuppositions of the universal rule of positive law in a way (both symbolic and specific) that serves as a visible and credible framework for our specific activities, such as the actualization of benches for a World Court system.

That is why we must begin, for example, to frame all the world courts as benches of the World Supreme Court as defined by the *Earth Constitution.* If we begin thinking of the ICJ as the bench for disputes between nations, the ICC as the bench for criminal cases, the courts of human rights as benches of the World Court Bench for Human Rights, and the bench being developed in Costa Rica as the World Court Bench for Public Cases, then the movement for universal positive law will be so much more powerfully enhanced because it is premised on appropriate assumptions. If we cater to the outdated paradigm presupposed by the very existence of a multiplicity of sovereign nation-states, we will be dragging down our endeavor, and our good-intentions are liable to lead to continuing chaos and disaster.

The *Constitution for the Federation of Earth* does not need to be ratified by the people of Earth prior to our using it as a concrete symbol for the appropriate universal presuppositions. It is these presuppositions (an aspect of the holism that embraces us) that influence our thinking and our actions. By assuming the *Constitution* as a model and embodiment of rationally grounded universal presuppositions, we are transforming human false assumptions into ways of thinking and acting evermore congruent with the correct assumption that universal democratic positive law is implicit in the human condition from the very beginning. With the very future of the human project at stake, the kind of assumptions we make become absolute vital to the possibility of realizing a truly humane and transformed future characterized by peace, sustainability, and justice. Framing the *Earth Constitution* in this presuppositional role, is basic to the very possibility of our being successful. Holism must be the first principle in all our endeavors to achieve peace, justice, or sustainability on Earth.

Chapter 4

From Disorder, No Order Can Emerge

When you see something clearly as being true—and clarity is always true—there is no other action but the action of clarity. . . . Look, nationality is poison: it has bred, and will continue to breed, wars and hatred. . . . What am I to do? I myself will not touch it. In myself I have wiped out nationality completely.

We live in great disorder; the society in which we live is utter disorder, with social injustice, racial differences, economic, nationalistic divisions. . . . Order is virtue and this order can only come about when we understand what is disorder. Through the negation of what is disorder, order comes into being. In denying the disorder of society there is order, because society encourages acquisitiveness, competition, envy, strife, brutality, violence. Look at the armies, the navies—that is disorder!

—Jiddu Krishnamurti

THESE statements by one of the world's great spiritual teachers also apply at the level of human political affairs and their genesis in a mistaken paradigm. If you see disorder in the world, and you see that it derives from false premises, you cannot reform that disorder. You must simply negate it, put it away. One cannot

131

create a civilized and humane social order from false premises, which imply disorder. The false premises of the present world logically imply disorder and empirically result in the massive planetary disorder that we see all around us.

Planetary political affairs must begin with true premises, which imply order. By "political affairs," I mean the principles by which we govern ourselves and organize our social, economic and civilizational relationships. The principles of political life are the first principles from which all order and civilized human relationships derive. Order derives from true premises. The true premises that have emerged from the 20th century revolutions in the sciences and the humanities involve holism. The principles of order (of social, economic, and political life) derive from holism.

The fragmentation that we inherit from the early-modern paradigm is a foundational or presuppositional fragmentation. Its basic premises assume that the world is fragmented. Such foundational disorder cannot be reformed because to evolve disorder toward the order of holism would mean giving up the premises themselves. Holism must take its place as the basic premise. Fragmentation must simply be negated so that a *founded* global society, premised on the holism of our human condition, can take its place. What is required is a global social contract.

One looks at a practice or institution and recognizes its disorder, discord, disgrace, even absurdity. On a personal note, I did that as a young collage age person in the US confronted with the horror of the Vietnam War and the military draft. I did this not from any philosophical or moral sophistication but simply from a gut feeling, a deep, intuitive recognition not only that this war was wrong, disgraceful, and absurd, but that all war was wrong, disgraceful, and absurd. I had not been taught this by my church, by my family, nor by my culture. But I simply saw that this practice is something ruinous not only for my life but for humankind as well. My gut reaction led me to negate war, to put it aside, to declare that I would never participate in this disgraceful human behavior.

We need to do this for all human practices and institutions that are disgraceful and absurd. We need to let the holistic heart of our emerging humanity (characterized by reason, intuition, and love) break into our distorted surface awareness that is conditioned by perverted institutions and held in place by routine, habit, social conditioning, powerful class interests, and fear. We need to put away war, the fragmented absurdity of militarized sovereign nation-states, the institutionalized greed and exploitation of global capitalism, and the vicious attacking of any and all persons labeled as "terrorists," and put on the cloak of peace and harmony that is emerging at the heart of our humanity.

Our immediate intuition described above by Krishnamurti, which can see the disorder and violence of life immediately and put it aside, is supplemented by our human rationality that can critically evaluate circumstances as to whether they promote the ideal of coherence, wholeness, harmony, and integration of unity and complexity. For these features are the very criterion of rationality and the presuppositions of its critical analytic and synthetic capacities. (I will be discussing "reason" in more detail in this chapter and again in Chapter Nine.) And for Krishnamurti, the dropping of the culture encapsulated ego of fear, envy, pettiness, hate, and violence frees us to see clearly the absurdity of the civilizational forms derived from this petty egoism.

I can also remember clearly the feelings and thoughts I had as a young child when it began to dawn on me that humankind could wipe itself out with nuclear weapons, that my family, my school, my city, my country—everything—could be wiped out in a few minutes of war. It took some time for this enormity to sink in. It was so monumentally absurd, so beyond comprehension, so seemingly insane that I could not come to terms with it. Yet this is what people called "reality." I understood in an inchoate way as a young child the terrible violations of all sanity, rationality, and human decency that were built into what many people just seemed to accept as "normal." I thought at the time that there was something wrong with me for having these feelings. It was only much later that I began to discover the psychologists and thinkers who understood this "normal" that surrounded me as deeply pathological.

A child may see immediately that the emperor has no clothes, but every mature, rational, clearly thinking person should also recognize these *a priori* presuppositions of human rationality and decency in one form or another and, by extension, the social principles of order that I will describe in this chapter. These principles can, however, be expressed, enumerated, and characterized in different ways. Here, I will discuss them as five most basic principles for human civilizational and political affairs, presupposed by our common humanity itself. They are (1) universality, (2) unity-in-diversity, (3) individual flourishing, (4) reason and love, and (5) a community of dialogue directed toward mutual understanding.

Before we enter upon our discussion of these principles of order, I want to say that we should not assume that the solution to our problems will be easy or without sacrifice. We long for a world community based on universal recognition of human dignity and the other self-evident principles that we will be examining. But our agony and our motivation must include our grief at the immense suffering of people worldwide: their immense suffering in wars and wanton violence; their immense suffering in cruel systems of economic exploitation and dehumanization; their immense suffering due to many forms of social, political, economic, or sadistic humiliation. We must think, write, and act out of our unspeakable grief at the holocausts going on everywhere on our precious planet. There are no easy answers. There is no magic formula for a world founded and sustained on human dignity. But, surely, with struggle, solidarity, clarity, and sacrifice, we can turn this mess around.

4.1   World Disorder and the Universality of Law

IN Chapter Three, we looked at several prominent philosophers of law with regard to the relation between ethics and law. In this chapter, I would like to review their thought from a slightly different angle, since they have also articulated something of what I mean by a world order based on human dignity in their analyses of the fundamental nature of law and lawmaking. The first thinker that I want to mention is Lon Fuller in his 1969 book *The Morality of Law*. We have seen that Fuller distinguishes the "morality of duty" from the "morality of aspiration." He says that the lawmakers cannot require the morality of aspiration from a population because this pursues human excellence beyond what is required for social harmony and good order, and this morality of aspiration separates into a great diversity of personal aspirations that cannot be generalized through consistent laws.

The morality of duty, however, links with the most fundamental requirements of social harmony, a harmony based on the reciprocity of contracts, kept promises, and exchange of goods and services. Here is the proper sphere of enforceable law and the sphere of sanctions and punishments, whereas the morality of aspiration is the proper sphere of rewards and honors. The notion of reciprocity, he says, is "implicit in the very notion of duty" (1969: 21). Hence, there is a sphere or dimension of morality, fundamental to all law, which establishes the social harmony that is essential for the morality of aspiration to operate successfully at all. That is the proper sphere of law enforceable by sanctions over individual persons.

Philosopher of law David Luban quotes Fuller as asserting that the function of the lawgiver is to "reduce the relations of men to a reasoned harmony" (2007: 103). Without law based on the morality of duty, therefore, the relations of men will be based on violence or chaos. Enforceable law introduces morality into human relationships, aimed at establishing a "reasoned harmony." In addition, law-makers themselves are under the obligations to make excellent law, laws that serve this "reasoned harmony." They are, therefore, under the morality of duty to make excellent laws as those in authority entrusted to govern others. As Luban puts this, "the rule of law establishes a moral relationship between those who govern and those whom they govern" (ibid. 99).

The obverse of Fuller's "morality of law" is a condition when there are no laws or no effectively functioning laws. The implication is that human beings are left in chaos or fundamental disharmony. The implication, as Immanuel Kant (1957) put it, is that they relate to one another merely with "senseless freedom," in "savage and barbaric" ways, not with the "rational freedom" of a reasoned harmony that is embodied in "republican" forms of government. These forms not only establish order but make possible life-opportunities to fulfill the morality of aspiration.

The second philosopher of law I wish to cite as a framework for this chapter is Ronald Dworkin in his 1977 book, *Taking Rights Seriously*. Dworkin argues that behind all legitimate law there are moral principles embedded in the very "logic of the law." There are principles such as fairness, equality, and due process that function behind the actual positive laws and judicial decisions on the books that every lawmaker and judge worthy of the name attempts to honestly consult. Embedded in the "logic of the law," therefore, are universal principles of order and harmony.

The Constitution of the United States, for example, presupposes human dignity and assumes "moral rights which individuals possess against the majority," as well as against the state (1977: 33). "The logic of the text demands" that lawmakers and judges face the "moral issues" embodied in the text (ibid. 136). Hence, part of the purpose of enforceable law is to protect human dignity by protecting individual rights against the majority and the state. Human rights are not some abstract ideal residing inside people in some ghostly manner, Dworkin states, but are embodied in the very nature of legitimate law and judicial decision-making.

If human rights, which Dworkin calls "trumps," arise from the internal logic of democratically legislated enforceable law itself, and if moral principles like equality, fairness, and due process similarly form the "interpretative principles" in the background of law, then what of situations when there is no law—like the condition that obtains between sovereign nation-states that, by definition, recognize no enforceable law above themselves? For nation-states, so-called international laws are mere treaties entered into by each signatory state to voluntarily agree to abide by certain (largely unenforceable) rules. Failure to abide by these rules does not, in the nature of the case, result in sanctions against individuals, because it is a representative of the nation as a kind of fictitious entity, as a quasi-legal territorially bound collective personality, that signs the voluntary agreement. Unlike the rules of contract within genuine legal systems, the violator of the contract does not face lawsuit, arrest, sanctions, or jail-time.

The regime of presupposed rights and implicit moral principles that Dworkin associates with genuine law and reasoned human order does not exist between nations. The system of so-called sovereign nations (interfaced with their multinational corporations) is really a fragmented system of disorder. Moral relations among nations or among individuals at the international level do not arise from any legal system in which they function as presuppositions or implicit principles. Rather the relation is largely ungoverned; it is a relationship of power in which multinational corporations, along with imperial nations, and transnational banking cartels make the rules for the entire world. Under these so-called "rules" the powerful can exploit the poor in dehumanized conditions or nations can send assassination teams to kill suspected enemies without due process of law.

The third philosopher of law I wish to cite as a framework for this chapter is John Finnis in his 1980 book, *Natural Law and Natural Rights*. Finnis begins the book by identifying the seven objectively real goods of human life that are self-evident to practical reason that we have already previewed: life, knowledge, friendship (sociality), aesthetic experience, play, practical reason itself, and religion. These are the primary goods of human moral life for every individual, and his book makes a powerful argument for this conclusion. The purpose of the law, he says, depends on its ability to secure justice (1980: 260), and justice means social arrangements based on the common good: laws that maximize the ability of individual citizens to successfully pursue any or all of these self-evident goods for their own lives.

There appear to be obvious similarities here between the thought of Fuller, Luban, Dworkin, and Finnis. The morality of duty involves the creation of laws that foster the common good of the society. This dimension of law creates a reasoned harmony making possible the pursuit of life, knowledge, friendship, etc., goods that may well be governed by the morality of aspiration. In the language of Dworkin, implicit in law and lawmaking are background moral principles that constitute justice in a legal system, a justice that makes possible the human flourishing that pursues the goods discerned by practical reason as identified by Finnis. Because there is no democratically legislated enforceable law for our planet itself (divided as it is into some 193 sovereign entities recognizing no effective law above themselves and with little individual accountability for agreements and treaties) there is also no moral dimension of reasoned order that obtains at the global level, only chaos, fragmentation, and naked power relationships.

There is, therefore, a broad sphere of overlap among these four philosophers of law. First, law includes the morality of duty which creates a reasoned harmony among human beings through establishing enforceable rules and their sanctions. Second, the logic of law presupposes fundamental moral principles, human rights, and human dignity that are not there in some ethereal "ghostly" way prior to the law itself. Third, law protects the common good (or the justice of equality) in order for people to be able to actualize real and concrete goods that apply to every human life and within every culture on our planet.

Finally, law cannot be merely localized in communities around the world, for law is inherent in human civilization and requires universal recognition of our common humanity and common human dignity that transcend all territorial divisions and national boundaries. We have seen above that serious thinkers have commonly recognized that 1945 was the "beginning of the end-time for human beings," as Moltmann puts it, or, as Hannah Arendt observes:

> For the truth of the matter was that by the end of the Second World War everybody knew that technical developments in the instruments of violence had made the adoption of "criminal" warfare inevitable. It was precisely the distinction between soldier and civilian, between army and home population, between military targets and open cities, upon which the Hague Convention's definition of war crimes rested, that had become obsolete. (1963: 256)

Warfare itself becomes a criminal enterprise at least in part because it can no longer distinguish clearly between innocents and combatants, between civilians and warriors. Traditional justifications were always weak and to be repudiated by those of maturity, conscience, and clear sense. However, today, warfare constitutes an immoral disorder of an immense magnitude that must be decisively repudiated. We have seen that the second half of the 20th century also signaled the recognition of multiple global problems beyond the scope of any territorial nation state to address, problems that absolutely require redress through the rule of law, yet without any transnational mechanisms for establishing enforceable laws to deal with these global problems.

Lacking such mechanisms warfare becomes inevitable. However, Arendt points out that what emerged from the Nazi phenomenon was not simply the realization that technical developments have made war obsolete, but that all so-called "international law" is also obsolete because it addressed only relations between nations, making them responsible for their own internal affairs, and attempted to govern international relations by formulating rules of warfare in the Hague and Geneva Conventions. International law never addressed *our common transnational humanity* that supersedes all national boundaries and makes us one human community.

International laws already covered the crime of aggression and war-crimes, Arendt points out, but the judges at Nuremberg were very uncomfortable about a new category of crime that had no precedent in prior national or international laws: crimes against humanity. Punishment of crimes, she observes, is not done simply as reparation for the victim of crimes, but because the criminal has violated the good order of the community itself. But "crimes against humanity" do not violate the good order of any territorial community but rather attack "the human status" itself. They violate our planetary human community that is premised on our common, universal humanity. The immense, horrific disorder of Nazi crimes against humanity call us to move to a higher level, beyond the international laws of territorial nation-states. She recommends the development of "international penal law," applying to all humanity beyond the boundaries of national states, to deal with this new level of law (1963: 273).

We have seen, however, that law cannot be law unless it is an integral part of all the institutional aspects that make law a genuine representative of the community: a constitution, a legislature, a court system, civilian police, administrative structures, recognition of human individual and social rights, etc. The great realization that came out of the 20th century (beginning with the world federalism of the Women's International League for Peace and Freedom that emerged during the First World War (Martin, 2010b: 8-14)) is that law, like justice, human rights, and human dignity, is *inherently universal* and all local territorial laws must be derived from the concept of world law: laws that derive from, and protect, "the human status" everywhere on Earth. Law derives from the primal relation of individuals and communities that characterizes our human situation. Local laws always imply this inherent universality. Human rationality itself, as I argued in section 3.4, which is always inherently social and implies the whole of civilization, thereby also presupposes universal, democratically legislated laws.

I contend that the five fundamental principles of legitimate law and order identified here can be taken from the broad vision about the meaning and purpose of law that I have derived from these prominent philosophers of law and from the understanding of our universal humanity that became explicit throughout the 20th century. All five of these principles, fundamental to human civilization and the rule of law, are lacking at the planetary level. They cannot be established at that level without negating the very disorder that blocks their actualization, and founding, in its place, a global social contract.

4.2   Five Fundamental Principles of Order: Universality, Unity-in-Diversity, Human Flourishing, Reason and Love, Dialogue

THE *first of these principles is universality.* Human dignity, rights, and responsibilities belong to all human beings without exception. Such universality has never been realized in human affairs even though it has been recognized by the most ancient texts and philosophical schools such as the Stoics of ancient Greece and Rome. It is a principle that became central to 20th century thought as expressed, for example, in the UN Universal Declaration of Human Rights and in Articles 12 and 13 of the *Constitution for the Federation of Earth.* In the early 21st century, we are long past the time when this universality has become an absolute necessity for the survival of humanity.

Human dignity, rights, and responsibilities must become foundational in human affairs. Yet without universally enforceable world law these rights remain abstract and disembodied. It is the rule of enforceable law that makes rights and dignity actual, since rights and dignity are implicit in the very nature of law.

Abstract ideals, like those embodied in the UN Universal Declaration of Human Rights, cannot create a decent world order. These moral principles must be embodied concretely within enforceable world law.

Our primary planetary institutions operate in direct violation of these principles. Both the global economic system and the system of sovereign nation-states violate the universality of human rights and dignity. The economic system operates as if economics were a set of inviolable quasi-scientific laws (supply and demand, free market, etc.), with the result that some two billion of the Earth's population live on less than two US dollars per day. Their human rights and dignity are violated by this system of division and fragmentation that ignores their humanity by making possible economic theft, systemic exploitation, commodification (turning human beings into market commodities), and consequent dehumanization.

Similarly, the system of sovereign nation-states divides the planet into approximately 193 independent territories recognizing no constitution and no enforceable laws above themselves. All so-called "international laws" are merely voluntary treaties on the part of these sovereign nations. Since they are voluntary, nations can withdraw, ignore, or withhold assent to any particular international agreement. In practice, under such a system the stronger dominate and exploit the weaker. Smaller or weaker nations are coerced into accepting so-called laws, including trade and monetary rules, imposed by the powerful nations and their financial institutions. Universality, the principle that human rights and dignity be applied systematically throughout civilization, is institutionally violated by this system of fragmentation.

There are many books on human rights (such as Jack Donnelly's 2003 book *Universal Human Rights in Theory and Practice*) that describe the tremendous growth of human rights recognition among all the nations of the world. But these books cannot account for why, in the face of this worldwide recognition, human rights are still so widely ignored and abused (cf. Posner, 2014).

Why does the emperor have no clothes? The answer is quite obvious to those who are no longer mesmerized by the pervasive nationalist mantra and unspoken assumption that this is the only possible way of organizing the world. We are historical and evolutionary creatures. The absurd system of sovereign nations, developed historically since the 17th century and based on false atomistic premises, is not an eternal verity. It is contingent and has profound negative consequences everywhere on Earth. Human rights can only be protected by the genuine rule of law, and genuine recognition of a single body and listing of these rights (not a plurality of contradictory treaties). As Donnelly's book points out repeatedly, the perceived self-interest of nation-states trumps their concern for human rights nearly every time.

These truths have been emphasized ever since Immanuel Kant's 1795 essay on "Perpetual Peace," yet little has changed in this system of world disorder since that time. National sovereignty contradicts the moral and legal *universality* of human dignity and human rights. We have noted that scholars commonly identify the Peace of Westphalia of 1648 as first recognizing this concept of national sovereignty. Under this historically constructed ideology (which is neither natural nor moral) each state is autonomous over its internal affairs and independent in its foreign relationships. The moral and legal universality of human dignity and human rights is systematically and institutionally ignored. As G.W.F. Hegel put it, "Each state is consequently a sovereign and independent entity in relation to others. There is no Praetor to adjudicate between States. . . .. Consequently, if no agreement can be reached between the particular wills, conflicts between states can only be settled by *war*" (1991, sections 331, 333-34).

There can be no true civilizational universality to human rights and dignity without a *Constitution for the Federation of Earth* that embodies this universality and translates it into enforceable world law. And we have seen that such universality is implicit in the "logic of law" itself. If there ever is to be a "reasoned harmony" in human affairs, it can only come through the rule of enforceable law, universal over all people. The principle of national sovereignty fragments the world into incommensurable territorial units, most of them militarized, in response to this condition of a lawless international world disorder.

Human beings can never become a planetary *community* as long as humanity is divided into "sovereign" states, for the principle of sovereignty gives states "rights" to act autonomously, that is, to recognize no binding legislative, executive, or judicial authority over themselves. An essential component of being a complete human community is becoming a *political community under a global social contract.* Only when humanity is bound together under the sovereignty of the people of Earth can human beings begin to act from, and protect, their *universal interests and a genuine common good.* To see the absurdity of this fragmentation that destroys our ability to form a human community is to see immediately that human relationships must be founded on universality.

From the principle that nations recognize no law above themselves, which is also the principle of war (disorder), you cannot derive the recognition of human rights and dignity through the universal rule of law (order). You can only derive more disorder. But seeing the horror and destructive nature of disorder (perpetual wars, destruction, dehumanization, deception, domination, and exploitation), one can simply negate that disorder, put it aside. No "evolution" of the present system is going to change false premises into true premises. We can continue to pretend that the emperor is wearing clothes, but a little child, who has not yet been mesmerized, can see through this nearly universal illusion. Our obligation is to *found* planetary systems of universal validity, for example, by recognizing the authority of a universal constitution from which civilization can derive all valid laws protecting the rights and dignity of every person on Earth.

The second principle of order is the principle of unity-in-diversity. For all phenomena within the universe, science has shown that the diverse parts cohere with one another within systems that unite them into unities. There are no autonomous parts not constituted by the wholes that embrace them and there are no wholes without parts. Unity-in-diversity constitutes the structure of the universe and operates on a multiplicity of levels composed of parts within wholes that are in turn parts within ever-greater wholes. Human beings form one or more levels of unity-in-diversity within this vast scheme. On the most basic level, our unity is that we are all human. Our diversity is that each person is a unique individual with a unique culture and historical background. Our humanity and individuality form an inseparable whole. In his book, *The Tao of Physics* (1975), physicist Fritjof Capra summarizes the insight of 20th century science in the following way:

> Thus modern physics shows us once again – and this time at the macroscopic level – that material objects are not distinct entities, but are inseparably linked to their environment; that their properties can only be understood in terms of their interaction with the rest of the world. According to Mach's principle, this interaction reaches out to the universe at large, to the distant stars and galaxies. The basic unity of the cosmos manifests itself, therefore, not only in the world of the very small but also in the world of the very large; a fact which is increasingly acknowledged in modern astrophysics and cosmology. In the words of the astronomer Fred Hoyle:
>
> "Present-day developments in cosmology are coming to suggest rather insistently that everyday conditions could not persist but for the distant parts of the Universe, that all our ideas of space and geometry would become entirely invalid if the distant parts of the Universe were taken away. Our everyday experience even down to the smallest details seems to be so closely integrated to the grand-scale features of the Universe that it is well-nigh impossible to contemplate the two being separated." (209-210)

At the cosmic level, and every subsidiary level throughout the universe, the diverse parts cannot be separated from the whole. This is exactly parallel to the human situation: parts and whole intrinsically belong together. As I argued in my book *Triumph of Civilization: Democracy, Nonviolence, and the Piloting of Spaceship Earth* (2010a), sound political principles are founded on unity-in-diversity. These principles must be universal to all human beings since the unity that unites us is precisely our common humanity, inseparable from the vast diversity of individuals, cultures, and specific differences.

Under global capitalism this unity is broken due to vast mechanisms of exploitation where people are dehumanized and alienated from their common humanity. The profits for a few are extracted from the cheap and dehumanized labor of the many who are being used as tools for production or services for the few. The present world provides no universal order of law that can regulate the effects of capitalism. Entire nations that are poor have little choice but to be victimized by a system that does not generate universal human rights to be respected by enforceable laws requiring companies to treat employees, subsidiaries, and outsourced contractual workers humanly.

As many thinkers today have pointed out, implicit in language and our human situation is the recognition of unity-in-diversity. As we cognitively and ethically mature, we become more and more aware of this. Swidler and Mojzes assert that:

> The very fact that we can differ is built on a fundamental commonality, a unity, within which context we can perceive differences, particularities. To be fully human, then, it is vital that we be aware of both the limited, particular, character of all statements, *and* at the same time the underlying unity within which differences can even appear. (2000: 154)

The unity of our common humanity (within which all languages, for example, are translatable into one another), forms the context within which we are able to dialogue with one another, to identify both similarities and differences, and to move toward mutual understanding. But global historically constructed institutions block and distort our ability to move toward universality of

consciousness through dialogue directed toward mutual understanding. They create institutional blockages to the actualization
of the unity-in-diversity of our human condition.

Under the disorder of sovereign nation-states, the world is
fragmented into competing territories violating the fundamental
principle of political order that all be united by a common constitution that recognizes and protects the great diversity of persons and groups. Persons outside of each nation have no rights or
freedoms according to the laws of the nation, for laws only apply
internally. The principle that some nations have in their constitutions that international treaties are part of the law of the land
does not mitigate this point. For conformity to international law
remains voluntary on the part of the government of each nation.
From the intertwined disorder of capitalism with that of sovereign
nations, order can never follow. Only by ratification of the *Earth
Constitution* can we negate the disorder and affirm the orderly
starting point of universal unity-in-diversity.

Recognition of the diversity of people is implicit within the
"logic" of genuine enforceable law. The logic of law generates
common duties for everyone, enforceable through sanctions, and
hence social harmony, but it also generates human rights as rights
against the majority, the state, and, we now see, the global economic system. Human rights apply to each individual person.
They represent the principle of diversity that allows each person
to pursue some or all of the objective goods identified by John
Finnis, or to pursue the morality of aspiration identified by Lon
Fuller. The *Earth Constitution,* in its Preamble, explicitly asserts the
principle of unity-in-diversity. This common universal law and
common constitution constitutes the unity, actualized through the
global social contract, for all peoples. Both the explicit and implicit logic of the *Earth Constitution* (universal, democratically legislated enforceable laws) generates the idea of human rights protecting each person's uniqueness and unique lifelong pursuit of
objectively identifiable goods.

The third fundamental principle of human and civilizational affairs is the principle of individual human flourishing. We have seen in several ways that the purpose of law and the function of legitimate constitutional government is to promote individual human flourishing. The right to the conditions that make flourishing possible belongs to each human being, as philosopher Alan Gewirth, for example, has underlined in his book, *Human Rights: Justifications and Applications* (1982). For Gewirth, human rights are the *logical presuppositions* of the free pursuit of humanly recognizable goods by each human being. Since each human being (qua human) pursues what he or she conceives of as good, human rights protecting both freedom and well-being form the logically required and morally grounded conditions for human life to exist at all.

Flourishing means that I have readily available opportunities for satisfying my physical needs for nourishing food, fresh water, sanitary conditions, shelter, clothing, social security in case of illness or old age, and other vital necessities. It means that I have easily available possibilities for education, for decent employment, for availing myself of the fruits of human knowledge and culture, and for political participation. It also means that my flourishing in these respects takes place within a framework of peace, social justice, and a decent, healthy planetary environment. The UN Universal Declaration of Human Rights identifies all of these except protection of the environment that is at the very heart of the *Earth Constitution*. Human rights protecting my freedom and well-being are the necessary conditions for human flourishing.

Some scholars have identified an evolution in philosophical thinking about human rights through three generations: first-generation political rights (free speech, association, due process of law, etc.), second-generation economic and social rights (education, health-care, social security, etc.), and third-generation rights to planetary peace and a protected environment (Wacks, 2008: 149-50). All three generations of rights are necessary features within a world that can protect individual human flourishing. Only the *Earth Constitution* is built on protection of all three generations of human rights as a whole. No constitution of any sovereign nation-state can give citizens guarantees of planetary peace and a protected, life-friendly planetary ecology. From the disorder of sovereign nations (no matter how enlightened their constitutions), these three fundamental categories of human flourishing cannot emerge.

Neither can the famous formula of utility give us the principle of individual human flourishing for the citizens of our planet. The idea of promoting the greatest happiness (or greatest good) of the greatest number of people fails in a number of ways, including regarding the well-known issue of means and ends. The idea of utility does not give us universality. With respect to human flourishing and human rights, we are not speaking of the greatest happiness of the greatest number but of the right of each person to live within conditions that promote his or her flourishing. These rights are implicit in the idea of legitimate law itself. But the world has no common legitimate law. Even most international laws apply only to nations (as subjects of the law) and not to individual persons, and, notoriously, none of these so-called laws are enforceable: and certainly not by and over individuals.

Individual human flourishing needs to be the principle of both means and ends, for it is the individual human being alone that has dignity and universal rights, both as an individual and as a member of the species. No human (as an end in himself or herself) may be used as a means for the happiness of others (to the extent of violating their dignity), whether this be workers exploited for the happiness of capitalists or presently living persons sacrificed for a greater happiness of future generations (or, indeed, the happiness of future generations sacrificed to our unsustainable desire for comfort and pleasure in the present). As stated above, this does not mean that the path to the future will be easy given the horrors of our present world disorder. But that path must be premised on the truth of human dignity, and rationally correct principles of order (holism), not on false principles of utility, "proportionalism," nationalism, private profit at the expense of others, or other forms of fragmentation.

Under capitalism individual human flourishing for vast numbers is destroyed by the process of supply and demand treating human beings as commodities to be used in the service of private profit. Under the nation-state system, the individual human flourishing of those outside the territorial boundaries is of little or no concern to national governments. Foreign policies conducted from national self-interest (inevitable within this system of fragmentation) invariably violate individual human flourishing for those outside these boundaries, and (because military expenditures deplete internal resources and destroy democratic openness) for citizens within nations as well. In contrast, Erich Fromm correctly declares that:

> The victory of freedom is possible only if democracy develops into a society in which the individual, his growth and happiness, is the aim and purpose of culture, in which life does not need any justification in success or anything else, and in which the individual is not subordinated to or manipulated by any power outside of himself, be it the State or the economic machine. ... The problem that we are confronted with today is that of the organization of social and economic forces, so that man—as a member of organized society—may become the master of these forces and cease to be their slave" (1958: 270-71).

Hans Jonas writes about the economic and political means by which we supply the necessities for human life: "the 'How,' which obligates humanity to a certain *quality* of life—i.e., which fills out the purely 'That' with a 'What'—forbids us to make out of this existence a wasteland for the soul" (1996: 105). Capitalism and the system of warring nation-states have done just this: made out of this existence "a wasteland for the soul." The only way to establish legitimate government directed toward providing the framework for true human flourishing is to establish a world constitution that supersedes the global institutions (including the UN system) that now impede universal individual flourishing for all persons on Earth.

The fourth principle of order in human civilization includes the right and duty to develop our reason and our love. This is related to the above three principles and is an extension of them. Perhaps the very core of individual human flourishing involves the development of our reason and our love. As Fromm has argued in *Beyond the Chains of Illusion: My Encounters with Marx and Freud,* and in other writings, reason and love, our two highest human qualities, should be holistically integrated within every human being.

Each of us needs to recognize ourselves, Fromm writes, "as part of humanity, of living according to a set of values in which the full experience of love, justice, truth, is the dominant goal of life to which everything else is subordinated; it means a constant striving to develop one's powers of love and reason to a point at which a new harmony with the world is attained; it means striving for humility, to see one's identity with all beings, and to give up the illusion of a separate, indestructible ego" (1962: 156).

The different forms of love relate to one another in a holistic way. In his book *The Nature of Love from Plato to Luther,* Irving Singer identifies four concepts of love that intersect in this tradition: *eros* (desire), *nomos* (law and justice), *philia* (friendship) and *agape* (the love of God). The latter, he argues, holistically makes possible all the others: "The concept of *agape*... makes no sense apart from *nomos* and philia, and it serves as a response to the entire attitude of *eros*" (1966: 276-77). *Nomos* is crucial because the law (including the natural moral law and the imperative for justice) asserts that the equality of all implicit in love simultaneously requires the equality of all before the requirements of justice and reason. "The Stoics," he asserts, "managed to throw wide the gate. ... It followed that mankind as a whole was one large fraternity bound by a common rationality, in principle benevolent and disinterested" (1966: 206). Both love and justice, I contend, can and must be promoted by good government.

The *a priori* framework of legally articulated social and economic conditions provided by government at all levels, from local to planetary, must maximize the possibilities for the development of reason and love in the citizens. This principle that the function of good government is to make possible this development of "virtue" (human excellence) in citizens was perhaps first elaborated in western political thought by Aristotle, some 2400 years ago, and is developed by a number of contemporary philosophers of law. For Lon Fuller, for example, good government, based on the morality of duty, *makes it possible* for people to participate in the morality of aspiration. For Alan Gewirth, the function of government is to provide the institutions of "freedom" and material "well-being" that *make possible* people's pursuit of what they take to be good in life (1982: 3).

Aristotle observed that the defining characteristic of the human animal was rationality and that the development of excellence also included informing our emotions and desires with this rational principle. He focused on "friendship" as a highest form of love in human relationships. In this same period, Plato developed the concept that love as *eros* is an inseparable complement to human reason. A human being is a synthesis of these two principles, reason and love. His *Symposium*, we saw above, articulated the role of love as desire in terms of a redirecting and shaping of that desire to become the indispensable ally of reason, ascending the "ladder of love," as he put it, toward true virtue (*arête*).

Four centuries later, Jesus Christ expressed the fundamental role of love (*agape*) in terms of caring for others, compassion, and deep respect for all, even "for the least of these my brethren" (Matt.25:40). In truth, love is properly a synthetic combination of friendship, right desire, affirmation of life, compassion, caring for others, social and political solidarity, respect for human dignity, and concern for justice. Love secures our right relationship to the world, its creatures, and other persons. As Moltmann puts this, "love is the self-communication of the good" (2012: 122). Love is our solidarity with human beings and all of life. It binds people together in friendships, families, communities, and the human community.

Reason, the complement of love, sees the universality of the human community that love binds together. Reason sees the self-evident truth of the natural-law principles articulated in these chapters and acts to secure these principles in human political, economic, and social affairs. Reason, like its complement, love, is also at the heart of the concept of legitimate law. For the "logic of law" includes principles of justice, fairness, nonviolent human relationships, and universal human dignity, which are also the principles of love. A law for the world would be the very embodiment of reason and love for the world. As Swidler and Mojzes write:

> To the degree that people remain fixed in injustice, whether intentionally or unintentionally, they are not free to trust and care for others. Instead, they turn to other people as if they were objects in the service of righting their own past hurts and disappointments. (2000: 126)

Love insists on justice and fairness for all people. When justice is denied (as it is, by and large, all around the world today), it blocks people's ability to trust and love. Love not only embraces all people without discrimination and therefore is itself a manifestation of unity-in-diversity; love also empowers reason in its task. Without love, reason can become heartless social engineering. Without reason, love can become self-indulgent and ineffective sentimentality. Love supplies energy and reason's universally affirmative character. It lifts reason to its highest potentialities. Like universal law, it embraces all without discrimination.

Reason here is not merely instrumental or technical reason, calculating how to achieve ends that arise from irrational, blind desires. In *Communication and the Evolution of Society*, Jürgen Habermas reconstructs Max Weber's famous study of capitalism in which Weber pessimistically concluded that human beings had little hope in the face of the domination of our highly "rationalized" economic and nation-state institutions. Habermas' critical analysis illuminates larger dimensions of reason (communicative and directed toward mutual understanding) that underline our potential for a higher synthesis of reason and love as articulated by thinkers like Fromm.

Weber largely missed the fundamental role of *communicative reason* that remains inescapable for all language-speaking beings. From Plato to Aquinas and Nicholas of Cusa, practical reason was most often understood as cognitive awareness of the moral dimension and the primary ends of human life, ends that are also comprehended directly by the love that binds us together with the world, other creatures, and the human community. Habermas shows that communicative reason carries forward this aspect of reason in several basic, "post-metaphysical" ways.

Hence, the idea that reason only deals with the means and not the ends of human life is a modern perversion of the tradition of reason in western thought, as John Finnis (1980) so clearly points out. Reason understands the moral dimension and the primary ends of human life, ends that are also comprehended immediately by the love that binds us together with the human community. Reason establishes social harmony through the morality of duty at the heart of genuine enforceable law. It also discerns the ends that appear through the morality of aspiration, ends articulated as self-evident human goods by Finnis and others.

Love is a principle of order just as much as reason, for love is the foundation of the relationships that bind us into families, communities, and the human continuum. Love also binds us to our wonderful planetary home and the ultimate cosmic miracle of the universe within which we live our lives. The conception of blind, heartless economic "laws" promoted by global capitalism is not only untrue, but it is a principle of disorder than cannot be reformed or evolved into an order premised on love, which would mean a world of peace, justice, and human flourishing. This disorder must be negated by our reason and our love, and a global social democracy must be founded and premised on the priority of human dignity and human rights within economic relationships.

The same is true of the system of sovereign nation-states. This "system" is no system, for it constitutes an institutionalized disorder dividing humankind into 193 incommensurate entities without any binding principles of law or justice above themselves. Whatever international rules of "global governance" they have developed to date are profoundly undemocratic and represent the few who dominate in the world, not all of humanity. One cannot evolve this system while retaining the principle of national sovereignty which is the essential component of this disorder. One must negate the disorder and establish an order *founded* on genuine principles, summarized by the five basic concepts articulated in this chapter. Sovereignty must be replaced by a global social contract founded on the human community itself.

Ratification of the *Constitution for the Federation of Earth* would establish universal order, based on reason and love, in human political affairs for the first time in history. All of us are under a moral obligation to develop our reason and our love, but our ability to pursue this marriage of human excellence is inhibited and blocked by both global capitalism and the system of sovereign nation-states. Reason and love, it may well be, cannot be significantly followed (for most people in most circumstances on Earth) or fulfilled apart from a global social contract both based on these principles and making possible their further development. Our capacity to follow the morality of aspiration indicated by the nexus of reason and love is made possible by universal enforceable laws under the *Earth Constitution*.

The final principle in universal human political affairs is a community of dialogue directed toward mutual understanding. Such a community of dialogue is and should be institutionalized within the universal laws under the *Earth Constitution*. The moral imperative for dialogue directed toward mutual understanding (as opposed to strategic or manipulative uses of speech) has been shown by Habermas (1998) and others as fundamental to language itself and hence to being human. Political life under laws characterized by universality, unity-in-diversity, human flourishing, and reason and love also must be structured to make communicative speech possible. The World Parliament created by the *Earth Constitution* transcends political struggle among self-interested parties by structuring speech to optimize the possibility for dialogue directed toward genuine understanding and communication.

Under the global capitalist system of disorder, speech is pressured to become manipulative speech directed toward maximizing self-interest and success at the expense of others. Under the nation-state system of international disorder, speech is institutionalized to become the speech of deceptive diplomacy, veiled threat, strategic maneuvering, and outright propaganda lies on behalf of perceived national self-interests. The so-called "free press" within the bourgeois democracies mostly serves as a lackey for both these systems of power and fragmentation.

Nowhere is communicative dialogue encouraged because the disorder of these global institutions leads to the disorder of dishonest speech. However, the principle of harmonious reason and order embedded within the very logic of legitimate, enforceable laws gives us, for the first time in history, the possibility of engaging with and between people invested with governmental authority, from all around our planet, in a reasoned dialogue concerning the future of our planet and its citizens and how to create laws that embody the common good, functioning to protect universal human rights and human flourishing.

Communicative dialogue directed toward mutual understanding among equals is a fundamental principle of order interrelated with the other four principles expressed in this chapter. Communicative dialogue invites and assumes universality. It invites and assumes unity and diversity. It invites and assumes human flourishing, reasoning, and love, just as these principles in turn invite and assume communicative dialogue. Our world does not have a viable future under its present fragmented systems of disorder. And one major missing element is that it lacks any mechanisms for an authoritative, meaningful dialogue concerning how to deal with and negotiate our gravely endangered future.

Swidler and Mojzes go so far as to identify the emergence of global dialogue as the fundamental character of the "Second Axial Period" that many thinkers today identify with the global transformation of consciousness presently occurring. They insist that "we must recapture the unity of tribal consciousness by seeing humanity as a single tribe. And we must see this single tribe as organically related to the total cosmos." Human beings are emerging into a holistic cosmic consciousness. But the shift in consciousness centers on the emergence of global dialogue:

> That shift from monologue to dialogue constitutes such a radical reversal in human consciousness, is so utterly new in the history of humankind from the beginning, that it must be designated as literally "revolutionary," that is, it turns everything absolutely around. (2000: 88-89)

For humankind as a whole, there is an absolute imperative that we create institutions that make global dialogue concerning the fate of humanity possible. Only the rule of democratically legislated enforceable law, therefore, can provide the possibility of dealing with our endangered future. The *Earth Constitution* establishes the World Parliament and the many agencies of government, staffed by qualified people from around the world, as institutional arrangements for people to dialogue with one another (both among those in the world government and with the people of Earth) about our endangered human future. If we want to really turn things around, to be really revolutionary, we must create an Earth Federation as the foundation for not only effective global dialogue but also the decision-making authority on behalf of the people of Earth.

The very *logic of law* embodies universal moral duties, one of which is global dialogue. It establishes a justice-oriented order making possible the universal pursuit of the most basic goods of human existence, and it establishes concrete legal principles of human dignity and inviolable human rights, providing both unity and diversity. The present lawless world must be superseded by a non-military, democratically founded, lawful world. We can

only *negate* the present global disorder by *founding* a global order
of peace, justice, and freedom of all human beings. Establishing
mechanisms for authentic global dialogue is the last principle of
order identified in this chapter, but, like the other four principles
with which it is intertwined, it is absolutely fundamental for a
complete concept of global order.

It may appear paradoxical that opening up people to the flux
and uncertainty of dialogue with those of possibly different ideas
and ideals is a fundamental principle of order. But the early-
modern paradigm from which we are now emerging, and the first
Axial Period from which individual consciousness first emerged,
resulted by and large, not in order, but in the disorder of fragmentation: people and nations talking past one another ("monologi-
cally"), often in instrumental forms of speech designed to promote
individual or national self-interests over and against the assumed
conflicting interests of others. Authentic dialogue directed toward
mutual understanding, articulated so eloquently by Habermas,
Swidler, and other contemporary thinkers, generates a human civilizational order, a common understanding and a common good
transcending the chaos of competing individual and national interests.

4.3   Summary and Conclusion

G LOBAL institutional respect for human dignity in a world that
   protects human flourishing cannot evolve or emerge from
disorder while continuing to embrace the false premises of that
disorder. True conclusions cannot derive from false premises.
Monologue and instrumental forms of communication cannot
give us order. The false premises of global capitalism and so-
called sovereign nation-states (both instrumental and monological) cannot provide the basis for an evolution of truth with regard to the human condition or human political and legal affairs. Such one dimensional speech has no ability to deal with
the global problems in the name of a planetary common good be-

cause monologue, in itself, cannot transcend its principle to dialogue without becoming something entirely different.

Dropping disorder, however, does not mean failing to preserve what is valuable about the United Nations or other global institutions that have some features premised on human dignity. For example, the World Health Organization (WHO) and the UN High Commission on Human Rights have important features premised on the promotion of global citizenship and dialogue, as does the UN Educational, Scientific and Cultural Organization (UNESCO). Such institutions must be preserved when the hopelessly inadequate Charter of the UN (premised on sovereign nation-states) is replaced with a genuine *Constitution for the Earth*, premised on the truth of human dignity. In place of the disorder of the current world anti-system, we must make a paradigm-shift to the principles of order and truth. Truth emerges from dialogue, from the common effort and interaction of innumerable truth-seekers, present and past.

Let us review and summarize the insights that have emerged in our discussions this far. The principles of order for human civilization on Earth can be expressed as follows:

1. Human beings as a species form a language-speaking and civilizational whole living on planet Earth (which is itself an ecological whole encompassing many parts or fields that fit within the Earth-system). The presupposition of our human rationality and sociality is democratic world law.

2. Human beings are divided into a multiplicity of subgroups: families, communities, cities, nations, cultures, languages, religions, races, ethnicities, genders, etc., all of which are parts of these larger planetary wholes. This multiplicity is embraced by world civilization, which again implies democratic world law.

3. The subgroupings in any holistic system function individually and together as unique parts of that system, each con-

tributing in various ways to the functioning, maintenance, and development of the whole.

4. Each person is also an individual whole related socially, linguistically, morally, and in many other ways, to the whole human project and to other human beings who are also all parts of the whole.

5. The primary unity (or part) within the whole of humanity is the individual person as bearer of inalienable rights and moral duties in relation to the whole, in relation to the lesser communities within which he or she is embedded, and to all other persons. Law is a fundamental form in which this unity-in-diversity is manifested everywhere on Earth and its inherent universality must be actualized in the form of world law reflecting this holism.

6. Therefore, human beings must govern themselves through a non-military, democratic world-system actualizing and embodying their holism, creatively addressing the challenges of moving into the future within a dynamic peace, freedom, justice, and sustainability world-system.

7. Each subgrouping and each person derives from this holism and, once established, all groups will find their proper places as unique, harmonious elements within the human system.

8. These subgroupings and persons will have voices, rights of dialogue and representation, within the whole according to a democratic constitution serving as a dynamic mechanism for human evolution and decision-making.

9. Human individuals will be the primary participants and valued elements within the whole system, which is directed toward their flourishing and development under the five principles of order specified in this chapter. Each individual and group will have rights and duties with regard to the

whole in a variety of unique ways. They will be morally and legally responsible to obey the rules and laws derived from the whole and to participate in the ongoing development of these rules and laws.

10. The whole, with its diverse subgroupings and human participants, will then function as a peace system, a freedom system, a justice system, a sustainability system, and a prosperity system, all these being part of a single system premised on universality, unity-in-diversity, human flourishing, reason and love, and dialogue directed toward mutual understanding. The ethical values immanent in creative holism will have become actualized in an earthly kingdom of ends, each person related to all the others through internal relationships recognizing that, on a very fundamental level, I am you and you are me.

We need a world that is institutionally structured on the principles of order identified in this chapter. In place of the disorder of the current world anti-system, we must make a paradigm-shift to the principles of order embodied within the legitimate, universal rule of law. We must simply negate and put aside disorder, for disorder cannot be evolved into order. Instead of attempting to evolve the fragmented world system, we need to cooperatively and collectively *found* a world peace system. We need a world that is rationally and lovingly organized on these five principles of order. We need to ratify the *Constitution for the Federation of Earth*.

Chapter 5

Sovereignty and the "Moral Autonomy" of Nations: Trashing the Rule of Law Everywhere on Earth

Thus they in mutual accusation spent The fruitless hours, but neither self-condemning; And of their vain contest appeared no end.

—*John Milton*, Paradise Lost

5.1 Private Morality versus Public Law

WE have looked at a number of philosophers of law who, whatever their differences, all see law as: (1) absolutely fundamental to human civilization, (2) intrinsically part of the moral dimension of human life, (3) universal and applicable to all human beings, and (4) intrinsically requiring premises of human equality, dignity, justice, and democracy. The anarchist vision of

163

people living together on Earth in moral and peaceful relationships without global law is not credible as an alternative to the rule of enforceable democratically legislated world law. The reason is not that people cannot be moral. Rather, the reason is the one hit upon by John Locke in his *Two Treatises on Government.*

Locke envisioned an earlier world as a collection of societies without government that was basically moral and peaceful because, as he put it, all men know the "natural law" of moral right and wrong. Rather, the problem in this earlier "state of nature" (prior to government) was one of *interpretation* of how to act within the complexity and "passionate heat" of difficult human affairs. Locke recognized that a few will always rob, exploit, dominate, deceive, or do violence to others. The issue is how to handle these situations on the level of complex societies.

The anarchist dream (that people can and should live without government) leaves how to deal with such situations as robbery, exploitation, or violence up to individual or group interpretations of the events: without any governmental authorities people must find ways to deal with the crime, the circumstances surrounding the crime, the extent of the injuries, the motivations of those involved, the punishment in relation to the crime, the theory of punishment (whether retribution or rehabilitation), etc. Locke understood that *interpretation* of these things could not be left to private judgment, whether group or individual, but must be regularized and publicly available through an "impartial" governmental authority.

Human life is just too complex and we could not live our lives if every situation required reinterpreting all these factors and if each group or person interpreted them differently (which would inevitably be the case). The result would be chaos and social paralysis. We saw H.L.A. Hart point out the many functions performed by the law across much of the spectrum of human affairs. And we saw David Luban declare: "Law enhances human dignity by knitting together thousands of details that make it possible for ordinary people to accomplish ordinary business smoothly" (2007: 4).

The anarchist does not understand that the issue is not whether or not people can be moral. The issue, beyond the smallest of local groups, is human dignity: our right to have a regularized system of law that can protect us by minimizing the chaos of personal feelings and interpretations, thereby allowing us to live flourishing lives framed by the reliability and regularity of the law.

The law protects human dignity in a number of ways, one of which is by creating a public regularity, a public and enforceable protection, a common, democratically arrived at set of interpretations that make it possible for people to flourish: to go about living life to the fullest without having to reinterpret and re-judge and re-negotiate each new situation on a daily basis. The law, therefore, is at the heart of civilized living. It provides, so to speak, a collective judgment and interpretation, ideally impartial and justice-oriented, that protects and empowers our dignity and ability to flourish.

If there is to be privacy from government intrusion in our lives, it is *the law* that will provide for this through placing strict enforceable limits on what government can do, with the ability of citizens through the courts to prosecute government officials who offend against this. If there is to be protection of our human rights from government interference, it is only enforceable law that can do this, necessarily including the due process ability of citizens to find redress of grievances. Only genuine law, carefully designed with checks, balances, transparency, and restrictions on governmental prerogative, can give us the necessary protection from tyranny and injustice.

In either case, it is the law itself that must be self-limiting, self-regulated, and transparent to citizens, operating to serve human flourishing. Under an anarchist regime (without government), relations between people and groups will be not only moral but also naked power relationships within a framework of unregulated interpretive perspectives, an impossible and immoral situation. Perhaps people can be moral but the framework itself is immoral.

As both Lon Fuller (1969) and Hannah Arendt (1963) point out, tyranny is always arbitrary, secretive, without checks and balances, and capricious when it comes to regulating restrictions on governmental prerogatives. Similarly, sovereign nations are not "free" in their self-regulated foreign policies. They are tyrannous. Only planetary law can eliminate the excuse now used by governments everywhere to restrict the human rights of their citizens: that they are protecting us in a dangerous world.

"Public order" is just that. In any community beyond just a few people, people need public rules to make the business of living and flourishing possible, objective, and equal for everyone. The law may indeed be "merely" conventional, as some point out (although it needs to be ultimately based on moral principles as we have seen several philosophers of law argue), and it may be somewhat arbitrary (occasionally dumb politicians may make bad, mistaken, or inadequate laws). But these features do not diminish the need for the law as a common framework for life in complex societies, up to, and including, the community of Earth as a whole. Without public order we have only private disorder, and today this private disorder is led by sovereign nation-states armed to the teeth and multinational corporations concerned only with maximizing profits.

Citizens within states with enforceable laws cannot take the law into their own hands, interpreting for themselves when and where to obey it. The law, however, normally provides for emergencies when citizens may make such decisions, such as breaking the law to save someone's life or in self-defense. But citizens who claim such emergencies must then go before the bar of public order and justify their actions using the "necessity defense." It is part of their human dignity, human right, and public freedom to go before the bar of public order. This does not diminish their freedom but protects it. Good law will provide for emergencies and exceptions, but it does not allow subjects of the law to act with impunity as lawless nation-states and corporations do today.

Citizens who claim the necessity of taking the law into their own hands can be held accountable and may be punished if they have violated public order beyond what is reasonably necessary. Unlike the US invasion of Iraq in 2003, citizens do not invade the next neighborhood claiming "preemptive self-defense," killing many thousands against the law and world public opinion, and get away with this atrocity scot-free. This so-called "freedom" of sovereign nation-states (to interpret for themselves when and where it is necessary to violate international law) does not reflect their dignity but rather their criminality. As Harris points out, at the international level "agreements are always between sovereign governments which interpret their terms as they wish" (2005: 48).

So-called international law is a collection of treaties signed by sovereign nations. The 1969 Vienna Convention on the Law of Treaties, posted like all such treaties on the UN website, makes this very clear. Like the world system as a whole, it still operates under the antiquated formula of *pacta sunt servanda* urged by Dutch thinker Hugo Grotius in his book *De jure belli ac pacis* in 1625. The Convention asserts that "every treaty in force is binding on the parties to it and must be performed by them in good faith." Treaties are entered into only by sovereign states, and no state is compelled (or can be compelled) to sign a treaty. This is voluntary for states. Moreover, any state signing a treaty may write in "reservations" for itself, stating that such and such provisions do not apply, etc. The Convention even has a section on "interpretation" that implicitly makes clear that each state interprets for itself its rights and duties under the treaties it has signed. Harris describes this system:

> The pages of history are littered with examples of wanton transgression and abrogation of treaties by signatories who no longer found them advantageous, as well as of arbitrary interpretations of the terms of a treaty by the participants to suit their own interests. ... The hallowed principle of International Law, *pacta sunt servanda*, thus becomes a dead letter. ... Although all treaties are supposed to be registered with the United Nations, that cannot guarantee that they

will be observed, because the parties are always sovereign states that have absolute discretion to interpret the terms as they think fit, or to abrogate the treaty at will, and have no compunction, when they consider their sovereign interests to be threatened, about simply ignoring their acknowledged commitments, usually on some pretext alleged to be permitted by International Law. Because the United Nations Charter is itself no more than a treaty, it cannot prevent these blatant aberrations from the professed norm, the more so in that, like International Law itself, it acknowledges the sanctity of sovereign rights and is committed (by Article 2 of its Charter) to uphold and respect the sovereign independence of its members. (2005: 59-61)

The world is therefore run by some 193 mostly militarized sovereign states, interfaced with gigantic multinational corporations, on principles that are merely voluntary, as all so-called international law is merely voluntary, with treaties from which nations can withdraw, or within which they can write "reservations" for themselves, and which they reserve the right to "interpret" as they please (although the Convention on Treaties urges that their interpretations be "in good faith"). To any clear thinking person, the *insanity* of this system could not be clearer. Our common human interests in peace, prosperity, security, dignity, and sustainability are all largely ignored by the self-interest of sovereign states. There is no planetary human *community*.

In *The Twilight of Human Rights Law*, philosopher of law Eric A. Posner studies the problem of sovereign states in relation to human rights treaties. He describes a world in which human rights are routinely violated throughout the globe at the same time that the majority of the world's nations are signatories to the nine major human rights conventions enacted since the advent of the UN system (2014: 28-38). Not only are these conventions entirely unenforceable over the signatory states but each state (as sovereign) reserves the right to *interpret* the convention it has signed as it sees fit. The system is known as RUDs (reservations, understandings, and declarations): any nation may insert qualifications or interpretations or reservations along with their signing of a treaty: "Some reservations," Posner writes, "specifically negate a treaty obligation as it applies to the reserving state" (ibid. 36).

Militarized nations, many with nuclear weapons, operate out of self-interest in a world system that explicitly rejects the rule of law (under the deceptive and disingenuous cover of promoting "international law"). Such a system is fragmented and anarchical, and therefore deeply immoral, to its very core. For the genuine rule of law is *never* merely voluntary, *never* subject to citizens making "reservations" for themselves, and *never* open to their own private interpretations of what the law requires. The rule of legitimate law results from people forming *a social contract that binds them into a genuine community* with a common good and common interests that supersede all particular interests.

5.2   The Rule of Law Among Nations after 9/11

THE book *War after September 11* (Verna V. Gehring, ed., 2003) contains essays by a number of thinkers concerning the issues of terrorism and the military responses to terrorism by nation-states. These essays can serve as a focal point for our discussion of the rule of law in relation to the actions of terrorists and the military responses of nation-states. One might look at terrorism as the ultimate disregard of the rule of law. As Benjamin Barber says in his essay "The War of All Against All: Terror and the Politics of Fear": "For the last four hundred years, we have traveled a road from anarchy, insecurity and fear (the state of nature postulated by social contract theorists like Hobbes and Locke) to law and order (lawful order), political safety and the enjoyment of civil liberty" (2003: 75-76). Terrorism, he says, threatens to take us back full circle.

But have we really traveled this route? Perhaps such conditions have been obtained within some countries at some times and places, but (as Barber goes on to point out) these conditions (of lawful order) have been linked with only a few territorial nation-states. Between states, and in a world dominated by neoliberal economics and multi-national corporations, Barber writes, chaos reigns: a so-called "free-market" that establishes "conditions as favorable to the globalization of crime, weapons, prostitution, drugs, and terror as to the spread of unregulated markets" (2003: 84). Indeed, my argument is that the doctrine of territorial sovereignty has actively prevented the development of the rule of law worldwide.

So-called "international law" has evolved as a set of guidelines for the behavior of sovereign nations from the mid-nineteenth century to the present, with its roots going all the way back to Grotius in the 17th century. International law is basically a set of treaties voluntarily agreed upon by the nations involved. Under the UN, all such treaties are supposed to be registered with, and mediated by, the UN system. However this does not make them significantly less voluntary. Nations are not required to sign onto the Convention against Genocide or the Kyoto Treaty on the environment. And if they do sign, it will be largely up to them how to interpret their own compliance.

And there are minimal, if any, penalties, for nations, especially powerful nations, that do not comply with their signed agreements. How do you penalize a nation anyway? Do you economically sanction an entire people for what their former or present leaders have signed onto or refused to sign onto? The most the UN has been able to come up with is some system of monitoring for some of its treaties, itself weak and fraught with difficulties. For example, the conventions on human rights are supposed to be monitored by the nations signatory to those treaties. But the reports, no matter how bad or good, have little consequence for sovereign nations, and a system that is largely *self-monitoring* on the part of those being monitored hardly produces objective results (cf. Posner 2014).

In fact, nations have jealously guarded their autonomy. Nearly all have signed the Nuremburg Treaty that prohibits war crimes, crimes against humanity, and crimes of aggression. But nations insist on the *right to interpret* when aggression has taken place, just as they insist on the right to determine when human rights violations have taken place. There is no independent tribunal that can publicly and objectively assess these things, and there is no civilian world police force that can enforce such decisions. Each nation interprets its own case. Under the UN system, the Security Council is supposed to determine when aggression has taken place, but, of course, this omits the five main aggressor nations: the US, China, France, the UK, and Russia, each of which has a permanent seat on the Security Council and has a veto over nearly anything the UN does.

In other words, each of the world's main aggressor nations insists on the right of private interpretation of all events, and none of the five, to date, has interpreted its own military actions as aggression. China invaded Tibet, Russia invaded Afghanistan and Georgia, the US massively attacked and invaded Vietnam and secretly bombed Laos and Cambodia, the US, France, and UK invaded Iraq and Afghanistan, and militarily attacked Yugoslavia and Libya (the list goes on and on as Michael Parenti points out in his 2011 book *The Face of Imperialism*). None of this was called aggression by the UN, so apparently being signatory to the Nuremberg Convention is hardly relevant to what actually happens in the world. If some nation were to give five private citizens veto power over their entire society and impunity from the laws of that society, this would be tyranny plain and simple, not public order. But that is exactly the mode of governing within the UN.

This is the situation that John Locke was arguing against when he said we need an independent, objective authority over everyone because everybody will interpret situations in their own favor and are unlikely to be objective in the "passionate heat" of difficult circumstances. Thus, in the passion of post-9/11 America, the decision was made to invade Afghanistan, a nation that never attacked the US, nor declared any sort of war on the US. Then, in 2003 the decision was made to invade Iraq, even though the UN wanted to wait until the inspectors had finished their work.

The US *interpreted* for itself the right to invade these countries because of a *new interpretation* of international principles that it had made up for itself: in the case of Iraq "preemptive self-defense." It asserted the right to invade on the far-fetched assumption that someday Iraq might attack the US. Sovereign nations insist on interpreting the world for themselves, including all the international treaties developed by the UN system. International law is no real law not only because it is unenforceable, as many have argued. It is no real law because the subjects of real law do not interpret the law for themselves, or withdraw from the law when it appears to go against them or is inconvenient for their purposes.

In her post-September 11 essay "The Ethics of Retaliation,"Judith Lichtenberg focuses on the rules of war that govern the military responses to terrorism. She focuses especially on non-combatant immunity, on the idea that it is not legitimate to target civilians. She considers the possible reasoning behind this prohibition, from the medieval doctrine of "the double effect" (if a civilian dies as a result of your good intentions to target only the guilty person, you are not morally culpable for that death) to modern consequentialist reasoning that targeting civilians would be very bad publicity and also might create more terrorists than it eliminates (2003: 17-19). She comments that "the idea that war is a rule-governed activity and not a free-for-all has always seemed somewhat strange, but the conduct of states in the international arena shows that, fortunately, it is accepted most of the time" (17).

What seems strange to the present writer, however, is not that the conduct of states is sometimes rule-governed, but that Lichtenberg appears to accept "rule-governed" war as a legitimate practice, at least for the US: "It is crucial that our conduct not blur the line between ourselves and those we condemn. If we abandon the moral high ground, we risk corrupting the standards that render our country worth defending" (19). Here we are back in Locke's state of nature in which we act on moral standards according to our own interpretation of *when* it is legitimate to use military action, *where* (anywhere in the world?) it is legitimate to use military action, and under what circumstances it is legitimate to kill civilians as part of targeting the enemy, keeping in mind that we want to conform to our own interpretation of what is "the moral high ground."

Lichtenberg appears to accept the system of sovereign nations without question and then describes the attitudes of those who attack or threaten, and those who ostensibly defend, as to their moral and pragmatic qualities. But a self-interested Pentagon, representing a self-interested ruling class (concerned with the control of people, resources, oil, etc., worldwide), all operating largely in secret, is hardly, as Locke understood, a prescription for a decent world order, nor for moral integrity, nor for defending anything of value. There is, ultimately, no genuine moral high ground from which to act in the state of nature. The only moral high ground is to leave the state of nature and turn to a public framework that binds everyone together so that we can then really discuss the moral issues.

War is not, as Lichtenberg points out, "anything goes," but is rule-governed. But who makes the rules? Who decides and interprets the circumstances for the use of lethal force or for risking the lives of civilians? Who decides who is guilty and what their level of guilt is? Who decides the meaning of the "international laws" of war and how to apply them? All this needs to be governed by the rule of impartial, enforceable law, not by the self-interested parties interested in "winning" in a self-defined, perpetual "war on terror." (But, then, if these things were so decided by law, it is likely that war itself could no longer exist.)

Perhaps that is why she enters the caveat that rule-governed conduct is "accepted most of the time." When the military system sees difficult circumstances, or feels outside pressures, or has faulty intelligence, it is free to alter the rules as its sees fit. Who decided to use illegal white phosphorous weapons in the Fallujah massacre? Who decided to humiliate prisoners in Abu Ghraib? Who decided that water-boarding was not torture? Who decided there was the right to kidnap anyone in the world in so-called "extraordinary renditions"? As Darth Vader declared to Lando Calrissian in the movie *The Empire Strikes Back*: "I am altering the deal. Pray I don't alter it any further."

It is apparently enough, in Lichtenberg's moral universe, that we follow the moral high ground "most of the time." But push us a little too far, and we immediately are on the same moral level as those we combat. We may look back on the firebombing of Dresden or the dropping of nuclear weapons on Hiroshima and Nagasaki and say "perhaps we went too far." But the war system itself, rules or no rules, makes this inevitable.

The moral failure is not only this excess in these trying circumstances. The moral failure is that we continue to affirm the system that makes such horrors routine. The warring states of the world are already poisoning our biosphere with immense amounts of low-level radiation from such sources as depleted uranium weapons, on-going nuclear weapons testing, etc. This is already "going too far." Yet at any time the next excess within this war system may be the slide into nuclear war that hopelessly destroys the Earth itself. The only truly moral choice is to leave the system of private tyranny and establish real public order for Earth.

Here we have the prescription for the disaster that is modern-contemporary human history. We think that the nation-state is something special and important because it allows voluntary interpretations of when to obey the rules, and what the rules should be—for people who possess nuclear weapons and operate almost exclusively with merely instrumental forms of reasoning. It is clear that this is precisely the problem. There is no moral high ground from which to defend our country, because the moral imperative (as Kant explicitly points out in his 1795 essay "Perpetual Peace") is precisely to abandon the state of nature (which is always a state of war) and enter into genuine civil society under a constitution providing for the enforceable rule of law. It is immoral to live in a situation in which such crucial decisions (and the possible fate of our Earth) are left to the interpretation of individuals, governments, military commanders, nationalistic pride, or public opinion.

Ironically, the war system is indeed not entirely chaos, because it is somewhat rule-governed—by rules that we either make up ourselves or international rules that we insist on interpreting for ourselves. It does, however, presuppose the chaos of limitless private interpretations, some perhaps moral, some immoral, but all abjuring the legitimate rule of law in human affairs. What is moral is to live under the rule of public, democratically legislated, enforceable law, as Kant pointed out. Even if Locke was correct that most know the moral law and follow it in the state of nature, that condition is still immoral, for it allows for the chaos of private interpretations in human relationships. The genuine rule of law requires an objective, enforceable public order (administered by democratically legislated laws, courts, and civilian police) beyond the reach of the private interpretations of any citizen or nation.

In his essay "The War on Terrorism and the End of Human Rights,"David Luban sees a world descending into chaos and lawlessness led by the US. For the US has amalgamated the "war model" (that treats human beings who are identifiable enemies of some other nation as legitimate targets for lethal violence) with the "law model," in which human beings are captured and tried for their criminal activities. Criminals do not have a right to defend themselves against police and fight back as enemies in a war situation do, but they do have a right to trial. In war, on the other hand, the "rights" of the enemy are vastly reduced. In the war model, soldiers are not considered criminals who are to be captured and tried but legitimate agents of a warring nation who may be targeted without due process of law. If captured, however, according to international law, they cannot be mistreated or tried as criminals.

The George W. Bush administration drew on a 1942 US Supreme Court decision concerning "enemy combatants" not in uniform who cross enemy lines to commit acts of sabotage or destruction. The Court determined that they are to be treated as criminals subject to trial, not as captured soldiers presumed innocent of criminal activities. The Supreme Court treated them according to the law model. The Bush administration, however, created a new category for its war on terror: "enemy combatants" are those at war with the US (and hence nearly anything goes in the attempt to kill them, including collateral damage to civilians, and, once captured, they can be held without charges or trial, as international law allows for captured soldiers).

However, *at the same time,* they are criminals who can be interrogated, tried, and punished for their conspiracies or actions against the US or its citizens anywhere in the world. As criminals they have no right to fight back against us. Because it is war, however, enemy combatants have no presumption of innocence or right to due process of law and there is very little need for certainty of "guilt" before they are targeted. Because they are criminals, on that other hand, they can be captured and tried and punished by military tribunals.

However, because they are also warriors, the US has argued that the International Convention on Civil and Political Rights (ICCPR) that requires bringing charges and accused persons to trial does not apply (Posner 2014: 90). It therefore also has the right to hold prisoners indefinitely without charges or trial. As Luban points out, the Bush administration (now followed by the Obama administration) created a hybrid war-law model that serves their own purposes to do whatever they damn well please. They are indeed rule-governed. It is just that they make up the rules and definitions as they go along to serve power or whatever other private purposes they may have.

The human rights of the people of Earth are thus effectively negated by this universal, endless, war on terror. Anyone arbitrarily designated by the US government as an enemy combatant (in secret, by secret criteria) will have his or her human rights stripped and will be subject to this "war-law hybrid approach" (2003: 55-60). Luban writes:

> That means that the real aim of the war is, quite simply, to kill or capture all the terrorists—to keep on killing and killing, capturing and capturing, until they are all gone. . ... The war has no natural resting point, no moment of victory or finality. It requires a mission of killing and capturing, in territories all over the globe, that will go in perpetuity. It follows as well that the suspension of human rights implicit in the hybrid war-law model is not temporary but permanent. (2003: 59-60)

The UN Universal Declaration of Human Rights recognizes the fundamental connection between human dignity, human rights, and the protection of the law. It is "universal" because these rights and protections before the law apply to everyone on Earth:

> Everyone has a right to life, liberty and security of person. (Art. 3).

> No one shall be subjected to torture or to cruel, inhuman or degrading treatment or punishment (Art. 5).

> Everyone has the right to recognition everywhere as a person before the law (Art. 6).

> Everyone is entitled in full equality to a fair and public hearing by an independent and impartial tribunal, in determination of his rights and obligations and of any criminal charge against him (Art. 10).

These stipulations of the Universal Declaration of Rights are, of course, in contradiction to the structure of the UN itself, whose charter affirms the lawless world-anarchy of sovereign nation-states. Hence, everyone has a right to life, liberty, and security of person (except when some nation decides you are a terrorist or an enemy); no one shall be subjected to torture (except when we decide national security requires this); everyone has the right to recognition as a person before the law (except if you are an illegal immigrant trying to escape poverty and injustice in your home country); everyone is entitled to a fair and public hearing (except when national security interprets the situation differently). The UN Declaration correctly affirms the rule of democratic law; the structure of the UN trashes the idea of democratic law.

Even though the UN system remains predicated on the system of sovereign nation-states, which allows it to formulate (in the Hague and Geneva Conventions) the "rules of war," the assumption is that war can be progressively eliminated through converting the world to the rule of law: "Everyone is entitled to a social and international order in which the rights and freedoms set forth in this declaration can be fully realized" (Art. 28). As Kathleen Barry points out in *Unmaking War, Remaking Men*, the UN conventions on war are self-contradictory. The UN Charter says that the purpose of the organization is to end war, yet at the same time, it implicitly legitimates war by formulating *rules of war* and specifying when it is acceptable to nations to go to war (either in self-defense or through Security Council authorization).

Thus the Universal Declaration of Human Rights insists that human rights and human dignity require the rule of public law, but the "international order" required to actualize these rights has not yet arrived. The UN's implicit sanctioning of war reflects the same contradiction as the UN's sanctioning of the system of sovereign nations. The system of sovereign nations is intrinsically a war system. Only democratic public order gives us a peace system, and this is exactly what the UN Charter repudiates.

Luban is correct that the war on terrorism means the end of human rights worldwide owing to the illegitimate combining of the war model and the law model. But his essay fails to point out that the war model is entirely illegitimate in the first place. The war model has us back in the state of nature and is in fundamental contradiction to the law model. It is a consequence of the system of sovereign nation-states which refuse to give up their exclusive "right" to interpret their treaties, agreements, and obligations for themselves rather than submit to some objective, universal, public set of rules which are the hallmark of the legitimate rule of law.

The US has not, therefore, simply gone to some extreme and become a rogue state (as William Blum, and many others, have declared); rather the US has *carried to its logical conclusion the assumptions behind the system of sovereign nation states*: that human beings remain in a state of nature in which they interpret their moral obligations for themselves and in which the publicly determined rule of law does not apply. The US has simply drawn the final conclusion implicit in this system and abjured the rule of so-called international law for the pretense that it is.

If nations have the "right" to interpret international law for themselves, then the next logical step is that they have the right to write new international laws to suit themselves, which is what the US has done in its hybrid law-war model. The world condition is one of war, of might makes right, of power relationships. Within this situation, there simply is no "moral high-ground." We make up the "rules" as we go along, based on our drives to power and self-interest. And the future of our planet is in the hands of these lawless crazies!

5.3   Private and State Terrorism

IN his essay "Terrorism, Innocence, and War," Robert K. Fullinwider quotes from the 1998 UN Convention on the Suppression of Terrorism. Terrorism is: "[a]ny act of violence, whatever its motives or purposes, that occurs in the advancement of an individual or criminal agenda and seeking to sow panic among people, causing fear by harming them, or placing their lives, liberty, or security in danger." Fullinwider points out that the UN convention goes on to distinguish such "criminal" activity from legitimate uses of violence in the service of freedom from oppression: "All cases of struggle by whatever means, including armed struggle, against foreign occupation and aggression for liberation and self-determination, in accordance with the principles of international law, *shall not be regarded as an offense*" (2003: 25)

He points out, however, that the definitions of when violence, even indiscriminate violence, is legitimate are highly complex and very difficult to determine. Adding to his point here, I ask why the bombing of Libya in 2011 from the safe distance of ships firing cruise missiles at supposed military targets, all the while killing many civilians, was not terrorism? And this attack, supposedly in defense of human rights, was against a country that never attacked or threatened the attacking nations (US, Canada, France, and UK) (cf. Petras, 2012, Chap. 7). Why was the use of cluster bombs and other anti-personnel weapons by the US against Yugoslavia in 1998-99 (again, supposedly in defense of human rights) not terrorism? (cf. Clark, et.al., 1998).

I would ask why the saturation bombing of civilian populations by the US in Vietnam, Cambodia, and Laos was not terrorism? Why was the dumping of toxic defoliants on Vietnam amounting to "more than 30 million liters" and "destroying 5 million acres of upland and mangrove forests and about 500,000 acres of crops (a total area the size of Massachusetts)" not terrorism? If people's cropland and ability to survive are destroyed *en masse* is that terrorism? (see, e.g.,http://www.aspeninstitute.org/policy-work/agent-orange/history)

Why is the US use of militarized drones in a number of countries such as Afghanistan, Iraq, Pakistan, Somalia, and Yemen not acts of terror? In his essay "The Paradox of Riskless Warfare" Paul W. Kahn points out that the US policy of attacking people around the world from a position that does not risk its own forces (from the air, for example, by drones or cruise missiles or bombers, against people who have no possibility of defending themselves) again calls into question the traditional moral justifications for warfare and becomes something else entirely. Each one of these examples I have given fits precisely the UN definition of terrorism.

Kahn argues that it becomes "policing" not warfare, but that policing requires different rules from warfare: police are to apprehend the guilty and protect the innocent while drone warfare still retains the war model of simply killing those suspected of being guilty while treating the innocent who are killed or maimed as mere "collateral damage." Policing requires, therefore, real government, world government. You cannot "police" the world without such an enforceable institutionalized due process framework, otherwise such violence is simply terrorism.

Here we have Luban's hybrid war-law model raise its ugly head again, threatening the human rights and human dignity of people everywhere. You cannot "police" the world using the "war-law" model without chaos continuing to ensue. Under the Geneva conventions and the traditional UN model, there was a clear distinction between war and the rule of law. Many people pointed out the paradox that soldiers were encouraged to do terrible things in the war situation that they were prohibited from doing when they returned home. But there were at least some lines drawn by this paradox that people were supposed to respect. The war-law model trashes all that and, in doing so, finally reaps the consequences implicit in the entire system from the beginning: anything goes. We make up the rules as we go along according to our private interpretations and secret machinations.

Journalist Tom Engelhardt underlines this total lawlessness:

> Since 9/11, the result has been a religion of perpetual conflict whose doctrines tend to grow ever more extreme. In our time, for instance, the NSS has moved from Dick Cheney's "1 percent doctrine" (if there is even 1 percent chance that some country might someday attack us, we should act "as if it is a certainty") to something like a "zero percent doctrine." Whether in its drone wars with presidential "kill lists" or the cyberwar—probably the first in history—that it launched against Iran, it no longer cares to argue most of the time that such strikes need even a 1 percent justification. Its ongoing, self-proclaimed Global War on Terror, whether on the ground or in the air, in person or by drone, in space or cyberspace (where the newest military command is already in action) is justification enough for just about any act, however aggressive. (2014: 7)

The fact that I want to underline here is that there is no significant moral difference between private terrorism and nation-state terrorism. The only difference is that nation-state terrorism kills millions of people (as in Vietnam), while private terrorism kills only thousands at the most. However, both are largely products of the same fragmented system of "sovereign" nation-states and global Neoliberal capitalism. To end terror means to change the system, to effect a paradigm-shift to democratic holism. The only realistic possibility for ending terror and endless war and destruction, possibly leading to the extinction of humanity (and certainly leading to climate collapse), is conversion to a global peace system, which means enforceable world law.

In the 2013 book by Medea Benjamin and Barbara Ehrenreich, *Drone Warfare: Killing by Remote Control,* the authors point out the terror felt by civilians in Pakistan and Afghanistan at the 24 hour a day buzzing of the drones overhead. They never know if there will be instant death, for example, with the kids in a school blown up (as happened), or a group of women and children in cars on the way to market blown up (as happened). Can there be greater terror (greater "threat of violence for social or political aims") than to live with the knowledge that some foreigner in a comfortable chair in Nevada or Florida who has little or no idea of your life or your customs might at any time wipe out your community, your loved ones, and your life?

We can declare that morally this practice is hideous, but that will help little as long as the system makes it possible and as long as there is no objective, enforceable planetary law to put the people in Nevada or Florida in jail where they properly belong. Electing "moral" people to office will not help. It is the system itself that is the root of the problem. Systems theorist and paradigm-shift advocate Ervin Lazlo points out what should be obvious:

> We could change direction: with a timely transformation we could create a peaceful and sustainable world. Will we create it? Einstein told us that we cannot solve a problem with the same kind of thinking that produced it. Yet,

> for the present we are trying to do just that. We are fight-
> ing terrorism, poverty, criminality, cultural conflict, climate
> change, environmental degradation, ill health, even obesity
> and other 'sicknesses of civilization' with the same means
> and methods that produced the problems in the first place.
> (2008: 14)

Terrorists are hardly the amoral psychopaths or nihilists often
portrayed by the media. They are often people who are aware
of the atrocities perpetuated on Vietnam, Laos, Cambodia, Iraq,
Afghanistan, Pakistan, Yugoslavia, Libya, Yemen, Somalia, Pales-
tine, and elsewhere who are attempting to fight back, not through
riskless slaughter of those suspected to oppose them but through
the willingness to die in lethal battle or a suicide struggle. But
Laszlo's statement (and perhaps the statement of the preceding
sentence) presupposes that the imperial attackers of these countries have some noble motives, as if they are genuinely trying to
deal with problems of conflict or private terror. But many serious
thinkers disagree.

Internationally known peace researcher, Johan Galtung, recognizes the inevitable link between private terrorism and state terrorism:

> Anyone surprised by 9/11 was ignorant, naïve or both. The
> bottomless, limitless US state terrorism elicited an unsur-
> prising answer: terrorism hitting back. With an estimated
> 13-17 million killed [by the US], and an average of 10 be-
> reaved for each, filled with pain, lust for revenge and re-
> vanche, acts of justified revenge seem probable. (2009: 39)

Scholars such as James Petras and Henry Veltmeyer in *Empire
with Imperialism: The Globalizing Dynamics of Neoliberal Capitalism*
(2005) reveal in detail the ways that transnational corporations
use the first world military domination of the world to protect
their system of exploitation. Naomi Klein in *The Shock Doctrine:
The Rise of Disaster Capitalism* (2008) points out that the CIA and
Pentagon doctrine of "counter-insurgency warfare" is not really

counter-insurgency but a directed attempt to shock and terrify civilian populations into compliance with economic policies that enrich foreign corporations at their expense.

Klein shows that the use of torture inevitably accompanied all attempts, led by US "Chicago School" economists, to impose the Neoliberal economic model on third world peoples. Like many other truly critical thinkers and scholars, Klein shows that the so-called "war on terror" is merely a cover for the attempt to destroy the will of peoples to resist their global exploitation, domination, and dehumanization. The discussions of scholars who have pointed this out could be greatly expanded, but I have already gone into some detail concerning this elsewhere, for example, in Chapters 4-6 of my *Triumph of Civilization* (2010a).

Given this background and the Cold War background from which it also emerges, many critical thinkers see the secret agencies of the nation-states as intentionally creating *false-flag* terrorist atrocities, and for a variety of reasons. In *Operation Gladio,* there is much evidence that terror bombings of public squares and buses carrying school children in Italy during the 1960s and 70s were false-flag operations designed to implicate and demonize the Communist Party. Information from an Italian Parliamentary Commission investigating these terror bombings and a report from the Guardian News Agency are summarized here:

> In 2000, a Parliament Commission report from the communist/center-left coalition *"Gruppo Democratici di Sinistra l'Ulivo"* asserted that a strategy of tension had been supported by the United States to *"stop the PCI, and to a certain degree also the PSI, from reaching executive power in the country"* It stated that "Those massacres, those bombs, those military actions had been organized or promoted or supported by men inside Italian state institutions and, as has been discovered more recently, by men linked to the structures of United States intelligence." According to *The Guardian,* "The report [claimed] that US intelligence agents were informed in advance about several rightwing terrorist bombings, including the December 1969 Piazza Fontana

bombing in Milan and the Piazza della Loggia bombing in
Brescia five years later, but did nothing to alert the Italian authorities or to prevent the attacks from taking place."
(http://en.wikipedia.org/wiki/Operation_Gladio)

The CIA denies involvement, but the Cold War attempt to dis-
credit the strong Communist Party of Italy was very real. Not only
have the major secret agencies of the world's powers (CIA, FBI, M-
6, Mossad, etc.) been repeatedly accused of sponsoring false-flag
terror operations, they may also know of terror plans in the works
(as the above quote asserts) that they allow to take place because it
promotes their "strategies of tension" or other political purposes.

We need only look at the perceived "benefits" the US administration received from these so-called terrorist attacks, including
the terrible attacks of 9/11, to question their professed motives
and strategies. David Ray Griffin, for example, writes:

> We need only look at the benefits the administration reaped
> from 9/11 to see several plausible motives: they wanted
> a huge increase in military spending, which, they knew,
> would be forthcoming after "a new Pearl Harbor"; they
> wanted a climate, consisting of fear and desires for re-
> venge, in which Americans would support a "war on ter-
> ror" that could be used as a cover for enlarging the empire;
> they wanted a pretext to carry out the preplanned wars to
> bring about regime change in Afghanistan and Iraq; and
> they wanted, more generally, a climate in which Ameri-
> cans would accept the new doctrines of preventive war and
> regime change. (2006: 21)

What are the moral differences between a CIA torturer or
strategist who allows a bombing to take place, and a terrorist? What are the moral differences between a country that
captures suspects in a program of "secret rendition" and sends
them to countries where it knows they will be tortured (or to
Guantanamo or Abu Ghraib where it does the torturing) and
a terrorist? If the tragedy of 911 was not a false-flag operation of secret elements within the US government, it was al-

most certainly something known about and allowed to happen for the obvious political purposes expressed in the on-line Project for the New American Century document, signed by leading hawks and Neocons within high levels of the US government (www.newamericancentury.org).

Terrorism scholar Webster Griffin Tarpley, in his 2008 book *9/11 Synthetic Terror: Made in USA,* describes this reality:

> We must stress again that international terrorism should never be seen as a spontaneous sociological phenomenon arising directly out of oppression and misery. International terrorism and national liberation struggles are always mediated through a level of clandestine organization in which the efforts of intelligence agencies come decisively into play. Many international terrorist groups are false-flag operations from the very beginning. Others assume false-flag status as the result of coordinated arrests, assassinations, and takeovers by intelligence agencies. Even where there is an authentic national liberation organization, intelligence agencies will create false-flag operations under their own control to mimic it, perpetrating atrocities in its name in an effort to isolate and discredit it. Here again, deception and dissembling are the rule. (2008: 385)

How can it be made clearer that this chaos of naked power relationships—whether private terrorism, state terrorism, or corporate exploitation and domination—are the result of the lack of democratically legislated enforceable public law in the world? More drones, more military, more secret trade deals, more trumped-up nationalist feelings, and more calls for a moral foreign policy are not going to bring human beings any nearer to peace, justice, or sustainability. Neither will a campaign to elect progressives such as Elizabeth Warren, Bernie Sanders, or some Green Party candidate as President of the United States.

The problem lies in the absolute refusal, under the system of sovereign nation-states, to give up the "right" of these states to *interpret* events in terms of their own viewpoints, interests, and feelings and respond with violence accordingly. The rule of enforceable democratically legislated law, which is the only system in the world that can promote peace, human dignity, and ability to flourish, is precisely what is lacking at the international level, and it is more and more lacking on the national level as nations militarize further, convert to national security states, and begin to treat their own citizens as potential threats.

If you maintain the lawless, Hobbesian state of nature at the international level, in a globalized world of instant communications and weapons of mass destruction, the lawlessness will erode whatever law is left *within* the nations themselves. Unlike the assumptions made by several of the essays we have examined—that there is a morality of war that differs from the morality expected of citizens internally within nations—these two dimensions cannot coexist: the chaos of war and terror will inevitably destroy the rule of law and the heart of civilization itself will be threatened.

5.4 Conclusion

I cited above Barber's statement that for the last four hundred years we have struggled out of anarchy and the state of nature toward the rule of "law and order (lawful order), political safety and the enjoyment of civil liberty." Barber blames the terrorists for having "in a certain sense undone the social contract, bringing us full circle back to a kind of 'state of nature'" (2003: 75). However, he also goes on to point out that the world's "democratic deficit" is not due to the terrorists alone, but to "fundamentalists" who use a religious absolutism to destroy tolerance and due process protections they disagree with, and to "American exceptionalism" that places the US above the common laws and rules formulated for the rest of humanity by the UN and other internationalist traditions, and to "unregulated transnational financial and corporate interests" which contribute to the prevailing anarchy (78-87).

Barber makes good points but misses the systemic dimension of the argument: *that both private terror and nation-state terror arise from the same failed "international" system.* Within the essays in this volume on war after September 11, however, the only essay suggesting that the entire world system needs to be transformed in a holistic and positive direction is this one by Barber:

> Ours is a new age in which borders have grown porous and the global social contract calls for a novel and unprecedented Declaration of Interdependence. Nation by nation, democracy can no longer survive. . ... Hobbes' contradiction that to overcome anarchy within nations, one had to create a sovereign nation-state system in which there would be anarchy among nations, can no longer stand. The costs have become too high, leaving the predators of international anarchy to feed not just on individual states but the nation-state system itself. The call today for the globalization of democracy, the globalization of law, the construction of strong international institutions that allow genuine participation, is no longer simply a romantic call of irrelevant world federalists for an impossible utopia. It has become a call of national security, an imperative of a new realism. (2003: 86-87)

As with Laszlo, quoted above, Barber sees that you cannot solve the problem of international violence and anarchy using more violence and anarchy, which is just what the nation-states are attempting (assuming, for the moment, that they want to solve the problem at all and are not simply accepting the premise that law is only a window dressing and that the rule of power and violence are all that is "real" and effective in human affairs). However, the vast majority of ordinary human beings in most countries simply want to flourish in peace.

They simply want to live their lives in an orderly and secure fashion and actualize some features of human flourishing: family, home, modest achievements, education, health-care, clean water, sanitation, a decent diet, a stable environment, and peaceful order within which to live their lives. All this is negated by the denizens of power, exploitation, domination, and violence: the few, the 1%, who want unreasonable and unequal power and domination (and whose policies largely govern the imperialist nation-states with their systems of war, terror, and violence) and by their opponents, the other few, the other 1%, who resist this horrific system with privately organized terror and violence.

Ironically, the first 1% insist on the balkanization of humanity through the system of territorial, sovereign nation-states as a key to their power and domination. They understand very well that human fragmentation is a key source of their power. They divide and conquer. They invade and dismember Yugoslavia, Iraq, Afghanistan, or Libya with the near certainty that other nations will not interfere. But the other few, the second 1%, who violently resist and struggle against this system of domination, also often insist on local autonomy and the principle of territorial sovereignty. They also want to balkanize the world. Both are equally wrong, both are two sides of the same coin of unprincipled anarchy: the arrogant insistence on the right to interpret events as each sees fit and to act, outside the law, as a sovereign agent, each promoting its own interpretation of what is right, appropriate, and necessary as served by violence and terror.

Hobbes' paradox is a fatal contradiction for humanity. He declared that establishing the rule of law within national territories required simultaneously establishing the chaos of the state of nature in the international sphere. This opened the door for the perpetual struggle of nations for ascendency and self-interest at the expense of the others, and of each nation's 2% of dominators and violent resisters at the expense of nature and the other 98%. Why do we allow a mere 2% of the world's population to continue this reign of lawlessness and terror on Earth while 98% of us want simply to live a decent, flourishing, law-abiding life?

Barber is right in this respect: unless we *globalize democracy* and the rule of public, enforceable law for everyone on Earth, it is unlikely that we will survive much longer on this planet. Traditionally, he says, world federalists were considered "utopian." But in the face of the growing threats to human existence on this planet we can now see that their insight was fundamentally correct: We establish the rule of enforceable law for the planet or we continue the route of violence and chaos and ecological destruction that will ultimately mean planetary death. World federalists were, and continue to be, the realists. And the most practical, concrete, and available option to actualize this realist program is ratification of the *Constitution for the Federation of Earth.*

Private morality is, by and large, lost and helpless outside of the framework of democratic public law. This does not mean that it does not have an important role, for democratic dialogue and debate about public order requires morally mature people to address the issues of the day with effective civic participation in the public order. And we have seen that the establishment of democratic public law is itself a moral imperative. It is immoral, strange as it may initially sound, to live by private morality alone. We are living with others, always in a social context, and the chaos of interpretations within the complexity of circumstances and events requires that we have enforceable, public standards within which we can nonviolently live our lives and debate the moral issues. The consequence of not acting on this fundamental insight is both state terrorism and private terrorism, two sides of the same coin.

Both nation-state and private terror involve the immoral use of violence in the service of fragmented ("sovereign" or "private") interpretations of events. There is no "morality of war" versus the "morality of law." We have seen Kathleen Barry point out that by formulating the "rules of war" the Geneva Conventions implicitly accept the legitimacy of war in contradiction to the stated purpose of the UN. However, under this paradigm-shifting insight, war, violence, and terrorism are not likely to be morally possible at all. The deeper moral imperative is that we nonviolently join together to solve the problem of different interpretations through courts, public laws, civilian police, dialogue, mediation, arbitration, and voting.

Holism is both the reality of the world discovered by contemporary science and the noblest moral ideal. Fact and value can no longer be torn apart. And as Harris explains, holism encompasses the other traditional Western ethical theories such as the morality of duty, the morality of self-gratification, virtue ethics, and even Jesus' ethics of love (1992: 30-31). Holism not only binds these all together but goes beyond them in revealing new dimensions of moral obligation.

Moral imperatives include the imperative of solidarity with all humanity, the imperative of sustainable living that preserves our planet for future generations, the imperative of worldwide human liberation from poverty and injustice, and, ultimately, enforceable democratic world law legislated by a World Parliament, administered by civilian world police, and adjudicated by impartial, professional courts. Today, our very survival requires this fundamental paradigm-shift.

Public law does not replace morality with arbitrary conventions. It is rather at the heart of the moral demand, since it makes possible dialogue and discussion among free and equal citizen participants, as Jürgen Habermas has pointed out (1998a). And global public law is the presupposition of our humanity itself, of our common rationality and sociality, as I have shown throughout this book. The moral principles deriving from this presupposition (from universal human rights and dignity to the Socratic and Pauline principles that evil should never be done that good might come of it) must be the basis of global public law.

Both state and private terrorism are deeply immoral, for they shatter solidarity and the imperative for a global nonviolent framework for discourse and lawful public order. The global framework, of course, would have to be free, equal, basically egalitarian, and peaceful, which is why the 1% with their wealth, power, and investments in the industrial-military complex hate the idea. This is also why many private terrorists fear this result as well, since a global framework would require that they grow beyond their current narrow rebellion and submit to a public framework for redress of grievances. However noble they believe their motives are in the violent struggle against global oppression, exploitation, and dehumanization, their methods would make them wanted criminals within a democratic world system.

Moreover, both the top 1% of dominators in the world with their state terrorism and the 1% who are violently resisting them with private terrorism believe we live in a condition of scarcity. All the trillions of dollars in wealth of the top 1%, the dominators say, if distributed equally, would not solve the problem of some four or five billion of the world's poor but only destroy the limited good that the top 1% are able to do. They claim that the laws of economics, that result in our present unjust and endangered world, operate "objectively" and independently of our subjective wishes that things should be different. But at least some of the 1% know that these are lies. Their wealth and power depends on perpetuating the lie of money scarcity and the lie of objective, value free economic laws. Their wealth and power depends on their lies that the present system creates jobs and is the best we can do under the conditions of scarcity on Earth. Matthew Fox writes:

> Economics is still running on the Newtonian mechanistic "laws" such as Supply and Demand, with little question-ing of what is supplied and for whom, and what is not being supplied and who is demanding, and how demands are channeled to manufacturers. Another "law" is that eco-nomic progress is synonymous with constant increase in Gross National Products. There is also a presumption, since Adam Smith's influential *Wealth of Nations*, that economics is primarily an issue of nationalist concern. In other words, that the proper 'home' for economics is the nation-state. People are beginning to question the frozen world of or-dained economists who are unable to halt rampant infla-tion, to redirect resources to ensure the survival of the very poor, to guarantee employment for all fit workers, to stop the rich from getting richer and the poor from dying of star-vation. (1990: 178)

The authors of the *Earth Constitution* saw through these de-ceptions. They understood that holistically sound economics is not separate from human values, that the proper "home" for economics is world legislation, and that scarcity is a myth supporting the old system of domination and exploitation. They wrote the *Earth Constitution* to empower all the people of Earth through an honest economic system. Above I concluded that "out of the new, holistic scientific paradigm there arises a new ethics, a new politics, a new economics, and a new conception of human life and civilization." This new politics, economics, and model of planetary civilization are embodied within the *Earth Constitution*. The Earth Federation government deriving from the *Earth Constitution* carefully transforms the current world economic system into one directed toward the flourishing of all human beings.

To establish a genuine world peace system you need a decent and honest world economic system. The holistic vision encompasses all aspects of our lives on Earth, including economics. The fundamental premise of economist Herman E. Daly's 1996 book *Beyond Growth: The Economics of Sustainable Development* is that you cannot foster perpetual quantitative growth within a finite planetary ecosystem. Our criterion for economic success must become *qualitative*. The empowerment of real freedom and the ability to flourish, requires a holistic economics in conformity with the holism of our planetary biosphere and with the holistic dignity of every member of the human community. For these reasons, the next appropriate chapter in a discourse on how to build a world peace system is to examine the question of economics. This next chapter draws from Chapter Three of my book *The Anatomy of a Sustainable World* (2013b).

Chapter 6

Economics, and the Earth Constitution as a Blueprint

> *The development of technology and of the implements of war has brought about something akin to a shrinking of our planet. Economic interlinking has made the destinies of nations interdependent to a degree far greater than in previous years. The available weapons of destruction are of a kind such that no place on earth is safeguarded against sudden total destruction. The only hope for protection lies in the securing of peace in a supranational way. World government must be created which is able to solve conflicts between nations by judicial decision. This government must be based on a clear-cut constitution which is approved by the governments and the nations.*
>
> *—Albert Einstein*

I N my view the best and most practical blueprint for establishing a holistic political and economic system for Earth is found in the *Constitution for the Federation of Earth.* Its Preamble explicitly invokes holism in a number of ways, including emphasis on the principle of unity-in-diversity, and its design establishes a matrix of holistic institutions cooperating with one another and the people of Earth in a planetary regime of harmonious and sustainable economic and political democracy. This constitution is the most important document produced in the 20th century and should be studied in every school, college, and university in the world. My book, *The Anatomy of a Sustainable World: Our Choice between Climate Change or System Change,* studies the holistic design of the *Earth Constitution* in some detail.

The Earth Federation government itself reflects the structures of creative holism: interdependency, dynamic internal relationships between its parts, as well as a conscious orientation for unity-in-diversity. This is fundamental to establishing a sustainable world civilization based on an efficient and morally responsible world economic and political system. As we have seen, institutions influence and condition people. If we want people to act sustainably in their lives and economic relationships, these principles must permeate the institutions of which they are part. The *Earth Constitution* does exactly this. It functions as a global social contract in which people institutionally agree to forgo war and live in peace according to the rule of enforceable laws.

The *Earth Constitution* was written with the participation of hundreds of world citizens meeting in four international constituent assemblies between 1968 and 1991. It can be found online at http://worldparliament-gov.org/constitution/the-earth-constitution/. Since 1991, it has been considered a finished document, ready for ratification by the people and nations of the Earth. Its conditions for ratification are divided into three distinct stages, making universal ratification both practical and possible, and its Article 19 allows the people of Earth to begin Provisional World Government in anticipation of, and preparation for, its final ratification. Indeed, the Provisional World Parliament has been meeting since 1982, with its 14th session scheduled for Kolkata, India, in December 2015. It has passed more than 50 provisional world legislative acts (all available on-line at www.worldproblems.net) that spell out, and empower, the kind of holistic world system that will be actualized under the *Earth Constitution*.

We have observed that a holistic world government will eliminate war and militarism and convert the many employed in these pursuits to a non-military civilian environmental and civil service corps. The world government will also end severe poverty and misery, employing millions of the underemployed in these same types of environmental and social service jobs. It will move rapidly to end reliance on fossil fuels and non-renewable resources. Where will the new global social democracy get the money to do all these things? I have already published accounts, in several places, of the holistic economic system written into the *Earth Constitution* and the new global economics that it engenders. Let us examine some of the most fundamental ideas of a global economics.

The ending of global capitalism and the conversion to social democracy will also end the scarcity of money and the systemic tendency of the economic system to funnel most of the world's wealth into the hands of the top 10%. The key to the conversion to a holistic economics is the ending of the global debt-based system and the conversion to truly public banking. There is no need to socialize all production or ownership, for banking is the key to converting all the rest to a cooperative and harmonious economics. From this starting point, a holistic economics will necessarily follow. Economist David Korten writes:

> To survive on a living spaceship we must create a system of economic relationships that mimics the balance and cooperative efficiency of a healthy biological community. It must distribute rights equitably and link power to the consequences of its use. In short, we must commit ourselves to establish an economic, as well as political, democracy. A substantial body of proven experience suggests that such systems can be built around smaller enterprises functioning as self-directing members of larger networks in ways that are efficient, flexible, and innovative, and thereby secure the freedom and livelihood of the individual while nurturing mindful responsibility. (1999: 181)

The *Earth Constitution* mandates that agencies in the "Integrative Complex" of the Earth Federation government study the biological communities of the Earth (and draw upon such knowledge from all the universities of Earth) to be able to adapt human economic activities to the balance and efficiency of the Earth's biosphere. As Korten points out, this means economic as well as political democracy. Citizens and communities all over the planet will be drawn into the process of creating a sustainable world, and restoring the already damaged environment as much as possible.

Reves points out correctly that the conception of "freedom" associated with capitalism was not socially mediated "positive" freedom, in which the freedom of each is mediated by law to be compatible with the freedom of all the others. Rather it was "absolute, unlimited and unrestrained" (1945: 36). He states:

> Our civic life is based entirely on the fundamental doctrine that the maximum individual freedom results from the prohibition of the free exercise of such human actions as would infringe upon the freedom of others. This is the meaning of political freedom. It is also the meaning of economic freedom.... *Economic freedom and the freedom of free enterprise have been driven into bankruptcy by the primitive, erroneous notion of unregulated freedom and by political nationalism, by the nation-state structure.* (Ibid. 41, 46)

To empower the flourishing and freedom of everyone on Earth, including future generations, we need to view the economic problem as part of the common good of the whole, overcoming both unrestrained capitalism and the system of sovereign nation-states. We need to establish "the integration of the scattered conflicting national sovereignties into one unified, higher sovereignty, capable of creating a legal order within which all peoples may enjoy equal security, equal obligations and equal rights under law" (ibid. 125). This is exactly what has been brilliantly done by the *Earth Constitution*.

6.1   The World's Current Unsustainable Debt-based Monetary System

TO understand the extraordinary power of the stipulations for the World Financial Administration and their implications for sustainability it is first necessary to look at the current unsustainable, debt-based world monetary system. The economists who have worked out the economics of sustainability (such as Herman E. Daly) call for fundamental changes in the way business and production operate. Specifically, Daly (1996) and others (e.g., Rifkin, 1989) show that economic formulas can no longer treat the economy as a self-contained institution ignoring the finitude of resources, the delicate balance of the planetary ecosystem, or the natural laws of energy and entropy.

Business can no longer operate with calculations of private profit that maximize gain by externalizing the true costs of production to society and the natural environment. The cost calculations must now take into account society, nature, and future generations, which means, as Daly puts it, that business is no longer independent of *values*, ecological principles, or the human community within which it functions. He writes:

> Distribution and scale involve relationships with the poor, the future, and other species that are fundamentally social in nature rather than individual. *Homo economicus* as the self-contained atom of methodological individualism, or as the pure social being of collectivist theory, are both severe abstractions. Our concrete experience is that of "persons in community." We are individual persons, but our very individual identity is defined by the quality of our social relations. Our relations are not just external, they are also internal, that is, the nature of the related entities (ourselves in this case) changes when relations among them changes. We are related not only by a nexus of individual willingness to pay for different things, but also by relations of trusteeship for the poor, the future, and other species. The attempt to abstract from these concrete relations of trusteeship and

> reduce everything to a question of individual willingness
> to pay is a distortion of our concrete experience as persons
> in community, an example of A.N. Whitehead's "fallacy of
> misplaced concreteness." (1996: 55)

The global economic meltdown that began in 2008 has led to
a chorus of voices from economists and monetary theorists who
believe that human welfare and the welfare of our planet should
be the central premise of economics. Some of the concepts associated with "democratic socialism" are now being widely discussed
by sustainability economists. Whether these thinkers use the for-
bidden "S-word," or speak in terms of some form of "cooperative capitalism" (Smith, 2003), or of economics premised on the
"public good" is irrelevant to their consensus. There are two central alternatives: either have money, debt, and the economy controlled by huge private financial monopolies structured around
the accumulation of ever-greater private wealth for themselves
(the present world-system) or place money, some essential forms
of production, and the economy democratically in the hands of
the people through a public banking system.

Economist Michael Hudson describes the latter alternative in
contradistinction to the bailout for the big private banks that was
arranged by the Obama administration:

> The alternative is a century and a half old, and emerged out
> of the ideals of the classical economic doctrines of Adam
> Smith, David Ricardo, John Stuart Mill, and the last great
> classical economist, Marx. Their common denominator was
> to view rent and interest as extractive, not productive. Clas-
> sical political economy and its successor Progressive Era so-
> cialism sought to nationalize the land (or at least to fully tax
> its rent as the fiscal base). Governments were to create their
> own credit, not leave this function to wealthy elites via a
> bank monopoly on credit creation. So today's neoliberal-
> ism paints a false picture of what the classical economists
> envisioned as free markets. They were markets free of eco-
> nomic rent and interest (and taxes to support an aristocracy
> or oligarchy). Socialism was to free economies from these

> overhead charges. Today's Obama-Geithner rescue plan is
> just the reverse. . . . The Treasury is paying off the gamblers
> and billionaires by supporting the value of bank loans, in-
> vestments and derivative gambles, leaving the Treasury in
> debt. (2009)

The issue is not the abolition of all private property. This idea functions as a red herring promoted by dominant elites to terrorize populations into not examining the present system carefully and honestly. The *Earth Constitution* explicitly affirms the right of private property (Article 12.1 and 12.16). The real issue involves the question as to whether *the economic infrastructure that provides the means for all business and trade* (banking) will be democratically owned by the people as a public utility to be used in the service of universal prosperity and sustainability or whether it will be privately owned to be used in the service of private accumulation of wealth for the rich and making a sustainable civilization nearly impossible. The central issues are banking, money creation, and the structure of property laws in general.

This is as much an infrastructure question as are roads and streets. Government normally builds and maintains roads, streets, electrical systems, water systems, sewage systems, and other vital infrastructure because these *make possible the free exchange of goods and services* that constitute a healthy economy. You cannot have all streets and roads as the private property of individuals or corporations to be used for private interests without throwing the society into chaos. But this is precisely what the dominant monopoly capitalist ethos advocates: The monetary system must be privately owned by giant financial interests while government must raise money through taxes on the people resulting in debt enslavement of the public to these private interests.

In her 2007 book *Web of Debt*, Ellen H. Brown traces the history of the struggle over money creation in the United States (and thus, to a great extent, in the world). She exposes the sleight of hand that led to the creation of the Federal Reserve Bank in 1913, which was and is really a consortium of giant private banks that create money for the people of the United States *as debt* to these private banks. These banks create the money they "lend" to the people of the United States out of nothing, and the indebtedness they create enslaves the people who must then pay taxes that are primarily used simply to keep up with the interest on this privately held debt (2007:4). Brown quotes Sir Josiah Stamp, director of the Bank of England and the second richest man in Britain during the 1920s, who spoke at the University of Texas in 1927:

> *The modern banking system manufactures money out of nothing.* The process is perhaps the most astounding piece of sleight of hand that was ever invented. Banking was conceived in inequity and born in sin. . . . *Bankers own the Earth.* Take it away from them but leave them the power to create money, and, with the flick of a pen, they will create enough money to buy it back again. . . . Take this great power away from them and all great fortunes like mine will disappear, for then this would be a better and happier world to live in. . . . But, *if you want to continue to be slaves of bankers and pay the cost of your own slavery, then let bankers continue to create money and control credit.* (2007:2)

The overwhelming agreement among economists and monetary theorists who are not indentured as propagandists for the monopoly capitalist system focuses on a socially-owned banking system. As Steven Zarlenga (2002) points out, democracy is effectively gutted when private interests control its financial infrastructure for society loses control over its own destiny. As Brown shows in detail, financial elites who control the money system use their control not to fund the productive economy but to maximize their wealth through the financial manipulation of markets and casino investments directed toward speculative windfalls. And as Hudson says, both classical economics and its successor progressive era socialism understood that "governments were to create their own credit, not leave this function to wealthy elites via a bank monopoly on credit creation." Zarlenga writes:

Lack of money to pay for crucial programs is again not a fiscal but a monetary problem caused ultimately by the false idea that government must get money only by taxation or borrowing. . ... Behind these problems is the fact that the nation is controlled more from behind the scenes by financial institutions than by citizens through elections. *When society loses control over its money system it loses whatever control it might have had over its own destiny.* It can no longer set priorities and the policies for achieving them. It can't solve problems, which then develop into crises and continually mount up. . ... This book has shown that it is historically self-evident that the best monetary systems have been controlled and monitored through law, by public authority. Leaving money power in private hands has invited, even assured, disastrous results. This is also consistent with the logic of money: since the money system is a creature of law, it rightfully belongs within government, just as the law courts do. (2002: 655-657)

Here we have a fundamental reason for democratic world law. Global money creation is in private hands worldwide, taking advantage, as we have seen, of the balkanization of the planet into some 193 competing quasi-independent entities. Even the IMF and the World Bank are financed and run by these giant, private banking cartels. The global crises beyond the scope of any nation or group of nations are in many ways a result of global financial indebtedness to banking cartels. *Only world law can solve these crises, for it is the only force on Earth that could convert banking globally from private to public banking.* Without disbanding any present banks, it would be relatively easy to convert the largest ones by law into public institutions serving humanity rather than the 1%.

Monetary theorist Richard C. Cook (2008) agrees with Hudson and Zarlenga. The ability of financial elites to speculate in the unproductive economy must be abolished by law and capital markets should be regulated to maximize the productive economy in which real goods and services are produced to serve human needs. All of these thinkers advocate the same basic principle. *Money and its democratic creation and regulation should be treated as a "public utility," available to all citizens as part of their social heritage and human rights.* Cook itemizes the key points:

- Private creation of credit for speculative purposes should be abolished, and capital markets should be regulated to assure fairness, openness, and freedom from predatory practices.

- Every national government should have the right to spend low cost credit directly into existence for public purposes— including infrastructure, environmental protection, education, and health care—without incurring new debt.

- The physical backing for every currency in existence should be the actual production of national economies.

- National governments should treat credit as a public utility—like clean air, water, or electricity—and should assure its availability to all citizens as their social heritage and as a basic human right. (Ibid.)

Economist J.W. Smith also agrees. The banking system must be "socially owned" and financial speculation by private financial interests must be abolished at the same time that public investment is made in the real productive economy that supplies goods and services to the people. "Due to a *socially-owned* banking system being more powerful than armies. . ..." he writes, "that power is denied a private banking system because their *property rights* are designed for maximum rights to monopolists and minimum rights for all others" (2009: 169-170). Smith affirms that:

> Monopolies claim a large share of the wealth produced, waste enormous amounts of resources, capital, and labor, restrict the efficiencies of an economy, claim unearned wealth, and all this doubles the cost of production. . .. In an efficient economy, with *full and equal rights for all*, there are no unearned values. Instead of financing unearned monopoly-created values, touchable and usable *use values*

are financed, created, and bought and sold. Both planning and financial control are primarily regional and local.
(Ibid.144-146)

Smith shows that the structure of property laws today actively *prevents* both social equality and a fully efficient economy.
A socially owned banking system not only enables production of
the general wealth that substantially eliminates poverty and creates universal prosperity, it also democratizes society, placing the
power back in the hands of the people's democratically elected
government rather than in the hands of financial elites to whom
the government is debt ridden and beholden. The key to an economically transformed world order and democratically run community in the service of the common good is clear and simple.
Banking must be a public utility in the service of the people and
the community, and property laws must be modified so that people gain full rights to the fruits of their labor and their creative
ingenuity.

However, as for many theorists of sustainability, this fundamental agreement among monetary theorists is marred by a fatal flaw in their thought: many of these theorists remain trapped
within the conceptual straitjacket of the sovereign nation-state.
They have liberated themselves from the concept of a privately
owned monopoly banking system as well as the property laws
supporting this system and have shown the path toward a real
salvation for humanity from poverty, misery, disease, war, and
ecosystem destruction. However, they fail to realize that there can
be no such salvation under the planetary war system of sovereign
nations each operating its own central bank on its own behalf.
Cook (2008), for example, writes:

- Monetary systems should be controlled by sovereign national governments, not the central banks which mainly
  serve private finance. The main economic function of the
  monetary system should be to assure adequate purchasing
  power to consume an environmentally sustainable and op-

timal level of production whereby the basic needs of every person in the world community are satisfactorily met.

- Income security, including a basic income guarantee and a national dividend, should be a primary responsibility of national governments in the economic sphere. A right to adequate purchasing power should be part of every national constitution. (www.richardccook.com/articles/)

Cook's excellent and sound monetary principles are undercut by his naïve assumption that each "sovereign" government of the 193 or so worldwide must have its locally controlled socially owned monetary system. His motivations are clearly in the right place, since socially owned monetary systems will create "an optimum level of production whereby the basic needs of every person in the world community are satisfactorily met." Yet one cannot liberate human beings through sound economic principles coupled with flawed political principles. We have seen the many ways in which the system of sovereign nation-states has devastated democracy, human rights, and peace for more than four centuries, existing, as they do, in a system that is intrinsically a war system.

Exceptions among these monetary thinkers are Ellen Hodgson Brown and J.W. Smith, both of whom acknowledge the need for a global monetary system under some form of an Earth Federation of nations, even though they both see this in the future and do not recognize its immediate necessity and viability. With regard to solutions to the world's financial mess, Brown writes:

> That sort of model has been proposed by an organization called the World Constitution and Parliament Association, which postulates an Earth Federation working for equal prosperity and well-being for all the Earth's citizens. The global funding body would be authorized not only to advance credit to nations but to issue money directly, on the model of Lincoln's Greenbacks and the IMF's SDRs [special drawing rights]. These funds would then be disbursed as

needed for the Common Wealth of Earth. Some such radical
overhaul might be possible in the future; but in the mean-
time, global trade is conducted in many competing currencies, which are vulnerable to speculative attack by pirates
prowling in a sea of floating exchange rates. The risk needs
to be eliminated. But how? (2007: 440)

Brown ignores the fact that the Earth Federation Movement
has *already* designed a universal currency to replace the "many
competing currencies" in their "sea of floating exchange rates."
She ignores the fact that the founding of the Earth Community is
not a "radical overhaul" of the present broken system (which cannot be repaired because it is based on false premises). Rather, the
establishment of the Earth community actualizes the very heart of
our civilizational project. Its founding on universal principles is
the only possible way out of today's mess. Smith puts the matter as
follows:

> The once powerless are getting stronger and they recog-
> nize that the imperial centers are getting weaker. Their
> many alliances and federations are forming a power that
> will be difficult to challenge and they can serve notice to
> the historic imperial nations that the UN be restructured
> into a democratic and moral forum or they will form their
> own world governing body, effectively a federation of 80%
> of the world.... World federalist organizations have been
> working to have a constitution ready for that momentous
> day. The World Constitution and Parliament Association
> (WCPA), as do others, has one ready for revision and ac-
> ceptance by just such an alliance of nations.... With a
> name picked and a constitution for that governing body
> in place, the first order of business should be on how best
> to move forward on world development and alleviation of
> both poverty and global warming. (2009: 155-156)

Smith sees that the immediate solution requires global transformation through a "world governing body," although he fails to
recognize how unlikely it is that the flawed premises of the UN
system can be "restructured" into such a body. We have seen the

fundamental ways in which the UN is based on self-contradictory premises. Unless its Charter is replaced with a genuine non-contradictory Constitution instituting planetary public order, efforts for "reform" will be self-defeating and inadequate.

While Brown and Smith appear to be far ahead of Hudson, Zarlenga, and Cook in their recognition that a solution to the world's immense economic inequality and instability will ultimately require an Earth Federation, neither of them sees clearly that a solution to today's economic nightmare is *effectively impossible without a real democratic world governing body under the Earth Constitution* having genuine legal authority to operate the monetary and banking systems, reform property laws, alleviate poverty, end war and militarism forever, and deal with climate collapse, creating a sustainable planetary civilization. These economists are not yet thinking in terms of the holism of our human situation.

We have seen above some of the ways that the relationship between economics and law are *interconnected and interdependent* within the modern world system. They cannot be solved piecemeal by changes within some of the 193 sovereign nations. Humanity is a whole and the ecosystem is a whole. An effective, holistic Earth Federation is a *necessary condition* for a sustainable and pacific world order. Its holism will include a market socialism in which human beings will achieve a rough and workable economic equality that does not fundamentally impair their right to buy and sell. Holism requires a reasonable economic equality that does not destroy their political equality and civil liberties as does capitalism. I choose to call this social democracy or *democratic socialism*. Boswell and Chase-Dunn articulate the connection between global democracy and socialism:

> Global democracy is the equivalent of social democracy at the world level. It is both the first step and the primary goal of world socialism. All other benefits for working people, from environmental protection to banning child labor, flow from their ability to contest the standards and rule of the

world order. Most important is the development of a true people's World Bank that would direct investment and adjust interest rates in order to support environmentally safe production for human needs and work to balance development worldwide. (2000: 12)

Both democracy and socialism derive from a holistic understanding of truth and reality. Mahatma Gandhi also affirmed these truths. We will see further in the chapters below that the coherent whole of our world, including its immanent and transcendent dimensions, are beginning to be grasped by our reason, intuition, and love. Gandhi called this process *Satyagraha* (clinging to Truth): "This I do say, fearlessly and firmly, that every worthy object can be achieved by the use of *Satyagraha*. It is the highest and infallible means, the greatest force. Socialism will not be reached by any other means. *Satyagraha* can rid society of all evils, political, economic, and moral" (1998: 130). "Realism" should best be defined as "clinging to the truth of the whole." This means at the very least, as Gandhi recognized, that every human being has the right to a social framework respecting his or her dignity, human rights and responsibilities, and freedom to flourish.

Social democracy simply means recognition that human freedom and successful flourishing are inseparable from the rule of democratic law predicated on the common good of the whole of society, and both of these, it should now be clear, are inseparable from the whole of humanity. Democratic socialism is, therefore, the realization that there can be no universal human flourishing or freedom without reasonable economic equality, and without the essential foundations of the common good (such as banking) being publicly owned, in other words, through economic holism. Market freedom must be defined by law in such a way that everyone benefits, so that extreme poverty is eliminated along with extreme concentrations of wealth, for both of these destroy democracy and freedom. Let us examine what social democracy looks like in terms of the *Constitution for the Federation of Earth*.

6.2   The World Financial Administration and Sustainable Economics

UNDER the *Earth Constitution*, the World Financial Administration is established in Article 8.7 with the directive to create a Planetary Accounting Office that makes cost/benefit studies and reports on the functioning of all government agencies including their "human, social, environmental, indirect, long-term and other costs and benefits." It is also directed to create a Planetary Banking System and make the transition to a common global currency, valued the same everywhere. Such a stable and reliable currency will be fundamental to both human prosperity and the ability to create a sustainable civilization. Bernard Lietaer, a European central banker who helped design the single European currency (the Euro), in his book *The Future of Money*, writes:

> Your money's value is determined by a global casino of unprecedented proportions: $2 trillion are traded per day in foreign exchange markets, *100 times more than the trading volume of all stocks in the world combined.* Only 2% of these foreign exchange transactions relate to the "real" economy reflecting movements of real goods and services in the world, and 98% are purely speculative. This global casino is triggering the foreign exchange crisis which shook Mexico in 1994-5, Asia in 1997 and Russia in 1998. (In Brown, 2007: 213)

Sustainability means, we have seen, a world community with the sense that we are all in this together and must work together to preserve and restore our planetary home. A system in which the well-being of people and their ability to operate sustainably is subject to the casino conditions of global financial speculations cannot be allowed to continue. Such a necessary step as the creation of planetary public banking with a single stable Earth currency is clearly a near impossibility for the system of militarized sovereign nation-states, with some of them relying for their wealth on the huge banks located within their domains, and for the UN, which is largely subject to this present system.

Article 8 of the *Earth Constitution*, sections 7.1.6 and 7.1.7, establishes the new economic model that will be absolutely essential for a sustainable civilization:

> 8.7.1.6: Pursuant to specific legislation enacted by the World Parliament, and in conjunction with the Planetary Banking System, to establish and implement the procedures of a Planetary Monetary and Credit System based upon useful productive capacity and performance, both in goods and services. Such a monetary and credit system shall be designed for use within the Planetary Banking System for the financing of the activities and projects of the World Government, and for all other financial purposes approved by the World Parliament, without requiring the payment of interest on bonds, investments or other claims of financial ownership or debt. 8.7.1.7: To establish criteria for the extension of financial credit based upon such considerations as people available to work, usefulness, cost/benefit accounting, human and social values, environmental health and aesthetics, minimizing disparities, integrity, competent management, appropriate technology, potential production and performance.

First, these articles establish for the Earth Federation the authority that all governments have—the power to create money. However, in the case of most governments and the present world monetary system, this power has been co-opted by private banking cartels to make most governments and people think that they can only create money as debt, by going ever-deeper into debt, as is the case with the 17.5 trillion dollar national debt owned by the people of the United States to the consortium of private banks known as the Federal Reserve. Under the Earth Federation government, there will be no shortage of money to create jobs to hire people for restoring the environment, nor to pay for planetary conversion to sustainable energies and technologies. For the money is to be created "debt-free." Bernard Lietaer, by contrast, describes our present system:

> Greed and competition are not the result of immutable human temperament. . . . Greed and fear of scarcity are in fact being continuously created and amplified as a direct result of the kind of money we are using. . . . We can produce more than enough food to feed everybody, and there is definitely enough work for everybody in the world, but there is clearly not enough money to pay for it all. The scarcity is in our national currencies. In fact, the job of central banks is to create and maintain that currency scarcity. The direct consequence is that we have to fight with one another in order to survive. (In Brown, 2007:31)

Global public banking will end this "system of scarcity" and put people and their needs before private profit by establishing planetary public, debt-free banking. The second major reform is found in section 8.7.1.7 quoted above: The purpose of the planetary banking system will not be to make money for the rich but to empower people to create businesses, jobs, social projects, and innovations that eliminate poverty, establish peace and harmony, and actualize sustainability. To this end, credit will no longer be available, as today, only to those with prior assets that serve as collateral. Credit will now be available based on "people available to work, usefulness, cost/benefit accounting, human and social values, environmental health and aesthetics, minimizing disparities, integrity, competent management, appropriate technology, potential production and performance." Every responsible adult or organization will have access to credit to be paid back at low or no interest rates, since the purpose of the credit is a sustainable and prosperous planetary community not the private wealth and power of a few.

Our global monetary system today is 99% composed of privately created debt-money (Brown, 2007). Because of this, we live in a world of global scarcity and desperation requiring, as we have seen, massive military training for counter-insurgency warfare and massive military interventions by imperial nations designed to protect and promote the present world domination by a tiny corporate and financial elite. The *Earth Constitution* is explicit that money must be created by the Federation as *debt-free money* addressed to the common good and planetary prosperity.

This debt-free, interest-free money is used to promote the prosperity, free trade, and well-being of the people of Earth while protecting the planetary environment. Individuals, corporations, state and local governments may all take advantage of very low cost development loans and lines of credit that are not premised on exploitation of the debtors in the service of private profit. In addition, primary created (debt-free) money will be judiciously spent directly for global infrastructure needs by the World Parliament. Money and banking can now be used in the service of the common good of the people of Earth and in protection of the "ecological fabric of life" on our planet. The rich can no longer exploit the poor through a system of World Bank and International Monetary Fund loans and debt that has so far created such misery for the peoples and nations of Earth.

The Earth Federation will coordinate the international actions of demilitarized nation-states through world laws legislated by the World Parliament. Under the *Earth Constitution*, conflicts are settled through the World Court system and violators are subject to arrest and prosecution by the World Attorneys General and the World Police. Similarly, transnational corporations are regulated through the democratic legislation of the World Parliament. Corporate expertise and organizational infrastructures can now be used to promote universal prosperity while protecting the environment.

Three features of the corrupt oligarchy that now dominate the world economy are eliminated from the start. *First,* military Keynesianism (or militarism used to artificially pump up the economies of nations) is eliminated, since under Articles 2 and 17 all militaries worldwide become illegal. *Second,* legal corporate personhood is abolished, something which has turned the once beneficial corporations of the world into monstrous, immortal super-humans, who use their billions of dollars and super-human legal rights to dominate the economy of our planet. *Third,* the *Constitution* also removes the ability of these corporate entities to influence politics, judges, and government officials through massive campaign contributions or other forms of monetary influence.

Hence, the key steps necessary to founding a truly democratic and prosperous world order take place with the ratification of the *Earth Constitution*: the hold of the militarized oligarchies now dominating the planet is broken along with the hold of the banking, corporate, and massive financial oligarchies, and the monetary system of the world is placed in the service of the people of Earth. The founding of world social democracy under the *Earth Constitution* accomplishes all this from the very beginning.

In the face of the ever-worsening planetary crises that threaten the future of human civilization on Earth, our best option is to ratify the *Earth Constitution*. The many valuable agencies of the UN will be integrated into the Earth Federation government, and empowered with adequate funding and staff to really do their jobs. At present these agencies are seriously compromised by the world-system within which they are attempting to function. The *Earth Constitution*, therefore, will only substitute for the UN Charter, not the UN in its entirety.

The Charter, as is well known, is undemocratic and unworkable, and structurally denies the holism of the Earth and humanity, even though certain other UN documents, such as the Universal Declaration of Human Rights, affirm this holism. We have seen that Article 28 of the UN Universal Declaration declares that "everyone is entitled to a social and international order in which the rights and freedoms set forth in this Declaration can be fully realized." The *Earth Constitution* is the living blueprint for that social and international order.

Under the *Earth Constitution*, there is a place for everyone and every nonviolent organization. NGOs, UN agencies, global citizens, nation-states, religions, cultures, and the diverse races of

Earth will all be empowered through its fundamental principle of holism. The people of Earth will soon begin thinking holistically, and the economic and social institutions of Earth will immediately begin to gravitate toward creative holism. The future requires a deep existential and scientific recognition of our wholeness, of the oneness of humanity, our Earth, and its biosphere. Both the ethics and politics of holism demand this fundamental paradigm-shift. Our best hope for actualizing this future is ratification of the *Constitution for the Federation of Earth*. The *Earth Constitution* serves as a living embodiment of these transformed practical possibilities that are the real source of hope for the people of Earth.

But what about the question of power, of a centralized power over all the nations and people of Earth? Is this going to lead to the same kind of corrupt oligarchy that now dominates our planet? Instead of an economic oligarchy, could a bureaucratic oligarchy or a planetary police state emerge? Such questions, which are frequently raised, fail to understand the paradigm-shift to genuine holism under the *Earth Constitution*. The *meaning of power itself is transformed* and the danger of totalitarianism becomes almost nil. In order to show that this is the case, we need to examine in some detail this issue of power in relation to the *Earth Constitution*.

Chapter 7

The Question of Power in Relation to Global Government: Is There a Threat of Global Tyranny?

All the greatest and most important problems of life are funda-mentally insoluble.... They can never be solved but only out-grown. This "outgrowing" proved on further investigation to re-quire a new level of consciousness. Some higher or wider interest appeared on the patient's horizon, and through this broadening of his or her outlook the insoluble problem lost its urgency. It was not solved logically in its own terms but faded when confronted with a new and stronger life urge.

—*Carl Gustave Jung*

WHAT are the pros and cons of the attempt to create demo-cratic world government under the *Constitution for the Fed-eration of Earth*? Some say it will save us from nuclear holocaust, ultimate climate collapse, and other such planetary disasters. Others claim it will open up the possibility of global totalitarianism. With the continuous technological revolutions in military and surveillance capability that have continued unabated since the Second World War, all these fears (of nuclear holocaust, ultimate climate collapse, and global totalitarianism) should be taken very seriously.

The first includes an understanding that the possibility of a major holocaust that has not significantly abated since the end of the Cold War. The second understands that human activity is destroying the planetary ecology on which we are dependent for our survival, and the third understands that totalitarianism, today, is a technological and military possibility exceeding anything previously dreamed of in human history. Such global domination might signal the end of human political freedom, perhaps forever.

The first and second concerns provide a fundamental argument for federal world government, the first articulated, for example, in Albert Camus' 1946 essay "Neither Victims nor Executioners," which called for a "world parliament" with authority over all the nations. The second has become a powerful force through the ecology movement that has largely developed since Rachel Carson's 1962 book, *Silent Spring*. The third concern, however, raises doubts in people's minds about the wisdom of placing governmental power in the hands of a single governing body for the entire planet. This chapter explains why these reservations concerning the danger of world government under the *Earth Constitution* are largely misguided.

Such doubts arise from the same outdated paradigm that gives rise to the possibility of totalitarianism in the first place. They involve a conception of "power" as "power-over" derived from the fragmented system of sovereign nation-states integrated with unrestrained global capitalism. This chapter attempts to draw on the new, holistic paradigm that this book seeks to articulate to show that this latter paradigm is behind the *Constitution for the Federation of Earth*. The new paradigm that informs the *Earth Constitution* substantially transforms our understanding of governmental "power." The "power" integral to the Earth Federation government will be qualitatively different from totalitarian or dictatorial power that we fear today. "Power" within a holistic paradigm is fundamentally different from "power" within the fragmented, early-modern paradigm.

We have examined the central paradigm of the modern period since the Renaissance that involved a fragmented conception of "power-over," what Moltmann calls "the boundless will for domination" (2012:67), manifested clearly in a system of sovereign nation-states characterized by multiple wars, dictatorships, and colonial empires of domination and exploitation. The new holistic paradigm embodied in the *Earth Constitution*, on the other hand, manifests a new paradigm of "power" best associated with holistic health and vitality. It manifests the holism that has been a fundamental discovery of science since Einstein. The old "atomistic" paradigm of modernity has been superseded during the 20th century by this new paradigm that demands a reevaluation of our conception of power in relation to properly constructed governmental authority.

Since the perpetual military revolution symbolized by the development of nuclear weapons during the Second World War, thoughtful people around the world have been deeply concerned about the possible fate of our Earth. We continue to live with the obvious possibility of a major war using chemical, biological, geodynamic, or nuclear weapons of mass destruction so devastating as to wipe out the human race or at least destroy the planetary environment to the extent that the human race is thrown back into a primitive and brutal Hobbesian struggle for existence in a poisoned world of mutants, unstoppable diseases, and global wreckage. Hollywood movies have exploited this scenario relentlessly for decades. The popularity of this dystopian genre indicates the credibility of these fears in people's minds.

Some scholars have also assessed the destructive possibilities of major nuclear war in empirical and objectively scientific terms. In 1966, for example, Errol E. Harris, published a study of the effects of "thermonuclear war" as part of his book *Annihilation and Utopia*. The study provides substantial scientific data concerning the effects of nuclear war, including the immense initial destruction, the radiation effects, long range effects on survivors, planetary shock, collapse of medical facilities, the devastating ecological effects, destruction of food sources, epidemics, and worldwide cultural disintegration.

Harris concludes this section of his book by quoting another scholar who asserts that "a nuclear disaster would be far worse, in both intensity and duration of suffering, than any previously recorded event in human history." Harris states: "For today men have in their possession weapons of such devastating destructive power that their full-scale use would, without doubt, completely destroy organized social life on earth, any standard worth the name of civilization. It would completely obliterate the human race (if not immediately, within a measurable period of the nuclear conflagration), and might even make the planet uninhabitable by any developed form of life" (1966: 11).

7.1   Conditions Fostering the Rise of Totalitarianism

THE funeral speech of Pericles, as written by Thucydides in the 5th century BCE, initiated a tradition of reflection on the best social arrangements and modes of governing that has continued down to the present. The speech raises the image of a meaningful and fulfilled human life involved not only with its private occupations but outwardly engaged with others in public participation in governing, and in making the decisions that affect everyone. This image of a free and meaningful life in relation to citizen participation in the community has become, over the centuries, an ideal that lives in the background of this on-going dialogue about the relation of persons to government and the role of citizens in governing.

Many people fear being subjected to the arbitrary will of another, and many long for freedom to determine their lives in satisfying and meaningful ways. Within society, criminal behavior will often subject individuals or groups to the arbitrary will of others (fraud, coercion, theft, intimidation, assault, blackmail, extortion, rape, murder, etc.), a phenomenon that usually requires government—the legitimate use of force under the rule of law—to control or mitigate. However, when the arbitrary will of another is instituted *in the name of* the legitimate use of force and the rule of law, when government itself becomes tyrannical, the situation becomes a totalized criminality even worse than ordinary criminal activity, for there appears to be no recourse other than submission or the attempt at violent revolution—the latter being a horrific and devastating affair when attempted against modern governments with their technologically sophisticated police and military powers.

Thinkers have studied the history of democratic thought and the history of totalitarianism in the attempt to reveal the salient conditions under which each arises and flourishes. Like all human social phenomena, there are causes and conditions for each that can be studied, articulated, and appropriated by future generations as they participate in the on-going effort to actualize the best social arrangements for human flourishing and dignity. The debate continues into our own day and is far from concluded, although we possess a wealth of insight accumulated from experience and past generations that was not available to them.

Thomas Hobbes famously argued in his *Leviathan* that, because human beings were basically selfish, competitive and egoistic creatures, when they exist in a "state of nature" (without government), their situation is that of a "war of all against all" in which life is "solitary, nasty, brutish and short." In relation to this imagined background, Hobbes argued that leaving this condition of the war of all against all required the creation of authoritarian government, a government against which citizens had no recourse and no rights except the right to preserve their

lives. Peace, for Hobbes, requires government, and the government must be authoritarian because of these characteristics in human nature. Yet subsequent thinkers have recognized that the
problem of peace runs deeper than governmental control of a supposedly greedy and selfish human nature.

Hannah Arendt's book *Eichmann in Jerusalem* goes beyond
simple description of the trial of Eichmann to a substantially detailed account of the totalitarian Nazi regime during the 12 years
of its existence (1933-1945). The experience of this trial, which she
attended, and her previous study of the Nazi regime that had been
undertaken for her monumental book, *The Origins of Totalitarianism*, provided the background for her assessment of Eichmann.
How to understand the Nazi phenomenon remains, of course,
controversial, and Arendt's assessment has been criticized from
a number of directions as documented, for example, by Richard
Wolin (2001).

Yet there is a very real element of truth in her account of the
ease with which ordinary people are co-opted and coerced by *institutional systems* that produce radically evil consequences. The
subtitle of this book on Eichmann, *A Report on the Banality of Evil*,
indicates one component in the origins of totalitarianism: human
personalities conditioned to conform to their social context and,
to an alarming extent, apparently incapable of forming an independent judgment or autonomous conscience that allows them to
discern and resist a developing totalitarian social context and its
inevitable crimes against the humanity of its citizens.

In Chapter Two we briefly discussed the Nazi legal theorist,
Carl Schmitt, who used what he claimed was the inherent ambiguity in the interpretation of law to argue for a "decisionistic" (totalitarian) form of government. We also saw some of the problems
inherent in capitalism as a form of class society in which the law
is tailored to the needs of the ruling class. Inherent in any class
society is a possible *telos* for totalitarianism. Schmitt, who emphasized the "decisionist" theory of law also spoke of the "state
of emergency" in which there is a transformation from the inher-

ent (concealed) power of the capitalist constitutional state to the actuality and "realism" of fascism. As Bloch describes this, for Schmitt:

> The "state of emergency" is always something other than anarchy and chaos; it always consists in a juridical order even if not a legal order. The existence of the state is confirmed by its undeniable superiority to the validity and value of the legal norm (*Political Theology,*1922, p. 13). Consequently both sovereignty and the politician are conserved; and even more, dictatorship disengages itself for the first time from the concealed dictatorship of the bourgeois constitutional state. (1986: 150)

Inherent in capitalism, as in any form of class society, is a "concealed dictatorship." As monopolization occurs and free market competition declines (inevitable under capitalism) philosophies of law arise, such as that of Schmitt, to justify the end of the pretense of democracy ("formal democracy") and the initiation of totalitarianism. Theoretical decisionism and state of emergency were key concepts necessary for the rise of totalitarian fascism in the case of Nazi Germany. In any class situation, the ruling class will use language and conceptual manipulation to further its power and open up the prospect of totalitarianism. Such factors must be kept in mind as we examine the question of the danger of totalitarianism under the *Earth Constitution.*

In Chapter One we also saw P.A. Sorokin, Karl Jaspers, Jacques Ellul, and Max Weber critically evaluate modern society (under the bourgeois Western democracies) in related contexts that found these societies functioning, in a multiplicity of ways, to diminish human freedom and the capacity for meaningful, fulfilled life. Ellul sees the threat of totalitarianism arising from the domination of technique, from an instrumentalization process in which intrinsic values are evacuated from human life and the organization of society focuses on technique for its own sake, assuming that all perception of intrinsic value and meaning in human life is merely subjective.

He links the development of totalitarian societies in the Stalinist Soviet Union and Nazi Germany with this domination of technique, and he sees a potential for the same slide into tyranny in the United States. Ellul's analysis does not necessarily disagree with the class-analysis perspective on the rise of totalitarianism put forward by Ernst Bloch and Karl Marx, but may well complement it. Capitalism and the class-based sovereign nation-state, we have seen, are indissolubly connected within the early-modern paradigm.

In Chapter Five we examined some of the essays in the book *War After September 11* in order to clarify this slide toward tyranny in relation to the US and examine ways in which it can be averted and transcended. We looked at David Luban's essay on the concept of "enemy combatant" used by the George W. Bush and Obama administrations in the US to create a "hybrid war-law" concept that allows the government and military to trash the rule of international and domestic laws in favor of a totalitarian (lawless) attitude toward possible internal and external enemies. In his 2007 book *Legal Ethics and Human Dignity* Luban similarly analyzes the "torture memos" created by lawyers for the Bush administration in which language and legal concepts were manipulated to legalize the torture of those captured under the label of "enemy combatant."

Concepts are manipulated to justify the assumption of ever-more absolute power: Torture is now called "enhanced interrogation," any struggle for liberation against oppression is now called "terrorism," a government department is created for "homeland security," a phrase reminiscent of Nazi Germany. At the same time statistics from multiple sources show the ever-greater concentration of wealth among the top 10 percent within the US and especially among the top one percent. As with Schmitt in relation to the rise of fascism in Germany, ideas appear, and language is manipulated, in ways that justify a "state of emergency" and the distortion of the traditional rule of law.

In previous chapters we also examined some basic features of the early-modern paradigm and its institutional progeny: the global capitalist system and the system of sovereign nation-states. The assumed separation of fact from value, the rapid rationalization of society to accommodate the growing power of both these institutions, and the growing power of instrumental thinking and technique concomitant with scientific progress in controlling nature all combined to create a civilization that substantially repudiated intrinsic values and replaced them with what Heidegger (1977) termed "the autonomous will and its desires" facing a world conceived of as "standing reserve."

Clearly, a totalitarian perspective is inherent in such a world: Power and domination are thought to be the "facts" of our human situation, and compassion, kindness, and morality are thought to be "merely subjective." We saw that positivism and so-called political "realism" are products of this paradigm, all the way from Machiavelli through Morgenthau to Bush and Obama. Nations and corporations pay lip service to universal human rights but act on the principles of a "realism" that entirely ignores these rights.

Chapter Four elaborated the conditions of human flourishing and thereby the conditions of legitimate, morally justifiable government. The only legitimate government is that in the service of human flourishing, providing the economic, infrastructure, social, and political conditions for people to live good lives. Non-democratic or non-republican governments of all forms (oligarchy, monarchy, dictatorship, etc.)   violate the fundamental moral and social imperative constituting legitimate government.

As human beings convert to creative holism through planetary government under the *Earth Constitution*, the basic conditions of good government will be established and protected. "Power" will be understood in entirely new ways. As Harris remarks: "The only consistent moral relationship between a truly good moral ruler and his subjects is that of friendship and service. The power of such a ruler cannot be physical force but can only be moral power, the power of inspiration and love" (1958: 148).

Harris also affirms my point, discussed in Chapters Two and Five, that power politics, and with it the danger of one power becoming tyrannous over the entire world, disappears under a world federal government that converts the world to a "community of communities" with a common interest and common welfare (in preventing nuclear holocaust, promoting human flourishing, etc.). Under an earth federation this "is not only possible but inevitable." A "community of Sovereigns," on the other hand, is impossible (1950: 173-74), whereas the tyranny of one Sovereign over others is clearly possible due to the imperialism and the quest for empire inherent in the early-modern world system. Let us examine, therefore, the conditions that foster totalitarian government and contrast these with the holism embodied in the *Earth Constitution*.

Reves affirms that the original democratic idea of sovereignty was the sovereignty of the community. The community meant the totality of people who established government to ensure freedom and their common good. "Our present system of national sovereignty," he writes, "is in absolute contradiction to the original democratic conception of sovereignty, which meant—and still means—sovereignty of the community" (1945: 135). For Reves, as for Baker and Dewey cited above, real freedom is only possible at the level of democratic world government, since nation-state capitalism, socialist dictatorships, and fascist governments are all inevitable by-products of the false "sovereignty" of nation-states (ibid. 100-102). Under a world government:

> Sovereignty would continue to reside in the people in accordance with the original conception of democracy, but institutions would be created to give realistic and effective expression to the democratic sovereignty of the people in place of the inefficient and tyrannical institutions of the nation-states. (Ibid. 143)

The world community, as the totality of the people who live on Earth, is the proper locus for the highest sovereign authority. To fragment that community into warring incommensurable territories, is to invite totalitarianism. It is to ensure "class domination" of one form or another because the military readiness in a world of secretive, dangerous adversaries requires a secretive militarized government to run each state.

From these reflections the first, and perhaps most fundamental, thing we can conclude is that several important factors (causes and conditions) are involved in the rise of totalitarian government. Fascism, dictatorship, Stalinist absolutism, or the fanatical social engineering of a Pol Pot, do not just come about by accident. By making ourselves aware of these causes and conditions we can also learn how to establish societies that protect against these dangers. We can build institutions that systematically and carefully avoid the factors that could lead away from peace, justice, democracy, and freedom and toward their destruction.

I have identified here nine factors that can be understood as fundamental to the rise of totalitarianism, with the proviso that any list and any analysis can be framed differently and that this list does not aspire to be exhaustive. Entire volumes can be, and have been, written on these or similar factors. Our purpose here is to examine the danger of totalitarianism in relation to establishing the *Earth Constitution*.

1. The paradigm. A paradigm is defined by the largely unspoken assumptions behind a culture or civilization. In the case of the early-modern paradigm, the possibility of the totalitarian state, we have seen, is clearly inherent. When human morality is effectively discounted as merely subjective, and "objective" fact and the realism of an "external world" are divided from mere subjective emotions and sentimentality, and, when technological rationality in the service of non-rational desires and the human will supersede the idea that reason can discern real objective value and moral principles, then all societies informed by this paradigm will be in danger of succumbing to totalitarianism. The result will be the "political realism" of sovereign nation-states and the economic determinism of exploitative capitalism.

2. System imperatives. We have seen the ways in which the *system* of sovereign nation-states intertwined with the *system* of corporate capitalism have fostered a war system, an exploitation system, and a global domination system throughout the world. System imperatives within these systems tend to foster totalitarianism as well as environmental destruction. The ways things are organized have consequences. Cause and effect here are not an impenetrable mystery. We can study systems and their consequences as we have seen Laszlo (2007) point out. If we change the fundamental and deep structures of this system, it is obvious that different consequences will emerge.

3. Class societies. Any time there is a ruling class with immense power in relation to the rest of society (whether a dictatorship of the proletariat, a ruling religious elite, an aristocracy, or a super-wealthy capitalist class), there will be a tendency for that class to use its power and influence to increase its power and influence. In the modern world, so-called political democracy without a substantial corresponding economic democracy always contains the threat that the "concealed" dictatorship of the ruling class will find excuses to unconceal itself and become totalitarian. In the United States, the 2010 Supreme Court decision referred to as *Citizens United* overturned restrictions on direct corporate involvement in election campaigns and allowed corporations to now spend unlimited amounts of money to influence elections, with devastating results for whatever democratic processes previously existed.

4. Crises. In any class society, domestic and international crises (both social and natural) are normally excuses for increasing executive powers and curtailing freedom. A "state of emergency" elicits the demand that those in power take extraordinary measures to save society. The "revolutionary" emergency of emerging civil war required the extreme measures that brought the Bolsheviks to (unconcealed) dictatorship in 1917. The chaos of hyperinflation and national degradation allowed the German people to respond to Hitler's promises to restore their greatness in

1933. In *The Shock Doctrine: The Rise of Disaster Capitalism*, Naomi Klein shows that totalitarian practices follow capitalism around the world as it uses both natural and human-made crises to circumvent democratic law in its drive to maximize profits. The George W. Bush administration and Congress (representing the US ruling class) responded to "the new Pearl Harbor" of an attack on American soil in September 2001 to radically curtail civil liberties and set up vast systems of spying on the American people.

In *The Origins of Totalitarianism*, Arendt outlines the multiple crises engendered by the First World War, one of which was that hundreds of thousands of stateless persons, refugees, immigrants, etc., had no legal rights as citizens of any nation-state (1958: 280). There were no legal mechanisms adequate to handle this immense social chaos, and the lack of legal rights of these people opened the possibility of denying legal rights to other classes of people. Such universal human rights, she says, should be the source of law independently of class privileges or of nations themselves (290). However, she does not see a way for this to happen, as she appears trapped by the early-modern fact/value separation: "How should one be able to deduce laws and rights from a universe which apparently knows neither the one nor the other category?" (298). Under the *Earth Constitution*, exactly this will be the case: all persons have legally protected rights of citizenship from birth, and such social chaos with such classes of unprotected persons will no longer exist. The principle of holism is itself the ground for universal human rights.

   5. **Threat of enemies internally and abroad.** One mode of crisis is the common claim that there are lethal adversaries who are without restraint in their desire to destroy or harm us. The George Bush administration claimed falsely that Iraq was building a nuclear weapon with the intention of attacking the US. Stalin claimed that global capitalism wanted to crush the burgeoning alternative of Communism. Hitler claimed that the nations of Europe wanted to forever humiliate Germany and its need for "liv-

ing space," that Hungary was "like a knife pointed at the heart of Germany," and that "opponents" of the German spirit were guilty of "Communism, Sabotage, Liberalism, and Assassinations" and that "sects" (Catholics, Protestants, Freemasons, and Jews) together constituted a social crisis polluting the purity of the German idea and German race (Arendt, 1963: 70).

In the Stalinist era, it was Trotskyites and Bourgeois compromisers who had to be eradicated. In the US, it was the threat of a worldwide Communist conspiracy (emanating from the Soviet Union) that fueled the rise of the national security state, a supposed danger that now has been replaced by a global terrorist threat (emanating from Arab cultures and radical Islam) bent on attacking and destroying the US from everywhere and nowhere. Arendt states that this is one of the basic totalitarian tenants: "that the world is divided into two gigantic hostile camps" (1958: 367). Under the all-inclusive unity in diversity of the *Earth Constitution,* such ideas will appear for what they are: ridiculous. In terms of our common human project, unity without diversity is tyranny. Diversity without unity is war. We need the holism of a global social contract.

6. Secrecy and "language rules." The manipulation of language and law is a common feature in the ascent of totalitarianism. Hannah Arendt points out that the "Oath of Secrecy" became more important in Nazi Germany than the Oath of Loyalty (1963: 84-85). In Nazi Germany, the use of the word for "murder" was avoided and code words were instituted such as "the final solution." "The word for 'murder' was replaced by the phrase 'to grant a mercy death'" (108). The Obama administration in the US now threatens journalists with prosecution if they fail to turn over their sources to the government (which largely operates in secret according to secret criteria of who is a terrorist, etc.), and it prosecutes whistleblowers under the 1917 Espionage Act, treating transparency, investigative journalism, and telling the truth as criminal acts. It continues the Bush administration's special use of language to cover its global policy of assassinations, murder, and attack on others without due process of law.

7. Totalitarian Ideologies and massive propaganda campaigns. Propaganda and illusory ideologies are not unique to totalitarian movements or regimes. Noam Chomsky in *Necessary Illusions: Thought Control in Democratic Societies* (1989) details the pervasive uses of propaganda to promote ideologies protecting the status quo and the system of private wealth, primarily in the US. Totalitarian discourse, however, political theorist Claude LeFort asserts, "before anything else. . .effaces the opposition between the State and civil society" (in Kroker & Kroker, eds., 1991: 71). Totalitarian propaganda, as Arendt points out, seeks to obliterate the impartial rule of law, which is intended, in significant measure, to protect human autonomy and rights, with an ideology of absoluteness in which atomized individuals are directly ruled by the will of the supreme totalitarian center, whether this be Hitler or Stalin (1958: 341-364).

8. The social character of citizens. Chris Hedges, in *War is a Force that Gives Us Meaning* (2002), describes the elation that comes with crisis, danger, lawlessness, and war that fascinates and attracts many human beings like moths to a flame. But along with the few attracted to the flame, there are the vast majority who are simply complicit. Jonathan Glover's *Humanity: A Moral History of the 20th Century* (1999) ponders the amazing complicity of ordinary citizens in every 20th century genocide—from the Armenian Genocide in Turkey after 1915, to Stalin's genocide through starvation in 1932-33, to the Nazi genocide during the 1940s, to Vietnam's genocidal mass murder by US forces in the 1960s and early 70s, to the Pol Pot Cambodian genocide in the 1970s, to genocide in Rwanda during 1994. Arendt reflects on the very ordinary social character of Eichmann (1963: 52-54), on the complicity of the German people, and on the apparent complicity of some Jewish leaders themselves in the systems of organized death during the Nazi period (1963: 117-125).

In his famous 1974 book *Obedience to Authority*, psychologist Stanley Milgram reveals the surprising proclivity of the students in his psychological experiments to obey authority, even to the point of giving potentially lethal shocks to the subject persons in the experiments. Milgram also interviewed many soldiers who had returned from Vietnam, virtually all of them having committed atrocities (such as wanton murder or torture). In a situation of apparent legitimate authority, those obeying the authority appear to routinely transfer responsibility for their actions to those who give the orders, or to the system as a whole with its vague utilitarian goals.

Eichmann spoke of his "duty to obey the law" and of the overwhelming authority of "acts of state" to determine his actions (Arendt, 1963). Milgram writes: "There is fragmentation of the total human act...no one man decides to carry out the evil act and is confronted with its consequences. The person who assumes full responsibility for the act has evaporated. This is the most common characteristic of socially organized evil in society" (1974: 11). Arendt writes: "this total responsibility for everything done by the movement and this identification with every one of its functionaries have the very practical consequence that nobody ever experiences a situation in which he has to be responsible for his own actions and can explain the reasons for them" (1958: 375). Institutions themselves can be organized to systematically produce evil consequences and to influence "good citizens" to obediently participate in producing those consequences.

Erich Fromm agrees. His 1941 study of totalitarianism, *Escape from Freedom*, attempts to show at length the relations between the "social character" of people in a social order and the rise of a totalitarian society. Certain types of "social characters" are much more open to blind obedience to authority, acquiescing to the dictates of government, being swayed by totalitarian propaganda, and mass conformity with popular emotions than are people with a social character that is mature, individualized, democratic, and free.

In today's "dangerous" world requiring immediate military and executive decisions, citizen participation in government is significantly reduced. Secrecy has replaced transparency and citizen questioning, investigation, and debate are considered detriments to the efficient functioning of the national security state. Police and administrators have been given ever-greater authority and the right of citizens to question this authority has been significantly reduced. The tendency to obey authority studied by Milgram and Fromm has only been exacerbated by government emphasis on security and the need to absolutely obey the authorities "for our own safety." The price paid for disobedience, as in Nazi Germany, is raised higher and higher as the regime slides toward totalitarianism.

9. Inadequate checks and balances. In any social system oriented to democracy, human rights, and human dignity, there will be checks and balances built into the constitution or the legal structure of the system to guard against abuses and the rise of totalitarianism. These checks and balances can be more or less effective, more or less deeply institutionalized, and more or less well designed and organized. Also, societies continually need to reexamine their checks and balances in order to update them in the light of new technological developments and new experiential levels of insight into the pitfalls and dangers. In the case of the Bolshevik revolution, these were practically nonexistent to begin with. In the case of the Weimar Republic, these were weak and plagued by the economic crisis, etc. In the case of the US, since the late 1970s the ruling class has systematically worked to promote its "Neoliberal" ideology that advocates removing the environmental, financial, and other restraints on its activities and to neutralize the checks and balances intended by the US Constitution.

In the US, the checks and balances intended to prevent tyranny were placed into the Constitution more than 200 years ago when high speed weapons were non-existent and instant life or death decisions did not need to be made by the Executive Branch. Since the advent of the Cold War, the invention of weapons of mass destruction, and the rise of a vast military industrial complex, the Executive Branch of government has taken on immense powers that have dwarfed the checks and balances that were supposed to be supplied by the legislative and judicial branches. Presidents, the military, and cabinet meetings of high level civilian and military officials in the Executive Branch have taken on a huge, largely clandestine, power significantly independent of the other two branches. In G-8 or G-20 economic summit meetings, the huge corporations and world's largest economies meet in secret to decide the economic rules for the rest of the planet. Checks and balances are practically nonexistent.

All of these nine factors are clearly interrelated and interdependent. They influence one another in the complex and difficult world within which nations and corporations act. They are clearly not all on the same conceptual level. The key factors are clearly at the level of numbers 1, 2, and 3, the levels of paradigms, system imperatives, and class societies. The key to preventing totalitarianism is to transform the fragmented paradigm that makes the drive to domination conceptually possible to a holistic paradigm in which it largely loses its meaning and possibility. Power then becomes health, harmony, cooperation: empowerment of people. Checks and balances must remain stringent. *But what is most fundamental is the transformation of paradigms, systems, and class societies.*The other six factors remain details to be guarded against through carefully designed democratic safeguards.

If we change the systems that follow from the early-modern paradigm: if we eliminate the system of sovereign nation-states and its alliance with the system of global capitalism within the context of a new, holistic paradigm, and if we substitute global economic and political democracy for the "concealed dictatorship" of class societies, the threat of totalitarianism will substantially disappear. If we convert to an economic system that transforms the class-structure of societies, and restrains the ability of the wealthy to influence the political process, we will substantially reduce the threat of totalitarianism. In spite of the special significance of items 1, 2, and 3, however, all nine factors that I have outlined here need to be considered when reflecting on the best social arrangements to establish peace, justice, democracy, and freedom.

In point of fact, all nine factors implicated in the rise of totalitarianism have been dealt with by the *Earth Constitution* and by the paradigm-shift to holism that is behind the *Constitution*.

1. The new paradigm is democratic, egalitarian, and holistic: reuniting fact and value and the recognition of inviolable human dignity, as well as the dignity of natural living things. All of human civilization on Earth will rapidly convert to the new paradigm since it comes from the sciences and is the basis not only of human flourishing but of preserving the ecology of our planet. The Earth Federation government reflects a direct embodiment of this new interdependent and cooperative paradigm.

2. The new paradigm results in new planetary institutions designed very differently from the early-modern institutions that foster war, exploitation, and environmental destruction. Our analysis of the "system imperatives" of capitalism and sovereign nation-states has revealed the totalitarianism implicit in these. By contrast, a holistic world system implies planetary democracy and public order. Moreover, the "federal" system mandated by the *Earth Constitution* will diminish centralized authority and distribute legitimate governmental authority around the world. The authority of national governments will *regain* legitimacy, once they become functioning parts within the whole provided by the *Earth Constitution*.

3. Simple economic changes (reviewed in Chapter Six) will substantially reduce the disparity between rich and poor and the condition of scarcity that exacerbates the greed and lethal competition among and between peoples. Corporations will be regulated by law to serve the common good, not the private profit of the top 10 percent. Class differences will be reduced to the point where the threat of totalitarianism implicit in them is close to nil.

4. The excuse of "crisis" will be vastly reduced in a world which is demilitarized, in which nation-states are administrative, non-military units (like states within the US or Pradesh within India), and in which nuclear weapons have been abolished and dismantled. Under the *Earth Constitution* the world administration has no power to declare a "state of emergency" and suspend the *Constitution.*

5. In a world in which every nation has an effective voice in the World Parliament and its equal rights with all the others effectively protected by the world courts, the World Ombudsmus, and the whole of the Earth Federation government, the threat of "enemies" will be virtually eliminated and will become, in the case of any remaining isolated terrorist groups, not a military, but rather a civilian police matter dealing with criminal behavior.

6. The need for the national security state in a dangerous world will virtually disappear: *Governmental transparency* is required by the *Earth Constitution* and citizen participation encouraged. Government will see no need to manipulate language to hide the true intentions and secret plans of a ruling or security elite. The propagandistic fictions emphasized by both Arendt and Fromm as essential to totalitarianism will find no place to flourish.

7. The capacity for propaganda itself can be associated with societies unclear about the nature and meaning of authentic democracy as well as societies in which there are concentrated class resources that have colonized big media to propagate their authoritarian interests and ideologies. Establishing reasonable economic democracy under the *Earth Constitution*, as well as the global educational practices described below, will radically reduce the danger of such propaganda "taking off." Under the *Constitution*, a diversity of news media, and freedom of research, reporting, and investigating (guaranteed under Article 12) are combined with a

requirement for government transparency that cuts off the possibilities for totalitarian propaganda at their roots. The distinction between civil society, replete with many citizen-watchdogs, and governmental authority (itself protecting citizen autonomy in numerous ways) is rigorously maintained.

8. The emphasis by governments on absolute obedience to authority will be vastly reduced since authorities will no longer have the excuse that there is a crisis (lethal terrorist, Communist, or some other threat) that requires such unquestioning obedience. Due process of law will then protect all citizens on Earth. Education, by law, will encourage confident, articulate, perceptive citizens capable of challenging authority and actively participating in political affairs. The civilian police force will truly be able to "protect and serve" for the first time in history. The World Ombudsmus will encourage independence, truth-telling, and critical evaluation of all aspects of government.

9. A highly sophisticated and carefully designed system of checks and balances have been built into the *Earth Constitution* in the several ways that we will examine below.

7.2   The Earth Constitution and Paradigms of Power

THE Preamble to the *Earth Constitution* provides the conceptual framework for the whole of the document. It gives us the language of a "new world... which promises to usher in an era of peace, prosperity, justice and harmony." Given the bleak and bloody history of humankind to date, how can the framers of the *Earth Constitution* be so confident? The answer is given in the second paragraph of the Preamble: "Aware of the interdependence of people, nations, and all life." This is a declaration of holism that could not be clearer: There is no such thing as autonomous independence from the rest of humanity, from the other nations of the world, or from the natural world.

The next four paragraphs in the Preamble address the consequences of the older fragmented paradigm: we are at the "brink of ecological and social catastrophe"; we are aware of the "total illusion" of "security through military defense"; we are aware of the terrible consequences of the global economic system that causes "ever increasing disparity between rich and poor"; and we are aware that we need to save humanity "from imminent and total annihilation." All these are caused by the older, dysfunctional world system of autonomous sovereign nation-states and a flawed, class-controlled economic system operating in coordination with this nation-state system. The seventh paragraph of the Preamble again returns to the new paradigm announced in paragraph two:

> "Conscious that Humanity is One despite the existence of diverse nations, races, creeds, ideologies and cultures and that the principle of unity-in-diversity is the basis for a new age when war shall be outlawed and peace prevail; when the Earth's total resources shall be equitably used for human welfare; and when basic human rights and responsibilities shall be shared by all without discrimination."

The statement of holism from paragraph two is here spelled out in greater detail. The "diverse nations, races, creeds, ideologies and cultures" of the world means that we are no longer faced with incommensurable fragmentation, war, and conflict. Human beings are united within this *Constitution* under a "principle of unity-in-diversity" that is the basis for this "new age" of peace, justice, protection of rights, and assumption of mutual universal responsibilities by the people of Earth. The new concept of "power" in the Preamble to the *Constitution* and everything that follows must be understood in terms of this fundamental paradigm-shift from fragmentation to holism.

The *Earth Constitution* is permeated with the concepts of holism, sustainability, interdependence, and unity-in-diversity.

The document emerges from the new holistic paradigm and therefore, once actualized as an Earth Federation Government, it will operate in a manner qualitatively different from traditional governments with their top-down, class based, structures. The *Constitution* makes clear that it operates through networks of relationships: the people of Earth with direct input into the World Parliament, itself based on unity-in-diversity, and the several agencies of the "Integrative Complex" operating within a cooperative and integrated system. Here we have the collective social mind for Earth described by contemporary science. We have the "global brain" awakening, described by Peter Russell, or the "deep heartfelt impulse to connect with others and co-create a world equal to our love and our capacities," described by Barbara Marx Hubbard. Fritjof Capra describes this new pattern of thinking:

> Understanding ecological interdependence means understanding relationships. It requires the shifts of perception that are characteristic of systems thinking—from the parts to the whole, from objects to relationships, from contents to patterns. A sustainable human community is aware of the multiple relationships among its members. Nourishing the community means nourishing those relationships. (1996: 298)

Study of the *Earth Constitution* reveals that the Earth Federation System set up by the *Constitution* is premised on this understanding of the *primacy of relationships* and the ecological understanding of sustainability as a healthy condition of the whole (of humanity in relation to one another and the biosphere). Under this new paradigm, totalitarianism will largely become a non-issue, for the holism of a now organized democratic global brain and global consciousness for Earth will operate on a *qualitatively* different level from the fragmentation of the early-modern paradigm where the threat of totalitarianism and arbitrary power were very real issues.

The *Constitution for the Federation of Earth* gives a number of substantial planetary powers to the Earth Federation government, many of which are detailed as "specific powers" in Article 4. This is done within the context of Article 1 that specifies the "broad functions" of the Earth Federation government: Its functions are to address those issues of governing that fall beyond the scope of nation-states. As Article 2.3 also reads:

> The authority and powers granted to the world government shall be limited to those defined in this Constitution for the Federation of Earth, applicable to problems and affairs which transcend national boundaries, leaving to national governments jurisdiction over the internal affairs of respective nations but consistent with the authority of the World Government to protect universal human rights as defined in this World Constitution.

The *Earth Constitution* wants to make clear that the "powers" of world government are not indiscriminate and are limited in their scope to what transcends national boundaries, as well as being subject to numerous checks and balances. In spite of the fact that the Earth Federation will be operating on a qualitatively different holistic principle, multiple checks and balances are built into the system. These checks and balances can be seen as clearly preventing abuse of power by any persons or agencies of the Earth Federation government. But they can also be understood as arising from an *integrated governing system,* outlined by the *Constitution,* that will *have no need* to place extraordinary powers in the hands of the Executive Branch, for example, and no need to place extraordinary powers in the hands of the World Police or any other agency.

In fact, the *Constitution* separates the World Administration from the World Police. The World Executive does not have police powers, and there is no military at all once the second operative stage has been reached under Article 17. The head of the executive branch is a "Presidium" of five persons, one from each continental division, and all elected by the World Parliament. Term of office for each is five years and can be renewed only once (Art. 6.3). The World Executive may not limit or abridge any provision of the *Earth Constitution*, has no veto power over world legislation, has no power to declare a state of emergency and suspend the rights guaranteed by the *Constitution*, and must faithfully execute the budget allotted to it by the World Parliament (Art. 6.6). In addition, any official violating the *Constitution* may be removed from office by due process vote of the World Parliament.

Regarding the nations as federated parts of the whole, the "self-governing" parts will not be "sovereign" autonomous, militarized atoms as in today's world-anarchy, capable of interfering with and destroying the whole. Hence, the world will also be safe from any one state dominating and colonizing the whole. Our planet is an ecological and geological whole, humanity is a biological and ethical whole, and civilization is an immense holistic tapestry of cultures, languages, and histories. All these wholes are made up of diverse parts integrated into the wholes. The parts will have self-governing integrity (and moral legitimacy) precisely to the extent that they function as parts integrated into the self-governing whole of humanity.

The *Earth Constitution* distinguishes its "power and authority" from that of national governments. Like human beings within any community that has effective government, the individuals are both parts of the whole (under binding, enforceable laws applicable to everyone) and they are self-governing individuals with rights vis-à-vis the whole ("inalienable" individual freedoms are specified with which government may not interfere). Ultimately the healthy functioning of the whole, however, can improve the lives of all the parts (as we saw above in the concept of "positive freedom"). We shall see further that woven throughout the *Constitution*, and specifically embodied in the "directive principles" of Article 13, is a *telos* directing these powers to perfect the human potential for developing civilization (in the form of peace, justice, prosperity, etc.) while simultaneously dealing with the global crises that are beyond the capacities of nation-states.

The very important Article 14 entitled "Safeguards and Reservations" makes this again clear. It assures "freedom of choice within the member nations and countries of the Federation of Earth to determine their internal political, economic, and social systems consistent with the several provisions of this World Constitution." These provisions of the *Constitution* that respect the internal autonomy and integrity of nations, however, should not be understood in terms of the older paradigm that sees nations as sovereign atoms with only external relations to the rest of the world system.

The many dimensions of authority attributed to the Earth Federation make clear that national freedom can only be understood and empowered as part of the planetary freedom provided by the *Earth Constitution* in relation to the multiplicity of the world's diverse nations and peoples. These disclaimers concerning "safeguards and reservations" give political weight to the idea of a *federation* in which the units are not lacking their share of authority and, as such, have a role in safeguarding the freedom and integrity of both themselves and the entire system. Nevertheless, the units and the system are holistically bound together if there is to be freedom, peace, protection of human rights, sustainability, and prosperity for the people of Earth.

Again, these "safeguards and reservations" do not hearken back to an autonomous national sovereignty assumed to be independent with respect to the whole system. The Earth Federation government will be no weak and impotent UN system premised on "the principle of the sovereign equality of all its Members" (UN Charter, Chap.1.2.1). For "sovereignty" under the *Constitution* lies with "all the people who live upon the Earth" and their representatives in the form of the Earth Federation government (Art. 2.2). This government is "organized as a universal federation, to include all nations and all people, and to encompass all oceans, seas and lands of Earth, inclusive of non-self-governing territories, together with the surrounding atmosphere" (Art. 2.1). The conception of holism could not be more specific. The Earth Federation represents the whole of humanity and the ecology of Earth on which we depend.

This government is delegated substantial "powers" by the *Earth Constitution* to save the ecological integrity of Earth, to create economics that benefit all human beings, to end war and militarism, and to establish peace upon Earth. These substantial powers are not only necessary to address the lethal global crises that we collectively face. They also derive from the fact that the planet has now been conceived as a holistic system in which all societies, nations, and persons are *interdependent*. Such a holism is in itself very powerful. Humanity as a whole is *empowered* as a collective world civilization of unity-in-diversity both transcending the individual powers of the parts and enhancing the power of each part through the healthy functioning of the whole.

7.3 The Question of an "Outside" to the System

WHEN we point out that "sovereignty" under the *Earth Constitution* no longer lies with territorial nation-states but now with the "people of Earth" (Article 2.2), skeptics may respond with something like: "Is this not likely to become a new form of domination and new totalitarianism?" Such skeptics might continue: "Perhaps this *Constitution* now projects all power into a unified governmental force for which there will be no outside force that could put up a fight for freedom and independence."

These questions are based on a misunderstanding of how the concept of sovereignty functioned during the modern era and also a misunderstanding of the nature of the conceptual paradigm-shift embodied in the *Earth Constitution*. In nature, the universe, and human life, there is no longer a physical, space-time "outside" that transcends the series of holisms within which we are embedded and to which we are integral. Even the transcendence of God, as Christian thinker Errol E. Harris points out, can no longer be conceived as another being exterior to the universe, which reduces God to just another being among beings (1993: 91-92).

And the "otherness" posited by Emmanuel Levinas (1969), discovered in the "infinity in the human face," is not such an outside. Levinas insists that the sacred depths of our humanity are not reducible to the "system" of the world studied by science. It is, therefore, not some territory from which we can fight for the freedom of some fragment of humanity. It is, rather, a depth that can more easily shine through society and civilization from within the holistic paradigm (see Chapter Eight).

Or, perhaps better put, the "outside" is now found in our inner human depth-perception and its freedom, a freedom that itself points to the "exteriority" of God and of human beings as truly "Other" in the depths of their being. This form of "exteriority," however, is really an *interiority* of human freedom and spiritual openness to inner transcendence as well as to a non-predetermined future. This lack of an external "outside" does not limit our political and social freedom, for genuine freedom of this kind can and does only emerge from cooperation among human beings. War, national security fears, and fragmented sovereign nation-states destroy freedom at every turn. As we will see in Chapter Eight, Levinas himself recognizes the present system as a "war" system.

Michael Hardt and Antonio Negri argue in their book *Empire* that both the ancient Roman Empire and the American Empire project (from the 18th century to the present) extended the dynamic republican "power of the people" through ever-greater territorial expansions. This territorial expansion included the developing of natural and human resources in the ever-newly acquired territories. In the US empire, therefore, the expansionism of capitalism appeared to synchronize perfectly with the territorial expansion across the continent as well as throughout Latin America and finally the world. While publicly repudiating "colonialism," the US empire has nonetheless established binding hegemony over the "grand areas" connected with the economic interests of its ruling class.

The postmodern "power" of the global empire of hegemonic domination, now administered by the US, is more diffuse and flexible than that of the earlier *colonialism* of modernity, and the postmodern power of the capitalist system is more tolerant of diversity among workers as long as the authority of the managers is obeyed within the regime of maximizing profits for the owners. The empire, still deeply integrated with global capital, now promotes a regime of discipline and power that is flexible and adapted to innumerable local situations around the planet, but the power of the empire remains one of domination, and the modes of production and consumption are still those of exploitation. The world already has a far-flung and internally conflicted system of power and domination, one that is merciless to its two to three billion victims who happen to live in the periphery of empire.

For Hardt and Negri, power, in these instances, becomes a complex mixture of power-over (the authority of the sovereign government over citizens), republican power arising from the dynamic politics of the people, and, finally, the power of ever-increasing scope of wealth and territory being appropriated by the ruling elite of the empire. This power of hegemonic domination and exploitation simultaneously serves the process of capital expansion, which is the goal of the ruling classes of the dominant imperial nations (2000: Chaps. 2.5-2.6). But none of these senses of power (expansion of the hegemony of empire, republican power represented in a territorial fragment, or political domination by an economic elite) will be able to function under the *Constitution for the Federation of Earth*.

7.4 Legitimate Power as the Alternative to Violence

THE people of Earth are sovereign (Article 2), not territorial fragments of Earth. The structure, spirit, and letter of the *Earth Constitution* underwrite the imperative of government to create *universal* peace, justice, and freedom. The mainsprings of

imperialism and class rule are broken: the paradigm fostering
totalitarianism has disappeared; the system supporting this tendency has changed, and the class structure that tends toward totalitarianism has been undermined. The sovereign people of Earth
retain for themselves many specifically enumerated "inalienable
rights" (Articles 12, 13, and 14) and the nations retain their integrity as parts of the whole. The paradigm and related system that empowered imperialism and exploitation are broken and
transformed into one that empowers universal solidarity and (its
complement) personal dignity and autonomy.

The recognition of the sovereignty of the people of Earth is
equivalent to recognizing the Earth as a *community*. A community
has common interests and a common good that bind it together
in a system of social cooperation under that good. A collection of
sovereign nations recognizing no law above themselves and each
operating out of its own national self-interest can never be a community. We have seen that the *Earth Constitution* legally establishes a human community. By superseding national sovereignties and recognizing the people of Earth (and their representatives
in the World Parliament) as sovereign, the *Earth Constitution* is
legally recognizing common interests of humankind (e.g., peace,
security, prosperity, human rights, sustainability) as more fundamental than the interests of individual states. Power becomes
something different. It is no longer the power of conflicting autonomous fragments, but the power of the human community to
represent the common good of humanity.

One of the political thinkers who began to recognize the implications of both democratic theory and the emerging holistic
paradigm discovered by science was Hannah Arendt. She points
out that power itself is not the enemy, for power can and should
be manifest in a many-faceted political process of recognition and
support by the people, resulting in that sense of the legitimacy
and authority of government that constitutes its proper power.
The enemy of legitimate power is *violence*, she declares. Insofar
as any government must resort to violence, it betrays its lack of

legitimate power and its fragility as a recognized authority. She writes:

> Power needs no justification, being inherent in the very existence of political communities; what it does need is legitimacy.... Violence can be justifiable, but it never will be legitimate.... We saw that the current equation of violence with power rests on government's being understood as domination of man over man by means of violence.... To substitute violence for power can bring victory, but the price is very high: for it is not only paid by the vanquished, it is also paid by the victor in terms of his own power.... Power and violence are opposites; where the one rules absolutely, the other is absent. Violence appears where power is in jeopardy, but left to its own course it ends in power's disappearance. This implies that it is not correct to think of the opposite of violence as nonviolence; to speak of nonviolent power is actually redundant. Violence can destroy power; it is utterly incapable of creating it.(1969: 52-55)

Similarly, in *Fallible Man*, Ricoeur understands that the power inherent in all organizational relationships need not be oppressive power associated with violence. Human intelligence, the power of the human imagination, can understand the difference between human power-motivations that are base (or "fallen") and those that are perfectly natural ("innocent") and directed toward our common human good:

> The fact remains that I could not understand power as evil if I could not imagine an innocent destination of power by comparison to which it is fallen. I can conceive of an authority which would propose to educate the individual to freedom, which would be a power without violence; in short, I can imagine the difference between power and violence; the utopia of a Kingdom of God, a City of God, an empire of minds or a kingdom of ends, implies such an imagination of nonviolent power. The imagination liberates the essence; and this essence governs all efforts to transform power into an education to freedom. Through this highly meaningful

goal I "endow" history, in fact, with a meaning. By means
of this imagination I discover power as primordially inherent in the being man.   In turning away from this meaning, in making himself foreign and alienated from this sense
of nonviolent power, man becomes alienated from himself.
(1967: 182-83)

As a holistic thinker, Ricoeur does not separate the feelings
and desires of human beings from their reason, intuition and capacity for imagination, for we cannot formulate a truthful "philosophy of perception prior to a philosophy of discourse." This
"binds one to work them out together, one with the other, one by
the other" (139). We are capable of discerning a primordial intentionality to our feelings and desires that points beyond their historically negative manifestations to a non-fallen human "essence"
that can be understood as the goal of culture and history (1967:
Chap. 4). This conception of an actualized human potentiality
is also present within the *Earth Constitution*; the concrete legal institutions that it constructs are designed to protect this vision of
planetary maturity.

The *Earth Constitution* does assume substantial legitimate
power and authority for the government of the people of Earth.
This precludes neither diversity of cultures nor local governments
within a federated system, but presupposes it, explicitly, for example, in its Preamble. The Earth Federation government will
lack power only if the diverse local governments of Earth are opposed to it, or serve as merely fragments upon which it has been
imposed, or become the victims of violence. This is not the proper
model, however. Under the *Constitution* the whole is presupposed
to be significantly more integrated than a mere "confederation" or
collection of fragments posing as "sovereign nation-states." This
is the difference between the UN system (a confederation of semi-
autonomous parts, and therefore not a whole) and the *Earth Constitution* (a holistic federation).

Local governments will flourish precisely because of the economic and political *integration* of the whole in a cooperating world

that *makes possible* their flourishing. In an ecologically and economically interdependent world, there is no local autonomy that can flourish excluded from the empowerment and cooperation provided by the whole. Power, therefore, becomes substantially different. It is no longer the power of economic and/or political fragments (like a ruling class or an imperial hegemonic nation-state) imposing domination and exploitation over other fragments, whether internally or externally. It is now the legitimate authority of the human *community*, with a universal common good that *ethically and morally* deserves recognition. The coercive power of government is only legitimate if it carries this moral authority.

The power of the Earth Federation government will not involve the sinister and corrupt aspects of imperial power and capital power, always linked with violence, as these have operated throughout the modern period. The imperial power of territorial expansion involves war and the destruction of those resisting the imperial encroachment on their territories. Even if the postcolonial imperial regime has the tendency to incorporate them into its legal universe, as Hardt and Negri assert, the process is an ugly and immoral one. Something similar is true of capitalist expansion, which necessarily generates wealth and productivity through the exploitation and dehumanization of large segments of the population of Earth as capital searches for ever-new markets and new ways of production and expansion, utilizing the structural violence of global poverty to maximize its profits and drawing on imperial violence as deemed necessary. As we have seen Naomi Klein point out (2007), torture and political repression follow wherever this economic system raises its ugly head.

The power of the Earth Federation deriving from the substantial worldwide consent of the people of Earth will not result in either the corrupt phenomenon of violent territorial expansion, nor in the ugly phenomenon of searching for new populations for exploitation in the service of capital expansion. It will be the power of *the human community*, bound together in unity and diversity, now recognizing a common humanity and a common good that supersedes all fragmented, particular goods and interests. If for some reason all power naturally seeks expansion (a hypothesis that should be questioned and that would require substantial justification), then that expansion under the Earth Federation will be intensive, *qualitative,* and internal to the system, not extensive and expansive. "Power" takes on an entirely different character within a holistic system.

7.5   Power as Qualitative rather than Quantitative

As economist Herman E. Daly points out (1969), "development" under a sustainable system will be "qualitative" not quantitative. So too, "power" under an ecologically and humanly sound holistic world system will be *qualitatively* different from the power-over of today's world. Violence, the failure of legitimate power, will be minimized and essentially eliminated, for violence is a product of fragmentation and injustice, or, as Gandhi puts it, violence is a product of deception (always used to cover up injustice).

Harris calls such processes that are intensive and internal to systems "teleological" (2000a: 132-164). The *logic of a holistic system* moves the parts toward synergy and harmony. The whole teleologically draws the parts together in a healthy unity-in-diversity. In the case of the Earth Federation, this means toward peace, justice, freedom, and reasonable prosperity. By contrast, the *logic of a fragmented system* necessarily leads to situations in which the parts become involved in conflict, war, domination, and exploitation. What is "expanded" under the *Earth Constitution* is the *telos* toward peace, harmony, and mutual flourishing. By uniting humanity into a genuine political whole (which mirrors its species-wholeness), the whole exerts a teleological influence toward harmony over the parts. Power means something qualitatively different.

The paradigm has now shifted. Power in a holistic system will involve "expansion" of the *quality* of life, not quantity for the sake of accumulation and evermore quantity. The technologies supporting environmental sustainability and the protection of human life, education, cultural flourishing, and the cultivation of our higher human capacities for love, compassion, justice, thought, reflection, and other aspects of human and civilizational virtue will become the beneficiaries of the integrated teleological and community-based power of the whole. Quality replaces quantity as the *telos* of life and society. As Harris points out, only this holism makes real political freedom possible (2000b: 121-22).

We should recall here the quotation from Paul Ricoeur in section 1.2 above. It is through "imagination" that we discover our human essence by "breaking the prestige of the fact." We can understand very clearly a situation in which "the quests for having, power and worth would not be what they in fact are.... In imagining another state of affairs or another kingdom, I perceive the possible, and in the possible, the essential" (1967: 170). We can easily imagine a qualitative transformation of the concept of power in human affairs. Indeed, we already experience this everyday in some of our relationships.

We want the power of living fully—God's cosmic joy in creation expressed through us—to manifest itself within the Earth Federation. Paradoxical as it may sound at first, by establishing the unity of humanity through uniting all together within a common democratic framework, we reaffirm the rootedness of every person in their distinct communities, languages, differences, and cultures that nourish the human soul and make it loving, harmonious, and healthy. The unhealthy "fetish of nationalism," Rabindranath Tagore affirms, distorts our fundamental "human truth" and leads to "living in the dense poisonous atmosphere of worldwide suspicion and greed and panic" (2011: 173). Power in the negative sense is linked to human fragmentation rather than to that fullness of our humanity that can be termed "perfect":

Man in his fullness is not powerful, but perfect. Therefore
to turn him into mere power you have to curtail his soul
as much as possible. When we are fully human, we cannot
fly at one another's throats; our instincts of social life, our
traditions and moral ideals stand in the way. If you want
me to take to butchering human beings, you must break
up that wholeness of my humanity through some discipline
which makes my will dead, my thoughts numb, my movements automatic, and then from the dissolution of the complex personal man will come out that abstraction, that destructive force, which has no relation to human truth, and
therefore can be easily brutal or mechanical. Take away
man from his natural surroundings, from the fullness of his
communal life, with all its living associations of beauty and
love and social obligations, and you will be able to turn him
into so many fragments of a machine for the production of
wealth on a gigantic scale. (2011: 177)

Another word for the *telos* generated from social wholeness
of humanity is "community." Persons are really free only within
communities that respect their uniqueness and use the common
power of the community to support their freedom and personal
flourishing. The *Earth Constitution* both treats and establishes human beings on Earth as a community of free, equal, and cooperative citizens. And a community, as a holistic social reality, carries
within it a *telos* (power) for both the common good of all and the
productive flourishing of every individual or group within it. As
Moltmann expresses this: "The opposite of poverty is not wealth,
but community. In community individuals become rich, rich in
friends who can be trusted, rich in mutual help, rich in ideas and
powers, rich in the energies of solidarity" (2012: 159).

Within our Earth community, the economy will no longer be
expansive in the sense of the gross (and inappropriate) indicator of an ever-increasing gross domestic product (GDP) produced
by the fragmented nation-states in competition with one another.
Under present methods of measuring GDP even destruction, pollution, and chaos can increase GDP and appear as an indicator
of economic "health." Under the new paradigm embodied in the

Earth Constitution, the economy will be "intensive" (and not disastrously growth-oriented) in the sense of searching for ever-better ways to increase the quality of sustainable production, environmental restoration and protection, and human well-being within this framework. People will not obsessively seek monetary wealth within this framework, for they will be rich in community. Similarly, the power of the Earth Federation, deriving from the consent and active cooperation of the people of Earth, will result in a continual improvement and perfectibility of the rights in the bill of rights (Art. 12) and the progressive actualization of the "directive principles" ("certain other rights") specified in Article 13.

Power is neither good nor bad in itself; it can have very different dynamics and very different consequences depending on how it is constituted and conceived. Power in the Earth Federation derives from the new holistic paradigm on which the *Constitution* is founded. It is power deriving from integration, cooperation, unity-in-diversity, and community, not from domination, which always finally perverts power and turns it into violence of one sort or another, delegitimizing itself in the process. Power as violence or domination denies holism, and operates from a conception of autonomous fragments, however diffuse these fragments may now be under the hegemony of today's postmodern empire.

Similarly, the new paradigm of holistic power does not involve exploitation, which requires structural violence, that is, exploitation requires poverty, scarcity of resources, and human desperation for its success. But the holistic world system initiated by the *Earth Constitution* eliminates all of that. It establishes a universal social democracy that retains private property but regulates its accumulation in corporate or private hands so that democracy is not undermined in the process. It places human dignity and well-being first, and transforms the present soulless sphere of market forces in large measure by removing the conditions of scarcity necessarily required for capitalist exploitation. Within a genuine community of free and equal citizens in a condition of reasonable prosperity, people do not exploit one another.

The consequence of the domination of power in the sense of resorting to violence is human misery and loss of freedom. The consequence of power resulting from holistic integration is precisely the flourishing of human freedom. We become free from fear of enemies, from food insecurity, housing insecurity, health care insecurity, educational deprivation and, therefore, free to formulate life plans according to our personal values and flourish within our communities and natural environments in pursuit of those life plans, or by simply living fully within the fullness of our humanity and our communities. As Moltmann expresses this:

> Power in itself is good. There is the power of love, the power to understand, the power of conviction and the forces of nonviolent communication. . . . With violence, we have to do with the perversion of the powers of life into destructive and ultimately deadly drives. . . . Life itself distinguishes between violence and power. Power strengthens and enhances life. Violence diminishes and destroys it" (2012:190).

Only a new holistic political, economic, and social paradigm (of an Earth community) can make the power of life prevail against the destructive forces of violence.

The power of people united in solidarity and creative cooperation within the Earth Federation transforms power into its proper civilizational dynamic. The holism of the people of Earth must be actualized across several dimensions—ethically, ecologically, culturally (as unity-in-diversity), economically, politically, and in terms of our "rational loyalty" to the whole. The loyalty to the Earth Federation under the *Earth Constitution* fosters the economic and political unity and encourages all the other forms of consciousness of interdependence within the whole as well. Theologian Sallie McFague expresses something of what the realization of holism means:

> We are not separate, static, substantial individuals relating in external ways—and in ways of our choice—to other individuals, mainly human ones, and in minor ways to other

> forms of life. On the contrary, the evolutionary, ecological
> perspective insists that we are, in the most profound ways,
> "not our own": we belong, from the cells of our bodies to
> the finest creations of our minds, to the intricate, constantly
> changing cosmos. (1987: 7-8)

This realization, she argues, generates a new understanding of power: power is no longer understood as domination, as power-over. The relations of power that arise from holism are now associated with "love" and bring to mind "the characteristics of love shown by parents, lovers, and friends, the words that come to mind included 'fidelity,' 'nurture,' 'attraction,' 'self-sacrifice,' 'passion,' 'responsibility,' 'care,' 'affection,' 'respect,' and 'mutuality' " (ibid. 20-21).

Theologian Matthew Fox says that the current paradigm advocates "the wrong kind of power—a power that is outdated and therefore deadly. Theirs is the power to control instead of the power to heal. It is a power over instead of a power with. It is the power of power instead of the power of nurturing and celebration" (1990: 246-47). The emergence of the Earth Federation within the context of humanity's conversion to holism will transform our conception of power across the board. People will literally begin thinking differently. Government officials as well as citizens will begin thinking and acting primarily for the common good, no longer out of greed, compulsive egoism, the fetish of nationalism, and the drive for domination.

7.6   Self-Limiting Features of the Earth Federation Government

THE Earth Federation government will also be *transparent*, and therefore any tendency of government officials to slide into corruption will be checked by public scrutiny. Indeed, by the second stage of the Earth Federation, as outlined in Article 17, the nations of the Federation will actualize a carefully designed and systematic process of disarmament. A militarized nation in a potentially hostile world requires governmental and military secrecy, which in turn always breeds corruption and a supporting industrial-military complex that enriches itself through violence and war. Democracy only flourishes in the light of transparent forms of government and authority. Secrets kept from the population under militarism and corporatism necessarily strike at the very heart of democracy.

Transparent government means that the income and assets of all government officials are publicly known and accounted for. There are no secret "offshore" bank accounts or assets. Public auditing of the workings of all government agencies, and the income and assets of all government officials, means that the potential for corruption will be substantially minimized. Similarly, the elimination of militarized nation-state sovereignty will mean transparency for all the federated governments of the world since there will be no more military and no more need for a national security state.

Secondly, the elimination of scarcity (food, health care, housing, educational, monetary, etc.) from the Earth (which will soon be accomplished under a cooperative, united Federation aiming at the common good) means that the incentive for bribery, extortion, fraud, or theft will be radically minimized. People will find their personal aspirations addressed in alternative ways. It will no longer be "me and my family against the world," since "the world" will be recognized as the nexus that empowers and sustains the freedom and security for me and my family.

Similarly, the limitations on the private accumulation of wealth that we may assume will be legislated by the World Parliament (since these have already been legislated by the Provisional World Parliament) will not result in a denial of entrepreneurial energy in creative and innovative people. The immense task of creating a sustainable global economic system and the continuing transformation of technology and innovation directed toward improving the quality of living for all persons (while reducing to a

minimum their environmental impact and the impact of the production process) will be more than sufficient to engage even the
most creative entrepreneurs. Their rewards will be recognition
and honored status, not wealth beyond the legal limits.

The limits to personal wealth and income set by the Provisional World Parliament are four to one (World Legislative Act
22). The "one" here indicates the (fully sufficient) minimum wage
and decent standard of living applied to all human beings. Under Article 13 of the *Constitution*, this includes health care, social
insurance, housing, clean water, nourishing food, education, a
protected environment, etc. The lowest income level, therefore,
will be *entirely sufficient* for a flourishing human life. Four times
this level will, therefore, be quite wealthy. If we include with this
"quite wealthy" status, social recognition and awards, the incentive for entrepreneurs will be entirely sufficient.

The power of the Earth Federation government, therefore,
will not result in a new system of domination and exploitation
as feared by those today who lack insight into the nature of the
paradigm-shift embodied in the *Earth Constitution*. The reification
of the nation-state as a new god on Earth (that began with the
Peace of Westphalia in 1648 and continues to this day), resulting
in its militarism and oligarchical systems of power and exploitation, is eliminated by the new paradigm, as is the "right" to unlimited accumulation of private wealth by individuals or corporations considered to have all the legal rights of persons. Such
"deifications of the state" resulting in totalitarian governments,
as Moltmann asserts, are today understood as an "idolatry" to be
repudiated (2012: 24).

Without the shibboleths of "national security" and "national
glory" in war to cover over the self-interests of the industrial-
military complex and the process of domination and exploitation
embedded within the capitalist system, the Earth Federation government will naturally enjoy a very different philosophical and
ideological environment. Lies, manipulation, and strategic uses
of language covering hidden greed and special interests will be

unnecessary and frowned upon. Like all other industries, the news media will also be transformed. There will no longer be a ruling class with the incentive to privately own the mass media and use it for status quo propaganda, nor a national-security war mentality using the media to terrorize the population with threats of enemies. Within the community of Earth, lying and manipulation (phenomena central to both capitalism and nation-state power politics) are no longer socially acceptable.

The articulation of a powerful Earth Federation government by the *Earth Constitution* is elaborated within a *Constitutional* system assuring its authentic legitimacy. Legitimate power has no need of violence, the use of which only diminishes its legitimacy. Realistically, in a decent world civilization, the use of force can be reduced to a minimum. The *telos* of the Earth Federation system is toward harmony under the principle of unity-in-diversity. Within the multiplicity of ways by which the *Earth Constitution* assures a legitimacy arising from the people of Earth, there are two more that I will briefly mention here.

The first is that the World Police will "only possess weapons necessary to apprehend individuals" (all production, possession, or deployment of military weapons will be banned everywhere on Earth). Police are also required to obtain warrants for searches and arrests. In addition, the police are mandated to engage in "conflict resolution" and to minimize the resort to force as much as possible in the course of enforcing the law (Art. 10.4-5). The specification of these goals for the civilian world police force is by no means arbitrary. The logic of holism provides an intrinsic goal for the police characterized by progressively reducing the use of force in their work and progressively increasing their role of conflict resolution.

When the police are no longer protecting the property rights of a dominating ruling class (as is the case everywhere in today's world), their role will become literally one of protecting and serving the people of Earth. They will likely be widely recognized public authorities for mediation, conflict resolution, and the defusing of potentially violent conflict situations. In fact, the *Constitution* explicitly assigns "conflict resolution" of one of their functions. The wide recognition of their vital and beneficent role will support the legitimate power of the Earth Federation government and, in turn, continually lessen the need for using force in any and all situations. The description of the role of the police in Article 10, therefore, is no utopian dream, but a mere drawing out the logic of holism on which the *Earth Constitution* is based.

Secondly the World Ombudsmus (Article 11), a worldwide agency assigned to protecting the human rights of the people of Earth, will function as a watchdog on the government itself, including the World Police. The Ombudsmus will have the power to investigate accusations of violence or other kinds of corruption and bring these before the courts. Like the many other checks and balances built into the *Earth Constitution*, this agency will underline the legitimacy (and hence the power) of the Earth Federation government in the eyes of the people of Earth.

Its relation to the World Police will not likely be hostile, however. Indeed, the World Ombudsmus also will have mediation and conflict resolution functions that somewhat mirror those of the World Police. But the *Constitution* explicitly places *conscious realization of the telos of its holism* into the functions of the World Ombudsmus. Among these functions are "to press for the implementation of the Directive Principles for the World Government as defined in Article 13 of this World *Constitution*" (Art.11.1.3), and "to promote the welfare of the people of Earth by seeking to assure that the conditions of social justice and of minimizing disparities are achieved in the implementation and administration of world legislation and world law" (Art.11.1.4).

The Directive Principles of Article 13, we have seen, include all those "intensive" uses of holistic power to perfect the quality of human life through universal nourishing food, housing, health care, education, social insurance, clean water, healthy environment, etc. The role of the World Ombudsmus is to see that this *telos* toward harmony and perfection is followed as efficiently and rapidly as reasonably possible. Here we have a worldwide agency whose explicit duty is to actualize the *telos* at the heart of the *Earth Constitution*. This, again, is neither utopian nor arbitrary, for it follows from the *logic of holism* embodied in that document.

The power of that government, therefore, will be directed, on the one hand, toward addressing the terrible global problems of climate collapse, resource depletion, pollution of air, land, and water, corporate crime, violent crime, militarism, terrorism, etc. Such problems can never be effectively addressed without substantial cooperation of the nations within the federation and the active participation of the people of Earth. On the other hand, the power of the Earth Federation government will also be directed toward actualizing the directive principles of Article 13 and perfecting the quality of human life for everyone on the planet. The logic of holism demands both these goals. The government will be powerful enough to address these apparently overwhelming tasks precisely because it will have the massive support of the people and nations of Earth. The beneficent roles of the World Police and the World Ombudsmus in this process will simply be manifestations of this holistic power.

The power of the Earth Federation, therefore, will now be authentically directed toward creatively moving into the future on behalf of the common good of the people of Earth. This explains how and why the great power accorded to the Earth Federation government by the *Earth Constitution* will be qualitatively different from power as it is now understood within the global capitalist and nation-state systems, as well as the system of global empire and hegemony currently promoted and defended by the world's imperial nations. As we have seen, a *holistic* system is qualitatively different from a system of fragmented autonomous parts. *In a holistic system the unity-in-diversity means that the whole functions well because of the parts and the parts function well because of their integration into the whole.*

There is an analogy with the power of health, for example, in a human body when all the organs are functioning and integrated into a harmonious whole. Parts and whole working cooperatively together create health in living things, in natural systems, and in the planetary ecosystem. Fragmentation in all these dimensions means death. Similarly, social and international fragmentation means war and violence, domination and exploitation. The power generated by social holism and world-system holism transforms these negative consequences into a synergistic flourishing of the whole with the harmonious integration of all its parts. This is what social power is and should be—the power of a genuine human community. Let us have this power, and work to establish this power, by ratifying the *Constitution for the Federation of Earth!*

7.7   Education as Empowerment

THE Earth Federation government will have tremendous influence over educational processes and practices worldwide. The Provisional World Parliament has already passed an "Education Act" as World Legislative Act 26 that outlines the kind of core syllabus that will be essential to Earth Federation schools and recommended to educational institutions worldwide. It stipulates that all students study the *Earth Constitution*, that all students study the fundamentals of democracy and good government, and that all students study the requirements of (world and local) citizenship as participation in government and the community pursuit of the common good of all.

Education will be directed to producing genuine "world citizens" who are loyal to the Earth and the common good of present and future generations, qualities that are also required for an ecologically sustainable civilization. Becoming such world citizens requires cognitive, moral, and spiritual development on the part of human beings, actualizing their capacities for reason, love, and intuition. The problems that I identified above in my list of nine factors in the rise of totalitarianism will be substantially overcome not only through the new world system but also through global education. Let us examine the dynamics of education from a holistic perspective in order the show the fundamentally transformed understanding of power that arises from holistic educational practices.

Every human being lives in the dynamic present, that is, every human being lives within a pervasive process of recalling and synthesizing the past within the ever-changing present in a process of projecting a future on the basis of perceived possibilities. Thinkers from Kierkegaard to Heidegger to Ricoeur have articulated these structures of human temporality. We live only in the present, a present synthesizing its past and envisioning its future in an ever-changing and ever-renewed process of projecting itself toward that future. This same dynamic holds true of families, groups, societies, nations, and cultures.

With the development of a universal consciousness of human beings and our common history upon Earth, the dynamic of a synthesized past, in a lived present, projected toward future possibilities begins to operate for humanity itself. We can ask about human destiny, human opportunities, human possibilities, and our common human future: about the gigantic hope for a transformed human future. In chapters eight and nine we will see further that a transformed future requires the realization of a human spirituality in which each person begins to live from a deeper level of awareness that connects them with the source, the ground of being. Education must take place with teachers and within a context that evokes development to higher levels of spiritual awareness in the learners.

Human beings possess immense possibilities for cognitive, moral, and spiritual development. Education, therefore, is about enhancing, refining, articulating and enlivening the creative process of actualizing these possibilities for individuals, for groups, and for humanity as a whole. It draws upon history and human knowledge in a dynamic interaction between the older generation and the younger generation directed toward a future of enhanced or transformed possibilities, including the possibility of living fully and blissfully in the present.

As Krishnamurti affirms, education is not simply about getting a job or fitting into some role in society, it is also about how to live, about living fully decently and fearlessly with love, beauty, and order (1964: 9-13). The development of spirituality cannot be turned into an ideology or doctrine imposed by a teacher on the students because spirituality involves inward awakening that must be realized by each individual person. Teachers can point the way and institutions can provide a harmonious, balanced and conducive environment for spiritual, moral, and cognitive growth, but none of this can be imposed. As Krishnamurti expresses this:

> Life is really very beautiful, it is not this ugly thing we have made of it; and you can appreciate the its richness, its depth, it extraordinary loveliness only when you revolt against everything—against organized religion, against tradition, against the present rotten society—so that you as a human being find out for yourself what is true. Not to imitate but to discover—that is education, is it not? (Ibid. 11)

The fullness of human life involves the mysterious duality of human existence: we need to live fully and blissfully in the present while at the same time synthesizing a past within a dynamic projection of our lives into the future. Education is about both these dimensions, for the structure of human temporality—moving from a recalled past through a dynamic present toward an imagined future—is always about *some future*, always projecting toward some set of imagined possibilities, while at the same time living fully and deeply in the present. In this book we have seen that these two dimensions of our cosmic-divine situation also characterize the cosmos: the blissful, eternal fullness of the present (what Whitehead calls God's primordial nature) and the evolutionary development of ever-greater, more complex holistic systems (what Whitehead calls God's consequent nature).These two dimensions, as they operate in and through human life, compose the subject-matter of authentic education.

Perhaps most people, much of the time throughout human history, have experienced life as a nightmare of scarcity of resources or the dehumanization of oppression of one form or another. History records experiences of domination, slavery, exploitation, war, hate and fear, clinging to a precarious and uncertain existence in the face of horrible possibilities of disease, suffering, death, and destruction. We may want to preserve some values, insights, and wisdom from the past, or an understanding of sacred scriptures, or some ideals of culture, but these preserved remembrances are invariably in the name of a better future, a future transformed in the direction of peace, justice, truth, love, community, and freedom.

Some contemporary Christians, such as Paul Tillich, Enrique Dussel, and Jürgen Moltmann, have understood the future in terms of God: the power of God and the call of God toward a transformed future. Moltmann writes:

> When we speak in such an absolute and dominant way of "the" future which defines all history and therefore itself does not pass away, God is meant as the power of the future. The power of the future affects people in such a way that they are liberated from the compulsion to repeat the past and from bondage to the givenness of what is already there. To speak of the history of the future means to speak of the history of human liberation. That is the basic thinking of the eschatologically oriented hermeneutic of history. (Italics in the original, 2007: 106)

Human history can be rightly understood as the story of the struggle for human liberation in general. Several of the world's great religions have understood history this way, as did Karl Marx who criticized religion as a fetter on the process of liberation. Since the Axial Period in human history 2500 years ago, there have been religious and philosophical thinkers who have seen humanity as one reality and history as the actualization and articulation of that one temporalized reality. By the 20th century the unity of humanity has become widely recognized and articulated in documents such as the UN Universal Declaration of Human Rights.

Authentic education is about human liberation into a decent future for everyone on Earth. It brings the experiences and knowledge of past generations into the present with a view to a better future. In situations of broad structural injustice, it is inherently revolutionary.

Law has also been a feature of most human societies throughout these past 2500 years. And thinkers have reflected on the nature and foundations of the idea of law in human societies. Is the law simply the expression of the arbitrary power of rulers or a ruling class? Or is there a moral basis behind the idea of law that makes arbitrary power illegitimate and only democratic systems of law morally legitimate? Ronald Dworkin (1978), for example, argues that the power of the law (legal coercion) only has moral legitimacy if it arises from a "true community," that is, if the members of the community consider that the obligations to the law that are an expression of their community are: (1) *specific* to their community, (2) *personal obligations* binding them to other members of the community, and (3) directed toward the *common good* or welfare of the entire community.

If a community of people operates according to these principles, he argues, then it will be a system of "integrity" based on fundamental moral principles and the equally recognized human rights of all. In such a society, the common understanding of the citizens creates a social and moral harmony that is bound together and enlivened by the rule of enforceable laws. It is clear that the conflict and chaos of the world as a whole today is linked to the fact that the world is not a community in this sense and that there is no morally legitimate regime of enforceable law over all nations and citizens that could establish and institutionalize a community of peace and harmony for the entire Earth. However, in the above chapters we have demonstrated that the idea of such a community is presupposed in the very concept of law.

The story of the human project as an emerging global community has only come to real prominence in the 20th century, and we have seen through Swimme and Berry that we can integrate the human story into that of the evolving universe itself. Yet the story of the rule of law within this emerging global community has yet to be fully told. How can the rule of morally legitimate enforceable law establish, enhance, and undergird a world of peace, justice, freedom, harmony, and sustainability? How can the human community as a whole appropriate a common past within a dynamic present of reflection and decision-making and project itself toward a future characterized by moral legitimacy and harmony?

Education, which clearly bears on enhancing the future possibilities of individual students, can also be about creating a transformed future for humanity, as we have seen Ricoeur assert. It can be about creating a harmonious civilization for all humanity on Earth, empowering both the individuals and the community. Indeed, every aspect of human knowledge, when taught, operates within this dynamic of a recalled past synthesized in a dynamic present with imagined possibilities for the future. If we study war, military training and strategy, we are similarly recalling a past and defining or imagining certain future possibilities. However, it is dawning on people worldwide that we do not have to study war, we can study peace and in doing so establish and articulate long suppressed possibilities for human liberation and a transformed future.

In this sense education is not simply about the transmission of knowledge from one generation to the next through classrooms, books, lectures, and electronic media. Education becomes a universal process by which each of us and society as a whole engages reason and imagination in a dynamic process of learning from the past, and the horrific failures of the human project throughout the past and present, and exploring the immense possibilities for a future beyond war, poverty, injustice, and oppression. Reason, imagination, love, and intuition do not stand as opposed faculties, but rather as complementary powers through which the processes of growth and transformation are energized.

Reason here is not the tired positivist reason that erroneously constructs the world as a collection of facts and maintains that the future must be merely an extension and continuation of these depressing facts. Rather, reason, with the power of imagination, opens up a world of possible alternative futures, understanding the immense creative and transformative powers flowing through human beings that can bring very different futures into existence. Reason also understands that the very possibility of parts presupposes the wholes that encompass them. Positivism fails to understand the creative power of values, principles, and imaginative vision within human life and history. It fails to understand the principle of holism at the heart of the cosmos and our common humanity. The tired and unimaginative study of war brings with it a future of war. The creative and hopeful study of peace and harmony draws with it a future of peace and harmony.

Education is also about cognitive, moral, and spiritual growth. Across the board, psychologists and spiritual thinkers show broad agreement about stages of growth, the higher stages being essential to universal harmony. It is understood that today perhaps a majority of persons remain at the lower stages of growth throughout their lives. In Abraham Maslow's "hierarchy of needs" (1970), people are understood to have a primary need for "belongingness" that often binds them to their local community and its conventions. Psychologist Lawrence Kohlberg (1984) and philosopher Jürgen Habermas (1979) call this lower stage "conventional." Carol Gilligan (1982) calls this stage "ethnocentric" and James Fowler (1981) calls it "synthetic-conventional." If one's identity is defined by local religion, local conventions, and national customs, then global harmony is not likely, since it appears from this level of growth that the other religions in the world and other national customs and perspectives are simply wrong or misguided.

These thinkers posit the higher stages of cognitive, moral, and spiritual growth as essential to universal harmony. Maslow speaks of self-transcendence, and Kohlberg of harmony with nature and the cosmos (embracing all people and cultures). Habermas (1998a) speaks of developing the capacity for dialogue directed toward mutual understanding, which assumes the equality of the other and makes possible the harmony of mutual understanding. He shows that the very possibility of language presupposes claims to truth, truthfulness, and normative rightness: making possible true mutual understanding among peoples. Fowler speaks of "conjunctive faith" in which truth is recognized as multidimensional and found in all faith traditions.

Following a century of advances in developmental psychology and cultural theory, integral philosopher Ken Wilber (2007) articulates a model of developmental stages applicable both to individual persons and the historical development of the human species. With regard to the ladder of development of the individual, lower stages move progressively from the "archaic" to the "mythic" and then to the "achiever self," none of which can harmoniously embrace the diversity of humankind. Higher and more inclusive stages move through the "sensitive self" to the "holistic self" to the "integral self" where people are now able to more and more fully embrace and affirm the vast unity-in-diversity of humanity. The educational process directed toward harmony must address the need for development toward these higher, more universal, moral, and spiritual stages of growth.

Wilber draws on his immense scholarly corpus of studies in the development of science, world cultures, planetary psychologies, and the history of mysticism embedded within the world's religious traditions to create a developmental model for humanity across four "quadrants": science, culture, individual consciousness, and organizational systems. He calls this model AQAL (All Quadrants All Levels, 2007: 72, 180). Wilber's model, therefore, provides a complete picture of our human situation. Any given moment of human existence can be understood from an individual or a collective standpoint and each of these standpoints has both an interior and an exterior dimension.

Wilber calls the first quadrant the *individual interior* (my inner consciousness, my "I"). He calls the second quadrant the *collective interior* (our "we" consciousness, the consciousness of my group, culture, or humanity as a whole). The third he calls the *imper-*

sonal exterior (as this is understood by developments in scientific paradigms), and the fourth he calls the *collective exterior* (the "its" consciousness—social systems, historical economic and political forms, and our collective ways of organizing society).

In terms of the history of thought, Wilber also articulates these dimensions in terms of the traditional philosophical ideals of the *good*, the *true*, and the *beautiful* as recognized by many thinkers such as Plato, Aristotle, Plotinus, Aquinas, and Kant. The *good* encompasses the moral dimension arising from the heart, from our collective "we" consciousness. The *true* indicates the objective truth as this is formulated for the exterior dimensions—scientific study of nature or human social systems, etc. Finally, the *beautiful* refers to the sense of beauty arising from the subjective consciousness of each individual person (ibid.: 67-70). In human civilization, an evolutionary emergent development has been taking place across all these dimensions.

Drawing on the insights of these same developmental and educational thinkers (Maslow, Kohlberg, Gilligan, etc.), Wilber has created a model of human development for all four quadrants that can serve as a fundamental guide to education. The pattern of development in each quadrant roughly parallels that of the others. Individual development culminates in the "holistic self" and the "integral self." World culture culminates in "holistic world culture" and then moves to the integral level. Science progresses to the cosmic and biospheric holism that we have been discussing in this book.

In the quadrant for the social, economic, and governmental "systems" by which human beings organize themselves, Wilber's developmental model culminates in "holistic commons" and "integral mesh networks" (ibid.). At the level of systems people begin to see that planetary ecology with its oceans, atmosphere, forests, and interdependent systems as part of a holistic commons belonging to all of us. In an on-line video discussion of planetary governance with Jim Garrison, Wilber advocates moving toward a "world federation government" that is capable of meeting the interrelated needs and problems of our planet with the spiritual maturity, authority and effectiveness (https://vimeo.com/12354463). My contention is that the *Constitution for the Federation of Earth*, that places the key resources of the planet, including its oceans and atmosphere, under a holistic commons belonging to the people of Earth, fulfills the vision articulated by Wilber in these works.

Education, if it is to be enlightened and informed, must show the students this developmental model across all four of Wilber's quadrants: scientific, cultural, personal, and structural. Education can and should bring the unity of humankind and human civilization into the awareness of students. But the structure of the systems by which we organize our lives is educative as well. Wilber's timeline includes the lower levels of "feudal empires," "early nations," and "corporate states." History shows clearly that people organized under these systems thought and acted in terms of the presuppositions of these system. If we organize the world as a "holistic commons" under the *Earth Constitution*, people will begin thinking and acting from these higher more integral levels.

We considered above the roles of law and education within this process. We examined the relation between law and harmony with respect to at least three dimensions. First, the function of the rule of law that establishes a unity-in-diversity that frees human beings from naked power relationships and establishes the primordial harmony of the social contract. Second, within the framework provided by the social contract, a dialogue directed toward mutual understanding is made possible through which racial, cultural, religious, and other forms of harmony can be pursued.

Third, within the framework provided by the social contract, freedom can develop from a mere "negative freedom" into an empowering matrix of "positive freedom" in which society as a whole pursues the common good of universal harmonies of peace, justice, freedom, and sustainability. People begin to understand that cooperation and mutual support give much greater freedom to all than do fragmentation and conflict. People are influenced by their institutional framework to grow to maturity. But maturity means freedom, autonomy in relation to that institutional framework. This understanding goes all the way back to Kant:

> *Enlightenment is man's emergence from his self-imposed immaturity. Immaturity* is the inability to use one's understanding without guidance from another. This immaturity is *self-imposed* when its cause lies not in lack of understanding, but in lack of resolve and courage to use it without guidance from another. *Sapere Aude!* "Have courage to use your own understanding!"—that is the motto of enlightenment. (1983: 41)

This effort to bring people to moral autonomy and maturity is fundamental to the purpose of education. But good laws under a universal social contract, Kant also insists, help bring people to moral autonomy and maturity. All three of these functions of good law are educational for the citizens who find themselves within the embrace of this law. The fact of a global social contract, establishing democratic world law for Earth, alone helps lift people from ethnocentric and partial perspectives to universal, more all-embracing perspectives. Erich Fromm stresses the relation between the individual and society that, as for John Dewey considered above, makes possible the actualization of our higher human potential:

> Positive freedom on the other hand is identical with the full realization of the individual's potentialities. . . . The victory of freedom is possible only if democracy develops into a society in which the individual, his growth and happiness, is the aim and purpose of culture. . . . I have stressed the psychological side of freedom, but I have also tried to show that the psychological problem cannot be separated from the material basis of human existence, from the economic, social, and political structure of society. It follows from this premise that the realization of positive freedom and individualism is bound up with economic and social changes that will permit the individual to become free in terms of the realization of his self. (1941:270-71)

The economic transformation of global society under the *Earth Constitution* and the guarantee of universal human rights and freedoms permit people everywhere to grow to maturity. The making possible of a dialogue directed toward mutual understanding by the law (what Fromm terms genuine democracy) also lifts people out of their parochial, strategic, and instrumental patterns of speech and helps them actualize the maturity of genuine openness to the other through authentic dialogue. Moral autonomy (the ability to use one's understanding without guidance from another) and openness to others through dialogue are not mutually exclusive but rather complementary, both essential features of moral maturity. The actualizing of positive freedom similarly helps bring citizens to a more and more universal understanding of what it means to be human and the role of a diverse global community in supporting freedom and the roughly equal capacity of everyone to live a decent, morally mature, human life.

The rule of democratic law is essential to this process. As Harris declared: "If the implications of this scientific revolution and the new paradigm it produces are taken seriously, holism should be the dominating concept in all our thinking." Holism is *revolutionary holism*, the source of our hope for a transformed future, for the emergence of new, holistic levels of human existence on the Earth. Education concerning our imagined future possibilities and the transformation effected by world law must also carefully study today's law—its nature, strengths, and limitations.

Education must reveal the law's role in our current conflicted and endangered human situation. It must also study the relation of law and the development of our higher human potentialities to the new holistic paradigm that encompasses all four of Wilber's quadrants, including the structural and organizational dimension. The law confers powers upon a particular group to govern society. Fragmented systems of law (under sovereign nation-states) confer this power in a fragmented way, leading to violence and repression. We must show the potential of holistically conceived law for contributing to a transformed and harmonious human future.

Education must show that this future is presupposed in the very concept of universal law, which directly follows from our common human rationality and sociality. It can show that power becomes something entirely different within this context. Our appropriation of the past within the dynamic present in the service of imagined future possibilities applies to our individual lives, our local communities, and to humanity as a whole. Power in all of these contexts now becomes the power of life, the power of human flourishing, the power of living blissfully and fully in the present, the power of free people using their understanding without guidance from another, the power that arises from a holistic and harmonious community. It is this transformed conception of power that will inform the Earth Federation government under the *Earth Constitution.*

But education does not provide our only hope. It will contribute substantially toward awakening humanity to its common vocation of becoming ever more fully human and creating a worldwide consciousness of world citizenship. Yet it is but one element within a holistic context that is creative, dynamic, dialectical, flexible, and in process. The mechanistic world view of the early-modern paradigm made no room for teleology, for dialectical emergence of higher levels of synthesis, nor for the influence of the unspeakable depths of existence on the surface dimensions of existence. It made no room for a future that is substantially different from the past.

That is why I want to place a chapter on "ethics and eschatology" next in this volume. The arguments in this book stand on their own and do not depend on an appeal to the "depths of existence" for their logic, coherence, or validity. But the "principle of hope," so eloquently elaborated by Ernst Bloch in his three volume work by that name (1986), arises out of a multiplicity of human intuitions that open up for us genuine possibilities for a truly rapid and transformed future. In the limited space of one chapter, let us examine some of these.

Chapter 8

Holism and Eschatology: Transforming the World's War System to a World Peace System and Breaking the Hold of One-Dimensional Thinking

Freedom— and this is something that was not made explicit in any of the previous concepts of freedom— in all of its levels as freedom of choice and of action, as ethical and religious, is only founded contra factum, *thus in a perspective of a still* open world, *on* not yet determined all the way to the end. *This is where the continual revolutionary accent on freedom comes from.... Only a* partial *determinability of the world, thus as yet unclosed possibility, makes freedom possible in this world.... Freedom is the mode of human comportment in the face of objective real possibility. Only thus does its purpose have any margin of play on the path that leads to the* content *of freedom: the un-alienated* humanum. (1986: 162-63)

—*Ernst Bloch*

THE dominant ways in which human beings organize their thinking in the modern world has resulted in what Emmanuel Levinas has called war and a war system: "The visage of being that shows itself in war is fixed in the concept of totality, which dominates Western philosophy" (1969: 21). Similarly, drawing on Christian biblical concepts, Enrique Dussel contrasts "this world" (of sin and evil) with the "reign of God" (the world to come). Our contemporary world is understood as "a system or structure of prevailing, dominant *social* actions and relationships under the hegemony of evil" (1988: 29), in other words, a war system intimately connected, for Dussel, with a system of domination and exploitation.

In the first part of this chapter, I attempt to elucidate further the closed off nature of the world's dominant system (which produces the world's dominant set of value-orientations) in contrast with the opened up or awakened nature of the ethical and its revolutionary child, the eschatological. In doing this, I want to show that the "totalizing" of the world, as understood by thinkers like Levinas and Dussel, is not the same as the philosophy of holism. Holism is open to the depths; it opens up the depths of existence. Von Brück speaks of "the eschatological tension between what is 'already' and what is 'not yet.' Within this eschatological differentiation we see only through a mirror (1 Cor. 13:12), which reflects the original image in a conditional way" (1991: 202).

In *Beyond the Big Bang: Quantum Cosmologies and God*, scientist-theologian Willem B. Dees states that: "'Holism', a contemporary label for pantheism, tends to underscore the brokenness of the world and to overemphasize harmony and unity" (1990: 101). We will see that this is not the case, holism has no need to deny transcendent dimensions to reality. Holism understands that the reality cannot be understood in reductionistic terms: the holistic structures are themselves realities that cannot be reduced to bare matter, atoms, or deterministic causal processes. In his book *One World: The Interaction of Science and Theology*, physicist-theologian John C. Polkinghorne writes:

Reality is a multi-layered unity. I can perceive another person as an aggregate of atoms, an open bio-chemical system in interaction with the environment, a specimen of *homo sapiens*, and object of beauty, someone who deserves my respect and compassion, a brother or sister for whom Christ died. All are true and mysteriously coinhere in that one person. To deny one of these levels is to diminish both that person and myself, the perceiver; to do less than justice to the richness of reality. (1986: 115-16)

The "richness of reality" clearly includes its transcendent dimensions. Reality is indeed a "multi-layered unity," but one that emerges out of the depths. In *God and the New Physics*, physicist Paul Davies declares: "The brain is the medium of expression of the human mind. Similarly the entire physical universe would be the medium of expression of the mind of a natural God. In this context, God is the supreme holistic concept, perhaps many levels of description above that of the human mind" (1983: 223).

We will see in Chapter Nine that a mature development of our reason, intuition, and love brings a person evermore deeply into awareness of the unsayable mysteries and depths of existence. There are indeed "levels of description" that cannot be intelligibly reduced to atomistic or mechanistic levels, and for Davies or Polkinghorne the concept of God may be one of these levels. But if we are attempting to conceptualize "Ultimate Reality" we will always run into limits imposed by our finitude, as 15th century thinker Nicholas of Cusa made so very clear in *De Docta Ignoranta* and as Whitehead, quoted in Chapter Two above, also made clear.

Nevertheless, it may be our human place, as Ricoeur asserts, to "function as a mediator of the infinite and the finite in things" (1967: 71). The concepts of immanence and transcendence, within a holistic perspective, point beyond finite concepts to infinitude, to the unsayable depths of existence beyond conceptualization. And one aspect of these concepts of immanence and transcendence has to do with the astonishing futurity of human existence: our eschatological potential.

We human beings, as persons who synthesize all of existence in our relationships and creatively engage an unknown and emergent future, emerge from the absolute mystery of these depths. Von Brück cites St. Paul's notion that now we see through a mirror darkly what will one day be illuminated. We can both cognize and intuit the truly transformative possibilities of this emergent future. Eschatology emerges from this tension between the present and the liberating possibilities of a redeemed future. This contrasts starkly with the paradigm, discussed by Levinas and Dussel in alternative ways, of those who "totalize" reality in such a manner as to close off its transformative possibilities. A human being is, most essentially, these transformative possibilities. Martin Buber writes:

> Man is the crystalized potentiality of existence. But he is this potentiality in its factual limitation. The wealth of possibility in existence from which the animals are kept away by their exiguous reality is exhibited in man in a sign that is incomprehensible from the standpoint of nature. Yet this wealth of possibility does not hold free sway, so that life might be able time and again to follow on the wings of the anticipation of spirit, but it is confined within narrow limits. The limitation is not essential but only factual. That means that man's action is unforeseeable in its nature and extent, and that even if he were peripheral to the cosmos in everything else, he remains the center of all surprise in the world. (1972: 437-38)

We are "the center of all surprise in the world"—"the crystalized potentiality of existence." In a holistic human being, the fullness of awareness includes reason, intuition, and love. All three of these can open the depths for us. Each of these aspects of human awareness (as we will see further in Chapter Nine) can open up what Tillich calls "levels of reality" (1957: 42) closed to the conventional paradigm of totality. The "totalization" of the world's "war system" (Levinas), or its "system of sin" (Dussel), closes off these depths. As Gabriel Marcel remarks "there can be totalization only of that which is homogeneous" (1951: 50). A holistic world of many dimensions and depths is anything but homogeneous in this sense. To be open to these depths makes us capable of eschatological transformation.

To accomplish this task of elucidating some of these eschatologically relevant depth dimensions, in this chapter I also draw on the work of Ludwig Wittgenstein, Immanuel Kant, Raimundo Panikkar, James Fowler, Jürgen Moltmann, and Paul Tillich. I try to show that the eschatological insight arises from a depth-dimension of human experience that is universally available to human beings. The eschatological dimension is thus available to us independently of any particular religious orientation and is itself integral to a holistic understanding.

In subsequent parts of this chapter, drawing on the ethical and eschatological insights developed in its opening sections, I attempt to show that neither ethical exhortation nor a philosophy of nonviolent action will suffice to deal with a world dominated by "totality." The key pivotal point for moving from the world's war system to a world peace system is ratification of the *Constitution for the Federation of Earth.* The ethical awakening culminates in eschatological vision, a vision that needs to include institutional transformation: I argue that the *Earth Constitution,* or something very similar, forms a necessary, but not sufficient, condition for actualizing the ethical and eschatological potential of our human situation.

8.1   Totality

THE concept of "totality" receives a multiplicity of meanings in the relevant philosophical literature. In *Marxism and Totality: The Adventures of a Concept from Lukács to Habermas*, Martin Jay distinguishes a number of different formulations of the concept, for example, "aesthetic," "normative," "decentered," "expressive," "latitudinal," "longitudinal," "individual," etc. What is more, he appears to use the term as equivalent to "holism" (1984: 31-32). Ricoeur points out that the idea of totality, deriving from the unity of consciousness, is implicit in the very possibility for human beings to be rational, developing creatures and is fundamental to all philosophical reflection. Nevertheless, he writes:

> Nothing gives rise to deception more than the idea of totality. All too quickly it has been said: It is here, it is there, it is Mind, it is Nature, it is History. Violence is the next step—first violence to the facts and then violence to man, if, to top it off, the philosopher of totality has power over man. (1967: 74-75)

For purposes of this chapter I am primarily following Levinas and Dussel who formulate their eschatology through a critical contrast with what they conceive of as totality. They use the word to indicate a certain *reductionism* endemic to much of western civilization and perhaps especially actualized in the early-modern paradigm. As will become clear, I define "holism" in contrast to totalization of the sort that Levinas and Dussel criticize. In my rendering, holism is open to "depths" and "dimensions" to which totalization closes itself off, and which simultaneously opens for us the eschatological possibility.

Taking these thinkers as my point of departure, I find that the negativity of war lies in the act of objectifying the other by an autonomous subjectivity assumed to be in external relationship with the other. The world is conceived as a totality of entities in objective relations of power, subservience, alignment, or disalignment with regard to my (or my group's) needs and interests. Other people, and the collective identities that I project on them in my objectifying of the world, are central to my assessment of threats to my security and well-being. War is the relation I have to all such threats (and ultimately even those now identified as allies continue to count as possible threats). The "I" here is most often a collective "I" involving nations, races, religions, or other groups.

When I am not actively fighting to eliminate threats and possible threats to my self-conceived collective or individual autonomy, I engage in politics (war by another name): maneuvering to enhance my strength, my position, my security and diminish the relative strength and position of others. "Morality" (in this objectified world of autonomous selves or autonomous groups versus others) lies in *loyalty to the collective identity and its norms,* for the "sticking together" with those identified as "we" over and against those understood as "them" is the foundation of my security and well-being. In a world "totalized" in this way, war, as Heraclitus declared, is king and master over all.

In such an objectified world in which other people appear as objects of threat or as allies, my autonomy and well-being also require a domination in which some are used as instruments to produce the wealth and security of others. The system of private property as defined by the laws of the society establishes relationships into owner and worker, manager and managed, those who produce and serve, and those who own and command. This system is an offshoot and corollary of the objectified negative relationship of war. My autonomous subjectivity, individual and collective, opposes its "we" to a "them" who are instrumentalized as enemies, subordinates, the labor force, the uneducated masses or poor people available for my corporate uses, or as my hired mercenaries.

In *Ethics and Community,* Dussel characterizes societies with this orientation as follows:

> In the totality of the *systems of practices* of the world, as objective and social reality, the "carnal" subject or agent desires the permanency of order, which, however, attempts to legitimate itself by appealing to the "gods" as its foundation. The "flesh" is idolatrized in the "kingdom of *this world,*" and promulgates its own law, its own morality, its own goodness. . . .
>
> This system is closed in upon itself. It has replaced the universal human project with its own particular historical project. Its laws become natural, its virtues perfect, and the blood of those who offer any resistance—the blood of the prophets and heroes—is spilled by the system as if it were the blood of the wicked, the totally subversive.(1988: 30-31)

The prophets and heroes whose blood is spilled by the system of conventional morality live from a depth of awareness largely unknown to the objectifying consciousness of the representatives of the system. This is awareness of a depth that is not a product of the totalized system of the world, but an awareness that is nevertheless there as a possibility in every human subjectivity: love for the other, love for the other as other, as a person with the dignity and holiness manifest in all persons as persons.

The prophets and heroes represent the relationship of *community*, Dussel maintains, a community of persons who treat one another as persons, each with attention to the needs of the others. They represent an "eschatological ethics" that lives from the demand for liberation at the heart of human existence, characterized by Bloch as "the unalienated *humanum*, "a "philosophy of the future." The autonomous objectifying subjectivity of this system is broken through in the person to person relationship of the community known as *agape* and its implicit demand for a transformed world characterized by *agape* in all its relationships (1988: 9-12).

Rudolf Bultmann asks the question: "Is the understanding of Jesus Christ as the eschatological event inseparably connected with the ideas of a cosmic eschatology?" (in Jonas, 1996: 148). Do we need to understand eschatology within the mythological framework of ancient cosmological thinking, or can the eschatological dynamic of human freedom, love, and historical existence emerge within a new image of being human? For Dussel and Bultmann, but not for Levinas or Bloch, that new eschatological image is provided by the life and teachings of Jesus Christ.

For Dussel, negating the other (in the system of objectification) means negating God (1988: 19). Our relationship with the other is our relationship with God: "when you have done it unto one of the least of these my brethren, you have done it unto me" (Matt.25:40). How is it that our relationship with God is identical with our relationship with the other? How is it that the Infinite can be reflected in the other in such a way that doing toward the other is identical with doing toward God? Perhaps we can discern something of the answer in the thought of Jewish philosopher Emmanuel Levinas.

Levinas attempts a phenomenological description of *subjectivity directed to revealing a primordial awareness of infinity in the depths of subjectivity prior to its constitution of the "objective world."* Infinity is prior to the correlative relation of a Kantian transcendental unity of apperception with the world in the subject-object relationship. Infinity, the not-finite, the idea of a depth beyond being and beyond saying, he says, does not first exist and then reveal itself. Rather:

> Its infinition is produced as revelation as a positing of its idea in *me*. It is produced in the improbable feat whereby a separated being fixed in its identity, the same, the I, nonetheless contains in itself what it can neither contain nor receive solely by virtue of its own identity. Subjectivity realizes these impossible exigencies—the astonishing feat of containing more than it is possible to contain. . . . Here intentionality, where thought remains an *adequation* with the object, does not define consciousness at its fundamental level. All knowing qua intentionality already presupposes the idea of infinity, which is predominately *non-adequation*. (1969: 26-27)

The human being is opened up to the depths through discerning that intentionality *presupposes* what intrinsically cannot be adequated to thought. Levinas focuses on the idea of infinity, within us primordially prior to the ego confronting its world. Infinity is not and cannot be an object of consciousness (since the intentionality of ordinary consciousness encounters only what is finite) but finds signification in the ethical demand that I be responsible for the other person.

> The exposition of the ethical signification of transcendence and of the Infinite beyond being can be worked out beginning with the proximity of the neighbor and my responsibility for the other. . . . It consisted in being struck by the *"in"* of infinity which devastates presence and awakens subjectivity to the proximity of the other. (1998: 166)

The "presence" of the world in my consciousness, which so easily lends itself to totalization in the thought of an objectified world sufficient unto itself and without depth, can be "struck by," in the first instance, an infinity that can be encountered in the presence of the other person. Levinas attempts to elucidate this infinity (there in the human face, in the proximity of others) that evokes in us the mysterious realization of something not part of the totalized "objective" world, something that he characterizes as "exteriority": infinity radiant in the human face—the realization that I am utterly responsible for the other (1969: Sect.III).

Human subjectivity can also be seen to become aware of a primordial depths to things through several other encounters or "being struck by" certain aspects of experience that cannot be adequated to thought. I want to point to some of these encounters as aspects of our ethical situation, all of which also point to an eschatological imperative at the heart of the human situation—an imperative that we transform the world in the direction of a liberated and fully human future.

In a famous passage within the *Critique of Pure Reason*, for example, Immanuel Kant writes:

> Two things fill the mind with ever new and increasing admiration and awe, the oftener and more steadily we reflect on them: the starry heavens above me and the moral law within me. I do not merely conjecture them and seek them as though obscured in darkness or in the transcendent region beyond my horizon: I see them before me, and I associate them directly with the consciousness of my own existence. The former begins at the place I occupy in the external world of sense, and it broadens the connection in which I stand to an unbounded magnitude of worlds beyond worlds and systems of systems and into the limitless times of their periodic motion, their beginning and continuance. The latter begins at my invisible self, my personality, and exhibits me in a world which has true infinity but which is comprehensible only to the understanding – a world with which I recognize myself as existing in a universal and nec-

essary ... connection, and thereby also in connection with
all those visible worlds. (1956: 166)

I am related to the boundless magnitude of worlds beyond
worlds in a number of ways that evoke ever "new and increasing
admiration and awe." Kant says that this magnitude is directly
related to him. The human mind comprehends this as a whole. Its
wholeness is correlative to the unity of the human consciousness,
to the "transcendental unity of apperception," as he points out in
the *Critique of Pure Reason.* The unity and order of the boundless
magnitudes are "associated directly with the consciousness of my
own existence." There is an *a priori* connection between the holism
of the human mind and the limitless universe.

But implicit in Kant's awe and wonder is also astonishment
at the existence of these worlds. Kant stands before the moral
law within and the boundless magnitudes without as a conscious
existing being, astonished at being so and at the existence of the
universe itself. The experience here is not only that of beauty, and
not only one of the vastness of the universe, but of the sublime, a
trembling and awe in the encounter with numinous presence.

There is a note here, implicit to be sure, of an awareness later
made explicit by Ludwig Wittgenstein in his 1929 "Lecture on
Ethics." Wittgenstein identifies three "absolute experiences" the
literal descriptions of which, he says, are strictly "nonsense." Yet
they illustrate what he means by "ethics" and by "absolute value."
These are experiences of astonishment *that* anything at all exists,
of feeling *absolutely* safe, and of feeling guilty (1965: 8-10).

The last of these "absolute experiences" links to Kant's declaration quoted above. The moral law, Kant says, "exhibits me in a
world which has true infinity but which is comprehensible only to
the understanding." The understanding can only comprehend the
categories of the world within which the unifying subject stands
in correlative relationship to the order and regularities of the finite
world open to science and human understanding. But the infinite
cannot be understood, only encountered. For Kant the essence
of "the moral law within" is the absolute command to always do

what is right regardless of one's inclinations, a command that cannot be understood in terms of the categories of the understanding but appears to break into my subjective consciousness from the infinity of the noumenal dimension (from an infinity beyond the understanding).

Human beings, in view of the moral law within, have dignity, that is, their dignity is "exalted above all price and so admits of no equivalent" (1964: 102). Further, this is to say that human beings have "intrinsic value" or "absolute value." They must be respected as ends in themselves and never reduced to mere means or instruments (1964:96). The concept of human dignity (that later became the premise of the UN Universal Declaration of Human Rights) points again beyond the closed system of finite and objective knowledge to an infinity incommensurable with that system.

8.2   An Absolute Command

AN absolute command, the demand to recognize something of *Infinite value* confronting a mere finite being means, at the same time (just as it does for Wittgenstein), "feeling guilty." Wittgenstein nowhere discusses at length the philosophical implications of the "absolute experiences" described in his "Lecture on Ethics," perhaps because, as he declares in the Preface to the *Tractatus,* he wants to put everything firmly into place by remaining silent about it. As I have pointed out elsewhere (1988), the whole of Wittgenstein's philosophy and life might serve as an elaboration of his encounter with the unsayable Absolute. Guilt here is an absolute experience (an experience of infinity) in the face of absolute demands and the sense that "God disapproves of our conduct." This in turn can be linked to Levinas' sense of an absolute obligation to the other, beyond understanding, reason, and prior to the egoistic constitution of subjectivity. Levinas begins by quoting Dostoyevski:

> "Each of us is guilty before everyone, for everyone and for
> each one, and I more than others," writes Dostoyevski in

> The Brothers Karamazov. ... But it is thus a position already deposed of its kingdom of identity and substance, already in debt, "for the other" to the point of substitution for the other, altering the immanence of the subject in the depths of its identity. This subject irreplaceable for the responsibility assigned to him finds in that very fact a new identity. But in extracting me from the concept of the ego, the fission of the subject is a growth of obligation in proportion as obedience grows, the augmentation of guilt that comes with the augmentation of holiness, the increase of distance proportionate to the approach. ... The subject as a hostage has been neither the experience nor the proof of the Infinite, but a witness borne of the Infinite, a modality of this glory, a testimony that no disclosure has preceded. (1998:168-69)

As with Wittgenstein, Levinas links the awakening to absolute obligation with guilt. Wittgenstein does not elaborate on his "absolute experience" of feeling guilty beyond the idea that God disapproves of our conduct. But the relationship appears significant, especially in the light of the other two "absolute experiences" described by Wittgenstein. The second of these is the experience of "feeling absolutely safe." He makes clear that this feeling has nothing to do with ordinary relative experiences of feeling safe or unsafe. To feel absolutely safe means "I am safe, nothing can injure me whatever happens."

He says that the metaphors characteristic of religious language would translate this into the idea that "we feel safe in the hands of God." But the idea can also be connected with Wittgenstein's insight into the deep unsayable reality of the self, what he calls in the *Tractatus* "*what is true about solipsism.*" Like the *anatta* of Buddhism, Wittgenstein understands the sense in which there is no self and hence the sense in which one can have the experience of "feeling absolutely safe."

For Wittgenstein, however, his "experience par excellence" is the experience of "wonder at the existence of the world. And I am then inclined to use such phrases as 'how extraordinary that anything should exist' or 'how extraordinary that the world should exist'." His subsequent discussion makes it very clear that this idea is "nonsense" to ordinary meaning and sense. Yet it is Wittgenstein's primary example of "absolute value." He tries to explain absolute value with the following: "I can only describe my feeling by the metaphor, that, if a man could write a book on Ethics which really was a book on Ethics, this book would, with an explosion, destroy all the other books in the world." "Ethics," he says, "if it is anything, is supernatural" (1965: 7).

In all these cases, we see that the experience cannot be adequated to the finite world of concepts, knowledge, and facts. We encounter the Infinite in the mystery of the starry skies above, in the *agape* for the other that is identical with *agape* for God, in the absolute commands of the moral law within transcending the totality of selfhood, in the face of the other that, as Levinas says, speaks to me as a master, in the experience of astonishment *that* the world exists, in the absolutely safe self, and in the feeling of guilt for which there is no expiation. Similarly, Christian theologian Paul Tillich (recalling the astonishment St. Augustine felt in his *Confessions*, Book X) finds in the present moment an experience that cannot be adequated to the finite world:

> The mystery of the future and the mystery of the past are united in the mystery of the present. Our time, the time we have, is the time in which we have "presence." But how can we have "presence"? Is not the present moment gone when we think of it? Is not the present the ever-moving boundary line between past and future? But a moving boundary is not a place to stand upon. If nothing were given to us except the "no more" of the past and the "not yet" of the future, we would not have anything....
>
> The mystery is that we *have* a present; and even more that we have *our* future also because we anticipate it in the present; and that we have our past also, because we remember it in the present.... The riddle of the present is the deepest of all riddles of time. We live in it and it is renewed for us in every new "present." This is possible because every moment of time reaches into the eternal. It is the eternal that

stops the flux of time for us. It is the eternal "now" which provides for us a temporal "now".... Not everybody, and nobody all the time, is aware of this "eternal now" in the temporal "now." But sometimes it breaks powerfully into our consciousness and gives us certainty of the eternal, of a dimension of time which cuts into time and gives us our time. (1963: 130-31)

In the *Tractatus* Wittgenstein declares: "If we take eternity to mean not infinite temporal duration but timelessness, then eternal life belongs to those who live in the present" (1974: sec. 6.4311). For Wittgenstein, as for Tillich, the present moment (as absolute) is not in time at all. There can be no adequation between the absolute present and the objective world of fact and knowledge, governed as it is by history and clock time. If the Infinite is what lifts us out of ourselves in "an awakening" as Levinas states (1998: 168), if we are held "hostage" by that which is within and around us at every moment to which we are usually half asleep, then the dimension of absolute value, ethics (intimating the "good beyond being" declared by Plato in *Republic*, Section 509b) is a key to liberation from the enclosed world of the totality and its social morality. Raimundo Panikkar perhaps sums up this awakening when he declares:

Every being has an abyssal dimension, both transcendent and immanent. Every being transcends everything – including and perhaps most pointedly "itself," which in truth has no limits. It is, further, infinitely immanent, i.e., inexhaustible and unfathomable. And this is so not because the limited powers of our intellect cannot pierce deeper, but because this depth belongs to every being as such. (1993: 61)

Every being, that is, every aspect of our encompassing being-in-the-world, contains a dimension that breaks the finite, closed world of "being as totality" and presents us with an infinity beyond adequation with human comprehension or knowledge. For the human being, and the dignity associated with these depths that live within us prior to our subjectivity and our knowledge, this means reverence for human freedom and personal uniqueness:

> Nothing which stifles human freedom can endure or be called truly human. Humanness demands the free fulfillment of Man. There is no justice if liberty is not respected. But there is no freedom where justice is violated. No monistic system or uniform worldview will ever satisfy the inexhaustible versatility of Man, whose greatest dignity is inseparable from his or her freedom and personal uniqueness. (1993: 8)

The awareness of an infinite depth that permeates our human situation gives rise to the realization that we are under an absolute command, a command also associated with our unfathomable freedom and dignity. This awareness may be at the very heart of the eschatological vision.

8.3 Beyond the Totality

WHAT spills the blood of the martyrs is the system itself, Dussel maintains, the so-called "natural order" of things, recognizing no non-idolatrous transcendence and no eschatological imperative for transformation. What constitutes the "Antichrist" is the self-contained system of institutionalized domination and exploitation, generating its own self-justifying norms, and living off the blood of the poor, the dispossessed, and their martyrs. It is the world of endless war in which "the other" is objectified as enemy, terrorist, or outsider (Moslem, Jew, Communist, Gay, Black, etc.), or in which the other is reduced to a member of some nation-state (Iraqi, Afghani, Iranian, Russian, Chinese, etc.). Subjectivity, within the closed totality of a world of objective knowledge, facts, and power relations, finds its security and defense in the preemptive attack on the not-self, on the other, different than we are.

But the self that has encountered the unsayable beyond being within which it is immersed at every turn, is broken open to an encounter with the other as (non-objectified) other and to the absolute responsibility for the other, in what Levinas calls "inspiration" (1998: 171):

> I am a testimony, or a trace, or the glory of the Infinite. . . .
> But this is without thematization; the sentence in which
> God gets mixed in with words is not "I believe in God."
> The religious discourse that precedes all religious discourse
> is not dialogue. It is the "here I am" said to a neighbor to
> whom I am given over, by which I announce peace, that is,
> my responsibility for the other. "Creating language on their
> lips. . . . Peace, peace to him who is far and to him who is
> near, says the Eternal" (Isaiah 57:11). (1998: 170)

Levinas understands that we are not speaking here of "belief." We are not talking about mere religious opinion, which is often contrasted, to its detriment, against the objectivity of knowledge. Knowledge thematizes categories and concepts within *commensurable* relationships of sameness and difference (as Nicholas of Cusa long ago pointed out in *De Docta Ignorantia*). "Thematization and conceptualization. . .," Levinas writes, "are not peace but suppression or possession of the other" (1969: 46). The Infinite permeates our situation prior to the distinction between knowledge and belief. It is incommensurable with both knowledge and belief and can only be pointed to in the claim that "I am a testimony." It speaks of a different world order, one of "peace to him who is far and to him who is near." That peace is actualized in my responsibility for the other, in my *agape*, in my obedience to the Good beyond being.

For Dussel, this is the reign of God promised by Jesus as the fruit of *agape* and the love of neighbor for neighbor (which is a fundamental way that persons manifest the love of God). The closed system of the world-totality, in which domination and exploitation have become institutionalized within the framework of a self-justifying ideology and set of "moral norms," is broken open in those who experience the Infinite at the heart of the human situation. Within the depths of our human situation lies the eschatological demand for transformation: "The reign that is absolute *transcendence* with respect to all praxis, to all historical face-to-face, to all community, is ever a 'beyond,' an approach to full human realization. ... As eschatological horizon the reign of God is the absolute principle of Christian ethics, which is the measure of *all* historical undertakings—reformist and revolutionary included" (1988: 15-16).

For Levinas, "the visage of being that shows itself in war is fixed in the concept of totality which dominates Western philosophy." The system opposes an objective world to a subject fully commensurate to that world and encompassing all things within it as objects or forces within the totality. "The state of war," he says, "suspends morality" (1969: 21). But the Infinite that can be encountered in the opening or inspiration of discovering the other as other, and our limitless responsibility for the other, opens history to eschatological hope:

> Eschatology institutes a relation with being beyond the totality or beyond history, and not with being beyond the past and the present. ... The eschatological as the "beyond" of history, draws beings out of the jurisdiction of history and the future; it arouses them in and calls them forth to their full responsibility. Submitting history as a whole to judgment, exterior to the very wars that mark its end, it restores to each instant its full signification in that very instant: all the causes are ready to be heard. ... The eschatological vision breaks with the totality of wars and empires in which one does not speak. It does not envisage the end of history within being understood as a totality, but institutes a relation with the infinity of being which exceeds the totality. (1969: 22-23)

That which is incommensurable with knowledge and history is the Infinite, an *a priori* encompassing our lives that is not thematizable. It cannot be adequated to the system of knowledge and history: like Plato's Good beyond being. It is this "beyond" of both knowledge and history that calls us forth to assuming full responsibility for the dignity of the other, for the "infinity in the

face" of the other, for the love (*agape*) of the other. This eschatological command lives at the heart of our human situation. Tillich
describes this call to assume our full responsibility:

> The demand calls for something that does not yet exist but
> should exist, should come to fulfillment. A being that ex-
> periences a demand is no longer simply bound to the ori-
> gin. Human life involves more than a mere development of
> what already is. Through the demand, humanity is directed
> to what ought to be. And what ought to be does not emerge
> with the unfolding of what is; if it did, it would be some-
> thing that is, rather than something that ought to be. This
> means, however, that the demand that confronts humanity
> is an unconditional demand. The question "Whither?" is
> not contained with the limits of the question "Whence?" It
> is something unconditionally new that transcends what is
> new and what is old within the sphere of mere develop-
> ment. Through human beings, something unconditionally
> new is to be realized; this is the meaning of the demand
> that they experience, and which they are able to experience
> because in them being is twofold. For the human person
> is not only an individual, a self, but also has knowledge
> about himself or herself, and thereby the possibility of tran-
> scending what is found within the self and around the self.
> This is human freedom, not that one has a so-called free
> will, but that as a human being one is not bound to what
> one finds in existence, that one is subject to a demand that
> something unconditionally new should be realized through
> oneself. (1987: 143)

Each human being is "unconditionally new" and is, as self-
aware, subject to the demand that something unconditionally new
be realized through his or herself. "Transcendence," as Dutch theologian Edward Schillebeeckx declared, "is no longer up. It is in
the future" (in Fox, 1990: 43). Similarly, in his well-known study
of the *Stages of Faith* (1981), James W. Fowler identifies the highest
stage of faith as "Stage 6," which he calls "universalizing faith"
that flows from a "universalizing compassion." It is a faith that
apprehends the "depth of reality" (199-200). In its highest stage,

faith is grasped by "the futurity of being" (203) and is reflected in Jesus' teachings of the coming Kingdom of God, of "the eschatological character of the Kingdom of God." Fowler characterizes freedom in a way very similar to that of Tillich: freedom is not "free will," but rather the transcending of what one finds in existence, discerning the demand that comes to us from the future. Fowler speaks of "the freedom of God's future for us and for all being" (209).

Christianity articulates this eschatological insight in one way, but expressions of Stage 6 faith may articulate the freedom of futurity through other symbolisms, for all forms of Stage 6 faith are universalizing, no longer limited by which symbols are used. For Christianity, Fowler says, it can be expressed as follows:

> Seen in the light of this vision the human vocation—and it must be understood as a universal human vocation—is to live in anticipation of the coming reign of God. The human vocation is to lean into God's promised future for us and for all being. It is to be part of the reconciling, redeeming and restoring work that goes on wherever the Kingdom of God is breaking in. It is to be part of the suffering rule of God, to oppose those structures of life that block and deny the future of persons and being in God. (1981: 210)

From apprehension of the depths of reality, which include the mystery of freedom and the future, flows the ability to live in terms of a vision of our human-divine possibilities. In a similar vein, Paul Gordon Lauren declares that "there are times when the visions seen of a world of possibilities provide a far better measure of a person's qualities and contributions than the immediate accomplishments of his or her lifetime. That is, those unique individuals who possess a capacity to go beyond the confines of what is or what has been, and to creatively dream or imagine what might be, sometimes have an impact on history that far transcends their own time and place" (2003: 1). Perhaps this "capacity to go beyond the confines of what is" becomes present through apprehension of the depths, the infinity that confronts us on every side. For Fowler:

> Stage 6...persons...have become incarnators and actualizers of the spirit of an inclusive and fulfilled human community. They are "contagious" in the sense that they create zones of liberation from the social, political, economic and ideological shackles we place and endure on human futurity....[which include] the criteria of inclusiveness of community, of radical commitment to justice and love and of selfless passion for a transformed world, a world made over not in their images, but in accordance with an intentionality both divine and transcendent.... In these persons of Universalizing faith these qualities of redemptive subversiveness and relevant irrelevance derive from visions they see and to which they have committed their total beings. These are not abstract visions, generated like utopias out of some capacity for transcendent imagination. Rather, they are visions born out of radical acts of identification with persons and circumstances where the futurity of being is being crushed, blocked, or exploited.... (Ibid. 200-203)

As for Panikkar, every being has an abysmal dimension, and part of the depth within human beings is their freedom, their radical otherness that radiates what Levinas calls "infinity in the human face." Political theologian Jürgen Moltmann declares that ethical eschatology appears in the struggles for economic justice, human rights, human solidarity, ecological peace with nature, and the struggle for "personal conversion from apathy to hope" (2007: 110). We have seen him proclaim that God is the power of the future that frees us from the bondage to the past and the often horrible facts surrounding us in the present.

Not only does the encounter with the unsayable depths of the present moment break open the assumption of a determined past and a blocked freedom, the reading of history as the struggle for liberation means reading history in terms of God's futurity. We break out of bondage to givenness into an ethical eschatology of radical praxis and liberating futurity. What circumstances and what institutions block or crush the futurity of being? What concrete possibilities can we point to for human liberation? Does everything have to remain in the realm of abstract symbols of a human liberation with no clear objects of focus for a concrete praxis?

For the war system of the world's disorder, everything is bound to the origin. Its premises assume an historically objectified world system locked into universal causal laws with fragments (such as nation-states, competitive corporations, or individuals) in struggle with one another for goods, wealth, power, and resources. Kant, Buber, Tillich, Fowler, and Moltmann do not see the ethical demand (what ought to be) arising from "the sphere of mere development." To be trapped in the paradigm of slow, evolutionary change, the model of "development," is to be bound to the origin and dragged down by the intransigence of the paradigm of oppression and slavery.

The "liberal" idea that we can work within the present world-system to evolve it in the direction of justice, equality, and freedom is largely an illusion. Kant had this idea that the form of "republican government" itself would bring societies ever-closer to acting on the moral principles of liberty and equality, and those who discern a *telos* or *nisus* in history toward emergent levels of freedom may well think this is operating within bourgeois democracies, but history has shown differently.

The capitalist system interfaced with the system of sovereign nation-states has proved to be a paradigmatic constriction on the possibility of human liberation. Levinas and Dussel, like Heidegger and Ellul whom we discussed in Chapter One, suggest this in different ways—the totalized self-enclosed system of the world is itself the problem. It cannot be reformed, at least not in time to prevent nuclear holocaust or climate collapse. The system itself must be changed. The paradigm of totalization that systematically blocks awareness of the depths of existence must be transformed into the ethical demand to respect the infinity, the infinite dignity, in every human life.

The totalized conventional world of objectification, alienation, domination, and sin often provides illusory mechanisms (like voting within bourgeois class-based societies) said to allow for nonviolent ways of evolving the system toward the good. But such evolution never takes place because the premises of the system systematically block awareness of the depths that demand fundamental and immediate transformation. Holism is not totality (the totalization of an "objective" world utterly lacking in depth) but an *integration and harmonization* of all aspects of our human situation, including openness to the depths.

With increasing human self-awareness, the reality of the absolute demand for something truly new in history can become conscious. Martin Buber correctly identified human beings as "the crystalized potentiality of existence"—as "the center of all surprise in the world." This includes the eschatological demand for what Kant called the "kingdom of ends": a world in which war has been abolished and human dignity, and the dignity of the natural world, becomes the foundation for economics, law, culture, and planetary unity. Buber, Fowler, Tillich, and Moltmann recognize the same eschatological imperative identified by Dussel and Levinas.

8.4   Nonviolence and World Transformation

PERHAPS it is easier to identify what is wrong with the contemporary war system of the world than it is to determine how to correct it. We need to move beyond war, that is, to move beyond the enclosed and truncated system of the world that has little or no non-idolatrous experience of any redeeming transcendence. We need to establish a regime that can free us from the tyranny of causal laws of technique, power, domination, instrumentalization, and objectification. We need to transcend the idea of a subjective will promoting its own irrational desires over against an objective world available for exploitation and manipulation. All these are fundamental roots of the war paradigm.

Moltmann affirms such a holistic vision of peace: "Peace means not only the absence of war but also the overcoming of suffering, anxiety, threat, injustice, and oppression. Peace is the blessed, affirmed, good, splendid life with God, with human beings and with nature: *shalom*" (2007: 118). And we have seen Levinas affirm that "the eschatological vision breaks with the totality of wars and empires in which one does not speak. It does not envisage the end of history within being understood as a totality, but institutes a relation with the infinity of being which exceeds the totality." The fullness of peace as the eschatological possibility of humanity does not involve an end to history but a living relation to that which exceeds the totality, providing history itself with a *telos* and meaning.

Fowler declares that eschatological persons create "zones of liberation from the social, political, economic and ideological shackles we place and endure on human futurity." Is it the case that Fowler's idea of "zones of liberation" or Dussel's idea of "ethical communities" or Levinas' "eschatological vision [that] breaks with the totality of wars and empires" necessarily implies an anarchism on Earth that cannot be institutionalized or structured? Can there be a *peace-system* on Earth that organizes social, political, economic, and ideological structures for liberation rather than slavery?

A peace system would derive from the holistic paradigm and organize life on Earth holistically, a system that would not close off awareness of the depths of existence but would make room for enhancing this awareness in multiple ways. There would seem to be no reason why a peace system could not be established that allows for "a relation with the infinity of being which exceeds the totality." Indeed, we have seen that the current dominant institutions of the world preclude and actively militate against such a transformation of human awareness.

For the past several centuries the war system has been closely linked with the system of sovereign nation-states and global capitalism, gigantic institutions and forces self-contained and implacable in their violence. These systems and the ego-centered subjectivities that populate them use violence as the fundamental form of social control: violence in the rule of the rich over the vast population of the poor worldwide, violence in enforcing laws over recalcitrant populations, violence in protecting "property rights" from masses of poverty-stricken citizens, violence in eliminating or torturing perceived enemies, violence in the implementation of "economic shock therapy" (Klein, 2007), violence institutionalized in the form of military and paramilitary organizations within nearly every one of the world's 193 sovereign states, and violence in maintaining the threat of nuclear holocaust hanging over the future of all humanity (see Martin, 2010a, Chaps. 4-6).

Fundamentalists in various faiths may abdicate responsibility for action and passively wait for a miraculous intervention that ends human history. But intellectually mature and honest people know better. If the eschatological promise is to be realized, it will be through human actions: intelligence, responsibility for the other, and establishing the foundations for a loving and compassionate planetary community. How can this be done? Dussel's liberation theology may have influenced the founding of some Christian-based communities in Latin America, but these have had little defense against the weapons of the death squads trained in the School of the Americas in Fort Benning, Georgia, by the imperial dominators of Latin America (cf. Gill, 2004).

Christian philosopher Jacques Ellul concludes that repudiating violence is the only path toward "a revolution in depth": "My study of politics and sociology have convinced me that violence is an altogether superficial thing; that is, it can produce apparent, superficial changes, rough facsimiles of change. But it can never affect the roots of injustice—social structures, the bases of an economic system, the foundations of society. Violence is not the appropriate means for a revolution in depth" (1978: 118). On the other hand, what have the vast movements for nonviolence that have occurred in many countries of the world (as described, for example, in Ackerman and DuVall's *A Force More Powerful*) accomplished in transforming the world-system itself? Very little, for we need not just nonviolent resistance, but nonviolent and holistic institutions, as Gandhi himself insisted. A real "revolution in depth," it appears, would result in institutions fundamentally free of structural, overt, and spiritual violence to replace today's worldwide institutionalized violence (cf. Martin, 2005: Ch. 3).

Peace educator Betty Reardon links violence to the process of turning others into instrumentalities: "Otherness connotes, . . . in its negative form, hierarchies in human worth, the fundamental assumption that makes possible the dehumanization of the other sex, another race or class, citizens of another state, or adherents to another political philosophy" (1985: 50-52 and 93). Can we found institutionalized systems that promote human equality and dignity rather than dehumanization of the other through hierarchical economic and social relationships? Surely, some institutional arrangements will promote a sense of community through unity-in-diversity more than others.

These proponents of nonviolence have positive insights, but not meaningful concrete proposals for institutional transformation. Eschatological hope needs to establish institutional conditions on Earth that make its realization of dignity and nonviolence possible. We need to oppose the *global war system* with a *global peace system*. Indeed, the establishing of such institutions (predicated on nonviolence rather than violence) appears as a necessary condition for the realization of that hope. A philosophy of nonviolence alone will not do it, unless this is supplemented by concrete ways to replace the dominant institutions with structures that allow the ethical and eschatological dimensions to flourish among human beings.

Neither will ethical exhortation do it in the face of gigantic systems of ideology deceiving human beings into thinking otherwise. The first step in our analysis must be to concretize Levinas' highly abstract notion of a totalizing world recognizing only "being and the same" and excluding the Infinite. What are the specific institutions that concretely dominate our planet and perpetuate the objectifying consciousness everywhere on Earth and how, specifically, can they be replaced by liberating institutions?

Philosopher of religion John Hick points out that human beings find the world meaningful in a variety of overlapping ways. They engage with the world in terms of their meanings and assumptions about reality, and, if those meanings are wrong about the world "in what would soon become a fatal encounter the larger system would inevitably prevail and ... should be eliminated" (2004: 137). The dominant ways of cognizing the world of the past several centuries are clearly incompatible with "the larger system" in that we are destroying the planetary biosphere that sustains us, confronting one another with weapons of mass destruction that can wipe out civilization, and funneling the wealth of the planet into the hands of 10% of its population (and primarily 1%) while the other 90–99% live in ever-greater poverty and deprivation.

8.5   The World System

THE dominant meanings by which human beings interact with the world involve assumptions about the self and the world that instrumentalize nature and other persons, seeing the world as a totality of forces, powers, and things, with no outside, no (non-idolatrous) transcendence, no infinity. The dominant assumptions reify human groups (nations, races, cultures, religions) into objectified entities governed by instrumental and power-over relationships. These assumptions are reproduced in subsequent generations because they are embodied in the dominant institutions governing the planet. They generate their own conventional moral norms that justify and reinforce these orientations. They have no place for the ethical or eschatological as we examined these in the earlier sections of this chapter and in this book. To the dominant modes of meaning, the voices of the ethical or eschatological are subversive, dangerous, traitorous.

The sovereign nations cannot but objectify the other nations in a world of political manipulation, competition, and reduction of one another to "enemies" or "allies" in a global struggle. Citizens of each state identify themselves as Russians, Chinese, or Americans and externalize those of other states as in some vague way different from themselves. According to Mahatma Gandhi, the modern state is "violence in a concentrated and organized form" (1972: 132).

The same is true for capitalism. For Gandhi "capitalism" (as opposed to the capitalist) must be destroyed, for "the entire social order has got to be reconstructed" (1972: 120). Gandhi's name for the reconstructed social order is a "socialism" in which "truth and *ahimsa* must be incarnate" (1957: 3). Capitalism, we have seen, amounts to institutional and overt violence in which legally defined private property relationships allow a tiny minority to dominate and exploit the vast majority. "Truth," for Gandhi, means an economic system that benefits all, not just the few. To the extent it embodies the truth of "all," it would also embody nonviolence.

Under corporate capitalism, weapons cover the globe and the production and sale of weapons is one of the biggest businesses on the globe. The military-industrial-security complex (nation-states integrated with corporate capitalism) thrives on war and disaster, as Naomi Klein demonstrates (2007). Gandhi argues that an anarchism of nonviolent resistance is clearly not enough. We need to transform the nation-state and global capitalism into institutions incarnating "truth and *ahimsa*."

Just as the nation-state is violence in a concentrated form, so the world of capitalism cannot help but treat all of nature and human beings as mere instruments and implements within the institutionalized mechanisms for amassing private capital. Capitalism is, in its very essence, at war with nature and humanity, just as nation-states are at war with the concept of law, respect for law, and recognition of a true human dignity inherent in the law. Chris Williams, in his 2010 book, *Ecology and Socialism: Solutions to Capitalist Economic Crisis*, concludes that "capitalism is thus systematically driven toward the ruination of the planet and we underestimate how committed the system is to planetary ecocide at our peril. As stated above, ecological devastation is just as intrinsic to the operation of capitalism as is the exploitation of the vast majority of humans in the interests of a tiny minority, imperialism, and war" (2010: 232).

Dussel describes capitalism in terms of its victims:

> The "poor" are those who, in the relationship of domination, are the dominated, the instrumentalized, the alienated. ... Because of this domination, and in virtue of the basic fact of sin, person 2 robs person 1 of the fruit of his or her toil. The poverty or want suffered by the poor (person 1) is not the sheer absence of goods. No, the poverty of the poor consists in having been despoiled of the fruit of their labor by reason of the objective domination of sin. Thus the alienation of the other (fruit of the praxis of the sinner) produces the poverty of the poor (fruit of sin) as robbery, or dispossession. ... The life of the poor is accumulated by the rich. The latter live the life of the rich in virtue of the death of the poor. The life of the sinner feeds on the blood of the poor, just as the idol lives by the death of its victims. ... (1988: 22-24)

There can be no liberation from war and violence through an *evolution* of this system that recognizes no outside to itself, only more of the same, decade after decade, century after century. In the language of Levinas, it is a totalized conception of "being," everywhere "the same." It remains, in Tillich's words, "bound to the origin." The Pentagon is still significantly operating on the basis of a 1902 paper, the "Geographic Pivot of History" by Sir Halford John Mackinder, which stated that Europe, Asia and Africa constituted the "world island" and "who rules East Europe commands the Heartland; who rules the Heartland commands the world-island; who rules the world-island controls the world" (in Escobar, 2006: 11). The subjectivity of the people in the Pentagon stands over and against the rest of the world in a war relation.

There is nothing whatever in the totalized world view of the Pentagon that might allow for an evolution to a humane, ethically based planetary community. The idolatrous character of the totalized world system is there for all who care to open their eyes and see. You cannot slowly "evolve" what is evil—denying a human community based on *agape* and objectifying the other as threat or enemy—into conformity with the Good beyond being. Even when they claim that their "intent" is not evil, Socrates and Plato (like Buddhism and much of Eastern thought) have all pointed out that evil can be ignorance, and ignorance is to a large extent willful: we are responsible for refusing to overcome our ignorance.

You can only *found* a new order on correct premises from the very beginning. Moltmann describes the global confluence of capitalism and militarism:

> Like a huge idol, like the Beast in the Apocalypse (Rev. 13), the present economic system covers the Earth with its open sewer of unemployment and homelessness, hunger and nakedness, despair and death. It destroys different ways of living and working, which are in antithesis to its own. In its hostility to the environment, it sullies nature. It enforces an alien culture on peoples which it has conquered. In its insatiable greed for prosperity, it offers people themselves as a sacrifice in a bloody holocaust, pre-eminently in the Third-world but increasingly in the First-world too. The Beast has become a ravening monster, armed to the teeth with tanks and guns, atomic bombs, warships with computer-guided missiles, radar systems and satellites, and it is bringing humanity to the verge of total and sudden annihilation. But in the worldwide struggles of the poor and oppressed against all forms of dehumanization, there is a sign of life and of victory. (1996: 216)

This assessment reveals the hopeless juggernaut of our present world disorder, inherited from a dark past of centuries of racism, slavery, conquistadors, torture, and naked exploitation. It should be clear that human beings must find an eschatological liberation through overcoming global capitalism and the system of militarized nation-states. What concrete steps could we possibly take if not to create a global democratic set of institutions with authority *over* the nations, the private banking cartels, and the multinational corporations, and with the authority to abolish the Pentagon?

Mahatma Gandhi was one of those who understood that nonviolence can and should be institutionalized. Just as the violence of capitalism needs to be overcome by establishing a nonviolent global economic system (regulated by laws), so the system of sovereign nation-states needs to be overcome by a world federalist system. In 1942, for example, he introduced a resolution to the Indian National Congress that read:

> While the Indian National Congress must primarily be concerned with independence and defense of India in this hour of danger, the Committee is of the opinion that the future peace, security, and ordered progress of the world demand a world federation of free nations, and on no other basis can the problems of the modern world be solved. Such a world federation would ensure the freedom of its constituent nations, the prevention of aggression and exploitation by one nation over another, the protection of national ministries, the advancement of all backward areas and peoples, and the pooling of the world's resources for the common good of all."(In Hudgens, 1986: 14)

At the outset of the Second World War, as Japan invaded China, Gandhi wrote an open letter "To the Japanese" that began in part:

> I must confess at the outset that though I have no ill will against you, I intensely dislike your attack upon China. From your lofty height you have descended to imperial ambition. You will fail to realize that ambition and may become the authors of dismemberment of Asia, thus unwittingly preventing World Federation and brotherhood without which there can be no hope for humanity. (1962: 296)

And in his correspondence with the government undertaken between 1942 and 1944, Gandhi wrote "The structure of a world federation can be raised only on the foundation of nonviolence, and violence will have to be totally given up in world affairs" (1945: 460). Gandhi understood that nonviolence as a culture, as a character structure, as a personal way of life, and as capacity for resistance, is not sufficient for the world's need. We need to institutionalize nonviolence in our planetary economic and political systems. For Gandhi, we have seen, we need an earth federation of nations operating under a planetary "socialism."

8.6   Eschatology and World Transformation

THE continuing process of human beings breaking out of the totalized world system into the creative freedom, compassion, and hope of the "awakened" or "inspired" self (aware of infinity permeating our human situation) is a necessity if there is ever to be a world peace system, which would necessarily include ecological sustainability, reasonable universal prosperity, abolition of the war system, and freedom for all the world's citizens. This process requires new modes of thinking, a new paradigm, for human beings (as Gandhi understood) in which they envision a planetary community under the rule of democratic laws with humane institutions and protected human rights. If we set up the appropriate institutions, the conditions will be set for the transformation of human consciousness from objectification, greed, fear, and aggression to compassion, love, and interactions based on the golden rule at the heart of all religions (Hick, 2004: 309-314).

The first step in the eschatological actualization of the promise of history, therefore, is the establishing of institutions that can defang the nation-state and transform capitalism from a cancer on Earth into a system of reasonable prosperity and ecological sustainability. Wittgenstein states that "you cannot lead people to what is good; you can only lead them to some place or other. The good is outside the space of facts" (1980: 3). However, the Good beyond being is also the ground of the reconciliation of fact and value. Fact and value flow from the Source beyond being and can be recognized by human reason, intuition, and love. (This Source, contemporary science and philosophy reveals, cannot be cogently conceived as another "Being" outside the world but rather as an infinite dimension holistically in its depths.)

The key to a new paradigm is that it not be closed off, that it not exclude a possible awareness of infinity, for it is based on the legal recognition of truly universal human rights and dignity. Gandhi insisted on an economics that recognized this dignity, for such recognition of human dignity opens up to the depths, to the Atman in every person and to the "infinity in the human face." The totalized world of the war paradigm can find no real space for such recognition of dignity.

In an essay examining the "messianic atheism" of the neo-Marxist philosopher Ernst Bloch, whose *Principle of Hope* articulates an eschatological framework for perpetual hope in the depth-possibilities of existence available to human beings at all times and places, Moltmann finds that Bloch's orientation diminishes the possibilities for concrete decisive action in the present.

> Bloch's philosophical messianism also puts the world in a state of suspension.... Bloch uses a rich variety of symbols to characterize this state of suspension into which the messianic idea brings the world and the experience of the world, symbols such as "open world-process," "process matter," and "experimentum mundi".... This contains within itself, however, the weakness which Gershom Scholem pointed out—nothing is done in a conclusive way; everything remains preliminary, revocable, provisional.... Every word remains open, every thought remains fluid, every act revocable. Everything is only an "experiment." (2007: 184-85)

Moltmann's criticism of Bloch leaves out the depth-dimension pervading our human situation, from which Bloch derives his sense of the eschatological possibilities of human existence. As such, I believe Moltmann misses the deeper significance of Bloch's thought for understanding our human situation. Bloch's life and writings show that he does not advocate postponing or avoiding definitive action for fundamental change.

Nevertheless, Moltmann's point is well taken if this is understood as a weakness in eschatological orientations that can lead us to what he calls a "life in deferment" defined by a perpetual feeling that everything is "not-yet-real" (ibid. 185). The eschatological awareness does not need to defer concrete action because some actions in the present really can open up the possibilities of a redeemed future, while other kinds of action close off such a future.

We need to be able to act in practical and definitive ways to bring the dimension of peace into concrete existence within human affairs. To do so, as Moltmann fully understands, we need a penetrating critique of our current situation (war) and its defining institutions (that perpetuate and promote war and a war-mentality among human beings). We also need to be capable of making concrete changes in our global system that open up possibilities hitherto blocked by the dominant war and exploitation systems. The eschatological depths of human existence provide the hope necessary to believe that human liberation is possible. Our critical intelligence and rational capacity must be concomitantly focused on the flaws in our current world disorder and specific actions by which we can transform that war system and exploitation-system into a peace and justice system, or how we can *establish* a peace and justice system for Earth.

Similarly, we need to ask how to convert human thinking from the fragmentation implicit in objectification of nature and human beings in terms of rigid categories, forces, and powers to a sense of the holistic unity of the creative human community living cooperatively together within a finite and fragile planetary ecosystem. How do we establish a sense of *unity-in-diversity* as part of our worldview in which each unique personality (as Panikkar puts it) is respected and preserved in its infinite dignity while uniting the species in the unity of a planetary community? How do we eliminate militarism in nations and the military-industrial-security complex, and transform economics into relationships that promote sustainability and reasonable equality? How do we actualize the sense of our ethical obligation for the other that Levinas sees as the deepest and most primordial aspect of our humanity (1988: 164 ff.), currently ignored and unrecognized?

The institutional framework necessary for the actualization of a world-peace system, and necessary in the process of converting humanity to a sense of our universal ethical interdependency, is given in the *Constitution for the Federation of Earth* (see Martin, 2010b). Only the establishing of a global, non-military set of institutions that have the legitimate authority to regulate the nation-states and global capitalism through democratically legislated laws will suffice. As Dussel and Levinas both emphasize, human beings are conditioned by the dominant institutions into adopting the self-justifying "morality" of those institutions: "the 'flesh' is idolatrized in the 'kingdom of this world',," Dussel writes, "and promulgates its own law, its own morality, its own goodness" (1988: 30). Sovereign nation-states with their objectifying of enemies, together with capitalism with its instrumentalizing of human relationships, constitute a global war system that must be transformed into a planetary peace-system.

8.7 Our Global Social Contract

THERE are many reasons for ratifying the *Earth Constitution*. Most of these reasons are comprehensible at a pragmatic level by nearly everyone. But those aware of the eschatological demand at the heart of human history can see in its ratification, and in the quest for its ratification, an additional set of reasons. The *Constitution* defines its specific political, administrative, and economic arrangements in terms of a world of *unity-in-diversity* and the foundations of a new era of cooperation, peace, justice, prosperity, and sustainability for all humankind. It presents itself as an eschatological document beyond the reign of objectification, alienation, and nihilism.

It announces in its Preamble the establishing of "a new age when war shall be outlawed and peace prevail; when the Earth's total resources shall be used equitably for human welfare; and when basic human rights and responsibilities shall be shared by all without discrimination." The *Constitution* presents a coherent set of institutions designed to overcome both uncontrolled capitalism and the sovereign nation-state, making possible the coming of the reign of God to Earth. It converts the world's war system into a world peace system.

A full philosophical grounding for a universal democratic constitution would require moving far beyond the scope of this book into areas that I have elaborated elsewhere (e.g., Martin, 2008). However, a compelling basis for my claim can be easily found in Kant's ethics and eschatology discussed in part one of this chapter. As is well-known, Kant drew conclusions that bear directly on the issue of a transition from a war system to a peace-system in his essay *Perpetual Peace* (1795) and related writings concerning his social contract theory emphasizing the universal moral obligation to live under republican government. He argued that, *first*, persons are morally required (by the categorical imperative) to leave the "state of nature" in which they live according to power-only principles without a republican constitution that ensures their common freedom and equality (a condition that he calls "war") and to become equal citizens under the rule of universal, enforceable republican laws, in other words, under a peace system (1983: 71-72).

Second, he pointed out that nations, similarly, are required to "leave the lawless state of savagery and enter into a federation of peoples" (ibid. 34). "The state of peace," Kant correctly says, "must be established." It can only be established through a global social contract forming the universal rule of enforceable law over all (ibid. 111). He states that philosophy has its own "chiliastic vision," its own eschatology. However, this is "anything but fanciful" since it is promoted by the philosophically justified idea of a cosmopolitan world of peace among all peoples (ibid. 34-38).

We find here another eschatological implication of the idea of human dignity and its consequent ideal of a future Kingdom of Ends. Human beings encounter an absolute moral imperative to unite in an earth federation ending war and bringing the rule of republican law to all. Kant also understood that the rule of law under a republican constitution cannot establish the Kingdom of Ends, but it can establish the conditions that make further progress possible. As John Ladd points out in his introduction to Kant's *Metaphysical Elements of Justice*, "this whole book may be regarded as an extended philosophical commentary on the relation between what is and what ought to be, both in politics and law" (1965: xxix). This could be said of Kant's entire philosophy. Global republican laws must be established that promote what *ought to be* (the Kingdom of Ends: all persons living morally within a peaceful world system), and do not merely ideologically cover up and justify what *is* (systems of war, exploitation, totalization, and domination).

Democratic government under the *Earth Constitution* is premised on ending the inherent lawlessness of the system of some 193 militarized sovereign nation-states. Only the rule of democratically legislated enforceable law can bring the nations to lawful (peaceful) behavior. So-called "international law" has proved entirely powerless in this respect. The *Earth Constitution* is also premised on awareness of our planetary community cooperatively living within a fragile ecosystem, and on recognition of the inalienable dignity and human rights of every citizen of the Earth (cf. Martin, 2008 and 2010a). Within this institutional framework, the violence of sovereign nation-states and the global structural violence of capitalism can be pacified and transformed.

Many people of Earth have understood the possibility of democratic government since at least the 18th century. They have understood the idea of inalienable human rights since the 18th century and the responsibility of government to promote the common good. But today, planetary crises beyond the scope of individual nation-states threaten human existence in a variety of ways. Democracy, human rights, and the common good can no longer be protected without a world government that can also deal simultaneously with these planetary crises.

The "broad functions" of the Earth Federation government, given in Article One of the *Earth Constitution*, mandate government to: (1) end war and demilitarize the nations, (2) protect universal human rights worldwide, (3) eliminate poverty and establish reasonable economic equity, (4) regulate and conserve global resources, (5) protect the environment and the ecological fabric of life, and (6) find solutions to all problems beyond the capacity of the national governments (cf. Martin, 2010b: 29).

Only an Earth Federation government could accomplish these things and only the accomplishment of these things can set the stage for a truly cooperative and loving planetary society. A fundamental premise of the *Earth Constitution*, given in its Preamble, is the principle of unity-in-diversity: the diversity of "nations, races, creeds, ideologies, and cultures" shall be united in a unity in which "war shall be outlawed and peace prevail" (ibid. 28). The eschatological and ethical demand for deep transformation necessarily passes through the *Earth Constitution*. Not only its Preamble, but the entire *Constitution* embodies fundamental principles resonating with the principle of unity-in-diversity and the concept of our common humanity and our common political, environmental, and economic needs, while at the same time protecting, in the words of Panikkar, every human being's "freedom and personal uniqueness."

In Dussel's terms, ratifying the *Earth Constitution* would be the necessary preliminary act for the coming reign of God on Earth, for Levinas it would be the preliminary act for the Messianic Age, for Kant, it would be the necessary (although not sufficient) condition for a possible "Kingdom of Ends." Nothing can be done without taming the war system of the raging sovereign nation-states or the structural and overt violence of the capitalist system of dehumanization and exploitation. The *Earth Constitution* abolishes militarism and disarms the nations, leaving the enforcement of law to civilian world police and local police. It does not abolish "free trade" but tames it, bringing economics under the rule of democratically legislated laws and the common good of the planet and its citizens. "Free trade" becomes "fair trade." These transformations derive from, and make possible for human beings, a new way of cognizing the world and our human situation.

Every generation, at present, inherits a more sophisticated technology and a more pervasive system of domination, surveillance, and social control. But can every new generation inherit an awareness of Creative Existence and Transformative Freedom? This may be the great dilemma of human liberation. The young begin again, and ever again, as children. Hence, they may well become unquestionably socialized within the domination system, thinking it is "normal" and assimilating the propaganda of "terror" and "security." Under this system the chances of awakening to the Mystery of Existence and the Transformative Freedom appear severely diminished. Does this mean that the death of "our ontological vocation to become more fully human" (Freire, 1974: 40-41) is a foregone conclusion?

On the other hand, we can find a freshness and impulse to creativity in many young people that the system of domination must be at pains to suppress or channel into neo-fascist violence, inner deadness, and fear. Young people may find out about factory farms and the institutionalized torture of animals for private profit by which we feed ourselves. Many may become vegan, for example, in reaction to these horrors. It is necessary for the system, therefore, to criminalize the taking of photos at factory farms, just as it is necessary for the system to criminalize real investigative journalism or solidarity with oppressed peoples (calling this "supporting terrorism"). Older people, perhaps two billion of them, may engage in a transforming "pedagogy of the oppressed," directed to liberating both themselves and their oppressors (Freire, 1974).

But this is exactly why the people of Earth must take control of technology as well as the social system of the Earth under the emerging Earth Federation. The system of technological domination works to defeat the transformation of human consciousness. I have tried to make it clear that we do not need a majority of people aware of Existence and Transformative Freedom (Creative Holism) to establish the Earth Federation. The imperative for democracy, sustainability, and compassion for the Earth and its creatures is sufficient for establishing the Federation. Its establishment may well be the key to further human liberation, to fulfilling our ontological vocation.

Articles 12 and 13 of the *Earth Constitution* draw on the human dignity that is at the heart of the UN Universal Declaration of Human Rights (a concept, we have seen, that points to infinity within human beings) and actualizes that dignity in a comprehensive list of political, economic, environmental, and peace rights. Unlike the UN Declaration, however, the *Earth Constitution* embodies dignity not simply in an abstract "declaration" of human rights but within a global social contract in which these rights become enforceable world law, world law that includes sustainability, humane treatment of animals, and harmony with the biosphere.

Enforceable law is now presented, however, within the eschatological context of "a new age when war shall be outlawed and peace prevail." Human dignity and the cooperative spirit of working together in the spirit of tolerance, dialogue, and even love (as *agape or karuna*) lies at the heart of the *Earth Constitution.* A carefully designed system of checks and balances assures that the old tyrannies cannot colonize the new paradigm, which is premised on holism rather than fragmentation, dialogue rather than war, and sharing of basic resources rather than private appropriation by the few.

The ethical dimension that functions as a framework for human life, and that gives us the eschatological demand for a transformed world system, is released and validated by the *Earth Con-*

stitution. The paradigm-shift from fragmentation to holism, under the principle of unity-in-diversity, makes possible the recognition of our common humanity in a multiplicity of ways that can transform our understanding of self and other, making possible recognition of the infinity within. We have before us a concrete road map, a specific set of steps we can take, a path to tread upon that we know will take us into the new paradigm that must be founded if we are to survive and flourish on this planet. To equivocate is to be lost. To mumble about the need for a slow "evolution" of existing institutions is to be tethered to the origin, to fail to see the real foundations of the matter and the real possibilities that inform human life. Peace, as Kant declares, must be *established*—through a global social contract that embodies universal principles from the very beginning.

World peace involves both an ethical awakening on the part of humanity and a world peace system in which the conditions for ethical awakening are institutionalized worldwide. "Man must awaken to wonder," Wittgenstein exclaims, "science is a way of sending him to sleep again" (1980: 3). We do not need to repudiate science, of course, since this is absolutely essential to living sustainably with a quality existence within the limits of our finite, ecologically interdependent biosphere. But we also must awaken in wonder to the absolute demands of the ethical that transcend the spheres of science, technology, and organization, and make it possible for us to use these spheres in the service of creative holism: peace, justice, freedom, and sustainability.

Awakening to wonder opens persons up to the depths of the mysteries of time, our present, the miracle of existence, and the ethical. It makes possible the awareness that flows from the futurity of God. The vision of a transformed set of world institutions is found in the *Earth Constitution*, a vision of what is possible for human beings in terms of peace, justice, freedom, and sustainability. We can found a world system that makes possible human liberation.

The *Earth Constitution* provides a concrete grounding for a world peace system that cries out, in the words of Isaiah: "Peace, peace to him who is far and to him who is near." It is an actualization of a presuppositional *telos* embedded in the very concept of law. Ratification of the *Constitution* and activation of a democratic Earth Federation perhaps makes possible, for virtually all humanity, the awakening to the Infinite that lies at the foundation of the universe and at the heart of our human situation.

Chapter 9

Twenty-First Century Renaissance: The Reconciliation of Reason, Intuition, and Love

Nothing is vainly repeated; you too, then, as an individual are unique. And (here is the central fact) just insofar as you consciously will and choose, you then and there insofar know what this unique meaning of yours is. Therefore, you are in action free and individual, just because the unity of the divine life, when taken together with the uniqueness of this life, implies in every finite being just such essential originality of meaning as that of which you are conscious. Arise then, freeman, stand forth in thy world. It is God's world. It is also thine.

—Josiah Royce

We are expressions of the universal designing intelligence.

—Barbara Marx Hubbard

CREATIVE holism, as we have elaborated it in this book, is revolutionary because it means a pervasive shift from a fragmented and fractured world disorder to a harmonious and integrated world order. We have seen that some thinkers have expressed this revolution, currently going on worldwide, as a "paradigm-shift;" others have identified the transformation going on as a new "Axial Age." However it is framed, the emergent holistic worldview derives directly from revolutionary 20th century scientific breakthroughs that revealed the holistic structure of the universe and all levels of reality within it, including humanity and the ecosystem of Earth.

This emergent evolutionary and civilizational process of actualizing the holistic structures implicit in the cosmos resulted in the emergence of mind, reason, knowledge, and values within the human phenomenon. Each of us is a self-conscious embodiment of the whole and, at the same time, a life history in process of actualizing our own potential for holism, a process that is inseparable from our relationships to the larger wholes of which we are part. We are all individual (biological and psychological) systems and are part of Earth's larger (ecological and civilizational) systems. Harris explains the logic of systems as follows:

> A whole, therefore, as a system of elements in relation, a continuum of overlapping moments, is always both unified and differentiated, both one and many, and is always a totality, fragmentariness being inevitably relative to completion. Its unity and multiplicity are mutually dependent and inseparable. Each implies and requires the other in order to be itself. There is and can be no unity without multiplicity and no multiplicity without unity, for it is nothing other than the interdependence of the differentiations that constitutes the unity of the whole. Conversely, the unity of each constituent element is dependent upon its interrelations with the other elements. Its specified position in the whole makes it a reflection or expression of the total structure from a particular viewpoint. (1987: 144)

Each of us is an expression of the total structure (of humanity, and, indeed, the cosmos) "from a particular viewpoint." Each of us "implies and requires the other" in order to be ourselves. The insights of Gandhi and Socrates, that I am you and you are me, are confirmed by the very logic of the systems that make up the cosmos. The insight that each of us is a living and unique expression of the cosmos itself, as recounted in Swimme and Berry's *The Universe Story,* is confirmed by the scientific and philosophical breakthroughs of the past century.

9.1 Reason and Intuition

THESE two words remain, of course, broad and vague, and the phenomena to which they refer cannot be defined with any great precision. This is not the result of fuzzy thinking, for we have been using them intelligibly and with some precision throughout this book. As Wittgenstein made clear in his *Philosophical Investigations,* every word encompasses a range of *conventional* meanings that may entail some conventionally central uses of the word but whose uses taper off into meanings that become evermore peripheral and ambiguous. There are many ways to use each of these words. The context of the whole, in this case the whole of this book and the literature upon which it draws, serves to illuminate the intelligibility and coherence of the terms involved.

Meanings are not defined in isolation from one another: what we are talking about at least in part arises from the juxtaposition of meanings. With some intelligibility, we can contrast the situations in which we use the words "reason," "intuition," or "love" with their apparent opposites (irrationality, lack of intuition, impersonality, and hatred). Nevertheless, no exact precision is possible, nor necessary for our purposes. Similarly, St. Augustine points out in the tenth book of his *Confessions* regarding the concept of "time"— that he uses the word with apparent perfect understanding every day, yet when he thinks about what "time" means and tries to define it precisely, it becomes deeply mysterious to him. Thus, as we have seen, each of these words points to the depths that encompass the profound mysteries of our human situation. We use them casually every day, yet they point to very deep aspects of our human reality.

In an article entitled "Reason" in the *Encyclopedia of Philosophy*, philosopher G. J. Warnock writes on the mystery of "reason":

> First, it is far from immediately clear what reasoning is—on what occasions, in what activities or processes, reason is exercised. And second, if we determine—probably with some degree of arbitrariness—what reasoning is, it may very well remain highly disputable whether this or that can or cannot be achieved by reasoning. (1967, Vol.7-8: 84)

Even an analytically based encyclopedia cannot define reason clearly. Similar conclusions can be drawn regarding "intuition" and "love"—it is impossible to define them precisely. I believe my central thesis here is strengthened by the lack of precise definability of these words. For I want to assert that they are all interrelated and interdependent in human awareness and within the human relation to the world, and in some sense, as we shall see further, they reflect dimensions of the cosmos itself present in us.

We associate reason with our capacity for analysis, for synthesis, for imaginative interpretation and reconstruction, for discourse that uses evidence and logic to argue from premises to conclusions, as well as for a number of other things. All these capacities presuppose a single, coherent, synthesizing, self-aware self, as we saw in Chapter Two, presupposing the world as a coherent whole of unity in diversity. Yet within this dynamic framework of a multiplicity of human capacities operating within these holistic presuppositions, perhaps it is not possible to isolate and define reason more exactly.

In 20th century philosophy, some phenomenologists and existentialists rebelled against the Western tradition that had elevated reason to a superior status to the exclusion of our more primordial relationships to our environment deriving from our bodily existence. In *Being and Time* (1927), Martin Heidegger identified the primordial human relationship to the world as care (*Sorge*), which was non-rational and from which our other human capacities arose. He repudiated abstract "representational thinking" on the grounds that it assumed a false relationship to being. Similarly in *Phenomenology of Perception* (1945), Maurice Merleau-Ponty argued that our relation to the world arises from the "lived body" within the experience of which thought, perception, feeling are all fundamentally intertwined. These great insights into our lived being-in-the-world are not abandoned by the new holism but incorporated into its broader understanding of the pervasive holistic structures of the world discovered by the sciences and what these mean for our understanding of reason and human life.

The meanings and uses of words like reason, intuition, or love expand under the new holism, which understands that truth is *coherence*, and that coherence within the holism of possible modes of awareness gives a much richer set of epistemological sources of truth than a doctrine that restricts "truth" to empirical experimentation or to what can be discerned solely through analytical modes of reasoning. Harris defines "coherence" as "characteristic of ordered wholeness...a coherent unity of differences." He goes on to show that "this concept is by no means simple" (2000a: 215) and that within the dynamic, temporalized world of unities-in-diversities the proper mode of reasoning is "dialectical": "The exposition of the whole can only be dialectical."

Contradiction is, therefore, "mutually involved" with coherence (2000a: 218). In his 1987 book *Formal, Transcendental, and Dialectical Thinking: Logic and Reality*, Harris systematically shows the very limited application that formal logic has in revealing the structures of the world. He contrasts this with the power of dialectical logic to illuminate the world, since the real world is an evolving process of wholes within wholes, and dialectic is precisely the logic of such wholes. As the systematic examination of the dimensions of human knowledge in the work of Harris shows, the concepts of knowledge, reasoning, and truth are being substantially enlarged under the impact of contemporary holistic philosophy.

The older medieval and Cartesian idea that reason is a "faculty" of our human nature is replaced today with the insight that reason is a dialogical project of ourselves as individuals and of the evolutionary emergence of our humanity, embracing both ourselves, humanity, and the cosmos. As Habermas (1998), Ricoeur (1967), Swidler and Mojzes (2000), and others have shown, language, founded upon the presupposition of a dialogical situation embedded in the very possibility of communication, includes within itself both the individual and universal projects of rationality, intertwined as these are with our other emergent projects that are part of what Paulo Freire called "our ontological project to become ever more fully human" (1990: 43-61).

The mysterious and wondrous depths of our human capacity for multidimensional awareness of the world through reason, intuition, and love, however, should not obscure from us the fact in the evolutionary process, the universe has become conscious of itself in us. We discern its holistic quality throughout the cosmos, in the unity of the whole cosmos, and in our own transcendental self that presupposes the unity of the cosmos and the coherence of knowledge. At the head of this chapter I posted Barbara Marx Hubbard's conclusion that "We are expressions of the universal designing intelligence." Teilhard de Chardin affirms that "Man discovers that *he is nothing else than evolution become conscious of itself*" (1959: 221), and Harris states that "the awareness of self and other, which finally emerges, is no less than ... the wholeness of the world and the evolutionary process come to consciousness.... In this consciousness, the world becomes aware of itself in us" (1988: 150-51).

Human beings themselves are the holism of the cosmos, concentrated like a laser beam, and actualized in us. However, we understand that the cosmos is an evolutionary and *emergent* process, and now comprehend that we are responsible for the further actualization of holism, harmony, and coherence, most fundamentally in relation to human civilization and our precious planet Earth.

Our gifts of reason, intuition, and love must be developed in order to fulfill this responsibility. Let us examine further the interrelation of reason and intuition (and reserve the discussion of love for subsequent sections).

I have been using the word "intuition" to characterize some noncognitive aspects of human awareness. There may be several modes of noncognitive awareness, for example, the experience of sheer "duration" (Bergson, 1975), the primordial perceptual openness of our human bodies (Ricoeur, 1967), the awareness of "the Encompassing" beyond subject and object (Jaspers, 1959), or the direct, unmediated awareness of the suchness of things prior to language and thought (Wittgenstein, 1974, cf. Martin, 1988). Bergson states:

> Numerous are the philosophers who have felt how powerless conceptual thought is to reach the core of the mind. Numerous, consequently, are those who have spoken of a supra-intellectual faculty of intuition.... Intuition, then, signifies first of all consciousness, but immediate consciousness, a vision which is scarcely distinguishable from the object seen, a knowledge which is in contact and even coincidence.... Intuition give us the thing whose spatial transposition, whose metaphorical translation alone, is seized by the intellect. (1975: 30, 32 & 71)

Bergson speaks of intuition as an immediacy prior to the representational function of intellect, an immediacy that cannot be captured by reason or intellect. It gives us, he says, "the thing," the immediate awareness of things prior to their representation in thought. Similarly, mystics from all centuries and all major cultures have spoken of an immediacy prior to reason, thought, and language that is fundamental to their awareness of the One, which they called Tao, *Dharmakaya, Nirguna Brahman*, or God. The One is not Bergson's "thing itself," but the matrix of all things.

As with Bergson, many mystics assert that this awareness does not give us "knowledge" in the ordinary sense as understood today, but nevertheless such a direct awareness remains a fundamental human capacity. Mystics testify that this awareness is revelatory, veridical, and utterly convincing. Early western mystics like Dionysios the Areopagite or Eriugena developed the famous *via negativa* from their understanding that language, conceptualization, and ordinary knowing must be negated and transcended in the process leading to direct "illumination." In his book on religious and mystical awakening, F. C. Happold quotes the *Kena Upanisad* of classical Hinduism: "The ignorant think the spirit lies with knowledge, the wise man knows it beyond knowledge" (1966: 16).

On the other hand some, like Seyyed Hossein Nasr in *Knowledge and the Sacred*, argue that the drive to "profane knowledge" (emerging largely during this same early-modern period) has "depleted knowledge of its sacred character" and that, traditionally, in all the great religions and cultures, knowledge involved "the possibility of knowing things in principle and the principles of all things leading finally to the knowledge of Ultimate Reality" (1981: 6). Catholic theologian and sociologist Andrew Greely calls mysticism a "form of knowledge" that derives from a "particular form of contact with Reality" (1974: 57-58).

The word "knowledge," like the words reason, intuition, and love, can be used in a multiplicity of coherent ways depending on context and intent. One thing clear is that the emerging holistic paradigm is much more open to a multiplicity of dimensions of which human beings can be aware and a multiplicity of *modes of awareness* through which we access these dimensions. Walter Stace in *The Teaching of the Mystics* confirms that the "nonsensuous" awareness ("formless, shapeless, colorless, odorless, soundless") with which mystics experience the One is "entirely unlike our everyday consciousness and is wholly incommensurable with it" (1960: 12). Sri Aurobindo writes: "The mind spiritualized by the ascent into Self has the sense of *laya*, dissolution of itself, its thoughts, movements, Sanskaras into a superconscient Silence and Infinity which it is unable to grasp—the Unknowable" (1970: 1139).

Yet reason is not necessarily in contradiction with these more immediate modes of awareness within the dynamic process, composed of many depths and dimensions, that constitutes our universe. Edward G. Ballard in his book *Philosophy at the Crossroads*, for example, affirms that philosophy cannot operate as sheer reason alone without the input from intuition. He writes that "philosophy is careful, analytic thought only when this latter is enlivened by some effective inspiration. Thus philosophy arises from the interchange between inspiration and disciplined thinking. Philosophy is, in short, inspired reason" (1971: 22).

"Inspired reason" means that reason works in harmony with noncognitive intuition and love in its drive to apprehend the world. However we wish to define "knowledge" in relation to our several noncognitive forms of awareness, it is clear that we must reach outside of narrow reasoning and reductionistic science in order to encounter the deeper realities of our situation and their holistic implications. Physicist Fritjof Capra affirms that:

> In the twentieth century, however, physics has gone through several conceptual revolutions that clearly reveal the limitations of the mechanistic world view and lead to an organic, ecological view of the world which shows great similarities to the view of the mystics of all ages and traditions.... The fact that modern physics, the manifestation of an extreme specialization of the rational mind, is now making contact with mysticism, the essence of religion and manifestation of an extreme specialization of the intuitive mind, shows very beautifully the unity and complementary nature of the rational and intuitive modes of consciousness. (1982: 47-48)

The "inspiration" of these deeper realities is capable of redeeming our constricted and fragmented being, split (as it has been by the early-modern paradigm) between an apparently horrific "objective" external world and a "merely subjective" set of reactions to that external world. Reason and intuition, both capable of coherent and credible perceptions of reality, complement one another. We must move beyond "problem thinking," as Gabriel Marcel puts it, to an openness that allows us to encounter the "mystery," to the depths of that which encompasses all knowledge and all of life. Marcel calls this new level of awareness "meta-problematical":

> If the meta-problematical can be asserted at all, it must be conceived as transcending the opposition between the subject who asserts the existence of being, on the one hand, and being *as asserted by that subject,* on the other, and as underlying it in a given sense. To postulate the meta-problematical...is to recognize the primacy of being over knowledge.... From this standpoint, contrary to what epistemology seeks vainly to establish, there exists well and truly a mystery of cognition; knowledge is contingent on a participation in being for which no epistemology can account because it continually presupposes it. (1980: 18)

If ordinary perception requires the subject-object split, awareness of the wholes that encompass both subject and object (awareness of "being") requires that we transcend the standpoint of subject versus object. It is not only the "mystery of cognition" that is revealed in this process; for Marcel encompasses all these reflections within the framework of an encounter with "the mystery of being," the title of his 1951 book. Holism transcends "the problematical," which is the world as it is limited to instrumental forms of reasoning. James Fowler expresses a similar idea: "In any holistic approach to the human construction of meaning, account must be given of the relations of reasoning to imagination, of moral judgment making to symbolic representation, of ecstatic intuition to logical deduction" (1981: 99).

The ancient Greeks affirmed that philosophy begins in wonder, but wonder does not mean wondering about how to solve the problems posed by the constricted analytical intellect with its spurious empiricist epistemology. Wonder, like love, opens up for us depths that encompass our lives and helps reveal their meaning and purpose. Cognition itself participates in this mystery. To be "in the presence of a mystery," Marcel writes, is to encounter "a reality rooted in what is beyond the domain of the problematical purely so-called" (ibid. 21). In the presence of mystery, human beings can encounter, not subjective fantasies, but "reality." Reason is immensely important, and has its place, but it must be complemented by an intuition of the depths of existence.

9.2 Mystery, Astonishment, and Wonder

MARCEL continues: "It might perhaps even be shown that the domain of the meta-problematical coincides with that of love, and that love is the only starting point for the understanding of such mysteries as that of body and soul, which, in some manner, is its expression" (ibid. 20). Love, for Marcel, opens us to a dimension of "being" beyond any set of empirical "facts" posited by the "problem thinking" of the early-modern paradigm. For love is *participatory* and *relational*, whereas classical epistemology divorced the observer from any participatory relation with the "objective" phenomenon being observed.

He also calls this apprehension "intuition": "The more an intuition is central and basic in the being whom it illuminates, the less it is capable of turning back and apprehending itself. . . . An intuition cannot be brought out into the light of day, for the simple reason that we do not possess it" (ibid. 25). Hence, there are levels of apprehension of the depths of our situation that carry a level of immediacy that cannot be objectified, cannot "turn back and apprehend itself." We saw Panikkar affirm that every being has an "abyssal dimension, both transcendent and immanent."

This immediate openness to the mystery of being can also be called love, which is "central and basic." Marcel's thought continually swings back and forth between descriptors of the closed, fragmented, and limited world that was bequeathed us by the early-modern paradigm and the encounter with depths that can redeem and reclaim the meaning and purpose of our lives. In the world of problems and techniques, he writes:

> In such a world the ontological need, the need of be-
> ing, is exhausted in exact proportion to the breaking up
> of personality on the one hand and, on the other, to the
> triumph of the category of the "purely natural" and the
> consequent atrophy of the faculty of *wonder*.... Being is
> what withstands...an exhaustive analysis bearing on the
> data of experience and aiming to reduce them step by step
> to elements increasingly devoid of intrinsic or significant
> value.... I shall also point out that, just because this phi-
> losophy continually stresses the activity of verification, it
> ends by ignoring *presence*—that inward realization of pres-
> ence through love which infinitely transcends all possible
> verification because it exists in an immediacy beyond all
> conceivable mediation. (Ibid. 13-15)

In these reflections of Marcel we have a clear example of the
integration of reason, intuition, and love. Marcel uses reason
to distinguish the analytic and verificationist approaches of the
early-modern paradigm from the openness to being that can be
mediated through love and intuition. The awareness of presence
through love involves an immediacy that cannot be objectified.
These three features of an authentic and healthy human awareness are interwoven in his thought.

What is beyond the "purely natural" is called "mystery."
However, this word is merely an indicator pointing to the encompassing depths of our lives from which meaning, purpose, and
"intrinsic value" arise. Reason in its broadest sense, like wonder,
love, and intuition, opens us up to these depths of being. Some
thinkers, like Marcel himself, refer to these depths as God or revelatory aspects of God's cosmos. Nicholas Berdyaev declares that
"the fundamental religious truth is that God is mystery and that
mystery lies at the heart of all things" (in Langiulli, 1971: 368).

Similarly, Karl Jaspers contrasts "false philosophy," which derives from the early-modern paradigm, and authentic philosophy
that "awakens, makes one attentive, shows ways, leads the way
for a while, makes ready, makes one ripe for the experience of
the utmost" (1959: 79). Authentic philosophizing leads to "the

Encompassing" that Jaspers says cannot be the object of scientific knowledge because it transcends the distinction between subject and object. Philosophy opens us to a direct intuitive encounter with the mystery:

> The world and everything that occurs in it is a mystery. The crudeness of finding everything to be self-evident through force of habit and the mania for mystery to the point of the sensational and the superstitious must disappear where genuine astonishment begins. Philosophy illuminates the mystery and brings it completely into consciousness. It begins with astonishment and increases the astonishment. (Only false philosophy, which carries on its thinking like scientific research into the things of the world, casts out astonishment through an alleged knowledge.) Then the world as a whole and in every individual feature shows infinite depth. This mystery is quiet; in flaring up it becomes revealed in an unfoldment. And this mystery is essential; in it Being itself speaks. (1959: 37)

As with Marcel, in Jasper's thought, reason, intuition, and love operate inseparably from what he describes as a continually increasing ecstatic "astonishment." The reductionist approach deriving from the early-modern paradigm casts out, not only astonishment, but the awareness of intrinsic value, "the origin that lies in God" (ibid. 79). This awareness is explicitly beyond knowledge, for Jaspers, yet there is nothing ambiguous about it; it is not speculation, nor fuzzily held religious sentiments.

In his 1929 "Lecture on Ethics," we saw that Wittgenstein is attempting to communicate what he means "by absolute or ethical value" by describing his "experience *par excellence*." In this experience, he says, "*I wonder at the existence of the world....*how extraordinary that anything should exist" (1965: 8). In *The Inward Morning*, philosopher H. G. Bugbee writes:

> In wonder reality begins to sink in. It sets us to a questioning which can only find a conclusive answer in terms of our deepening of our response to things, which is the deepening, and not the allaying, of wonder." (1976: 162)

Wittgenstein's astonishment that anything at all exists elicits in him a fundamental *response* of his whole being. He has encountered "absolute value" and stands in an entirely different relation to the whole of existence. For Wittgenstein, it is this *responsiveness* that is at the core of authentic religion (see Martin, 1988). Under the influence of the early-modern paradigm, we have lost the ability to fully respond. The same for Bugbee. Reality begins to sink in when we deepen "our response to things," which is the deepening of wonder. Nicholas Berdyaev places the responsiveness of wonder at the heart of the spiritual life:

> A true realism and a true idealism issue from the recognition of Mystery beneath and beyond this world: it is the attitude of him whose eyes do not tell what they know or do not know. He who knows no mystery lives in a flat, insipid, one dimensional world. If the experience of flatness and insipidity were not relieved by an awareness of mystery, depth and infinitude, life would be no longer livable. In childhood all things, even a dark corner in the room, appear as mysterious. Later the realm of mystery narrows: the objective world around becomes more and more commonplace, and even the infinite depth of the starry night loses its mysteriousness. But for him who does not yield to this objectivity mystery abides and only moves on to another sphere. Then the very emergence of the objective world becomes a source of wonder. (1962: 299)

For Berdyaev, all "objectivity" of the commonplace world becomes suspended and framed within the absolute wonder that is the encounter with the mystery of existence, from the depths and infinitude that fall away from us on every side. For all these thinkers (examined here and in Chapter Eight), as for Marcel and Jaspers, deeper aspects of reality are only encountered through relationship and responsiveness (love), within the framework of an abiding wonder. As Marcel declares, love opens a relationship with being that cannot be captured by empirical investigations.

Nearly all such thinkers who have encountered the depths of being through some form of direct intuition remain absolutely clear about their encounter with these depths. The experience, as Bergson says of intuition, is primordial: more certain than empirically verifiable knowledge. Stace affirms that the experience is "more real (in some sense) than any other experience" (1960: 10). Søren Kierkegaard speaks of "a critical moment when everything is reversed, after which the point becomes to understand more and more that there is something which cannot be understood" (1959: 172).

Recognizing the ambiguity of the words "reason, intuition, and love" does not indicate an epistemology that is itself fuzzy, vague, or ill-conceived. What is going on in these thinkers is not superficial or sentimental. They are clear and on the mark in what they experience and understand. Just as contemporary physics as an "extreme specialization of the rational mind" discerns the value-laden holism of the cosmos, so mysticism as an "extreme specialization of the intuitive mind" becomes directly aware of that value-laden whole in an immediacy prior to language and knowledge.

Nevertheless, we do not need to appeal to direct intuition, or any form of mysticism, to confirm the holism of the cosmos and our human situation, for the "rational mind" also apprehends what the intuitive mind directly experiences. Much philosophical and spiritual work that is going on today can be linked with the paradigm-shift toward revolutionary holism, or to the emergence of a redeemed and holistic mode of consciousness characteristic of the Second Axial Age.

We need to explore this confluence of reason, intuition, and love further with a focus on these characteristics, not simply as human phenomena, but as manifestations of the holistic cosmos itself, allowing us to realize evermore fully that human beings truly are microcosms of the macrocosm. We will find that the astonishing "inwardness" that we experience in ourselves—the inwardness that makes us think that we are not "merely animals" struggling for survival within a Darwinian struggle of the fittest, that we really are, in some profound way "the measure of all things"—

is today confirmable through reason and science. Jonas declares that this work "admits to the much-scorned offense of *anthropomorphism*. And this after four centuries of modern natural sciences":

> Yet perhaps, in a properly understood sense, man *is* the measure of all things—not, of course, by virtue of laws promulgated by his reason but by the paradigm of his psychophysical wholeness, which reveals the maximum degree of concrete ontological completeness known to us. *From this pinnacle downwards*, the classes of being would then be described in terms of privation, by progressive subtraction down to the minimum of mere elementary matter. In other words, instead of the higher forms of life being reduced to the lowest, beings would be characterized in terms of "a less and less," an evermore distant "not yet." Ultimately, the deterministic nature of lifeless matter would be interpreted as sleeping, not yet awakened freedom. (1996: 62)

The entire process of evolution can be understood as leading to what Pierre Teilhard de Chardin called the "hominizing of the world"—nature running into the emergent properties that characterize her most complete and developed forms. As we move back down the evolutionary levels toward the framework of lifeless matter and energy, we discern progressive loss of consciousness, reason, feeling, love, and freedom. Contemporary reason and science show that we can understand evolution as being about these properties. The framework expresses not dead, disparate, material processes, but holistic integration and emergent higher properties.

9.3   Holism and Consciousness

HUMAN consciousness (which includes reason, intuition, and love) represents an emergent development of the cosmos itself. Unless we realize this within our deepest awareness and sense of self, we will likely feel dwarfed and insignificant in the face of the immense reaches of space and galaxies. But there are powerful arguments as well as intuitions that relate our consciousness to the consciousness of the universe itself. If the principle of systemic order in the universe has given rise to human consciousness, does this not imply that the same order is manifested in a cosmic consciousness? In reflecting on the revolutionary implications of contemporary science, Kafatos and Nadeau write:

> This argument also leads to an even more extraordinary conclusion. If consciousness is an emergent property of the universe in the case of human beings, would not this also imply, given the underlying wholeness of the cosmos, that the universe is itself conscious? In other words, if consciousness emerges out of this undivided wholeness at any stage in the evolution of the cosmos, would the temporal and spatial non-localities that are complementary aspects of this wholeness imply that it was present at all stages? We believe, providing of course that we refrain from viewing a conscious universe in anthropomorphic terms, that it does. (1990: 170)

Contemporary thinkers are beginning to apply the concept of "mind" (beyond definitions limited to the human mind) to the dynamics of the natural world itself. Gregory Bateson, in his 1972 book in *Steps to an Ecology of Mind*, argues that it is an epistemological error to limit mind to human beings. He states that:

> Mind is a necessary, an inevitable function of the appropriate complexity, wherever that complexity occurs. But that complexity occurs in a great many other places besides the inside of my head or yours. . . . For the moment, let me say that a redwood forest or a coral reef with its aggregate of organisms interlocking in their relationships has the necessary general structure. . . .The unit of survival is *organism* plus *environment. . . . The unit of evolutionary survival turns out to be identical with the unit of mind.* (1972: 482-83)

Bateson argues that mind is evidenced in the ecological structures of nature, that the dogma of an isolated human mind over nature and dominating nature is an "epistemological error" that has had devastating consequences for our planet. Mind for him permeates not only nature but human society as a whole: "But when you separate mind from the structure in which it is immanent, such as human relationship, the human society, or the ecosystem, you thereby embark, I believe, on fundamental error, which in the end will surely hurt you" (ibid. 483 & 485).

Mind emerges in relationships of the appropriate complexity: human relationships, human societies, localized ecosystems, the planetary biosphere, and, by extension, in the cosmos as a whole. With respect to the conception of "mind versus nature" characteristic of the early-modern paradigm, Bateson characterizes this as "insanity," and states that "it is characteristic of the system that the basic error propagates itself" (ibid. 484). In the language of Chapter Eight, this propagation of basic error involves a "totalized" world, a paradigm that systematically excludes mind and any form of holism from the non-human world, and that systematically denies any epistemology that is open to the depth dimensions.

In relation to the conscious universe and the absolute oneness of the universe, mystics of all ages have intuited this absolute oneness: beyond duality, that is, beyond subject and object. It may well be that God, as Whitehead (1978) argued, has both a primordial aspect (absolute oneness in this case) and an emergent aspect (the actualization of progressive harmony and integration within the evolving cosmos). It may be that mystics of all ages have intuited the primordial aspect of reality, while the theory of evolution and contemporary science have discerned the emergent aspect. But since these two aspects are integrated in the absolute wholeness of the cosmos as recognized by science, these two sides of reality necessarily implicate one another.

On the primordial side, through various ways of developing noncognitive forms of awareness and in every century and culture, a few have transcended the subject-object duality of human consciousness and encountered the absolute, non-dual consciousness of the whole. S. Abhayananda, in his *A History of Mysticism: The Unchanging Testament,* writes:

> These assertions by the great mystics of the world were not made as mere philosophical speculations; they were based on experience—an experience so convincing, so real, that all those to whom it has occurred testify unanimously that it is the unmistakable realization of the ultimate Truth of existence. In this experience, called *samādhi* by the Hindus, *nirvāna* by the Buddhists, *fanā'* by the Muslims, and "the mystic union" by Christians, the consciousness of the individual suddenly becomes the consciousness of the entire vast universe. All previous sense of duality is swallowed up in an awareness of indivisible unity. (1996: 2)

Porphyry, a disciple of Plotinus during the third century of the Roman era, reported in his famous biography of Plotinus that his master experienced the absolute non-dual *One* four times during the years he lived in Rome. The worldwide testimony for this non-dual consciousness is impressive and overwhelming, but there are also many who experience the *One* in what Walter Stace calls an "extrovertive" manner:

> There appear to be two main distinguishable types of mystical experience, both of which may be found in all the higher cultures. One may be called extrovertive mystical experience, the other introversive mystical experience. Both are apprehensions of the One, but they reach it in different ways. The extrovertive way looks outward and through the physical senses into the external world and finds the One there. The introvertive way turns inward, introspectively, and finds the One at the bottom of the self, at the bottom of the human personality. The latter far outweighs the former in importance both in the history of mysticism and in the history of human thought generally. The introvertive way is the major strand in the history of mysticism, the extrovertive way a minor strand. I shall only briefly refer to extrovertive mysticism and then pass on, and shall take introvertive mysticism as the main subject of this book. (1960:15)

We can ask why the extrovertive should be a "minor strand" in the history of mysticism. In Chapter Five of my *Millennium Dawn* I argued, using many references, that this is not the case. I termed this form of mysticism "integrative" and argued that this may well be the primary and fundamental form of mysticism in the process of human awakening. Human beings, in this Second Axial Age, are beginning to "look outward" and rationally (through science), intuitively (through forms of integrative mysticism), and lovingly (often through religion or forms of spirituality). We are beginning to experience the wholeness of things in and through our everyday conscious experiences.

Through various modes of awareness human beings encounter depth dimensions of the whole, the One, the primordial cosmic unity of all things that Laszlo (2007) terms "the Akashic Field," what traditionally was also often called the Tao, Suchness, *Ein Sof, Nirguna Brahman, Dharmakaya,* God, or Godhead. Yet today's emergent evolutionary perspective no longer sees the cosmos as "maya," as if it were merely a dream or playful illusion of the One. Integrative mysticism, combining reason, intuition, and love within self-aware everyday life, encounters, in and through its awareness of the One, an eschatological dimension and promise deeply connected with science, holism, harmony, and the ethical meaning of human life.

The ultimate principle not only transcends the universe but is also identical with the universe: the universe must now be understood, in the image of Jewish thinker Eric Gutkind, as "the body of God" (1969). For Panikkar, "the great challenge of Christian thought for the incoming third millennium consists in overcoming theism, deepening the experience of the Trinity in the direction of a cosmotheandric intuition" (Matthews & Varghese, 1995: 298). Theism as he uses the word, would appear to mean the idea of God as a being separate from the world. The "cosmotheandric intuition" becomes aware of the immanence of the divine in the world and human life. I would describe this as a form of "integrative mysticism."

In the discussion of education in Chapter Seven, we examined the commonly recognized developmental model embraced by many psychologists: Kohlberg, Erickson, Maslow, Gilligan, Fowler, Wilber, etc. In every case, despite differences in language and terminology, there is a progress in human development from a conventional level that takes its ideas and values from a community group, to a more autonomous level that critically examines the group values, to a higher "integrated" level that transcends group identification to experience and recognize the whole, embracing the unity-in-diversity of the world. And most of these thinkers draw a parallel between individual human development and the historical development of human consciousness. In this Second Axial Age, we human beings are experiencing a leap in this growth process to a new maturity in which we recognize, identify with, and participate in these holistic dimensions of the world.

Human consciousness is not divided into separate "faculties" such as reason, intuition, desire, or love, except for heuristic or stipulative purposes. Rather, human consciousness itself is a whole in which all these functions operate together simultaneously, and which ultimately transcends itself, as Bateson suggests, in being part of the social mind and biospheric mind. As we develop and swing out of our selves, into modes of self-actualization and self-transcendence, we encounter the holism of the universe through all these integrated functions and on many levels. Wilber expresses something of this process in his book *The Integral Vision*:

> If we pull all the scientific research on human development together, it appears that there are indeed at least three broad arcs of human psychological growth: prepersonal to personal to transpersonal, or pre-rational to rational to trans-rational, or subconscious to self-conscious to super-conscious. Each of the states in those arcs continues to transcend and include its predecessor(s). As each new level unfolds, it enfolds its predecessor—a development that is envelopment—so that the cumulative effect is integral indeed, just as with atoms to molecules to cells to organisms.

> Nothing is lost, all is retained, in the extraordinary unfold-
> ing and enfolding, developing and enveloping, transcend-
> ing and including, negating and preserving, that is con-
> sciousness evolution. (2007: 125)

At the highest level in each of these broad arcs (the trans-personal, the trans-rational, and the super-conscious), human beings experience something of the consciousness of the cosmos, which can be called, with Sri Aurobindo (1962), "super-consciousness" because it transcends the duality of subject and object that characterizes ordinary human consciousness. Aurobindo speaks of "the capacity to reorganize experience on a higher than the mental plane.... What was superconscient becomes conscient, one begins to possess or else be the instrument of the *dynamis* of the higher planes and there is a movement, not of liberation into Nirvana, but of liberation and transformation" (1970, SABCL: 1139). The evolutionary upsurge embracing the human project lifts us beyond the "human-all-too-human" toward a transformed and divinely inspired existence.

Can there be a consciousness that transcends the subject-object duality? Can there be a non-anthropomorphic reason that structures all things in the dynamism of holism? Can there be a cosmic love that transcends and completes the highest potentialities of human love? Summarizing the latest findings of science, Kafatos and Nadeau write:

> Since the universe evinces on the most fundamental level an
> undivided wholeness, and since this wholeness in modern
> physical theory must be associated with a principle of cos-
> mic order, or there would be no order, this whole manifests
> order in a self-reflective fashion. It must, in other words, be
> self-reflectively aware of itself as reality-in-itself to manifest
> the order that is the prior condition for all manifestations of
> being. Since consciousness in its most narrow formulation
> for human beings can be defined as self-reflective aware-
> ness founded upon a sense of internal consistency or order,
> we can safely argue that the universe is, in this sense, con-
> scious. In order to avoid this conclusion, one must deny

the existence of order as well as consciousness. Since the universe would not exist in the absence of the former, and physics would not exist in the absence of the latter, denying this conclusion based on appeal to scientific knowledge seems, in our view, rather futile. (1990: 178-79)

Just as the very logic of a "system," for Harris, reveals that human beings are simultaneously both one and many, so Kafatos and Nadeau argue that the very logic of the undivided wholeness of the universe, which manifests itself in the principle of cosmic order, necessarily implies consciousness on the part of the whole. The implications are tremendous, for human beings again (just as for the Ancients) now recognize themselves as microcosms of the macrocosm that embraces us. Our dignity is immeasurably enhanced. Each of us is a microcosm of humanity, the bio-system of the Earth, and the cosmos. Our subjectivity is no longer a mere insignificant epiphenomenon of biological processes. In *A Sense of the Cosmos*, Jacob Needleman writes:

Obviously, there is a great difference between contemplating a universe which exceeds me in size alone or in intricacy alone, and one which exceeds me in depth of purpose and intelligence. A universe of merely unimaginable size excludes man and crushes him. But a universe that is a manifestation of great consciousness and order *places* man, and therefore calls to him.

So much is obvious, for a conscious universe is the only reality that can include human consciousness. And only when I am completely included by something does the need arise in me to understand my relationship to it in all the aspects of my inner and outer life. Only a conscious universe is relevant to the whole of human life. (1975: 18-19)

We can now truly celebrate life, life as it is integrally related to the "primal flaring forth" and "universe story" of cosmogenesis with its emergence of beings capable of experiencing the cosmos in terms of universal, trans-personal dimensions of oneness, love, harmony, beauty, and compassion. A human being is not a detached subjectivity encased in a body with "access" to the world through the "doors" of the five senses as early-modern empiricism tended to assume. A human being is a whole, a perceptual, rational, emotional, desiring, intuitional, and loving whole—a whole that is in turn embraced by more encompassing wholes: humanity, planetary ecology, and the cosmos itself.

Just as the process of evolution creates increasingly complex systems that can be characterized as "mind," and the universe as a whole can be characterized as "consciousness" that transcends our anthropomorphic images and our subject-object duality, so the universe must be understood as increasing levels of personhood. We have seen that a person is defined as a center of relationships, an ever transcending and widening its circle of relationships. Von Brück understands this as a description of the holistic processes in the cosmos itself:

> Person, therefore, is a unity that is becoming and which integrates within itself the process of becoming, i.e., it stores up "experiences." Any complete concept of person, therefore, includes consciousness and consciousness of self, for it is only here that relationality can be realized as a reciprocity. Less perfect forms of the personal occur everywhere in reality where energy is held together in a relatively constant pattern. The power of integration increases as the degree of perfection of the personal increases, leading to consciousness as a storehouse of experiences, and consciousness fulfilled as self-consciousness. *Reality is thus a hierarchy of gradually differentiated levels of integration of universal consciousness.*(1991: 198)

All these features of a human being arise together, and our awareness of the world involves all of them simultaneously. To be a person is to live as something that infinitely transcends one's individual physical existence, to ecstatically exist in dimensions utterly transcending one's limited existence in time and space.

The bifurcation of human beings into reason and emotion, into rational cognition and irrational intuition, even into faith and reason is at an end. We encounter the world as whole persons. Our awareness is a synthesis of all these dimensions, and we understand that this holistic unity of human awareness has emerged from cosmic evolution making us, in very real ways, microcosms of the macrocosm, our self-awareness the fulfillment of a cosmic process of emerging consciousness and personhood. We can now be open to our eschatological possibilities for harmony, love, peace, sustainability, and justice that can be concretely actualized within a holistic world system under a holistic world paradigm.

Edmund Husserl argues that the consciousness of human beings is *intentional*, that we are in a perpetual process of transcending our subjectivity in the direction of the world. In *Being and Time,* Martin Heidegger understands the primordial human relation to the world as *care*. Before reason, cognition, analysis and synthesis, human beings operate in a relation of caring to the things, people, and conditions of their lives. Emmanuel Levinas phenomenologically evokes a primordial infinity within the depths of human subjectivity and prior to our constitution of the objective world, an infinity that we recognize in the faces of others.

There are important truths in all these contentions, for they all recognize a basic relation to the world prior to sense experience and "objective" rationality. I want to maintain that we relate to the world in the first instance holistically, through our whole being-in-the-world. My contention here is similar to what philosopher Joseph Kockelmans calls "existential philosophy":

> Thus, existential philosophy defends the thesis that a genuine 'ontology', which focuses all of its attention on the question concerning the meaning of the Whole, must take its point of departure in an interpretative analysis of the mode of being characteristic of man. This analysis now shows that human subjectivity is intentional; man necessarily transcends himself in the direction of the world. His mode of being is, therefore, to be characterized as a being in and toward the world. Man exists and as such he is open toward the world. Man is not an ego wrapped up in itself, nor is he a complicated mechanism which is causally inter-

> woven with his environment. From the very beginning and in the deepest core of his being man manifests himself as being-with, being-open-to, being-in-and-toward-the-world. It is through his dialogue with the intramundane things that man lets these things and the world be what they are, uncovers them, and brings their meaning to light. (In Wood, 1970: 240)

Not only from the deepest core of our being are we openness toward the world but the world itself becomes "open" through us. Holism is always dialectical, dynamic, and reciprocal: we both experience the whole and are manifestations of the conscious whole. A human being is profoundly distorted through the early-modern picture of reason as a detached, analytical function, using formal inductive and deductive logic to "objectively" observe an "external" world, all the while suppressing its primal intuitions and energies of love and compassion. The world is only experienced truly and objectively through the wholeness of human consciousness, which includes reason, intuition, and love.

The truth that is being discovered (or rediscovered) worldwide today, not only by mystics and religious thinkers but by philosophers, researchers, and scientists, is that we relate to the world, and properly cognize the world, as a whole. Reason, intuition, and love are integrated within the holism of our bodyminds, within human consciousness, manifesting the fundamental structures of the cosmos itself. These are not "merely subjective" but open us into ecstatic awareness of the depths, mysteries, structures, patterns, dynamics, and unspeakable beauties of existence.

We are truly microcosms of the macrocosm as the ancient thinkers and religious teachers affirmed. We are truly "children of God" as Judaism, Islam, and Christianity have always taught. We are truly embodiments of the divine, or of a cosmic oneness, as Buddhism, Hinduism, Confucianism, and Taoism taught. "God in man," Sri Aurobindo writes, "is the whole revelation and the whole of religion" (1972: 714).

Our job as human beings, our *telos* or *nisus*, is to sort out what is holistic in our selves, in our communities, in human civilization, and within the biosphere. Our mission and destiny is to creatively act from that holism, to foster ever higher levels of holistic institutions and consciousness. The ethical imperative is to overcome fragmentation, division, hatred, and war, and to establish peace and harmony. This means overcoming capitalism through a sustainable and equitable economic system for Earth and overcoming the sovereign nation-state system by creating a lawful, just, and peaceful democratic system for the world.

None of this should displace, of course, rigorous intellectual integrity in thought, investigation, philosophy, and science. Gandhi's expression of this ethical imperative as "clinging to truth" (*satyagraha*) means literally that. The truth, for Gandhi, includes both the whole and the parts. The truth of the whole, like the truth of each and every part, requires careful intellectual honesty, not wishful thinking, gratuitous emotion, religious dogmatism, or dishonest ideology. Socrates' quest to distinguish knowledge from belief, as presented in the *Apology* and other Platonic dialogues, remains fundamental. We don't want "mere beliefs" about the universe; we want knowledge, wisdom, clear understanding, and direct apprehension.

It is precisely this that we are talking about when we identify reason, intuition, and love as fundamental to a veridical and truthful experience of reality. As we have seen Whitehead proclaim: "The task of reason is to fathom the deeper depths of the many-sidedness of things. We must not expect simple answers to far reaching questions. However far our gaze penetrates, there are always heights beyond which block our vision" (1978: 342). As Aristotle pointed out in his *Nicomachean Ethics*, the degree of precision in our investigations must be appropriate to the subject matter, context, and scope. At the cosmic level there may be "heights beyond which block our vision," but the task of holistic cognition, nevertheless, remains to "fathom the deeper depths" with all the intellectual honesty and integrity that we can muster.

The categorical imperative of ethics is to discover the patterns of holism everywhere and actualize them further, to create holism in our personal lives, in our communities, and for the whole of Earth. The ethical imperative is to create authentic democracy, sustainability, and reasonable economic prosperity, as well as harmony, reunion, rebirth, reconciliation, and redemption for ourselves and the living creatures on our planetary home, first and foremost for the billions of marginalized and dehumanized persons living in vast horrific slums in every corner of the globe. All these goals inherent in our human situation go together. There can be no reunion and redemption, no planetary community of love and nonviolence, without democratic world law instituting an equitable planetary economic system.

The meaning of life becomes clear to us when we focus our lives, through reason, intuition, and love, on this process of experiencing life holistically and of creating harmony and healing for Earth. It is not sufficient to do this only on a local scale, within our local communities, for we have seen that each of us is both a unique individual and a generic embodiment of all humanity. We cannot be individual human beings without also being *human beings*. Each of us is responsible to the whole as well as to ourselves and our families. To act responsibly toward the whole is to act on behalf of enforceable democratic world law under a decent and just economic system. The meaning of our lives emerges as each of us, in our unique ways, engages our life-energies in this task of rebirth and redemption. Celebration is indeed in order.

9.4   Holism and Freedom in the Thought of Hans Jonas

JONAS published his *Imperative of Responsibility* in 1979. In this book he argued that inherent within our human situation itself was an immense responsibility to preserve the human project (and the natural world that makes the human project possible) in the face of the terrible threats to that project posed by modern

technology's capacity to destroy nature and human civilization altogether. He argued that this responsibility was grounded in the
evolutionary upsurge of nature itself, culminating in human freedom as the highest form of freedom known to us. His account of
the emergence of freedom out of the natural world is, therefore,
deeply holistic, and will enhance our discussion of these issues.

Jonas provided fundamental reflections with respect to the
holistic development of living systems and the emergence of
freedom out of the process of evolution. Unlike some of the
thinkers reflecting on the "consciousness" of the universe considered above, Jonas calls his approach "anthropocentric." He is examining the evolution of our distinctively human qualities holistically and reflecting on their significance for the theory of evolution and for a philosophical anthropology. He provides a non-
reductionistic account of the development of what he recognizes
as our astonishing range of higher human qualities, focusing especially on freedom. His approach is non-reductive because he
sees "reality" as establishing its "freedom" and its "feeling" in us.
We are the emergent freedom of the cosmos compacted like a laser
beam, opening before us an "astonishing" range of human possibilities.

Jonas discusses the rise of early-modern science, which led
to strong reactions in people for and against the presumption of
materialism. There were those such as Thomas Hobbes who appeared to reduce human life to just another form of the causally
determined, machine-like character of the physical world. And
this reductionism and materialism later appeared to be reinforced
by the mid-nineteenth century Darwinian revolution claiming
that human beings existed in fundamental *continuity* with animals
and the rest of nature.

On the other hand, many of those who wished to preserve
the apparent ontological dignity and nobility of the human form
clung to a Cartesian dualism between matter and spirit, between
body and mind, that denied the complete identity of human being with the natural world. In the understanding of Jonas, nei-

ther position made sense. The materialist position completely ignored the tremendously significant "inwardness" that has developed in human beings: an inwardness consisting of consciousness, thought, feeling, and, perhaps most significantly, *freedom*; the
inwardness we associate with *human dignity*. But the dualist position made little sense either; it arbitrarily inserted into human life
a mysterious ontological substance that was not discernible by science and human reason, and the metaphysical arguments for this
substance were not very credible (1996: 62-64).

Jonas points out the astonishing differences that appear with
the emergence of even the most primitive forms of life. With the
beginnings of "motility" and "metabolism" in the simplest life-
forms, *form* (the biological life-form) has taken over from matter. The material world of inert, apparently causally determined
processes, has transmuted into a *life-process* that continually ex-
changes matter with itself (through a process of intake and excretion) but that does not exist *as* that matter but as a living form
unique and independent of the matter that it takes in and excretes:
"*metabolism*, the basic substratum of all organic existence, already
displays freedom—indeed that it is the first form that freedom
takes" (60).

With the emergence of simple life forms, matter is now transcended by form. The form is never identical with the matter
that makes it up but is independent in relation to its intake and
excretion, while at the same time, it is not anything apart from
that matter except as a single, enduring form maintaining itself
between its birth and death. The first primitive forms of *freedom*
have developed, in which the organism must act in response to its
feeling or perception of an environment in order to persist as an
independent organism. It must avoid what harms its persistence
and pursue what maintains its existence. Here we have, in its first
primitive emergent form, the dynamics of the freedom inherent in
life forms that have continually transcended (through a dynamic
inherent in the very process of life itself) to find their maximum
completeness in humanity. This process of developing freedom in

relation to a material environment on which organisms are absolutely dependent can be traced from the primitive organisms all the way to the human level:

> The great contradictions that man discovers in himself—freedom and necessity, autonomy and dependence, ego and world, connectedness and isolation, creativity and mortality—are present *in nuce* in life's more primitive forms, each of which maintains a perilous balance between being and non-being and from the very beginning harbors within itself an inner horizon of "transcendence." This theme, common to all life, can be traced in its development through the ascending order of organic capabilities and functions: metabolism, motility and appetite, feeling and perception, imagination, art, and thinking—a progressive scale of freedom and danger, reaching its pinnacle in man, who can perhaps understand his uniqueness in a new way if he no longer regards himself in metaphysical isolation. (60)

With this understanding, we can now see in what ways the Darwinian breakthrough has provided the tools for appreciating the "inwardness" associated with our human dignity. While at first it seemed as if human dignity was diminished by the assertion that we were direct relatives of the animals and distant relatives of all life-forms, a deeper understanding of the implications of evolutionary theory reveal our fundamental *relatedness* to a cosmos in which freedom may be seen as the implicit goal of a continual process of "self-transcendence" inherent in the very structure and logic of living organisms.

> The *continuity* of descent linking man with the animal world made it henceforth impossible to regard his mind, and mental phenomena in general, as the abrupt intrusion of an ontologically alien principle in the total stream of life. Man's isolation, the last citadel of dualism, disappeared, and he could once again use his knowledge of himself to interpret the totality of which he was a part. . . . In this manner,

Darwinism undermined the Cartesian structure more effectively than any metaphysical criticism had been able to do. The affront to human dignity posed by the theory of man's descent from animals provoked outrage, but this reaction overlooked the fact that the same principle restored a degree of dignity to the phenomenon of life as a whole. If man is related to the animals, then the animals are also related to man and therefore, in degrees, possess that inwardness which man, their most highly advanced relative, is aware of in himself. . ... Thanks to evolutionary theory, the principle of qualitative continuity, which permits infinite gradations of obscurity and clarity of "perception," became an integral logical complement to the scientific genealogy of life. . ... But if inwardness is coextensive with life, then a purely mechanistic interpretation of life, framed in external terms alone, cannot be sufficient. (1996: 63)

We find, of course, the same dynamics in ourselves. As Jonas puts it, we have direct "inward" experience of feeling, perception, mind, and freedom. The material that composes our human bodies does not persist through time: the process of intake and excretion changes the entire material substance of our bodies repeatedly during our lifetimes. Nevertheless, we have a tremendous transcendence with respect to this process. We can plan to grow and store food for long periods of time. Unlike the primitive organism, we do not need to be constantly pursuing nourishment and avoiding threats. With our tremendous freedom comes "imagination, art, and thinking," indications of the concentrated wholeness of the human creature but comprehensible in terms of the evolutionary process itself: the ever-growing transcendence and independence of organisms vis-à-vis their environment.

On account of these evolutionary developments, our human being is "suspended in possibility" (62); in us a much more fully developed freedom evolves within the universe, a freedom radically open to the future, raising the question "what for?" Jonas argues that the early-modern tendency to see human reason in increasingly *instrumental* terms, that is, to interpret human capacities as pragmatic means for survival under a Darwinian theses of an evolutionary struggle for survival, is an example of "the genetic fallacy." "This explanation of its origin, he writes, "that is, nature's approval and nurture of it—can be mistaken for knowledge of its essence. . . . This fails to explain the enormous surplus of those characteristics that have emerged in man beyond what is needed for purposes of survival" (76).

He argues that the "task of a philosophical anthropology" is to "give thought to what is essentially beyond the animal in man without denying the features common to both" (77). And the result of this thought, for Jonas, is the realization that the very "essence" of humanity is its freedom and concomitant responsibility. "Man is the only being known to us," he writes, "who *can* assume responsibility. We immediately recognize this 'can' as more than a simple empirical fact. We recognize it as a distinguishing feature of human existence" (105-6). We are responsible not only for ourselves but for our collective future on this planet: "Our sense of responsibility must be commensurate with the magnitude of our power and therefore involves, *like it,* the entire future of humanity on this Earth" (99). Jonas' work evokes the sense of the *cosmic significance* and importance of this defining attribute of responsibility:

> If. . .there is the assumption—again an ontological one—that what exists is of value, then its being will have a claim on me; and since the valuableness of being as a whole speaks to me via this special instance. . .since its value has a justified claim on me. . . . then the universal call issuing from all transitory and valuable being is very concretely meant for me and becomes an imperative for me. . . . The Being of the whole in its integrity is the authority to which our act is responsible. This act itself, however, presupposes freedom. (1996: 102)

The mysterious upsurge of emergent evolution has resulted in a qualitative leap in freedom and the emergence of a human creature responsible for both itself and for the future of freedom and responsibility within the Cosmos through the preservation of future generations. The "Is" of the being of the Cosmos gives rise to the fundamental "ought" of human freedom. Human existence has this cosmic significance. Existence itself has value, and human beings must both respect that value, harmonize with it, and take responsibility for preserving and enhancing the flourishing of future generations.

Here, again, human beings are a microcosm of the macrocosm. We are the "one world" of the ancients reborn in freedom and responsibility within an emergent, open, and future-oriented cosmos. If we are truly responsible for the future of freedom and responsibility on this planet, what concrete steps can we take to ensure that future? Jonas' own reflections on what political arrangements might be best for addressing the threat to human existence leave much to be desired. By his own testimony he is not a political philosopher (2008: 209). He considered, he says: "Which among the various types of states, ideologies, social designs, or existing social systems offers the greatest likelihood that for the sake of preserving life, which is threatened, we will be willing to undergo the painful process of saying no to the development of all possible technologies?" (2008: 210-11).

He expresses doubt that the western democracies could successfully address this crisis, and he rejects "utopianism" and Bloch's *Principle of Hope* because "We can't afford a utopian notion of individual fulfillment, of achieving an ideal society; it's simply too dangerous" (ibid.). Jonas reflects that some form of planned and authoritarian politics, the leadership of a political elite with undemocratic powers, may be necessary if human beings are to survive into the future. However, in these thoughts Jonas abandons the very holism that inspired his account of freedom and the natural world. The options he considers involve the existing bourgeois democracies and other possible political systems that are all products of the fragmented early-modern paradigm.

He leaves out the insights taught by systems theory: that peace and sustainability will arise as products of the way we organize our economic and political system for Earth, and not as mere good intentions of leaders within the present utterly war-like and unsustainable systems that today dominate our planet. Holism must transform our political, economic, and social lives in addition to serving as a theoretical account of our relation to the Cosmos. He never considers the paradigm-shift to a holistic world-democratic system in which the notion of power is trans-formed from a quantitative authoritarianism to a qualitative full-ness of life.

Jonas misunderstands the immense possibilities for joyful, sustainable, simple, and austere forms of living that are under-lined by Bloch and many others we have considered in this book. Yet hundreds of world citizens had already been working on the *Earth Constitution* for close to 20 years before the *Imperative of Responsibility* appeared, and they had already approved the first draft of the *Constitution* in the Second Constituent Assembly meet-ing in Innsbruck, Austria, in 1977. Jonas' theoretical holism and consequent political conclusions were seriously impaired by his lack of social, political, and economic holism, and by his lack of *world* citizenship: not truly seeing the world and the human con-dition as a whole within an integrated vision embracing reason, intuition, and love.

9.5   Holism and Love

STRANGE as it may appear at first, we cannot rightly formulate an epistemology or theory of knowledge without reflecting on love as a component within human knowing. Knowledge cannot be intelligibly formulated as a human capacity without a concomi-tant consideration of human maturity, perfection, and liberation, and all of these include love. Jonas' thought, like that of so many others, fails in this regard. We may formulate a theory of truth as coherence, but proper perception of coherence itself requires love.

For the coherent universe is also a multidimensional universe, in which some of its dimensions are only accessible through a human holism that includes love. Human consciousness relates to the world as a whole, in which all its elements function together, ideally, in harmony. Love is fundamental to this relationship. Despite the fact that love has different senses and involves a number of related aspects of our lives (as discussed in Chapter Four), Tagore points out that there is an important sense in which love is an end in itself:

> When we find that that state of *Nirvana* preached by Buddha is through love, then we know for certain that *Nirvana* is the highest culmination of love. For love is an end in itself. Everything else raises the question "Why?" in our mind, and we require a reason for it. But when we say, "I love," then there is no room for the "why"; it is the final answer in itself. (2011: 161-62)

Love can and should be a dimension of our knowing, for through it human consciousness can manifest the creative joy in simply being: knowing as ecstatic consciousness: "Inspired by the breath of the universe," Tagore writes,"the heart, like a reed sings" (2011: 158). Love in its many dimensions expresses itself in wonder, seeks knowledge and understanding, joins together what is separated, and manifests itself in the simple joy in living, a joy that is often at the same time an apprehension, an "integrative mysticism."

In *An Interpretation of Religion,* philosopher and scholar of world religions John Hick argues not only that the ultimate principle of the universe (which he calls the "Transcendent" or the "Real") is love, but that the common worldwide criterion by which all the major religions recognize those who know the ultimate reality directly is love or compassion (*agape* or *karuna*). In Chapters 17 and 18, Hick quotes key passages from the scriptures of each of the world religions to illustrate this point. Hence, one of the ways that we know the ultimate principle, in addition to reason, direct experience, scriptural testimony, etc., is by seeing it manifested in the saints or holy persons of each of the religions:

> Thus the ideal of love, compassion, generosity, mercy has always been a basic factor in the recognition of someone as an authentic mediator of the Real. And having been recognized partly by their embodiment of this ideal such persons have then by their lives and teachings deepened and clarified our understanding of the ideal itself. (2004: 326)

The life of Mohammed, the life of Buddha, or the life of Jesus manifest the Real in human form and speak authentically about the Real to whomever they meet. God is love. The holism of God encompasses all: "inasmuch as you have done it unto one of the least of these my brethren, you have done it unto me" (Matt.25: 40). This holism of love need not be linked up with religion alone. Christian thinker José Miranda in his scholarly work *Marx against the Marxists* sees the work of Marx on behalf of the oppressed as the work of justice, which means that Marx affirms God because that recognition is necessarily embodied in someone who recognizes the "absolute moral imperative for justice" (1986: 191). To recognize a universal moral imperative for justice is itself a form of love.

Similarly, philosopher William Sadler in *Existence and Love: A New Approach to Existential Phenomenology* reviews Husserl's phenomenology revealing universal structures of human intentionality: the swinging out of ourselves that is the basic mode of human being-in-the-world. Sadler studies a range of literature and psychology to demonstrate that one intentional structure of human existence is love, an insight that changes our conception of human life from the isolated ego and its development to the relation with others and the community:

> From the perspective of love it becomes apparent that the main aim of human life is not to become oneself as an autonomous agent. Man's existential goal is to transcend his singular self by becoming a person in relation with others. The basic existential structure within which a human being becomes a person is loving coexistence. (1969: 186)

For Marx, the ethical imperative to overcome dehumanization and exploitation and to create a free, equitable, and just society for Earth, is fundamental to being human. Marx writes:

> Let us suppose we had carried out production as human beings. Each of us would have...*affirmed* himself and the other person. I would have been for you the mediator between you and the species, and therefore would become recognized and felt by you yourself as a completion of your own essential nature and as a necessary part of yourself, and consequently would know myself to be confirmed in your thought and your love. (In Hewitt, 1995: 52; see Marx, 1972: 124-26).

For Sadler, the possibility of such love is part of the very structure of intentionality. Love and the imperative for justice are not subjective, contingent feelings experienced by certain human beings. They are fundamental, objective structures of our being-in-the-world. For Marx, we are estranged from our essential nature, from our communal *species being*, and the overcoming of that estrangement would mean relationship, solidarity, and love.

Sadler insists that the intentional structure of love goes beyond even ethics, or, expressed differently, with Hick, we can assert that the ethical criterion is itself love, going beyond the more formal principles of ethics to the real point: not just proper behavior following abstract principles but compassion, solidarity, reconciliation, reunion, and reintegration. As Sadler concludes, the *telos* or goal of human life is "loving coexistence," but loving coexistence transcends simply relating to other people in predominantly formal relationships to an attitude of living in *community* with other persons, creatures, nature, and the cosmos itself. Spiritual thinker Jiddu Krishnamurti describes this development as the purpose of education:

> Now, is it the function of education merely to help you to conform to the pattern of this rotten social order, or is it to give you freedom – complete freedom to grow and create a

different society, a new world? We want to have this freedom, not in the future, but now, otherwise we may all be
destroyed. We must create immediately an atmosphere for
freedom so that you can live and find out for yourselves
what is true, so that you can become intelligent, so that
you are able to face the world and understand it, not just
conform to it, so that inwardly, deeply, psychologically you
are in constant revolt; because it is only those who are in
constant revolt that discover what is true, not the man who
conforms, who follows some tradition. It is only when you
are constantly inquiring, constantly observing, constantly
learning, that you find truth, God, or love; and you cannot
inquire, observe, learn, you cannot be deeply aware, if you
are afraid. So the function of education, surely, is to eradi-
cate, inwardly as well as outwardly, this fear that destroys
human thought, human relationship and love. (1989, pp.
4-5)

Fear binds us to ourselves or our ethnocentric group, block-
ing the *openness to being* described in Section 9.3 by Kockelmans.
The function of education is not merely "formal" education but
the perpetual process of learning and awakening that should be
fundamental to every human life and a process of constant attention, constant mindfulness of one's inner and outer environment,
of the world-process and the miraculous cosmos. This passage is
one of the rare places where Krishnamurti uses the word "God,"
and it is not insignificant that he uses it in relation to love: "truth,
God, or love."

Fear arises from the sense of being an isolated atom threatened
by external forces. The process of learning, and loving, for Krishnamurti, is the negation of fear. It is the swinging out of oneself in
a deep attention that transcends even the subject-object split, that
"state of silent alertness" in which "there is no division between
the person who is aware and the object of which he is aware" (ibid.
203). As with Marx and Sadler, this is not a merely subjective idea,
but an actualization of the holistic capacity for awareness that is
the miracle of being human.

The opening up of ourselves (that Sadler argues is our basic existential structure, and Kockelmans argues is the very definition of being human, and that is the true meaning of education according to Krishnamurti) leads to "truth, God, or love," suggesting that ultimate Reality is itself love. Indeed, some of the thinkers who recognize the holism of the cosmos identify this holism as love. We will look at what some thinkers have said about cosmic love—love as a fundamental reality of the universe itself.

But here I want to point out that there is another sense, expressed by some mystics such as Meister Eckhart, in which the primal oneness, the "Akashic Field," the "Godhead," or the *Ein Sof* is beyond love—for it is beyond all name and form, beyond all language and description (1981: Sermon 83, cf. Martin, 2005: Chapter 5). The absolute unity of the One, transcending subject and object (what might be called, with Whitehead, the "primordial nature of God") also transcends all predicates and languages.

The "introvertive" mystics who experience this dimension insist on "non-attachment," what in Zen has been called "no-mindedness," non-judgment.   D.T. Suzuki writes that he has sometimes translated this as "intuition or immendiate experience" (1972: 35). However, even though direct intuition of the Akashic Field is possible anytime, anywhere, it may be far more likely in the deep spiritual traditions where this opening to the "beyond" of name and form is systematically cultivated. But the human self is a dynamism of many forms of love (as we saw in Chapter Four) all interrelated: *eros, philia, nomos, agape,* etc.

The "non-attached" love called *agape* in certain traditions may correlate with the Akashic field in some ways. However, it is crucial not to ontologically prejudice a field of transcendence to the point of considering the natural world as *maya*: magical dream, illusion, the mere "play" of God—thereby ontologically diminishing the Cosmos and its astonishing "universe story." The evolving, growing self moves beyond what Nolin Pliny Jacobson (1986) calls "the culture encapsulated ego" toward ever more sophisticated forms of not only *agape* but also *eros, philia,* and *nomos.*

Unsayability permeates everyday experience, and becomes ever more apparent with non-attached mindfulness, but the ever-growing and evolving self experiences progressively more meaningful forms of love in multiple dimensions. William Johnston writes of *agape*: "This is the love that is universal, that is going out to the Infinite, that is going out to all men and women, to enemy as well as to friend; it is a love that brings much human joy" (1981: 125). The Akashic Field and the flowing out of the cosmos reciprocally embrace one another in the dynamic wholeness of reality.

Ervin Laszlo affirms the absolute imperative to love emerging from this holism:

> We are part of a series of large wholes, wholes within wholes. What it takes is to recover the intuitive feeling that we are part of it, that we are connected. So I could say, coming right down to it: it takes love, the deep, embracing feeling of love. Love is the recognition that the other is not other.... This is the key to what we should look for when we are asking which way we must go. I don't see even the remotest possibility of creating a sustainable and flourishing world on this planet unless we embrace this embracing love.... But this has never happened for mankind as a whole. Yet now it must happen, because we have become a planetary species. We must extend the embracing love that members of families felt for each other to all people on the planet. Doing this is not an option but a necessity.... We can discover that we are all one family. Utopia becomes a possibility at this juncture in our history. (2014: 79-80)

The *flowing out* of the cosmos from the divine core, itself holistic and still manifesting the primal unity, now experienced as process, order, and structure, perhaps can and should be called love. Paul Tillich writes:

> In social ethics, it is the new mysticism of love now stirring everywhere that signifies a theonomous overcoming of the autonomous ethical forms without a relapse into the heteronomy of a specifically religious community of love....

Kant's formula of ethical autonomy, his demand that man should do good for the sake of the good itself, and his law of universal validity are unassailable principles of autonomous ethics; and no interpretation of ethics as a divine commandment or of love as the overcoming of the law can be allowed to shake this foundation; but the content of love overflows the narrow cup of this form in an inexhaustible stream. The world that merely exists and is split up into individual beings is destroyed and experienced as an empty, unreal shell. The man who thinks in terms of the individual; the man who thinks in terms of the end to be attained does not know what love is: for love is pure experience of being, pure experience of reality. The man who tries to impose a limit or a condition upon love does not know that love is universal, cosmic, simply because it affirms and embraces everything that is real as something real. (1973: 172-73)

Love is the "pure experience of being, pure experience of reality." For Tillich, the *agape* taught by Jesus is not an emotion, nor a purely human form of love. *Agape* is attributed by Jesus to the love between human beings, between humans and God, and between God and humans. For Tillich love is the "ontological principle" that unites all things. It is the principle of holism: the drive toward the reunion of the separated, the drive of the parts to unite in a higher whole of solidarity and reconciliation:

Whereas faith is the state of being grasped by the Spiritual Presence, love is the state of being taken by the Spiritual Presence into the transcendent unity of unambiguous life. Such a definition requires a semantic as well as an ontological explanation. Semantically speaking, love, as faith, must be purged from many distorting connotations. The first is the description of love as emotion. . ... Love is the drive toward the reunion of the separated; this is ontologically and therefore universally true. It is effective in all three life processes; it unites in a center, it creates the new, and it drives beyond everything given to its ground and aim. It is the "blood" of life and therefore has many forms in which dispersed elements are reunited. (1967: 134)

For Tillich the point of religion is the experience of faith and love through being "grasped by the Spiritual Presence." The rituals and beliefs of religion are pointers to this existential experience, itself an ontological encounter, the living experience of love and the authenticity of faith as "ultimate concern." In Chapter Four we have already seen Moltmann and Harris speak of "rational love," for the discernment of holism by our reason is at a fundamental level also the discernment of love: both a love that discerns and a love that is discerned in the cosmos.

To be human is to be a beacon for this two-fold nature of love. Perhaps this is why Jesus links the two aspects of rational love together in the great commandment of Matthew 22: "You shall love the Lord your God with all your heart, and with all your soul, and with all your mind. This is the great and first commandment. And a second is like it, You shall love your neighbor as yourself." Von Brück writes: "Interior love of God and exterior love of neighbor are therefore two aspects of *one* love. The one cannot exist without the other" (1991: 104).

Each of us is an expression of the cosmic love that is focused like a laser beam in human consciousness, and it is only in the holistic realization of this fact ("You shall love the Lord your God") that we are capable of genuinely rational love for our neighbor as ourselves. We need to be conscious microcosms of the macrocosm, for this is the very condition of having *agape* for all, including ourselves. Not recognizing this is to live with a distorted, alienated, and severely limited form of consciousness.

And love of oneself is not in principle different from the *agape* for others. Others are "ends in themselves." This basic Kantian formula of respect for "humanity" in myself and others remains the bedrock for holistic ethical reflection. Like myself, others are *temporal beings* whose fundamental *telos* is for what Ricoeur calls the "image of humanity" that emerges from our temporal process of growth and learning as an end of intrinsic worth both for myself and for the human project as a whole. "If humanity is what I esteem in another and in myself," Ricoeur writes, "I esteem myself as a thou for another. . .. I love myself as if what I loved were another" (1967: 188-89). Psychologist Erich Fromm expresses this principle of the holism of self and others in similar terms. One's love, for Fromm, necessarily includes both self and others:

> From this it follows that my own self, in principle, is a much an object of my love as another person. The affirmation of my own life, happiness, growth, freedom, is rooted in the presence of the basic readiness of and ability for such an affirmation. If an individual has this readiness, he has it also toward himself; if he can only "love" others, he cannot love at all. (1941: 115)

Kafatos and Nadeau assert that "the alienated mind" is necessarily a result of seeing the world incorrectly, of failing to see that our own consciousness "participates" in the consciousness of the universe, which may now be called the "love" of the universe and the love that is the context of authentic human life. How to bring human beings to this holism is the problem of education today. How to lift human beings out of the fragmented early-modern set of assumptions and allow them to participate in the process of cosmogenesis itself. They write:

> In the grand interplay of quanta and field in whatever stage of complexity, including the very activities of our brain, there is literally "no thing" that can be presumed isolated or discrete. In these terms we can "infer" that human consciousness "partakes" or "participates in" the conscious universe, and that the construct of the alienated mind, no matter how real feelings of alienation might be in psychological terms, is not in accord with the scientific facts. (1990: 177)

Holism is not some dreamy idealism incongruent with the reality of the human situation. It is rather a deep discernment of the truth of our situation, confirmed by "the scientific facts." The minds of those who dominate in the power system of sovereign nation-states, the minds in the Pentagon and the militaries of the various countries, are literally alienated, that is out of touch with the reality of our situation. They are mostly operating under assumptions derived from the early-modern paradigm that have been entirely disproved by science and completely discredited by those who see the human situation clearly.

Needleman critically evaluates the turpitude of even many scientists to perceive the implications of holism, and he sees similarly that the thinking of non-scientists remains fragmented and distorted by early-modern assumptions:

> Thus, although we begin by asking for a new way to think about science, we end in need of a new attitude toward ourselves, especially the part in us that gravitates toward mere explanations of reality. All around us, both within and outside of the sciences, there is a yearning to heal the fragmentations and divisions that separate man from nature, man from man and man from God. The search is for new, unifying concepts of the universe and the social order. But can *the integration we long for ever* be reached through the part of ourselves whose function is to divide and categorize? (1975:162-63)

The integration we long for cannot be achieved through analytical reasoning, but through the synthesis of reason, intuition, and love. It is our own holism that integrates us with the holism of reality. Holism provides us with these "new, unifying concepts of the universe and the social order" as well as "a new attitude toward ourselves." It shows scientifically the absolute unity of the universe and the relative unities of all the dynamic fields within it, all interdependent and integrated as the processes of evolutionary and historical emergence continue. It shows our unique and central role as microcosms of the macrocosm. It makes possible a rebirth of the one world and spiritual unity of humankind envisioned by the ancient philosophers, saints, and founders of the great religions: Jesus, Plato, Plotinus, Buddha, Lao Tzu, Baha'u'llah, Lord Krishna, Moses, and Mohammed.

But the rebirth of "one world" is now raised to a higher conceptual level in terms of a dynamic understanding of emergent evolution and scientific holism. These new concepts and attitudes can be summed up, Needleman affirms, in the reality of love:

> But it is time to call things by their proper names and admit that we are speaking here about love—love both as a cosmic and as a human phenomenon. Surely one cannot speak for long about the idea of the microcosm without attempting to think about the meaning of love. A conscious universe, a universe that is more, not less, than man must contain love. The difficulty, the enormous difficulty, arises as we come to see how shallow, crude or sentimental is our understanding of love. Even people willing to entertain the thought that there is a great intelligence and purpose in the cosmos balk at the possibility that love is an attribute of reality. (1975:119)

We have seen that the human mind is a unique embodiment of the creative upsurge that characterizes *the universe story*. Human consciousness and mind-body reality are not a mere epiphenomenon but rather a central feature of the cosmic story, embodying "love both as a cosmic and a human phenomenon." Physicist Henry Stapp characterizes the human mind as "an integral part of the highly nonlocal creative activity of the universe" (in Kitchener, 1988: 57). Hence, for Stapp, it participates in the creative upsurge of the universe itself. It is not a mere localized subjectivity arbitrarily facing a mechanistic, causally determined material reality.

Whitehead concludes that the actualization of love and harmony in the world by human creatures is internalized within "the consequent nature of God" and returns to us from God to influence the course of future events. For human beings, God is the "lure for feeling, the eternal urge of desire," and my no means simply an object of reason alone. Our symbolic notion of the Kingdom of God arises from this lure informing human desire: "It dwells upon the tender elements in the world, which slowly and in quietness operate by love" (1978: 343):

> For the kingdom of heaven is with us today.... What is done in the world is transformed into a reality in heaven, and the reality in heaven passes back into the world. By reason of this reciprocal relation, the love of the world passes into the love in heaven, and floods back again into the world. (Ibid. 351)

Ethics, love, intuition, values, religion, and culture are not "merely subjective" reactions to an impartial "objective" reality. There is "great intelligence and purpose in the cosmos," Needleman affirms, and that intelligence and purpose is also embodied in us. As Spinoza declared in the 17th century, God "forms the essence of the human mind" (*Ethics* II, xi), and part of this essence is love. Our purposes are to create harmony, reconciliation, integration, respect for human rights and human dignity, the just rule of democratic world law, universal friendships, and loving relationships. In other words, a renaissance: *one world reborn*. Our vocation is to become evermore fully human.

Harris, in his book *The Reality of Time*, argues that love pervades the universe and, very much like Tillich, Sadler, Krishnamurti, and Needleman, is the primal relation both between people and within the cosmos. It inevitably leads beyond the love of individual persons, he says, to communities, to humanity as a whole in the form of the Kantian ideal of all humankind as a "Kingdom of Ends," or to the Christian ideal of bringing the "Kingdom of God" to Earth. (I quote him at some length because he is known as a major *rationalist philosopher,* and therefore his conception of the relation of reason and love appears particularly significant):

> There is a sense in which love pervades the entire universe as that universal tendency towards unity and coherent harmony previously stressed. Teilhard refers to it as "the radial zone of spiritual attractions." At the biological level it surfaces as sexual attraction, parental tenderness, and filial dependence, as well as in the gregariousness of many species. But these are only the precursors of human life, in which they become transformed by self-reflection into something

more than mere sentiment. While the emotive and conative aspects are not lost, love now becomes rational. It is genuine concern for the welfare of each and every individual, it is the universal respect for persons, that treats each as an end and none merely as a means. And because every individual is a social being, it is a concern for the welfare of the entire community, in which all are integrated and on which all depend. Nor can that welfare, for which this rational love is concerned, be confined to any one local or national community, because the welfare of every community depends, like that of each individual, upon the welfare of all. Genuine rational love, therefore, must extend to the entire human race. . ..

As human rational activity is socially organized and embodied in political institutions, love comprehends and transcends all political and social virtues. It is the emotional and sentimental counterpart and expression of the unity of the perfected human community—referred to as "the Kingdom of God." Thus, it is precisely in and as love that Omega reveals itself to us. . ..

Love of neighbor, in the full sense, transpires as love of the entire community and devotion to the ideal Kingdom of Ends. It is an unreserved devotion to that ideal—Christ's love, through which, by his service and sacrifice for the salvation of mankind, God is revealed; and in which again human and divine are united. It is the love and comfort of the Holy Spirit; in short, it is the love of God. Love of one's neighbor and love of God are therefore one and the same.

As the living organism is presided over by an all coordinating brain, by which it is maintained in balance and organic health; while and because the brain itself is served by those very organs and physiological cycles that it coordinates—so the corporate suprapersonality of Omega maintains itself by and in the mutual love of its component personalities. This love they can sustain in its proper strength and purity only through their devotion to the sovereign principle of unity. Its immanence in and operation through them is the Grace by which it gives them power to love one another.

> So Spinoza contends that man's intellectual love of God is
> identical with God's love for man. (1988: 162-64)

Harris uses Teilhard de Chardin's concept of the *noösphere*
(from the Greek *nous* or mind) to elucidate the growing process of
unification in human civilization (characterized by universal language translations, global information transmissions, global compassion, and other aspects of "mind") that has encircled and en-
compassed our planet, with one emerging consciousness becoming evermore unified and integrated and leading toward the cul-
mination of holism in the transformed communion of "Omega."
(A comprehensive overview of this process can be found in *The
Coming Interspiritual Age* by Kurt Johnson and David Robert Ord
(2012).) Like Teilhard (and Whitehead), he understands this integrative process (which is both cosmic and human) as love. In a
manner similar to Tillich, he sees that love transcends and encompasses all the social and political virtues that we associate with the
history of ethics. This process of evermore integrated and encompassing rational love "must extend to the entire human race."

Harris understands the emergence and power of the
paradigm-shift to holism as the emergence and power of love as
this is bequeathed to us by many thinkers, saints, and incarna-
tions in world civilization such as Teilhard, Spinoza, and Jesus.
For all of them, "love of one's neighbor and love of God" are one
and the same. We can see this identity relation now as perhaps the
supreme statement of holism. The holism of the cosmos brings the
universe forward to emergent levels of consciousness, mind, and,
at the highest current stages, rational love. The holism of humanity manifested in the rational love of neighbor, which, as Jesus
made clear in his parable of the Good Samaritan, means love of
every person as an end in him or herself.

Harris ends his book with a criticism of much contemporary
philosophy that cannot bring itself to recognize holism: "Those
who employ analysis without synthesis, and insist on a bogus
'precision', are incapable of comprehending systematic holism"
(ibid. 166). To be able to comprehend the universe that we live

in at all, or the meaning and purpose of human life within that universe, requires synthesis, a creative and dialectical use of our reason as well as the recognition that reason is helpless unless it is "inspired" reason, working together with intuition and love.

"Analysis" (the breaking things into parts to be inspected minutely and logically) tends to continue as a legacy of the early-modern paradigm—the outmoded narrow empiricism and positivism that today constitute a drag on human knowledge and understanding. Today, philosophy needs synthetic vision more than anything. It needs to become an embodiment of the rational love that is perhaps the central emergent feature of the human evolutionary upsurge.

The universal principle of order that is emergent within human life results in self-consciousness, and with self-consciousness the development of reason. The universal *nisus* or holistic *telos* that is emergent in us becomes rational, Harris affirms, and with this process love also becomes rational in us. This *telos* derives, at least in significant measure, from the lure toward ever-greater wholeness implicit within the holistic context itself.

We have seen that democratic world law is the presupposition of our human rationality and sociality. We are inextricably both individual and social beings. The implicit holism of our context appears as the love that draws us to actualize that holism in concrete institutions and associations. The rational love emerging in us extends to the community and society, to law and ethics, which are all products of the organizing and integrating power of reason and love. Harris writes: "The morality of love does not abolish the law, it presupposes it" (1966: 132).

Reason experiences the universal, structural, and dialectical features of the cosmos. It flourishes as a dynamic integrated process of identifying what is universal: through analysis, synthesis, imagination, and conjecture; it is always moving, always in process. It cannot be reduced to any formal logic or calculus. Intuition complements reason through a direct pre-theoretical awareness of the integrated oneness of all existence, ecstatic in its immediacy.

Reason contributes to meaning in life, and is absolutely fundamental to our human vocation. But it is limited in its ability to give us the ecstatic joy indicated by Krishnamurti in the quote below. And love, involving both reason and intuition, draws our world together into an ever more harmonious and transformed future, binds us passionately to one another, and invites each of us into the morality of aspiration, seeking to actualize the good. We need all three working together to correctly discern the world and the way into a redeemed future. You cannot separate the rational demand for universal law predicated on our common humanity from the demand of love for universal harmony, equality, and justice, also predicated on our common humanity. As I concluded in *Millennium Dawn*:

> What is significant is this sacred life "in the flesh," within this holy cosmos. Krishnamurti affirms the simplicity of this revolutionary awakening: "Live, live in this world. This world is so marvelously beautiful. It is our world, our earth to live upon, but we do not live, we are narrow, we are separate,..we are frightened human beings.... We do not know what it means to live in that ecstatic, blissful sense" (1973: 14). Planetary maturity is just such an adventure in perpetual growth, wonder, and spontaneous joy in living. We discover ever again a life of simplicity and joy in which democratic socialism, the sharing with others in mutual work for our own welfare and the common good, becomes as simple and self-evident as the ecstatic unity-in-diversity of life itself (2005: 138).

This is why reason, intuition, and love tell us clearly that the only legitimate form of government is non-military democratic government, founded on the equality, freedom, and dignity of all. Those who live fully and maturely have no need to exploit or dominate others. They have no need to reify the capitalist economic system with the pretense that "these are the objective laws of economics and I am not responsible for living off the labor and misery of others." Rational love tells us differently. We are morally responsible for both the economic-social order that allows us to live off the unpaid labor of others and the world's disorder of sovereign nation-states that perpetuates endless war and violence.

This alone can give us a world where the common good of democratic socialism and integrated harmony becomes the dominant motivation in every mature human life. And reason tells us clearly that ultimately the only legitimate form of democratic government itself is *non-military democratic world government*, since the holistic *telos* of rational love cannot be realized at the level of sovereign nation-states, nor can it be realized in an anarchic world without the rule of just and enforceable law. As Laszlo declares: "Utopia becomes a possibility at this critical juncture of our history." Reason, intuition, and love point forward to a social democratic federation for Earth, a basic precondition for a 21st century renaissance: *one world reborn.*

Epilogue

> *There is then no transcending of hope without the paradoxical counter-movement of the incarnation of love, no breaking out of new horizons without the sacrifice of life, no anticipating the future without first investing in it. It is in the incarnational movement even unto passion and death that, paradoxically, the kingdom of God can even be lived and not just hoped for.*
>
> —Jürgen Moltmann

IN this book I have attempted to show that creative, revolutionary holism is capable of transforming the human condition from one of sickness and fragmentation to one of health and harmony. This requires holistic transformations that are both structural and spiritual. Even if a spiritual maturity involving awakening to the fullness of reason, intuition, and love were to inform the majority of humanity, health and harmony would not prevail as long as the global institutions of capitalism and sovereign nation-states remain in place. Moreover, under these institutions the likelihood of such maturity developing at all is practically nil.

As Moltmann points out, we need not only an abstract hope for a transformed future but also an "incarnation of love" in the concrete world of here and now, perhaps requiring redeeming "sacrifice of life," like that of Jesus, Martin Luther King, Jr., or Mahatma Gandhi. Such an incarnation necessarily requires system transformation: really incarnating freedom, peace, and justice into human planetary institutions. We cannot simply turn aside into our private lives and narrow our immense love of life, the Earth, and the depths of *being* into vessels too small to contain this immensity.

We must express our love for humanity, Earth, and for the astonishing divine-anthropic project of the Cosmos through system transformation encompassing us all. In an important sense, we may say that *democratic world law is the 21st century form of love.* The *Earth Constitution* concretizes the unity of humankind in legal, social, spiritual, and cultural forms. Its unity in diversity is the principle of love expressed in institutional form. It not only embodies the unity of love but fosters the unity of love as well.

There is a dialectic between the structural and the spiritual. Transformation in one influences the other and vice-versa. As Fromm expresses this: "man reacts to changing external situations by changes in himself, and...these psychological factors in their turn help in molding the economic and social process" (1941: 297-98). To promote "a culture of peace" or an alternative lifestyle "off the grid" is not going to be sufficient as action, nor as a model for planetary transformation. *"Another world is possible,"* as the protest slogan truly proclaims. But it is only possible if humanity is united in a planetary community of law, justice, and reasonable economic equity, which is the 21st century form of love. The way we live our lives in the here and now is intimately and dialectically related to our eschatological possibilities for a transformed future.

And this is precisely why sovereign nation-states can never give us peace—they effectively recognize no law above themselves and reserve the right to "interpret" international laws as they see fit. And the UN, as a treaty of such nations, has clearly failed to give us peace or prevent the collapsing of our environment. It has been colonized by both the power politics of sovereign nations and by globalized corporate capitalism. Sovereign nations are forever compromising with evil—the evil that they themselves dialectically generate. The present world anti-system perpetuates a never-ending cycle of violence and corruption.

Only the rule of democratic law, with representatives from all around the world debating the way into the future and how to deal with the multiplicity of global crises, can give us the peace necessary for both sustainability and human flourishing. A federated Earth is the only practical step that can transform world economics and disarm the world's power-crazed militarized nation-states, along with their allies the transnational corporations. A federated Earth binds humanity together into a planetary community for the first time, recognizing a common good and linking together the structural and spiritual aspects of our human condition.

The harmonious convergence of spiritual and structural transformation is seen in the work of Errol E. Harris, among many others that we have considered in this book. The goal inherent in the emergent holistic upsurge of rational love, identified by him and others, can indeed be understood as working toward the Kingdom of Ends or the Kingdom of God on Earth. But a necessary part of this process, for Harris, is the foundation of democratic world government. Only the concrete transformation of our global institutions can genuinely open up our higher human possibilities.

The practical organization of societies and communities that flows from the social nature of our humanity (inseparable from our unique individuality) is itself a product of emergent rational love, a step on the way to the Kingdom of God on Earth. Just so is the overcoming of fragmentation and warring among the nation-state entities of Earth and joining them together under democratic world law, which would manifest a much higher level of rational love. As Harris declares in *The Reality of Time*:

> The common interest....can be served only by the formation of a world community presided over by a world authority with appropriate power to enforce world law and maintain world peace. ... This is the totality that must be realized in the historical process, to embody the universal principle of human welfare that we have postulated, and to give direction to historical time. If it is not realized within the foreseeable future, there is a high probability of the destruction of all civilization and the extermination of all historical agents, literally bringing history to an end. (1988: 142-43)

It is no accident that the book where Harris discusses rational love at the greatest length is named *"The Reality of Time,"* for *time* (the conception of an evolutionary and historical world process) is indeed real. There are very real historical developments that have characterized both the evolutionary process on Earth and in the cosmos. Similarly, there are very real historical developments that have characterized the emergence of human civilization and rational self-awareness (especially since the Axial Period in human history in the first millennium BCE).

Time must be taken seriously in terms of the *telos* of evolution, in terms of the ends of human existence, and in terms of the enormous threat of disaster for the human project that we now face. As Jonas expresses this, "From the discovery of man's basic historicity to the ontological elaboration of the innermost temporality of his being, it has been borne in upon us that time, far from being a mere form of phenomena, is of the essence of such things as selves, and that its finitude for each of us is integral to the very authenticity of his existing" (1996: 119).

We have a genuine present that demands our responsibility and our action precisely because of our human historicity and temporality. According to Jonas: "Responsibility is the moral complement to the ontological constitution of our temporality." He asserts that "only for the changeable and perishable can one be responsible, for what is threatened by corruption" (1996:15). The reality of time, a temporality in which we are holistically embedded, bestows upon us an immense responsibility toward nature and the future of our human project. Part of our celebration of the holism of the cosmos must be the celebration of the responsibility that we have to promote a harmonious and glorious future, that future under God envisioned by many of the ancient religious teachers and prophets.

There really is, therefore, an inspiring "universe story" (a chronicle of the time of the universe) worthy of the "celebration" of the "unfolding of the Cosmos." We ourselves are ecstatic manifestations of that unfolding, characterized by reason, intuition, and love. Yet, for Harris, and many others we have considered in this book, time must also be taken seriously in terms of the terminus we are facing as the global environment threatens to collapse and weapons of mass destruction threaten to wipe out humanity. Hence, the tremendous seriousness of Harris' lifetime philosophical project is reflected in the title of his 2005 book: *Earth Federation Now! Tomorrow is Too Late.*

In this book, Harris argues that the absolute historical imperative at this crucial moment in human history is the founding of democratic world government under the *Constitution for the Federation of Earth*. This constitution is our best option. It is brilliantly and holistically constructed and ready for ratification. It both embodies the emergent rational love of holism and makes possible the further development and integration of rational love for human beings in the future. It establishes a reasonable economic equality and prosperity for the people of Earth, and it holistically transforms "power" from power-over to the power of community, life, health, integration, justice, reconciliation, and sustainability. It provides a positive vision of a truly transformed future.

But here is the crux of the matter: A holistic consciousness that integrates reason, intuition and love, achieved by, say, at least ten percent of humanity, is clearly a necessary condition for a transformed world of sustainability, peace, and justice. But this would not be a sufficient condition. For the world is held hostage by two gigantic institutions deriving from the early-modern paradigm: the system of capitalism and the system of sovereign nation-states. Simply promoting a "culture of peace" or a "culture of ecological living" will not be sufficient to our need. The rationality of a *holistic systems approach* to world transformation needs to complement and complete the encouragement of cultural and spiritual transformation. Both our cultures and our systems need to be manifestations of love and thereby reflect the eschatological potential of love.

Systems quite naturally influence the consciousness of those within them. These fragmented systems continue to produce a fragmented consciousness in the majority of people on Earth. Change the systems and you have gone a long way toward changing the consciousness. Create a genuine *community* and people begin to think in terms of the community. The demand for a breakthrough to a holistic consciousness must be supplemented by a *systems analysis*, a *systems awareness*, and concrete action for *system change*: all possible through ratification of the *Earth Constitution*. A holistic social system for the Earth and a holistic spiritual consciousness will clearly complement one another. Yet even here, even many of the advocates of the new holism fail to provide a complete analysis or an effective *praxis*. Let me give just two examples.

Fritjof Capra in *The Turning Point* (1982) spends much time describing the Newtonian features within the capitalist system and describing the features of an alternative economics. So too Goerner, Dyck, and Lagerroos in *The New Science of Sustainability* (2008) give an excellent analysis of the many unsustainable features of the present endangered world under capitalism. Yet both books miss one gigantic feature of today's utterly unsustainable world disorder: the sovereign nation-state. It is as if this were too close to see, too pervasive in its diabolical omnipresence, or too overwhelming to contemplate, to allow even critical thinkers insight into the most destructive and pervasive system that one can imagine.

Similarly, many people teaching courses in peace studies over the past 60 years have used Albert Camus' famous essay "Neither Victims nor Executioners" as a text but appear to have failed to comprehend what he is saying. Is his language so literary that we cannot discern his impeccable reasoning? There can be no "revolution" in values or in society, Camus declares, no way to avoid being either "victims or executioners," under the present system of sovereign nation-states. Camus understood (in 1946) what perhaps most advocates of paradigm-shift have yet failed to comprehend:

> They will admit that little is to be expected from present-day governments, since these live and act according to a murderous code. Hope remains only in the most difficult task of all: to reconsider everything from the ground up, so as to shape a living society inside a dying society. Men must therefore, as individuals, draw up among themselves, within frontiers and across them, a new social contract which will unite them according to more reasonable principles. (1986: 49)

Clearly, by "present-day governments" Camus means the present historical era, for the governments of the world in the 21st century operate according to this same "murderous code." For the code is built into the very structure of national sovereignty, which structurally insists on maintaining a lawless and war-mongering world disorder. Terrorism is largely a consequence of this murderous system.

State terrorism reciprocally encourages private terrorism and only continues to reproduce the cycle of lawlessness and violence, as many have pointed out. Private terrorism cannot be combated by the lawlessness of the war system. It is a criminal activity and can only be combated by the rule of enforceable, due process of law, and by addressing the terrible injustices that inspire most terrorists in their rebellious quest. And we cannot properly prosecute terrorists until we have the rule of law, not the rule of war, in the world.

If the new categorical imperative is to create harmony in ourselves, within human civilization, and in relation to our planetary biosphere, then it confirms what Camus clearly argues and what Kant in his 1795 essay explicitly concludes: to live under a system of sovereign nation-states is to live in a perpetual condition of *de facto* war, which is immoral. *The moral imperative* is to leave this "barbarous" condition as rapidly as possible and establish "republican" government for all: protecting the "freedom and equality" of all persons as "subjects under a single legislation" establishing peace and ending war once and for all. We need a truly positive vision of a transformed future that can animate all our concrete efforts in the present. This is indeed the principle and manifestation of love.

In the decades following Camus' essay, hundreds, perhaps thousands of citizens from around the world did indeed "draw up among themselves...a new social contract" (cf. Martin, 2010b), based on "more reasonable principles" under which people around the world are no longer forced to be either victims or executioners. It was a social contract guaranteeing an extensive list of protected human rights to every person on Earth and institutionalizing the freedom that only the due process of law can bring. When the world is seen by most people as free, just, and equitable, most terror (whether of victims or executioners) will end of its own accord.

That new *global social contract* was called the *Constitution for the Federation of Earth.* Yet how many today comprehend Camus' simple and clear logic, fundamental to a genuine paradigm-shift? How many comprehend Kant's insight that this social contract is "an end that is an unconditioned and primary duty with respect to every external relation in general among men" (1983: 71). And in conformance with these insights, under the *Earth Constitution* world citizens have been holding sessions of the Provisional World Parliament (13 sessions to date in locations around the world), actively shaping "a living society inside a dying society." Camus was explicit: "The only way of extricating ourselves is to create a world parliament through elections in which all peoples will participate, which will enact legislation which will exercise authority over national governments" (1986: 45).

The ratification of either the *Earth Constitution* or of something very much like it is, therefore, also an *absolutely necessary* (although not a sufficient condition) for a world of sustainability, justice, freedom, and peace. We need a concomitant spiritual transformation as well, empowered through establishing humanity as a legal community. Bringing the rule of enforceable world law to the Earth will encourage a spiritual transformation in which all people begin to see the *multiple connections* (that we have explored in this book) between the universal rule of law, human morality, and the on-going spiritual development of humanity.

The criminals and murderers that run militarized nation-states (people like Bill Clinton, George Bush, or Barack Obama, and their counterparts in other states) should be indicted and tried in world courts under due process of law, likely to be placed in jail where they belong. For under the present world anti-system, all nations are "rogue nations." All nations are "gangster nations," as they used to say of Nazi Germany and Fascist Italy, spurning the rule of law, universal morality, and human decency. All nations must be demilitarized, and there is no way that this can possibly happen without a democratic earth federation under a global social contract that abolishes and transcends national sovereignty giving us the rule of enforceable, democratically legislated, law for every person on Earth.

Fundamental structural changes transforming today's fragmented Newtonian world system are absolutely necessary if we want to survive much longer on this planet. A holistic consciousness can and should demand a holistic world economic and political system. It is just such a system that is offered by the *Constitution for the Federation of Earth*. Ratification of the *Earth Constitution* is the most important step we can take at this point in history.

This constitution provides a concrete, positive vision of a transformed future. It is the key to actualization of the "practical utopia" that Ernst Bloch and others insist is at the heart of our present possibilities. It sets the stage for the world community of peace–*al Islam*–that Allah envisions through the Prophet. It is time to let the "messianic hope" advocated by Jean-Paul Sartre in *Hope Now* "engender Humanity,"for "the unity of the human enterprise is still to be created" (1996: 96). The *Earth Constitution* legally establishes "the unity of the human enterprise."

Our situation at the present moment in history has no real antecedents in the history of thought. We are aware of ongoing climate collapse disrupting the ecology of the planet and, with it, human civilization, perhaps to the point of extinction. We are aware of our technical capacity to wipe out human life with weapons of mass destruction and the continuing development of ever more of these hideous weapons. Our hope in the present does not derive primarily from deterministic antecedents constricting us from the past but from our capacity to envision a truly transformed future. It springs from the holistic expression of our reason, intuition, and love.

Drawing on the wisdom of the great religious and spiritual teachers of all ages, and drawing on our understanding of the fundamental role of democratic law at the heart of civilization, we must act in the present with the *Earth Constitution* as a model and guide for moving into the future. Our vision of the future will be the key to transforming the course of history and creating a decent planetary civilization. We must establish a planetary human community, one with legal, ethical, and spiritual legitimacy.

The universe story is significantly about us. It is a story about the emergence of consciousness, reason, freedom, and love out of the dynamics of the cosmic process, a process in which the entire universe is implicated at every stage. On planet Earth these qualities develop under a *telos* for wholeness, harmony, and love emerging out of the process among human beings—a wholeness, harmony, and love in relation to one another, in relation to our planetary biosphere, and in relation to the astonishing, divinely-inspired cosmos of which we are a part. A necessary feature of this process is a world united under democratic law that legislates a decent global economic system of sustainability and justice, and universally protects our human dignity and ability to flourish.

The *Earth Constitution* is, therefore, a key component on the way to a redeemed and transformed future. It is a key step on the way to Teilhard's emergent Omega Point, which is the unification of the noösphere in a higher integration that can be termed "super-consciousness," signaling "the unity of the human enterprise." It can be considered a key step on the way to Kant's actualization of a universal "Kingdom of Ends" in which all human beings relate to one another through moral relationships and the recognition of our universal human dignity in "a systematic union of different rational beings under common laws" (1964:100), a formulation that resonates closely with the world-peace vision of Islam. It can be understood as a key step on the way toward the eschatological fulfillment, envisioned by Karl Marx, of a non-alienated, ethically just, and communal human civilization.

Or it can be understood as a key factor in the creative realization of the Kingdom of God on Earth, announced by Jesus, in which all people will then celebrate *the universe story*—because what they now "see through a glass, darkly," they will then see "face to face." They will then perceive directly that "the heavens declare the glory of God," reason enough for celebration of life, our planet, and our common human unity-in-diversity. Ratification of the *Earth Constitution* is the next step in the process of rebirth of One World: holistic, sustainable, peaceful, just, and free.

At the outset of this Epilogue, Moltmann declares: "There is then no transcending of hope without the paradoxical countermovement of the incarnation of love." Our vision of the holistically transformed future depends on our love, on the ability of human beings everywhere to actualize their potentiality for love. We need to "incarnate" our highest human possibilities, live them in the here and now. For there is "no anticipating the future without first investing in it." Delay, postponement, is no longer an option.

Everyday, more people from all around the world are signing the "pledge of allegiance" to the *Earth Constitution* and declaring that the highest law for humankind is not that of illegitimate militarized nation-states but the *Constitution for the Federation of Earth*. They are living the reality of the future in the here and now and thereby bringing it to actuality. "The kingdom of God can be lived and not just hoped for," declares Moltmann. But in the face of our devastating planetary crises, we might better say, "The kingdom of God *must be lived* in the here and now and not just hoped for." Let's make it happen.

Appendix

Preamble of
the Earth Constitution

Realizing that Humanity today has come to a turning point in history and that we are on the threshold of a new world order which promises to usher in an era of peace, prosperity, justice and harmony;

Aware of the interdependence of people, nations and all life;

Aware that man's abuse of science and technology has brought Humanity to the brink of disaster through the production of horrendous weaponry of mass destruction and to the brink of ecological and social catastrophe;

Aware that the traditional concept of security through military defense is a total illusion both for the present and for the future;

Aware of the misery and conflicts caused by ever increasing disparity between rich and poor;

Conscious of our obligation to posterity to save Humanity from imminent and total annihilation;

Conscious that Humanity is One despite the existence of diverse nations, races, creeds, ideologies and cultures and that the principle of unity in diversity is the basis for a new age when war shall be outlawed and peace prevail; when the Earth's total resources shall be equitably used for human welfare; and when basic human rights and responsibilities shall be shared by all without discrimination;

Conscious of the inescapable reality that the greatest hope for the survival of life on earth is the establishment of a democratic world government;

We, citizens of the world, hereby resolve to establish a world federation to be governed in accordance with this Constitution for the Federation of Earth.

Holistic Planetary Democracy

The predicates of a redeemed World derive from the integrated unity in diversity of the whole: World Peace, Global Justice, Human Rights, Reasonable Prosperity, Ecological Sustainability

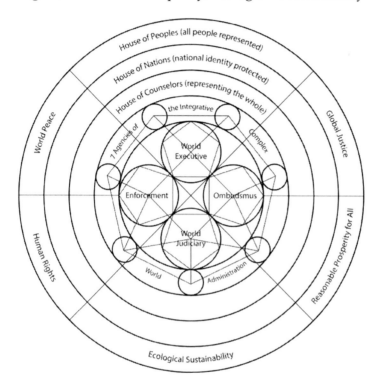

The central agencies of the Federation are structured in terms of councils of five leaders, one from each Continental Division, who rotate as President of their respective agencies. The seven agencies of the Integrative Complex and 28 departments of the World Administration, staffed by professionals in the global civil service, bring order and intelligence into all global processes. The House of Nations, The House of Peoples, and the wise ones in the House of Counselors bring unity in diversity to integrating all nations and peoples and to governing our precious planet Earth.

A Pledge of Allegiance
to the Earth Constitution

I pledge allegiance to the Constitution for the Federation of Earth, and to the Republic of free world citizens for which it stands,

One Earth Federation, protecting by law the rich diversity of the Earth's citizens, One Earth Federation, protecting the precious ecology of our planet.

I pledge allegiance to the World Parliament representing all nations and peoples, and to the democratic processes by which it proceeds,

One law for the Earth, with freedom and equality for all, One standard of justice, with a bill of rights protecting each.

I pledge allegiance to the future generations protected by the Earth Constitution, And to the unity, integrity, and beauty of humankind, living in harmony on the Earth,

One Earth Federation, conceived in love, truth, and hope, with peace and prosperity for all.

Bibliography

Sources for the Epigraphs

Dedication: Rabindranath Tagore, *The Essential Tagore*, p. 158

Chapter One: William Wordsworth, "Ode on the Intimations of Immortality from Recollections of Earth Childhood," lines 1–9.

Chapter Two: Alfred North Whitehead, *Process and Reality*, 1978, pp. 342 & 339.

Chapter Three: Marcus Tullius Cicero, *On the Commonwealth and On the Laws*,1999, pp. 120-121.

Chapter Four: Jiddu Krishnamurti, *You Are the World*, 1972, pp. 112 & 90.

Chapter Five: John Milton, *Paradise Lost, Book IX*, lines 1187–89.

Chapter Six: Albert Einstein, *Out of My Later Years*, New York, Philosophical Library, 1950, p. 138.

Chapter Seven: Carl Gustav Jung, *Jung: Psychological Reflections. A New Anthology of His Writings. 1905–1961*, 1970, p. 304.

Chapter Eight: Ernst Bloch, *Natural Law and Human Dignity*, 1986, p. 162.

Chapter Nine: Josiah Royce, *The World and the Individual*, 1959, p. 470; Barbara Marx Hubbard, *Emergence*, 2012, p. xxviii.

Epilogue: Jürgen Moltmann, "Messianic Atheism," in Leroy S. Rouner, ed. *Knowing Religiously*, 1985, p. 204.

Works Cited

Abhayananda, S. (1996). *A History of Mysticism: The Unchanging Testament.* Third (revised) Edition. Olympia, WA: Atma Books.

Ackerman, Peter and DuVall, Jack (2000). *A Force More Powerful: A Century of Non-Violent Conflict.* New York: Palgrave Publishers.

Agar, Herbert, Christian Gauss, Frank Aydelotte ,Oscar Jiszi, G. A. Borgese, Alvin Johnson, Hermann Broch, Hans Kohn, Van Wyck Brooks, Thomas Mann, Ada L. Comstock, Lewis Mumford, William Yandell Elliott, William Allan Neilson, Dorothy Canfield Fisher, Reinhold Niebuhr, Gaetano Salvemini (1941). *The City of Man: A Declaration on World Democracy.* New York: Viking Press. On-line at: http://zeitwort.at/files/the-city-of-man.pdf.

Arendt, Hannah (1958). *The Origins of Totalitarianism. Second Enlarged Edition.* New York: The World Publishing Company.

—. (1963). *Eichmann in Jerusalem. A Report on the Banality of Evil.* New York: Penguin Books.

—. (1969). *On Violence.* New York: Harcourt Brace & Co.

Aurobindo, Sri (1962). *The Human Cycle, The Ideal of Human Unity, War and Self-determination.* Pondicherry, India: Sri Aurobindo Ashram.

—. (1970). *Letters on Yoga, Part Four.* Pondicherry: Sri Aurobindo Ashram.

—. (1972). *Bande Mataram: Early Political Writings.* Pondicherry: Sri Aurobindo Ashram.

Ballard, Edward G. (1971). *Philosophy at the Crossroads.* Baton Rouge: Louisiana State University Press.

Banathy, Bela H. (1992). *A Systems View of Education: Concepts and Principles for Effective Practice.*Englewood Cliffs, NJ: Educational Technology Publications.

Barish, David P. (2000). *Approaches to Peace: A Reader in Peace Studies*. New York: Oxford University Press.

Bateson, Gregory (1972). *Steps to an Ecology of Mind: A Revolutionary Approach to Man's Understanding of Himself*. New York: Ballantine Books.

Bergson, Henri (1975). *The Creative Mind: An Introduction to Metaphysics*. Totawa, NJ: Littlefield, Adams & Co.

Barker, Ernest (1967). *Reflections on Government*. London: Oxford University Press.

Berry, Thomas and Swimme, Brian (1992). *The Universe Story: From the Primordial Flaring Forth to the Ecozoic Era – A Celebration of the Unfolding of the Cosmos*. San Francisco: Harper San Francisco.

Birch, Charles and Cobb, John B., Jr.1990). *Liberation of Life*. Denton, TX: Environmental Ethics Books.

Bloch, Ernst (1986a). *The Principle of Hope. Three Volumes*. Neville Plaice, Stephen Plaice, and Paul Knight, trans. Cambridge, MA: MIT Press.

—. (1986b). *Natural Law and Human Dignity*. Dennis J. Schmidt, trans. Cambridge, MA: MIT Press.

Boswell, Terry and Chase-Dunn, Christopher (2000). *The Spiral of Capitalism and Socialism: Toward Global Democracy*. Boulder, CO: Lynne Rienner Publishers.

Brown, Donald E. (1991). *Human Universals*. New York: McGraw Hill.

Brown, Ellen Hodgson (2007). *Web of Debt—The Shocking Truth about Our Money System*. Revised and Updated Edition. Baton Rouge, LA: Third Millennium Press.

Brück, Michael von (1991). *The Unity of Reality: God, God-Experience and Meditation in the Hindu-Christian dialogue*. James V. Zeitz, trans. New York: Paulist Press.

Bugbee, Henry G., Jr. (1976). *The Inward Morning: A Philosophi-*

cal Exploration in Journal Form. New York: Harper Colophon Books.

Camus, Albert (1986). *Neither Victims Nor Executioners.* Philadelphia: New Society Publishers.

Capra, Fritjof (1975). *The Tao of Physics.*Berkeley: Shambala Press.

—. (1982). *The Turning Point: Science, Society, and the Rising Culture.* New York: Bantam Books.

—. (1996). *The Web of Life: A New Scientific Understanding of Living Systems.* New York: Random House.

Carson, Rachel (1962). *Silent Spring.* Boston: Houghton Mifflin Company.

Chase-Dunn, Christopher (1998). *Global Formation: Structures of World Economy.* Updated Edition. New York: Rowman & Littlefield.

Chomsky, Noam (1998). *On Language.* New York: The New Press.

Cicero, Marcus Tullius (2006). *On the Commonwealth and On the Laws.* James E. G. Zetzel, ed. Cambridge: Cambridge University Press.

Clark, Ramsey, et. al. (1998). *Nato in the Balkans.* New York: International Action Center.

Cook, Richard C. (2008). "Petition for a Monetary System that Puts People First: Open Letter to the G-20." www.richardcook.com/articles/.

Daly, Herman E. (1996). *Beyond Growth: The Economics of Sustainable Development.* Boston: Beacon Press.

Daly, Herman E. and Cobb, John B. (1994). *For the Common Good: Redirecting the economy toward community, the environment, and a sustainable future.* Boston: Beacon Press.

Daly, Herman E. and Townsend, Kenneth N., eds. (1993). *Valuing the Earth: Economics, Ecology, Ethics.*Cambridge: The MIT Press.

Davies, Paul (1983). *God & the New Physics.* New York: Simon & Schuster Publishers.

Dewey, John (1993). *The Political Writings.* Debra Morris and Ian Shapiro, eds. Indianapolis: Hackett Publishing Co.

—. (1963). In *Social and Political Philosophy,* John Somerville and Ronald E. Santoni, eds. New York: Doubleday Books.

Donnelly, Jack (2003). *Universal Human Rights in Theory and Practice.* Ithaca: Cornell University Press.

Drees, Willem B. (1990). *Beyond the Big Bang: Quantum Cosmologies and God.* La Salle, IL: Open Court Publishing.

Dussel, Enrique (1985). *Philosophy of Liberation.* Aquilina Martinez and Christine Morkovsky, trans. Maryknoll, NY: Orbis Books.

—. (1988). *Ethics and Community.* Robert R. Barr, trans. Maryknoll, NY: Orbis Books.

Dworkin, Ronald (1986). *Law's Empire.* Cambridge: Harvard University Press.

—. (1978). *Taking Rights Seriously.* Cambridge, MA: Harvard University Press.

Ellul, Jacques (1965). *The Technological Society.* Robert K. Wilkinson, trans. New York: Alfred A. Knopf.

—. (1978). *Violence: Reflections from a Christian Perspective.* Oxford: Mowbrays.

Engelhardt, Tom (2014). *Shadow Government: Surveillance, Secret Wars, and a Global Security State in a Single-Superpower World.* Chicago: Haymarket Books.

Escobar, Pepe (2006). *Globalistan: How the Globalized World is Dissolving into Liquid War.* Ann Arbor, MI: Nimble Books LLC.

Fingerette, Herbert (1972). *Confucius—the Secular as Sacred.* New York: Harper & Row Publishers.

Finnis, John (1980). *Natural Law and Natural Rights.* Oxford: Clarendon Press.

—. (1983). *Fundamentals of Ethics*. Washington: Georgetown University Press.

Fowler, James (1981). *Stages of Faith: The Psychology of Human Development and the Quest for Meaning*. San Francisco: Harper & Row.

Fox, Matthew (1990). *A Spirituality Named Compassion*. San Francisco: Harper & Row.

Freire, Paulo (1974). *Pedagogy of the Oppressed*. Mira Bergman Ramos, trans. New York: Continuum.

Fromm, Erich (1941). *Escape from Freedom*. New York: Rinehart & Company.

—. (1947). *Man for Himself An Inquiry into the Psychology of Ethics*. New York: Holt, Rhinehart, and Winston.

—.(1962). *Beyond the Chains of Illusion. My Encounter with Marx and Freud*. New York: Simon & Schuster.

—.(1981). *On Disobedience and Other Essays*. New York: Seabury Press.

Fuller, Lon L. (1969). *The Morality of Law*. Revised Edition. New Haven: Yale University Press.

Galtung, Johann (2009). *The Fall of the US Empire—And Then What?* NP: Transcend University Press.

Gandhi, Mahatma (1945). *The Mind of Mahatma Gandhi*. R.K. Prabhu and U.R. Rao, eds. Ahmedabad, India: Navajivan Publishing House.

—. (1957). *Socialism: My Conception*. A.T. Hingorani, ed. Bombay: Bharatiya Vidya Bhavan.

—. (1962). *The Essential Gandhi: An Anthology of His Writings on His Life, Work, and Ideas*. Louis Fischer, ed. New York: Vintage Books.

—. (1972). *All Men are Brothers*. Krishna Kripalani, ed. New York: UNESCO and Columbia U. Press.

—.(1998). *Gandhi: The Science of Satyagraha.* Anand T. Hingorani, ed. Mumbai: Bharatiya Vidya Bhavan.

Gehring, Verna V.,ed. (2003). *War after September 11.* Intro. by William A. Galston. New York: Rowman and Littlefield.

Gewirth, Alan (1982). *Human Rights: Essays on Justification and Applications.* Chicago: University of Chicago Press.

Gill, Lesley (2004). *The School of the Americas: Military Training and Political Violence in the Americas.* Durham, NC: Duke University Press.

Gilligan, Carol (1982). *In a Different Voice.* Cambridge: Harvard University Press.

Glover, Jonathan (1999). *Humanity: A Moral History of the Twentieth Century.* New Haven: Yale University Press.

Goener, Sally J., Dyck, Robert G., and Lagerroos, Dorothy (2008). *The New Science of Sustainability: Building a Foundation for Great Change.* Chapel Hill, NC: Triangle Center for Complex Systems.

Greeley, Andrew M. (1974). *Ecstasy: A Way of Knowing.* Englewood Cliffs, NJ: Prentice-Hall.

Green, Thomas Hill (1964). *Political Theory.* John R. Rodman, ed. New York: Appleton-Century-Crofts.

Griffin, David Ray, et al. (2006). *The American Empire and the Commonwealth of God: A Political, Economic, Religious Statement.* Louisville: Westminster John Knox Press.

Gutkind, Eric (1969). *The Body of God: First Steps Toward an Anti-Theology. The Collected Papers of Eric Gutkind.* Lucie B. Gutkind and Henry Le Roy Finch, eds. New York: Horizon Press.

Habermas, Jürgen (1971). *Knowledge and Human Interests.* Jeremy J. Shipiro, trans. Boston: Beacon Press.

—. (1979). *Communication and the Evolution of Society.* Thomas McCarthy, trans. Boston: Beacon Press.

—. (1998a). *On the Pragmatics of Communication.* Edited by Maeve Cooke. Cambridge, MA: MIT Press.

—. (1998b). *Between Facts and Norms: Contributions to a Discourse Theory of Law and Democracy.* William Rehg, trans. Cambridge: MIT Press.

—. (2001). *The Postnational Constellation: Political Essays.* Cambridge: The MIT Press.

—. (2003). *The Future of Human Nature.* William Rehg, et. al, trans. Cambridge MA: Polity Press.

Happold, F. C. (1966). *Religious Faith and Twentieth-Century Man.* Baltimore, MD: Penguin Books.

Harris, Errol E. (1958). *Revelation Through Reason: Religion in the light of science and philosophy.* New Haven: Yale University Press.

—. (1966). *Annihilation and Utopia: The Principles of International Politics.* London: George Allen & Unwin.

—. (1988). *The Reality of Time.* Albany: State University of New York Press.

—. (2000a). *The Restitution of Metaphysics.* Amherst, NY: Humanity Books.

—. (2000b). *Apocalypse and Paradigm: Science and Everyday Thinking.* Westport, CT: Praeger.

—. (2005). *Earth Federation Now: Tomorrow is Too Late.* Sun City, AZ: Institute for Economic Democracy Press.

Hart, H.L.A. (1994). *The Concept of Law. Second Edition.* Oxford: Oxford University Press.

Hedges, Chris (2002). *War is a Force that Gives Us Meaning.* New York: Anchor Books.

Hegel, G.W.F. (1991). *Elements of the Philosophy of Right.* Alan Wood, ed. Cambridge: Cambridge University Press.

Heidegger, Martin (1962). *Being and Time.* John Macquarrie and Edward Robinson, trans. New York: Harper & Row.

—. (1977). *The Question Concerning Technology and Other Essays.* William Lovitt, trans. New York: Harper Colophon Books.

Henion, Hunt, ed. (2012). *The Sacred Shift: Co-Creating Your Future in a New Renaissance.* Shift Awareness Books.

Hewitt, Marsha Aileen (1995). *Critical Theory of Religion: A Feminist Analysis.* Minneapolis: Fortress Press.

Hick, John (2004). *An Interpretation of Religion: Human Responses to the Transcendent.* Second Edition. New Haven: Yale University Press.

Hobbes, Thomas (1963). *Leviathan.* John Plamenatz, ed. New York: Merridian Books.

Hubbard, Barbara Marx (1998). *Conscious Evolution: Awakening the Power of Our Social Potential.* Novato, CA: New World Library.

—. (2012). *Emergence: The Shift from Ego to Essence.* San Francisco: Hampton Roads Publishing Co.

Hudgens, Tom A (1986). *Let's Abolish War.* Denver: BILR Corporation.

Jacobson, Nolan Pliny (1986). *Understanding Buddhism.* Carbondale: IL: Southern Illinois University Press.

Jaspers, Karl (1953). *The Origin and Goal of History.* New Haven: Yale University Press.

—. (1957). *Man in the Modern Age.* Eden and Cedar Paul, trans. Garden City, NJ: Doubleday & Company.

—. (1959). *Truth and Symbol.* Wilde, Kluback, and Kimmel, trans. New York: Twayne Publishers.

—. (1967). *Philosophy is for Everyman.* Hell and Wels, trans. London: Hutchinson Publishers.

Jay, Martin (1984). *Marxism & Totality: The Adventures of a Concept from Lukás to Habermas.* Berkeley: University of California Press.

Johnson, Kurt and Ord, David Robert (2012). *The Coming Interspiritual Age.* Vancouver: Namaste Publishing.

Johnston, William (1981). *The Mirror Mind: Spirituality and Transformation.* San Francisco: Harper & Row.

Jonas, Hans (1984). *The Imperative of Responsibility: In Search of an Ethics for the Technological Age.* Chicago: University of Chicago Press.

—. (1996). *Mortality and Morality: A Search for God after Auschwitz.* Evanston, IL: Northwestern University Press.

—. (2008). *Memoirs.* Christian Wiese, ed. Krishna Winston, trans. Walthan, MA: Brandeis University Press.

Jung, Carl Gustav (1970). *C.G. Jung: Psychological Reflections. A New Anthology of His Writings, 1905–1961.* Jolande Jacobi, ed. Princeton: Princeton University Press.

Kafatos, Menas and Nadeau, Robert (1990). *The Conscious Universe: Part and Whole in Modern Physical Theory.* Berlin: Springer-Verlag.

Kant, Immanuel (1957). *Perpetual Peace.* Louis White Beck, trans. New York: Macmillan.

—. (1956). *Critique of Practical Reason.* Lewis White Beck, trans. New York: Bobbs-Merrill.

—. (1964). *Groundwork of the Metaphysic of Morals.* H. J. Paton, trans. New York: Harper & Row.

—. (1965a). *The Metaphysical Elements of Justice.* John Ladd, trans. New York: Library of the Liberal Arts, Bobbs-Merrill, Inc.

—. (1965b) (first published 1781). *Critique of Pure Reason.* Norman Kemp Smith, trans. New York: St. Martin's Press.

—. (1983). *Perpetual Peace and Other Essays.* Ted Humphrey, trans. Indianapolis: Hackett Publishing Co.

Kateb, George (2011). *Human Dignity.* Cambridge: Harvard University Press.

Kitchener, Richard F. (1988). *The World View of Contemporary Physics: Does it Need a New Metaphysics?* Albany: SUNY Press.

Kierkegaard, Søren (1959). *The Journals of Kierkegaard*. Alexander Dru, ed. New York: Harper Torchbooks.

Klein, Naomi (2007). *The Shock Doctrine: The Rise of Disaster Capitalism*. New York: Henry Holt and Company.

Kockelmans, Joseph (1970). In Wood, Robert E., ed., *The Future of Metaphysics*. Chicago: Quadrangle Books, pp. 229-250.

Kohlberg, Lawrence (1984). *The Psychology of Moral Development, Volume Two: The Nature and Validity of Moral Stages*. San Francisco: Harper & Row.

Kohlberg, Lawrence (1984). *The Psychology of Moral Development, Volume Two: The Nature and Validity of Moral Stages*. San Francisco: Harper & Row.

Korten, David (1999). *The Post-Corporate World. Life After Capitalism*. West Hartford, CT: Kumarian Press.

Krishnamurti, Jiddu (1964). *Think on These Things*. New York: Harper & Row.

—(1971). *The Flight of the Eagle*. New York: Perennial Library of Harper & Row.

—(1972). *You Are the World*. New York: Harper & Row.

Kroker, Arthur and Kroker, Marilouise, eds. (1991). *Ideology and Power in the age of Lenin in Ruins*. New York: St. Martin's Press.

Küng, Hans (1991). *Global Responsibility: In Search of a New World Ethic*. New York: Crossroad.

Langiulli, Nino, ed. (1971). *The Existentialist Tradition: Selected Writings*. Garden City, NY: Doubleday & Co.

Laszlo, Ervin (2007). *Science and the Akashic Field: An Integral Theory of Everything*. Second Edition. Rochester, VT: Inner Traditions.

—. (2014). *The Self-Actualizing Cosmos: The Akasha Revolution in Science and Human Consciousness*. Rochester, VT: Inner Traditions.

Lauren, Paul Gordon (2003). *The Evolution of International Human Rights: Visions Seen.* Philadelphia: University of Pennsylvania Press.

Lawrence, D.H. (1976). *Apocalypse.* New York: Penguin.

Leech, Garry (2012). *Capitalism: A Structural Genocide.* London: Zed Books.

Levinas, Emmanuel (1969). *Totality and Infinity.* Alphonso Lingis, trans. Pittsburg: Duquesne University Press.

—. (1998). *Collected Philosophical Papers.* Alphonso Lingis, trans. Pittsburg: Duquesne U. Press.

Locke, John (1963). *Two Treatises of Government.* New York: New American Library.

Luban, David (2007). *Legal Ethics and Human Dignity.* Cambridge: Cambridge University Press.

Marcel, Gabriel (1980). *The Philosophy of Existentialism.* Manya Harari, trans. Secaucus, NJ: Citadel Press.

—. (1951). *The Mystery of Being. II. Faith and Reality.* Chicago: Henry Regnery Company.

Martin, Glen T. (1988). "The Religious Nature of Wittgenstein's Later Philosophy." *Philosophy Today,* Volume 32, Number 3, pp. 207–220.

—. (2005). *Millennium Dawn: The Philosophy of Planetary Crisis and Human Liberation.* Pamplin, VA: Institute for Economic Democracy Press.

—. (2008). *Ascent to Freedom: Practical and Philosophical Foundations of Democratic World Law.* Appomattox, VA: Institute for Economic Democracy Press.

—. (2010a). *Triumph of Civilization: Democracy, Nonviolence, and the Piloting of Spaceship Earth.* Appomattox, VA: Institute for Economic Democracy Press.

—. (2010b). *Constitution for the Federation of Earth. With Historical Introduction, Commentary, and Conclusion.* Appomattox, VA:

Institute for Economic Democracy Press.

—. (2013a). "Tagore's Mystical Humanism and the Future of Humanity," In Santi Nath Chattopadhyay, ed. *Rediscovering Tagore*. Kolkata: Punthi Pustak.

—. (2013b). *The Anatomy of a Sustainable World: Our Choice between Climate Change or System Change*. Appomattox, VA: Institute for Economic Democracy Press.

Marx, Karl (1972). *Karl Marx: The Essential Writings*. Federic L. Bender, ed. New York: Harper & Row.

Maslow, A.H. (1970). *Religions, Values, and Peak-Experiences*. New York: Penguin Books.

Matthews, Clifford N. and Varghese, Roy Abraham, eds. (1995). *Cosmic Beginnings and Human Ends: Where Science and Religion Meet*. Chicago: Open Court Publishers.

McDaniel, Jay (2005). *Gandhi's Hope: Learning from Other Religions as a Path to Peace*. Maryknoll, NY: Orbis Books.

McFague, Sallie (1987). *Models of God: Theology for an Ecological, Nuclear Age*. Philadelphia: Fortress Press.

Merleau-Ponty, Maurice (1962). *Phenomenology of Perception*. Colin Smith, trans. New York: Routledge & Kegan Paul.

Milgram, Stanley (1974). *Obedience to Authority: An Experimental View*. New York: Harper & Row.

Mill, John Stuart (1956). *On Liberty*. Currin V. Shields, ed. New York: Bobbs-Merrill Publisher.

Miranda, José Porfiro (1986). *Marx Against the Marxists. The Christian Humanism of Karl Marx*. John Drury, trans. Maryknoll, NY: Orbis Books.

Moltmann, Jürgen (1996). *The Coming of God: Christian Eschatology*. Margaret Kohl, trans. Minneapolis: Fortress Press.

—. (2007). *On Human Dignity: Political Theology and Ethics*. M. Douglas Meeks, trans. Minneapolis: Fortress Press.

—. (2012). *Ethics of Hope*. Minneapolis: Fortress Press.

Morganthau, Hans (1993, first published 1948). *Politics Among Nations: The Struggle for Power and Peace.* New York: McGraw-Hill.

Munitz, Milton K. (1986). *Cosmic Understanding: Philosophy and Science of the Universe.* Princeton: Princeton University Press.

Nasr, Seyyed Hossein (1981). *Knowledge & the Sacred.* New York: Crossroad Publishers.

Needleman, Jacob (1975). *A Sense of the Cosmos: The Encounter of Modern Science and Ancient Truth.* Garden City, NY: Doubleday & Company.

Nicolas of Cusa (1985). *Nicolas of Cusa on Learned Ignorance: A Translation and an Appraisal of De Docta Ignorantia. Second Edition.* Jasper Hopkins, trans. Minneapolis: The Arthur J. Banning Press.

Panikkar, Raimundo (1993). *The Cosmotheandric Experience.* Maryknoll, NY: Orbis Books.

Parenti, Michael (2011). *The Face of Imperialism.* Boulder, CO: Paradigm Publishers.

Petras, James and Veltmeyer, Henry (2005). *Empire with Imperialism: The Globalizing Dynamics of Neoliberal Capitalism.* London: ZED Books.

Petras, James (2012). *The Arab Revolt and the Imperialist Counterattack.* 2nd Edition. Atlanta: Clarity Press.

Pinker, Steven (1995). *The Language Instinct: How the Mind Creates Language.* New York: Harper Perennial.

Plato (1957). *The Republic of Plato.* A.D. Lindsay, trans. New York: E. P. Dutton & Co.

Polkinghorne, John C. (1986). *One World: The Interaction of Science and Theology.* Conshohoken, PA: Templeton Press.

Posner, Eric A. (2014). *The Twilight of Human Rights Law.* Oxford: Oxford University Press.

Reardon, Betty (1985). *Sexism and the War System.* New York: Teachers College Press.

Ricoeur, Paul (1967). *Fallible Man.* Charles Kelbley, trans. Chicago: Henry Regnery Company.

—. (1992). *Oneself as Another.* Kathleen Blamey, trans. Chicago: University of Chicago Press.

Rifkin, Jeremy (1989). *Entropy: Into the Greenhouse World.* Revised Edition. New York: Bantam Books.

Roberts, Paul Craig (2014). *How America was Lost: From 9/11 to the Police/Warfare State.* Atlanta: Clarity Press.

Rosen, Michael (2012). *Dignity: Its History and Meaning.* Cambridge: Harvard University Press.

Rosenberg, Marshall (2005). *Speak Peace in a World of Conflict: What You Say Next Will Change Your World.* Encinitas, CA: PuddleDancer Press.

Rouner, Leroy S., ed. (1985). *Knowing Religiously.* Notre Dame: University of Notre Dame Press.

Royce, Josiah (1959). *The World and the Individual.* New York: Dover Books.

Russell, Peter (1983). *The Global Brain Awakens: Our Next Evolutionary Leap.* Palo Alto, CA: Global Brain, Inc.

Sartre, Jean-Paul (1996). *Hope Now: The 1980 Interviews.* Adrian van den Hoven, trans. Chicago: University of Chicago Press.

Schmidt-Leukel, ed. (1989). *War and Peace in the World Religions.* London: SCM Press.

Schmitt, Carl (1988, first published 1923). *The Crisis of Parliamentary Democracy.* Ellen Kennedy, trans. Cambridge: The MIT Press.

Shannon, Thomas Richard (1989). *An Introduction to the World-System Perspective.* Boulder, CO: Westview Press.

Singer, Irving (1966). *The Nature of Love from Plato to Luther.* New York: Random House.

Smith, J.W. (2003). *Cooperative Capitalism: A Blueprint for Global Peace and Prosperity.* Appomattox, VA: Institute for Economic Democracy Press.

Sorokin, P.A. (1941). *The Crisis of Our Age.* New York: E.P. Dutton, Inc.

Speth, James Gustave (2005). *Red Sky at Morning: America and the Crisis of the Global Environment.* New Haven: Yale University Press.

Spinoza, Baruch (1967). *Ethics. Preceded by On the Improvement of the Understanding.* James Gutman, ed. New York: Hafner Publishing Co.

—. (2002). *Spinoza: Theological-Political Treatise*, Samuel Shirley (trans.) & Seyour Feldman, eds. New York: Hackett Publishing Co.

Stace, Walter T. (1960). *The Teachings of the Mystics.* New York: New American Library.

Suzuki, D. T. (1972). *What is Zen?* New York: Harper & Row.

Swidler, Leonard, ed. (1987). *Toward a Universal Theology of Religions.* Maryknoll, NY: Orbis Books.

Swidler, Leonard and Mojzes, Paul (2000). *The Study of Religion in an Age of Global dialogue.* Philadelphia: Temple University Press.

Swimme, Brian and Berry, Thomas (1992). *The Universe Story – From the Primordial Flaring Forth to the Ecozoic Era, A Celebration of the Unfolding of the Cosmos.* San Francisco: Harper San Francisco.

Tagore, Rabindranath (2011). *The Essential Tagore.* Fakrul Alam & Radha Chakravarty, eds. Cambridge: Harvard University Press.

Teilhard de Chardin, Pierre (1959). *The Phenomenon of Man.* New York: Harper & Brothers Publishers.

Tillich, Paul (1957). *Dynamics of Faith.* New York: Harper Colophon Books.

—. (1963). *The Eternal Now.* New York: Charles Scribner's Sons.

—. (1967). *Systematic Theology. Three Volumes Collected.* Chicago: University of Chicago Press.

—. (1973). *What is Religion?* James Luther Adams, trans. New York: Harper Torchbooks.

—. (1987). *The Essential Tillich.* F. Forrester Church, ed. Chicago: University of Chicago Press.

Wacks, Raymond (2006). *Philosophy of Law: A Very Short Introduction.* Oxford: Oxford University Press.

Warnock, G. J. (1967). "Reason." In *The Encyclopedia of Philosophy, Volume Seven.* New York: Macmillan.

Weber, Max (1954). *Max Weber on Law in Economy and Society.* Edward Shils and Max Rheinstein, trans. New York: Simon & Schuster.

—. (2001). *The Protestant Ethic and the Spirit of Capitalism.* New York: Routledge.

Whitehead, Alfred North (1978). *Process and Reality. Corrected Edition.* New York: Macmillan.

Wilber, Ken (1996). *Eye to Eye: The Quest for the New Paradigm.* Boston: Shambhala.

—.(1998). *The Marriage of Sense and Soul: Integrating Science and Religion.* New York: Random House.

—.(2000). *Integral Psychology: Consciousness, Spirit, Psychology, Therapy.* Boston: Shambhala.

—.(2007). *The Integral Vision.* Boston: Shambhala.

Williams, Chris (2010). *Ecology and Socialism: Solutions to Capitalist Ecological Crisis.* Chicago: Haymarket Books.

Wittgenstein, Ludwig (1929). "Lecture on Ethics."*Philosophical Review* (January 1965): 3–12. Also at http://www.mv.helsinki.fi/home/tkannist/

—. (1974). *Tractatus Logico-Philosophicus.* Pears & McGuinness, trans. Atlantic Highlands, NJ: Humanities Press.

—. (1980). *Culture and Value: A Collection of Notes from Wittgenstein's Journals.* G.H. Von Wright, ed. Chicago: University of Chicago Press.

Wood, Robert E., ed. (1970). *The Future of Metaphysics.* Chicago: Quadrangle Books.

Wolin, Richard (2001). *Heidegger's Children: Hannah Arendt, Karl Löwith, Hans Jonas, and Herbert Marcuse.* Princeton: Princeton University Press.

Young, Arthur M. (1976). *The Reflexive Universe: Evolution of Consciousness.* San Francisco: Delacorte Press.

Zarlenga, Stephen (2002). *The Lost Science of Money: The Mythology of Money—the Story of Power.* Valatie, NY: American Monetary Institute.

Index

CPSIA information can be obtained at www.ICGtesting.com
Printed in the USA
BVOW02s0245220915

419052BV00010B/32/P